ARAB FALL

ARAB FALL

How the Muslim Brotherhood Won
and Lost Egypt in 891 Days

ERIC TRAGER

Georgetown University Press | *Washington, DC*

Library of Congress Cataloging-in-Publication Data

Names: Trager, Eric, author
Title: Arab Fall : how the Muslim Brotherhood won and lost Egypt in 891
    days / Eric Trager.
Description: Washington, DC : Georgetown University Press, 2016. |
    Includes bibliographical references and index.
Identifiers: LCCN 2016001902 (print) | LCCN 2016005194 (ebook) |
    ISBN 9781626163621 (hc : alk. paper) | ISBN 9781626163638 (eb)
Subjects: LCSH: Jamiyat al-Ikhwan al-Muslimin (Egypt) | Hizb al-
    Hurriyah wa-al-Adalah (Egypt) | Egypt—Politics and government—
    21st century. | Mursi, Muhammad, 1951–
Classification: LCC DT107.88 .T94 2016 (print) | LCC DT107.88 (ebook)
    | DDC 962.05/6—dc23
LC record available at https://lccn.loc.gov/2016001902

⊜ This book is printed on acid-free paper meeting the requirements of
the American National Standard for Permanence in Paper for Printed
Library Materials.

17 16   9 8 7 6 5 4 3 2 First printing

Printed in the United States of America

Cover design by Jen Huppert. Cover image by the Associated Press.

To my best friend—my wife, Alyssa—
and to our two sons, Max and Theodore

CONTENTS

Acknowledgments   ix
A Note on Transliteration   xiii
Abbreviations   xv

Introduction: Rapid Rise, Faster Fall   1

1. Late to the Revolution   13

2. An Islamist Vanguard   37

3. Postrevolutionary Posturing   57

4. Preparing for Power   77

5. The Road to Parliament   93

6. Powerless Parliamentarians   109

7. The Road to Ittahidiya Palace   127

8. The Power Struggle Continues   145

9. Power, Not Policy   163

10. The Power Grab   175

11. In Power but Not in Control   189

12. The Rebellion   205

Conclusion: Broken Brothers   227

Appendix: Interviews   235
Notes   247
Selected Bibliography   311
Index   313
About the Author   327

ACKNOWLEDGMENTS

"Why don't you write a book on the Muslim Brotherhood? Call it '*The Rise and Fall of the Muslim Brotherhood*.'" When Rob Satloff suggested this to me in the spring of 2013, I was a bit hesitant. Mohamed Morsi was clearly losing support and control, yet I wasn't convinced that he would be toppled anytime soon. But, as usual, Rob was way ahead of the curve, and I want to thank him for his tremendous mentorship throughout my five years as a fellow at the Washington Institute for Near East Policy.

I would also like to thank my Washington Institute colleagues for their encouragement, advice, and friendship throughout the process of writing this book: David Schenker, Patrick Clawson, Andrew Tabler, Simon Henderson, Mike Singh, Dennis Ross, Neri Zilber, Aaron Zelin, Marc Sievers, Ghaith al-Omari, Lori Plotkin Boghardt, Anna Borshchevskaya, Soner Cagaptay, Mohammed Dajani, Mike Eisenstadt, Sarah Feuer, Jim Jeffrey, Mehdi Khalaji, Matt Levitt, David Makovsky, Ehud Yaari, Jacob Olidort, Kate Bauer, Nadav Pollak, David Pollock, Vish Sakthivel, Margaret Weiss Tam, Jeff White, Lauren Emerson, Rebecca Erdman, Dan Heckelman, Laura Hannah, Jeff Rubin, Gina Vailes, Mary Kalbach Horan, Scott Rogers, George Lopez, Brittany Parker, Ian Byrne, Alison Percich, Jeanne Epstein, Jacqui Schein, and Judy Cole.

I also want to thank the Nathan and Esther K. Wagner Family Foundation for its generous support of my work. I was honored to be named the Washington Institute's Esther K. Wagner Fellow in July 2013. Many thanks to Nathan Wagner, Susan Wagner, Michael Lippitz, Joyce Croft, Linda Wagner Weiner, and their families for cultivating young scholars such as myself.

I owe a special thanks to my outstanding research assistant Marina Shalabi for her tireless work throughout the drafting of this book. Marina transcribed many hours of Brotherhood videos, translated key Brotherhood statements, sifted through hundreds of pages of Brotherhood tracts, and offered vital

feedback throughout the drafting process. I would also like to thank my former research assistant Gilad Wenig, who is now studying at Cambridge University, for providing timely feedback on my first draft and serving as a constant sounding board for my research ideas. Many thanks as well to the many
research assistants and interns who contributed to the years of research that
went into this book: Katie Kiraly, Gavi Barnhard, Adam Rasgon, Noam Ray-
dan, Heba Dafashy, Adam Sadick, Haisam Hassanein, Nour Chaaban, Oula
Alrifai Abdulhamid, Erica Wenig, Yara Hattab, James Bowker, Talia Rubin,
Noah Bricker, Leah Schulz, Timna Medovoy, Samy Saad, Eliot Calhoun, Coo-
per Klose, Grace Abuhamad, and Sonia Hinson.

I also owe a special thanks to Maged Atef. I first met Maged in February
2013 when I needed a fixer to assist my research in rural Egypt, and I have
worked with him on almost every research trip that I have taken since then.
In addition to being outstandingly resourceful and analytical, he is a wonderful friend. I would also like to thank my two prior interpreters in Egypt,
Mohamed Hemeda and Ahmad Khader.

Many thanks as well to my friends and colleagues in Egypt, including those
who have moved elsewhere, for making my research trips so enjoyable: Nancy
Youssef, Amina Ismail, Wendy Steavenson, Jon Argaman, Mohamed Abdel-
baky, Mahmoud Salem, "The Big Pharaoh," Mahmoud Ibrahem, Ahmed
Samih, Amr Bargisi, Emma Deputy, Bonnie Wei, Hany Nasr, Yasmin Amin,
and Maryam Ishani. I would also like to thank Steven Cook and Samuel Tadros, two Washington-based colleagues, for their insights and encouragement
over the years. And special thanks to Donald Jacobs of Georgetown University Press, who guided me through the process and shepherded this project
to publication. I would also like to thank Kathryn Owens, Don McKeon, and
Terri Rothman for their outstanding editorial work.

Parts of this book emerged from my doctoral research, and I'd like to thank
my committee at the University of Pennsylvania's Political Science Department—Bob Vitalis, Brendan O'Leary, and Tulia Falleti—for guiding my general interest in Egyptian politics to a full-bodied dissertation. I would also like
to thank the department and the Christopher H. Brown Center for International Politics, both of which provided vital fellowship support for the earlier
stages of my fieldwork, and the American Research Center in Egypt, which
administered the grant for the second half of my dissertation research in early
2011. Many thanks as well to (now former) department chairs Ed Mansfield
and Avery Goldstein for making Penn such a warm community for learning

and growing and to my classmate Chris Russell for being a great friend, colleague, and study partner.

Most of all, I am extremely grateful for my family's unyielding love and support throughout the many years of research that went into this book. My parents Cara and Mike, sister Rachel, and grandfather Papa Sy urged me to follow my fascination with Egyptian politics long before the "Arab Spring" made it fashionable. I want to thank my father as well for suggesting the title of this book. I am also blessed to have wonderful in-laws, Rhonda and Jeff, who have been extremely supportive.

The true saint of this project, however, is my wife and best friend, Alyssa. For her tremendous love, support, and patience during the many months I was away—whether in Cairo doing research or in my office writing it up—this book is dedicated to her. It is also dedicated to our two sons: our eldest, Max, arrived in February 2015 just as I was completing the first draft, and our youngest, Theodore, arrived in August 2016 just before this book went to press.

A NOTE ON TRANSLITERATION

Consistent transliteration for Egyptian history and politics poses a number of problems because there is no agreed-upon system. For this reason, when mentioning Arabic-language terms, places, and proper names, I have opted to use common transliterations in most circumstances. This means that in some cases, names that are written identically in Arabic have been spelled differently in this text (such as in the case of "jihad" and Muslim Brotherhood figure Gehad el-Haddad's first name) to match the way they are commonly spelled in English-language writing on the subject.

ABBREVIATIONS

AR   In Arabic
BDP   Building and Development Party
CSF   Central Security Forces
EGIS   Egyptian General Intelligence Service
ESDP   Egyptian Social Democratic Party
FJP   Freedom and Justice Party
IAEA   International Atomic Energy Agency
IRI   International Republican Institute
IMF   International Monetary Fund
ISIS   Islamic State of Iraq and Syria
NDI   National Democratic Institute
NDP   National Democratic Party
NGO   nongovernmental organization
NSC   National Security Council
NSF   National Salvation Front
RDP   Reform and Development Party
SCAF   Supreme Council of the Armed Forces
SCC   Supreme Constitutional Court
SPEC   Supreme Presidential Elections Commission
UAE   United Arab Emirates
UN   United Nations

Introduction
Rapid Rise, Faster Fall

On June 24, 2012, I stood among many thousands of Islamists in downtown Cairo's Tahrir Square, awaiting the results of Egypt's first-ever fair and free presidential election.

The mood was extremely tense. Ten days earlier, the Supreme Constitutional Court dissolved Egypt's freely elected, Muslim Brotherhood–dominated Parliament. The Brotherhood believed that the state institutions were conspiring to keep it from power and feared that the presidential elections results would be rigged against its candidate, Mohamed Morsi. So it mobilized its cadres from all over Egypt to Tahrir Square and told them to prepare for battles with security forces if former prime minister Ahmed Shafik was named the winner.

"If Shafik wins, I will be a dead man," one Muslim Brother told me as he set up his Tahrir tent a few days earlier. "I will fight to the end."

Elsewhere in the square, pro-Morsi Salafists marched in formation, carrying white cloths that were meant to represent burial shrouds. "This is my coffin," one of them told me, pointing to the cloth in his hands. "We win or we die."[1]

Two hours later, however, those dire pronouncements were quickly forgotten. The elections commission declared Morsi the winner, and Tahrir Square exploded in celebration. Chants of *"Allahu akbar!"*—"God is great!"—rang out across downtown Cairo as many of Morsi's supporters thrust themselves to the ground in prayer.

For the Muslim Brotherhood, it was a moment of profound ecstasy. Founded in 1928, the Brotherhood had struggled in Egypt's opposition for more than eight decades—often under severely repressive circumstances. The "Arab Spring," however, radically changed the organization's fortunes. Only seventeen months after the mass uprising that toppled longtime dictator Hosni Mubarak in February 2011, a Muslim Brother was now Egypt's president. And while the Brotherhood still anticipated a power struggle with the country's military, it nevertheless saw Morsi's presidency as an unprecedented opportunity to establish an "Islamic state" in Egypt, which it would use as a foothold for establishing a "global Islamic state."[2]

That did not ultimately happen.

One year later, the country was in crisis again. Morsi's autocratic edicts and failed governance catalyzed a mass movement against him, as well as a mutiny within the state's institutions. The crisis climaxed on June 30, 2013, when millions of Egyptians poured into the streets to demand his ouster. Morsi, however, refused to negotiate a political resolution, and with each passing day the situation on the ground deteriorated further.

Outside the presidential palace, uniformed police officers joined the anti-Morsi protesters and declared that they wouldn't return to work until the president was toppled. In Tahrir Square, protesters waved banners calling for Morsi and other top Brotherhood leaders to be hanged. And at its protest site in northern Cairo, the Brotherhood tried to intimidate the opposition by organizing its cadres into makeshift vigilante units, equipping hundreds of Brotherhood youths with helmets, shields, batons, and in some cases iron pipes.

"We will stay until Morsi has full power," one Muslim Brother told me. "Or we die."

Meanwhile, as deadly clashes between Morsi's supporters and opponents escalated throughout the country, many feared a civil war was imminent.

On the evening of July 3, four days after the anti-Morsi uprising began, I stood in the lobby of downtown Cairo's Semiramis Intercontinental Hotel, right next to Tahrir Square, awaiting a major announcement from the military. When Defense Minister Abdel Fattah al-Sisi appeared on air and declared Morsi's toppling, I could hear the surrounding streets explode in celebration. As I headed outside to observe the festivities, I noticed a middle-aged man—probably a hotel worker—pump his fist in victory.

"Allahu akbar!" he whispered to himself, smiling.[3]

• • • • • • • •

How did the Muslim Brotherhood rise to power so rapidly after Egypt's 2011 Arab Spring uprising? And why did it fall from power even more quickly, culminating in the popular uprising and military coup that toppled Morsi in July 2013?

To be sure, the Brotherhood's post-Mubarak story unfolded in an extremely fluid political environment. At every point during the Brotherhood's rapid rise and dramatic collapse, a complex set of factors impacted its decision making, as well as that of Egypt's other relevant political actors, including the military, judiciary, Salafists, non-Islamist political parties, revolutionaries, "remnants" of the Mubarak regime, and the private media establishment, among others. But as I argue in this book, the Brotherhood's particular organizational structure, which was designed to pursue a very specific set of political goals, conditioned it toward certain behavioral tendencies. More to the point, the very characteristics that helped the Brotherhood win power so quickly also contributed to its downfall.

So what kind of organization is the Brotherhood? Unlike Egypt's other political forces, the Brotherhood is neither a protest movement nor a political party, though it has occasionally behaved like both. It is first and foremost a vanguard—a rigidly hierarchical organization that seeks to transform Egyptian society, the Egyptian state, and ultimately the world according to its highly politicized interpretation of Islam. Specifically, it seeks to promote its interpretation of Islam as an "all-embracing concept" within the society, achieve sufficient support so that it can establish an Islamic state in Egypt, and use this Islamic state as a foothold for establishing a global Islamic state, or neocaliphate. As Hazem Kandil notes, the Brotherhood equates participation in its organization with Islam, claiming that it "is sacred because what it represents is sacred—that is, Islam. Without the movement, there can be no return to Islamic rule."[4]

To ensure that its members are fully committed to pursuing and implementing this theocratic project, the Brotherhood maintains a strict system of recruitment and internal promotion. Joining the Muslim Brotherhood entails a five-to-eight-year indoctrination process, during which every Muslim Brother is steeped in the Brotherhood's politicized interpretation of Islam, vetted for his belief in the organization's ideology, and closely monitored for his obedience to following Brotherhood leaders' orders. This system is designed to engender a uniformity of purpose, ideology, and—when commanded by leaders—activity among the Brotherhood's rank and file. As a result, the typical Muslim Brother sees himself as a foot soldier for the organization—meaning, again, that he sees himself as a foot soldier for Islam.

The Brotherhood further promotes its unity of purpose and action by maintaining a rigid nationwide chain of command. The Brotherhood's hundreds of thousands of members are organized in five-to-ten-person cells known as *usar*, or "families," which receive orders from the Brotherhood's leadership in Cairo and execute them locally.[5] This pyramidal structure enabled the Brotherhood's leadership to direct its cadres in virtually every Egyptian neighborhood for a wide range of purposes, including operating social services, organizing political protests, and mobilizing electoral campaigns.

The Brotherhood thus won Egypt's post-Mubarak elections thanks to its unparalleled organizational infrastructure. Indeed, during every post-Mubarak election, none of the Brotherhood's competitors could count on a similarly committed membership or possessed the Brotherhood's well-oiled, nationwide chain of command.

But, at the same time, the Brotherhood's particular organizational characteristics meant that it was deeply insular—and this became a tremendous liability once it achieved power. After all, the Brotherhood equates its organization with Islam. It therefore regards outsiders with tremendous suspicion and casts its political opponents as enemies of Islam. Moreover, the Brotherhood sees its hierarchical, nationwide chain of command as the proper mechanism for implementing its theocratic vision, which means that it cannot integrate other political and societal factions effectively. This exclusivism alienated many Egyptians, as well as many within Egypt's sprawling bureaucracy, which was a major factor in its rapid fall from power.

The Brotherhood's totalitarianism was another cause of its downfall. Its hierarchical organizational culture, in which internal dissenters are banished and external critics are often viewed as enemies of Islam, meant that it was poorly prepared for governing in the more competitive political environment that followed Mubarak's ouster. Indeed, rather than accepting checks on his power or compromising with his opponents, Morsi tried to obliterate them during his yearlong presidency. As a result, many Egyptians regarded Morsi as a new dictator—and a very weak one at that—and this fueled the escalating protests that culminated with his ouster in July 2013.

• • • • • • • •

My analysis of the Brotherhood as a cohesive organization differs from previous accounts of the organization, which portray it as internally fractious. Prior to Morsi's overthrow, it was common to study the organization in terms of the competition between the organization's "reformists" (sometimes referred to as "moderates") and "hardliners" (sometimes referred to as "conservatives," "radicals," or "Qutbists"). The reformists, as Alison Pargeter notes in her excellent book on the organization, sought to broaden the Brotherhood's base by occasionally embracing more inclusive ideas and engaging other non-Islamist movements. The hardliners, alternatively, sought to ensure that the organization was "anchored in its own traditions," which meant prioritizing ideological purity even if this limited the Brotherhood's appeal and slowed its progress toward power.[6] Carrie Rosefsky Wickham similarly analyzes the Brotherhood as an internally divided organization, emphasizing that Islamists "are not monolithic entities whose members think and act in lockstep."[7]

These scholars have a point: While the Brotherhood's recruitment mechanisms and internal hierarchy are designed to promote internal unity, there have often been profound disagreements within the organization. As this book documents, for example, prominent Brotherhood youths rejected their leaders' decision not to participate in the initial anti-Mubarak protests on January 25, 2011. A top Muslim Brother, Abdel Moneim Abouel Fotouh, defied the Brotherhood's leadership when he declared his presidential candidacy in mid-2011. And when the Brotherhood ultimately decided to nominate one of its leaders for president in March 2012, the decision passed by a very narrow 56–52 vote within the Brotherhood's legislative body—indicating that Brotherhood leaders were deeply divided over one of the most pivotal decisions in the organization's history.

Yet, in all of these instances, the Muslim Brothers' disagreements were about tactics and strategy—not about core principles. Indeed, the reformists and hardliners equally embraced the Brotherhood's theocratic goals of establishing an Islamic state and ultimately a global Islamic state.[8] They only disagreed on *how* this vision could be implemented most effectively—whether it should be done more gradually or immediately, whether establishing a political party would better promote this vision or alienate people from it, and whether the Brotherhood should seek the presidency now or in the future. And as this book documents, all of these internal debates ended once the Brotherhood's leadership took its final decision. The overwhelming majority of Muslim Brothers mobilized to support it, and those who dissented were often sidelined or banished.

Still, the fact that the Brotherhood was Egypt's most organized and cohesive political force hardly dictated that it would seek outright power when it did. After all, during the early months after Mubarak fell, the Brotherhood indicated that it would approach power gradually. It feared that rushing to power would invite backlash either within Egypt or from abroad. The Brotherhood thus promised to compete for only half of the parliamentary seats and vowed not to nominate a candidate during the first post-Mubarak presidential elections.

Perhaps the Brotherhood never intended to keep these promises in the first place. But this book offers a different explanation: The Brotherhood broke these promises because they threatened its internal unity, which the organization prized above all else. Had the Brotherhood not nominated a presidential candidate, for example, Muslim Brothers might have split their votes among any number of non-Brotherhood candidates. And an Islamist organization that views its internal cohesiveness as essential to establishing an Islamic state cannot tolerate this kind of chaos in its ranks. Yet just as the Brotherhood's emphasis on maintaining organizational unity impelled its leaders to pursue power immediately, it also engendered the exclusivism and insularity that precipitated that Brotherhood's rapid fall.

The Brotherhood's exclusivism wasn't the only cause of its undoing. Ultimately its aimlessness on policy matters and incompetence in government were far more damaging. As this book documents, the Brotherhood never bothered to articulate what it would do once it reached power—what "implementing *shari'ah*," for example, actually meant when it came to economic, social, or foreign policy. As Kandil argues, this was also a product of the Brotherhood's particular organizational culture: The Brotherhood feared that taking clear policy stances would alienate either the "zealots" or moderates in its ranks, and thus undermine its internal unity.[9] Once again, the very factors that helped the Brotherhood win power—in this case, its vagueness on policy questions—became a tremendous liability once it achieved power.

Of course, the Brotherhood wasn't the only key player in the story of Egypt's Arab Spring. After all, a diverse group of revolutionary youth activists sparked the original uprising and then continued their protests sporadically after Mubarak fell, hoping to influence the transition process in directions that the Brotherhood often opposed.[10] The Salafists similarly burst onto Egypt's political scene during this period, challenging the Brotherhood's support among Islamists by promising a more fundamentalist interpretation of *shari'ah*, while at other times cooperating with the Brotherhood against Egypt's weak, non-Islamist parties.

Much more significantly, the Supreme Council of the Armed Forces (SCAF) governed Egypt ineptly and often ruthlessly for the sixteen months that followed Mubarak's ouster. While the military's internal dynamics and deliberations are secretive, the generals' actions suggested a willingness to accept the Brotherhood's rise—but only so long as the military remained an autonomous entity, with its perquisites protected from any civilian government's oversight. And although the generals stepped away from day-to-day governance shortly after Morsi's election, the military never left the political scene entirely: It retained significant economic power, and signaled its independence from the elected president as opposition to Morsi mounted in late 2012.

Other groups' and institutions' roles during the post-Mubarak period are even more opaque. This includes the domestic security services, the Interior Ministry, the judiciary, the business community, rural clans and tribes, and the "remnants" of Mubarak's former ruling party, which are often referred to as "*feloul*." Of course, these were the state institutions and societal interests that supported Mubarak's rule. They thus took a dim view of the 2011 uprising that ousted Mubarak (and in some cases tried to suppress it) and later supported the 2013 uprising against Morsi.

Yet, as this book illustrates, the behavior of these groups and institutions vis-à-vis the Brotherhood between its rise and fall does not fit a clear pattern. They tolerated the Brotherhood's rise in certain instances, such as when judges certified Muslim Brothers' electoral victories. They aided the Brotherhood in other instances, such as when police reportedly helped Brotherhood cadres beat anti-Morsi protesters outside the presidential palace. And they undermined the Brotherhood in still other instances, such as when the police mutinied against Morsi in the spring of 2013. But because these groups and institutions are secretive, it is difficult to assemble a complete picture of their overall activities. It is therefore impossible to disprove the Brotherhood's claim that they undermined Morsi from the moment he won power.

Either way, the Brotherhood's significant influence over Egypt's post-Mubarak trajectory isn't debatable. It emerged from the 2011 uprising as the country's strongest political force, helped determine the country's transition process, and won the 2011–12 parliamentary and presidential elections. To be sure, it rose to power in a very uncertain environment and confronted a wide variety of challenges. But the Brotherhood's rapid rise and faster fall were both paved, to a large extent, by its own decisions. Those decisions are the subject of this book.

While the Brotherhood's rise and fall is overwhelmingly an Egyptian story shaped by domestic Egyptian political actors and circumstances, this book also examines US policy during this period. On account of its deeply anti-Western ideology, the Brotherhood expected the West to prevent its rise to power. The Brotherhood was therefore shocked when Washington did quite the opposite: The Barack Obama administration sent high-ranking officials to "engage" the Brotherhood and frequently signaled its acceptance of the organization's political emergence. This assuaged the Brotherhood's fears and contributed to its decision to seek power more rapidly than it initially intended. The Obama administration then bolstered its outreach to the Brotherhood after Morsi won the presidential election: It aided the Morsi government economically, intensified its diplomatic engagement, and rarely criticized Morsi's autocratic abuses.

From the administration's standpoint, this policy was grounded in realism: Egypt is an important American ally, and the United States therefore had little choice but to work with the Brotherhood once it held power. And while the administration had significant concerns about whether the Brotherhood would abide by the 1979 Egyptian–Israeli peace treaty and cooperate on counterterrorism, it believed that "engaging" the Brotherhood was the only way to influence its decision making. Meanwhile, the administration maintained its $1.3 billion in annual military aid to Egypt as insurance against a foreign policy shift.

In a narrow sense, the administration's policy was successful: The Brotherhood did not ultimately alter Egypt's foreign policy. But, at the same time, by engaging the Brotherhood unconditionally and often uncritically, the administration's leverage for slowing the Brotherhood's rise or deterring its autocratic excesses diminished. Meanwhile, the administration alienated Egypt's non-Islamists, who interpreted Washington's outreach to the Brotherhood as support. And although many American policymakers understood that US policy toward the Brotherhood carried these downsides, they accepted them on the assumption that the Brotherhood would govern for many years to come.

Which brings me to the core argument of this book: While the Brotherhood's rapid rise and even quicker fall might seem inevitable in retrospect, nothing about it seemed inevitable at the time.[11] In examining every step in the Brotherhood's post-Mubarak story, this book strives to recapture what the Brotherhood and other relevant actors knew, felt, and feared at that time, setting aside what the reader knows will happen next. The title of this book is meant to reflect the uncertainty of this period: What looked like a democratizing "Arab Spring" to many foreign observers was in fact a deeply uncertain "Arab Fall" for many Egyptians, in which the political climate grew colder and darker as time wore on.

• • • • • • • •

This book marks the culmination of five years of research, which began with my doctoral dissertation fieldwork in Cairo during the summer of 2010. My dissertation examined Egypt's opposition parties under Mubarak, and for the most part I gained access to these parties very easily. The Wafd, Tagammu, and Ghad parties were all extremely cooperative and gave me their full leadership rosters, complete with cell phone numbers. And since oppositionists under Mubarak had nothing better to do than talk to me, I breezed through most of the research, racking up over a hundred interviews in approximately seven weeks of work.

Interviewing Brotherhood leaders, however, was much more challenging. Given the significant repression it faced, the Brotherhood didn't hand out its executives' phone numbers, and its full leadership roster wasn't public. Indeed, when I approached the Brotherhood's media coordinator during the summer of 2010 and asked to interview ten Brotherhood leaders for my dissertation, he looked at me skeptically. Still, he arranged for me to interview Morsi, who was then a barely known Brotherhood apparatchik.

The interview went poorly. Morsi refused to answer many of my questions about his personal background and threatened to end the meeting when I asked him why he decided to become a Muslim Brother in his twenties. The Brotherhood's media coordinator was monitoring the entire exchange, and when my hour with Morsi was over, the coordinator told me that I wouldn't interview any other Brotherhood leaders. I was devastated: How could I complete my dissertation with only one interview from Egypt's strongest opposition group?

A few months later, at the annual meeting of the Middle East Studies Association in San Diego, I shared my frustration with Kent State University professor Josh Stacher, who studies Egyptian politics. "You're going about this all wrong," Stacher told me. To understand the Brotherhood, he said, I needed to start from the bottom—to find young and former Muslim Brothers, ask them about their experiences in the organization to better understand it, and work my way up the Brotherhood's hierarchy. This would help me better frame my questions and also enable me to get access to more Brotherhood leaders.

It was excellent advice. When I returned to Cairo for my second round of dissertation research in early 2011, I located a few young and former Muslim Brothers, who generously explained the organization's structure and recruiting techniques and, in many cases, gave me the phone numbers of Brotherhood leaders. My study of the Brotherhood intensified after Mubarak's ouster that February, when it became clear that the Brotherhood would be Egypt's most pivotal political force. By the time my dissertation research concluded in early April 2011, I had interviewed twenty-seven current and former Muslim Brothers, including ten top leaders.

My interviews with Brotherhood figures, which I continued through ten subsequent research trips to Egypt during the next three years, differed from those of other scholars in some important respects. During my interviews, I spent as little time as possible asking about the Brotherhood's ideology. After all, one doesn't have to travel six thousand miles to learn that the Brotherhood wants to "implement *shari'ah,*" since this is plainly stated in the organization's literature. I also avoided questions about typical Western obsessions, such as the Brotherhood's views on democracy, since I knew that this was a recipe for hearing the Brotherhood's well-rehearsed talking points to Western audiences. Instead, I focused on how the Brotherhood functioned as an organization: how it recruited members, how it chose its leaders, how it made decisions, how it gave orders, and how it organized its political work.

To facilitate this research, I collected dozens of top Brotherhood leaders' phone numbers, which enabled me to interview deeply within the organization. My goal was to interview the Brotherhood's lesser-known leaders at every level—the individuals who attended the same meetings as their more prominent colleagues but who were less media-trained and therefore less guarded in sharing information. Indeed, much of my information about the organization's internal operations and decision making during the post-Mubarak era comes from these figures.

The more I wrote about the Brotherhood's internal dynamics, however, the more its media team became aware of me, and not in a good way. By September 2012, and possibly earlier than that, I was on the Brotherhood's "blacklist"—an actual list of researchers and journalists with whom Muslim Brothers are instructed not to talk. (The Brotherhood also maintained a list of Western journalists and scholars to whom it gave preferred access, on the assumption that these individuals would write about it favorably.[12])

Of course, by putting me on its blacklist, the Brotherhood's media team sought to prevent me from continuing my research. But I was determined not to let their ban on me succeed. So during my subsequent trips to Egypt, I traveled more frequently outside of Cairo, randomly popping up at Brotherhood offices in Nile Delta cities and scoring interviews with local leaders. These folks, it turned out, hadn't received that blacklist memo—and they weren't media-trained either, which meant that they shared information about the organization's internal dynamics quite freely. And on occasion I was still able to interview the Brotherhood's more prominent leaders, though this became much harder.

While I continued interviewing Muslim Brothers in Egypt during the first year following Morsi's ouster, the government's severe crackdown on the organization makes that nearly impossible today. At the time of this book's publication, many of my interviewees are either in prison or exile, and Muslim Brothers risk arrest if they are identified while meeting a Western researcher. It is therefore difficult to assess fully the changes within the Brotherhood since July 2013. Still, certain key developments—such as some Muslim Brothers' embrace of violence and the deepening rift between its "old guard" and younger leaders—have been quite visible.

1 Late to the Revolution

Mohamed al-Qassas was a rising star in the Muslim Brotherhood, Egypt's oldest and best-organized opposition movement. The son of an Azhari sheikh, al-Qassas grew up in Cairo's upscale Heliopolis neighborhood and joined the Brotherhood as a student at Cairo University during the 1990s. Within the organization, the charismatic al-Qassas developed a strong following among younger Muslim Brothers, so the Brotherhood leadership tasked him with recruiting university students to the organization.

Given that the Brotherhood was arguably the greatest political threat to Hosni Mubarak's regime, al-Qassas's Islamist activism came at a personal price. He was arrested four times, once stood before a military court, and faced various professional restrictions. But al-Qassas's outreach work on university campuses also had a major upside: It enabled him to break through the Brotherhood's rigidly insular internal culture and meet a broad range of relatively young opposition activists from across Egypt's political spectrum.

It was through these contacts that al-Qassas learned on January 15, 2011, that opposition activists were planning major protests against the Mubarak regime ten days later. He immediately publicized the demonstrations on his Facebook page and coordinated with peers in other—mostly non-Islamist—groups to spread the message.

But al-Qassas knew from prior experience that social media activism didn't always translate into protesters on the streets. Getting a significant turnout required convincing the Brotherhood's executive bureau, known as the Guidance Office, to mobilize the organization's hundreds of thousands of members to participate in the demonstrations from the moment they started.[1]

That, it turned out, was a tall order.

• • • • • • • •

By early 2011, popular frustration with the Mubarak regime had been building for many years. Despite posting an impressive average 5.9 percent real GDP growth from 2005 to 2010, there was limited trickle-down, and a 2010 Gallup survey found that only one-fifth of Egyptians believed that economic conditions were improving.[2] Meanwhile, following the 2008 global economic crisis, unemployment rose from 8.7 to 10.1 percent during the next two years,[3] and youth unemployment was especially high at 23 percent, including 60 percent among women fifteen to twenty-four years old.[4] The final decade of Mubarak's rule also witnessed a surge in labor strikes, with over two million workers participating in nearly 3,400 strikes and other collective actions.[5]

Egypt's calcified autocracy exacerbated these frustrations. To many Egyptians, Mubarak's apparent attempt to anoint his younger son Gamal as his successor was a throwback to the pharaohs. The severely rigged 2010 parliamentary elections, during which Mubarak's ruling party won over 86 percent of the seats, and rampant governmental corruption added to popular distrust of the regime.[6]

Yet, even as Egyptians frequently warned that mounting anger might yield a popular *infigār*—an explosion—there appeared to be no party or group that could channel this distress into an impactful anti-Mubarak movement. After all, Egypt's legal opposition parties were small and thoroughly co-opted by the regime.

Meanwhile, the Muslim Brotherhood, which was Egypt's largest and best-organized opposition group, feared greater repression if it challenged the Mubarak regime too directly.[7] So the Brotherhood downplayed its political ambitions. It instead focused on building relationships among other sectors of society through its involvement in the professional syndicates and spreading its Islamist message through the social services it provided in Egypt's neediest areas. It also appealed to the public by occasionally organizing anti-Western protests, which was a useful tactic for criticizing the Mubarak regime's cooperation with the United States and Israel without challenging the regime's political legitimacy directly.

Like many of his colleagues, al-Qassas had participated in these protests since his earliest days as a Muslim Brother. His first political act was marching in a Brotherhood-organized, pro-Palestinian demonstration in 1992, and he increasingly participated in organizing these protests as he emerged as a Brotherhood student leader at Cairo University during the 1990s. In the pro-

cess, al-Qassas befriended leftist activists who disagreed with the Brotherhood's Islamism yet flocked to the Brotherhood's pro-Palestinian demonstrations at a time when few other outlets for protest activity existed.[8] Away
from the heat of the protests, al-Qassas spent long evenings with these leftist counterparts, debating a wide range of political, social, and philosophi-
cal questions. Before long, they located various points of agreement and, in
1996, formed the Committee on Collaboration among Political Forces, which
protested the Mubarak regime's prosecution of Brotherhood leaders before
military courts.[9]

Al-Qassas continued his campus activism even after he graduated from
Cairo University in 1998. He remained one of the Brotherhood's foremost student recruiters at the university and continued organizing protests as a mechanism for raising the Brotherhood's campus profile. Al-Qassas's network of
opposition youth activists thus expanded considerably, and a loose coalition
of Muslim Brothers, socialists, communists, and Nasserists coalesced amid
the various waves of protest that emerged in the years that followed.

The first protest wave began in late 2000, shortly after the outbreak of the
second Palestinian intifada. The intifada engendered mass sympathy for the
Palestinian cause within Egypt, and al-Qassas worked through the Brotherhood to organize campus protests against Israel, which the regime initially
tolerated.[10] But as these demonstrations increasingly criticized Mubarak's relations with Israel, the regime began cracking down. Central Security Forces
(CSF) police would surround the protests, clash with demonstrators, and detain activists by the dozens.[11]

Egypt's response to the US invasion of Iraq in March 2003 intensified the
activists' ire. While the Mubarak regime publicly criticized the invasion, it
nevertheless permitted US warships to pass through the Suez Canal.[12] In an
apparent attempt to contain the mounting popular outrage in the run-up
to the war, the regime permitted the Brotherhood to hold a major antiwar
protest at Cairo Stadium on February 27, which over a hundred thousand
reportedly attended.[13] But it was to no avail. On March 20, the day after the
US invasion began, tens of thousands of protesters occupied Tahrir Square
before CSF police beat them back. The massive outpouring included strong
denunciations of the Mubarak regime's foreign policy, and protesters tore
down a Mubarak poster hanging outside the ruling party's downtown Cairo
headquarters.[14]

Then in late 2003, a coalition of older Nasserist, leftist, and Islamist political opposition figures jointly established the Popular Campaign for Change,

which ultimately became known as Kefaya, meaning "Enough." The campaign demanded a variety of political reforms, including competitive presidential elections.[15] From December 2004 through the spring of 2005, Kefaya held a series of antiregime protests in downtown Cairo, representing the first sustained antiregime protest activity.[16] Al-Qassas participated in Kefaya, and the movement's ideological diversity made it another important meeting ground for Islamist and non-Islamist activists. But the ideological diversity of Kefaya also contributed to its downfall: Its leadership failed to offer a coherent political program beyond opposing Mubarak, and it fizzled due to regime pressure two years later.[17]

The youth activists who joined Kefaya, however, soon built other, often narrower anti-Mubarak movements. These included Haqqī ("My Right") and Gami'atunah ("Our University"), which protested the heavy police presence on campuses.[18]

But the most successful of these movements was April 6 Youth, which took its name from the date of a 2008 labor strike at Egypt's largest textile factory in Al-Mahalla al-Kobra, during which workers confronted riot police for two days.[19] In the run-up to these strikes, youth activists created a Facebook page to express their solidarity with the workers. The page rapidly attracted over seventy-six thousand members and thus became an important forum in which young Egyptians vented their frustration with the Mubarak regime.[20] Al-Qassas had met April 6 Youth founder Ahmed Maher during the Kefaya protests, and the two continued their collaboration through the mostly small protests that April 6 Youth organized in the years that followed.

Yet, as al-Qassas's involvement with non-Islamists became more frequent and visible, Brotherhood leaders in Cairo urged him to back off. "Those people are not Islamists," they would tell him, apparently worrying that cooperation with non-Islamists would damage the organization's ability to pursue its narrow Islamist agenda. But the Brotherhood leaders also had another, less ideological concern: They feared that the regime might use al-Qassas's anti-Mubarak activism as a pretext for a broader crackdown on the organization. To assuage the Brotherhood's leaders, al-Qassas and his fellow Brotherhood youths agreed that they would only participate in these protests as individuals, meaning that they wouldn't carry Brotherhood insignias.[21]

Mohamed ElBaradei's retirement from the International Atomic Energy Agency (IAEA) in late 2009 added a new dimension to these anti-Mubarak activities. A Nobel Peace Prize winner, ElBaradei was an outspoken critic of Mubarak's autocratic rule, and his global stature made him far less susceptible to the regime's repression. Activists thus started an online campaign to support a prospective ElBaradei presidential candidacy and held their first major event on February 19, 2010, when they mobilized approximately one thousand people to Cairo International Airport to greet ElBaradei as he returned to Cairo after decades abroad as a diplomat.[22] Shortly thereafter, activists named ElBaradei chairman of their newly formed National Association for Change, and he released a manifesto calling for seven constitutional reforms.[23] Despite the Brotherhood's tepid outreach to ElBaradei, al-Qassas collaborated with his non-Islamist peers to petition for ElBaradei's reforms.[24]

Then on June 6, 2010, police officers grabbed twenty-eight-year-old Khaled Said from an Alexandria Internet café and beat him to death as horrified pedestrians looked on. Images of Said's severely mangled face went viral on social media two days later, and activists established a Facebook group titled "We Are All Khaled Said," which drew over a hundred thousand members within days.[25] The Facebook group became another platform for organizing protests, including one that drew over four thousand activists on June 25 in Alexandria,[26] and al-Qassas gathered his colleagues to participate in protests outside of the Interior Ministry's headquarters in Cairo.[27]

By the autumn of 2010, however, this opposition activity suddenly cooled off. Activists staged dozens of demonstrations, but they were mostly small and had little impact. The severely forged November 2010 parliamentary elections and the bombing of a Coptic Orthodox church in Alexandria on New Year's Day 2011, in which twenty-three people were killed, each catalyzed new blips of protest activity but nothing sustainable.[28]

As a result, the Mubarak regime felt quite secure. When 118 former opposition parliamentarians, including some Muslim Brothers, created a "shadow parliament" in December 2010 to protest the rigged elections, Mubarak wryly remarked, "Let them have fun."[29] Protests came and went, it seemed, but the regime was still standing strong.

· · · · · · · ·

Tunisia is approximately one-sixth the size of Egypt, has only one-eighth the population, and its capital is situated 1,328 miles from Cairo. Historically, its impact on Egypt has been meager, and contemporary Egyptian rulers typically looked eastward—toward Israel and the Arabian Peninsula—in projecting their power and competing for regional supremacy. But on January 14, 2011, Tunisia suddenly moved into the center of Egyptians' political imagination. After three weeks of protests that began when a fruit vendor immolated himself in response to police harassment, dictator Zine el-Abidine Ben Ali fled to Malta, thereby ending his twenty-four-year rule.

Within hours of Ben Ali's ouster, approximately a hundred Egyptian youth activists rallied outside the Tunisian embassy in Cairo before security forces beat them back. The following afternoon's planned demonstration was less impressive: Approximately twenty protesters turned out, and security forces quickly surrounded them. But the activists were already looking ahead: They hoped to use Tunisia's successful uprising to build momentum for a mass anti-Mubarak protest in downtown Cairo's Tahrir Square on January 25.[30]

January 25 was National Police Day in Egypt, marking the anniversary of a 1952 battle in which forty-one Egyptian police officers died while fighting British forces along the Suez Canal. Mubarak declared it a national holiday in 2009, but Egypt's youth activists regarded it as a propaganda effort to white-wash the regime's police brutality.[31] So they staged Police Day protests in 2009 and 2010, which attracted only a few dozen participants.[32] Yet Ben Ali's ouster in Tunisia suddenly gave the activists new hope, and they intensified their efforts for 2011's Police Day protests.

Al-Qassas first learned of these preparations on January 15, the day after Ben Ali's fall, and immediately started spreading the word. He stayed in close contact with his longtime friends in April 6 Youth and the socialist Justice and Freedom Movement, who took the lead in assembling the overall route map, and flooded his Facebook and telephone contacts with exhortations to partic-ipate. Meanwhile, al-Qassas and some of his Brotherhood colleagues lobbied the Brotherhood's Guidance Office to mobilize the organization's hundreds of thousands of cadres in support of the protests.[33]

· · · · · · · ·

For the Brotherhood's leaders, the Tunisian Revolution was both inspiring and threatening. In their analysis, Ben Ali's relatively quick ouster in the face of mass protests demonstrated the inherent weakness of secular Arab dicta-torships. But the Brotherhood also feared that it would be the Mubarak re-gime's first target if a similar uprising erupted in Egypt.

It was a risk that the Brotherhood could barely afford because it had been the target of a significant government crackdown for much of the past five years. The Brotherhood's impressive performance in the 2005 parliamentary elections, in which Muslim Brothers won 88 of 444 contested seats, greatly unnerved the Mubarak regime. So in March 2006, the regime arrested twenty prominent Muslim Brothers, and hundreds of lower-ranking Brotherhood activists were arrested by May. Then, when the Brotherhood participated in a series of demonstrations to support two judges who had been arrested for exposing rigging during the parliamentary elections, the regime arrested an additional five hundred Muslim Brothers, including six top leaders.[34]

The crackdown intensified in December 2006 after dozens of masked Muslim Brotherhood–affiliated students staged a martial arts demonstration at Cairo's al-Azhar University in front of approximately two thousand students. The demonstration's militancy shocked the regime, which responded by arresting several hundred more Brotherhood members, including seventeen senior officials. Among them was Deputy Supreme Guide Khairat al-Shater, a millionaire businessman widely considered the Brotherhood's most influential leader. A military tribunal ultimately sentenced him and another prominent Brotherhood businessman to seven years in prison, and the state seized their assets.[35]

Thereafter, the crackdown intensified with each new election. Thirty Brotherhood members were arrested prior to the 2007 elections for the Shura Council (Egypt's upper parliamentary house), seven hundred Muslim Brothers were arrested before the 2008 local council elections, and over one thousand Muslim Brothers, including sixteen top leaders and eight candidates, were arrested as the November 2010 parliamentary elections approached.[36]

The Brotherhood thus had good reason to fear that it would end up "paying the bill" for any revolutionary activity and responded to the Tunisian Revolution very carefully.[37] The morning after Ben Ali's ouster, the Brotherhood released an official statement offering its "heartfelt congratulations" to the "brotherly Tunisian people" and saluting the Tunisians' "victory in the first round of their struggle for freedom and dignity." But the statement was otherwise quite vague, urging "Arab regimes and the whole world to listen to the voice of the people demanding freedoms and democracy" and warning "global powers" against "interfering in the affairs of the region."[38] It contained no mention of Mubarak and certainly nothing that could be construed as a call for an uprising in Egypt.

As news of the forthcoming January 25 protests spread, however, the Brotherhood's leadership suddenly felt compelled to offer a stronger statement. But it faced a significant dilemma: If it openly embraced the protests, it risked an intensified crackdown, and if it distanced itself from the protests too forcefully, it would alienate younger Muslim Brothers like al-Qassas, who were determined to participate in the demonstrations either way.

So in a lengthy statement on January 19, the Brotherhood tried to split the difference. On one hand, it endorsed the demonstrations' basic thrust, explicitly warning the Mubarak regime that "the reasons and motives that catalyzed the blessed uprising in Tunisia exist in many of the countries in the region in which we live, and particularly in our homeland Egypt," and argued that the regime's "corruption" and "injustice" could prove explosive. Yet, rather than backing the mounting calls for protests, the Brotherhood said that it was "keen for stability and social peace" and believed that the "current regime" was "most capable of undertaking reforms." It then proceeded to list ten demands, including various constitutional reforms and that the regime "support the Palestinian jihad" against Israel.[39]

The Brotherhood's call for "stability" instead of protest, however, did little to assuage the regime. The following day, officials from State Security—the domestic security service tasked with monitoring opposition groups—called the Brotherhood's provincial leaders nationwide and threatened them with arrest if they demonstrated on January 25.[40] Meanwhile, in a separate call to the Brotherhood's senior leadership in Cairo, a top State Security official warned that the regime would respond to the Brotherhood's participation in the January 25 protests by arresting the supreme guide.[41]

It was a very severe threat. For all of the repression that the Brotherhood had experienced under Mubarak, his regime had never arrested a supreme guide.

· · · · · · · ·

Beyond the fear of greater repression, the Brotherhood hesitated to join the January 25 anti-Mubarak demonstrations for another reason: It didn't trust the youth activists who were organizing them. To some extent, this reflected some Brotherhood leaders' fear that cooperating with non-Islamists would undermine the organization's pursuit of an Islamic state in Egypt. But for the most part, the eighty-three-year-old organization just didn't take the youth activists seriously. The Brotherhood's leaders viewed them as ragtag up-starts—amateurish newcomers who bloviated on Twitter and Facebook but had no coherent ideology and little real support.

The Brotherhood's impression of the activists was informed by experience. In recent years, the Brotherhood had twice endorsed the activists' demonstration calls and then watched with embarrassment as the protests fizzled on both occasions. The first such incident occurred shortly after the April 6, 2008, protests to support the workers strikes in Al-Mahalla al-Kobra, when activists declared follow-up protests for May 4, Mubarak's eightieth birthday. The Brotherhood, impressed by the initial protests' success, signed on. But when the regime announced a 30 percent increase in public wages a few days before the protests, the plans for new demonstrations crumbled.[42] A year later, the Brotherhood endorsed the activists' demonstrations marking the one-year anniversary of the original April 6 protests. Again, the protests failed, and state-run media highlighted the Brotherhood's involvement to declare that the organization had lost its popularity in the streets.[43] These episodes, and the activists' inability to mobilize the masses at any point thereafter, led the Brotherhood's leadership to conclude that the activists spoke loudly but carried small sticks.

Al-Qassas, of course, had a different view. He valued his years of cooperation with non-Islamist activists and wanted the Brotherhood to support their efforts. So on January 22, he lobbied Guidance Office leader Mahmoud Abuzeid, who oversaw the organization's "students file," to endorse the January 25 demonstrations.

Abuzeid refused. The Brotherhood didn't know the individuals behind the protests, he explained, and the organization was wary of participating in an event that it hadn't organized. Abuzeid also alluded to the recent threats from State Security and said that the Brotherhood would pay a significant price if protesters marched with Brotherhood banners. Still, the Brotherhood was feeling the pressure from a certain segment of its youths, who badly wanted to participate in the January 25 demonstrations. So Abuzeid made one concession to al-Qassas: Muslim Brothers could participate as individuals.[44]

Other Brotherhood youths held similar meetings with Brotherhood leaders during this period, but the response was always the same. On January 23, Brotherhood activist Anas al-Qassas (no relation to Mohamed) met with Guidance Office leader Essam el-Erian and alerted him to the significant activity on Facebook in support of the upcoming anti-Mubarak protests. But el-Erian declined, adding that the Brotherhood might get involved if the demonstrations were sizable. That same day, the Brotherhood's political chief, Mohamed Morsi, summoned Abdel Galil al-Sharnouby, the organization's thirty-seven-year-old Web editor, and ordered him not to publish a call for a revolution. "We will not call for a revolution and won't adopt the idea," Morsi said, according to al-Sharnouby, referring to the activists as "a bunch of kids."[45]

Yet, the Brotherhood's youths weren't the only ones itching to join the demonstrations. Many of the Brotherhood's former parliamentarians were members of the shadow parliament, and when the shadow parliament announced that it would protest on January 25 on the steps of Egypt's High Court, its Brotherhood members lobbied the Guidance Office to endorse their participation.

For the Guidance Office, this request posed a significant challenge. It couldn't simply tell the ex-parliamentarians that they were free to participate as individuals. Most of them were Brotherhood officials, and their participation would therefore be interpreted as the Brotherhood's endorsement of the protests. So Guidance Office member Saad al-Katatny, who had served as the Brotherhood's parliamentary bloc chair from 2005 to 2010, reached a compromise: Fifteen of the Brotherhood's eighty-eight former parliamentarians could participate, thereby ensuring that Muslim Brothers were not overrepresented on the steps of the High Court when the demonstrations started. To reinforce the Guidance Office's control over its organization, al-Katatny personally selected the fifteen.[46]

Indeed, in the days before the January 25 protests, the Brotherhood's leadership faced two sets of pressure: internal pressure from members who wanted to participate in the demonstrations and external pressure from the regime that threatened to destroy the Brotherhood if it endorsed the protests. So in its final statement prior to the demonstrations, which it released on January 23, the Guidance Office tried to strike a balance.

Signed by Supreme Guide Mohamed Badie, the statement sharply criticized the regime, accusing it of "tyranny, corruption, and state terrorism," and acknowledged that the authorities had "called the Muslim Brotherhood officials in the governorates and threatened them with assault, arrest, violent and perhaps bloody confrontation if they go to the streets to call for . . . popular demands." But rather than embracing the demonstrations, Badie called for "a comprehensive national dialogue" as a way out of the "crisis" and reiterated the Brotherhood's desire to "protect the security of the homeland and its stability."[47]

The youth activists who were organizing the January 25 protests derided the Brotherhood's statement as evidence of regime co-optation.[48] Al-Qassas and his fellow Brotherhood youth activists were similarly disappointed with their leaders' decision. But they nevertheless continued their preparations for January 25, as the Brotherhood leaders permitted them to do unofficially.[49]

• • • • • • • •

The Brotherhood youth activists and former parliamentarians weren't the only Muslim Brothers who disagreed with the Guidance Office's decision. Despite State Security's direct threat against them, a number of local Brotherhood leaders in Cairo actively lobbied the Brotherhood's top leaders to accept the risks and join the January 25 protests. When these efforts similarly failed, the local Brotherhood officials took matters into their own hands and organized their cadres to demonstrate in defiance of the Guidance Office.

The leader of this effort was Osama Yassin. A charismatic figure in the Brotherhood's central Cairo office where he served as media spokesman, Yassin had joined the Brotherhood during his university days at Ain Shams Medical School and quickly rose through the ranks in the Brotherhood's students division. Now forty-six, Yassin enjoyed a wide following within the organization and was considered one of the Brotherhood's rising stars—a possible future supreme guide, some said.[50]

On January 24, Yassin convened a meeting of thirty local Brotherhood leaders at his home to plan for the next day's demonstrations. Given the regime's threats, the group decided that the highest-ranking leaders would stay away from the protests but that its mid- and lower-level officials could participate. Most important, the group decided to send a message down the Brotherhood's chain of command urging—though, out of respect for the Guidance Office's decision, not commanding—Brotherhood cadres to participate. To ensure the decision's confidentiality, this decision was transmitted via face-to-face meetings. The Cairo Brothers worked quickly: By midnight, the message had reached the organization's lowest ranks.[51]

Perhaps recognizing that many Brotherhood youths planned to join the following day's protests, Guidance Office leader Saad al-Husseini posted a YouTube video on January 24 imploring the Brothers to stay peaceful. "We have to remember as Muslim Brothers—as extensions of our religion—not to injure people," he said. "Violence should not be used, [nor] destruction nor damage to public or private property, because this is a crime."[52]

• • • • • • • •

On the morning of January 25, the leading youth activists went to prearranged starting points all around the Cairo metropolitan area and began marching at approximately ten in the morning. Al-Qassas and some of his Brotherhood youth colleagues marched from Nahia Street in Giza, along with activists from the Democratic Front Party, the socialist Justice and Freedom Movement, and the ElBaradei campaign.[53] A second march began in northern Cairo's densely populated Shobra neighborhood and included the April 6

Youth Movement, Revolutionary Socialists, the Nasserist Karama Party, and various Christian activists.[54] A third protest march began in Imbaba, a low-income community in northern Giza along the Nile's western bank, and included local April 6 activists, another contingent of ElBaradei's supporters, and independent activists.[55] A fourth protest, which the Justice and Freedom Movement organized, began in northern Cairo's Matariya neighborhood, and a fifth demonstration, led by the non-Islamist Ghad Party, emanated from Bab al-Shaariya, a neighborhood just northeast of downtown Cairo.[56]

Each of these marches started with a few dozen activists, who called people into the streets as they wound their way through low-income neighborhoods. At the same time, the activists posted a list of major demonstration sites on social media, expecting a few hundred protesters to arrive at each. The activists' goal was to arrive at these publicly listed sites with enough marchers to overwhelm the security forces that would be stationed there and then proceed onward from multiple directions toward Tahrir Square. They dubbed this the "snowball" strategy, meaning that the protests were designed to grow as they pushed forward.[57]

At approximately one thirty in the afternoon, the shadow parliament, with fifteen Brotherhood ex-parliamentarians among them, gathered on the steps of the High Court in downtown Cairo, as planned. The Brotherhood, however, was hardly inconspicuous. Mohamed al-Beltagy, a forty-seven-year-old Brotherhood ex-parliamentarian with a strong following among the organization's youths, carried a banner calling for Mubarak's resignation and led a group of supporters in chanting for "change, freedom, and social justice."[58] Meanwhile, one block south, a small group of protesters gathered at the Lawyers Syndicate, and a second small group gathered on the steps of the Journalists Syndicate just around the corner. Riot police scrambled to all three locations and surrounded them, with small skirmishes breaking out around the Lawyers Syndicate as activists attempted to push into the streets.

For a few moments, security forces held the protesters at bay. But then a few hundred protesters suddenly streamed into the area from the north and overwhelmed the police. The police responded by redeploying into the streets, which enabled the small protests at the High Court, Lawyers Syndicate, and Journalists Syndicate to converge. The growing mass then pressed southward toward Tahrir Square, breaking past successive lines of security forces, which stood no chance of preventing the snowballing procession's progress. Within an hour, the demonstration hit Tahrir Square, and, as news of the protesters' feat spread, the crowds swelled further. By the early evening, tens of thousands of Egyptians had gathered in Tahrir Square.[59] The activists then tried to organize a sit-in, and al-Qassas called more of his Brotherhood colleagues, urging them to join the growing masses in the square.[60]

The day ended far less exuberantly, however. While most protesters stayed in Tahrir Square, a few hundred pressed further southward toward the prime minister's office and attempted to break through the gates and occupy the building. The regime responded forcefully, shooting foul-smelling water at the demonstrators, deploying plainclothes thugs to beat them, and arresting dozens. The regime then blanketed the side streets with tear gas, pushing the protesters toward Tahrir. Once night fell, the regime aggressively cleared the square with a mix of tear gas and birdshot.

By the following morning, Tahrir Square was empty. But the ubiquity of security forces in downtown Cairo reflected a severely shaken regime. And the protesters were already preparing their second punch: mass protests on Friday, January 28, which they dubbed "Friday of Rage."

Like almost everyone else, the Brotherhood hadn't anticipated the size of the January 25 protests. The suddenly escalating calls for Friday of Rage demonstrations thus presented the Guidance Office with a familiar dilemma: to participate or not to participate?

• • • • • • • •

At seven o'clock in the evening of January 25, three Brotherhood youths visited the Guidance Office and told Brotherhood leaders Mohamed Morsi and Mahmoud Ezzat that the square was full of Muslim Brothers.[61] Morsi seemingly didn't realize how big the Tahrir demonstrations were and responded angrily. "How dare you go without informing your leaders!" he shouted.[62]

The Brotherhood youths reassured him that the Brothers in the square were participating as individuals, and Morsi calmed down. The youths then informed the Brotherhood leaders of the new calls for a Friday of Rage and urged the Brotherhood to join officially. After much discussion, the Brotherhood leaders offered a conditional response: If the activists successfully rallied their base, the Brotherhood would endorse the Friday protests.[63] The extent of the Brotherhood's participation, however, had not yet been decided, and the Brotherhood leaders didn't promise a complete mobilization of the organization's cadres.

The Brotherhood's public pronouncements were similarly ambiguous. In its first statement on "The Events of January 25 and Their Aftermath," which it released the following day, the Brotherhood insisted that "the movement of the Egyptian people that began on January 25 and has been peaceful, mature, and civilized must continue against corruption, oppression, and injustice." But it didn't echo the activists' calls for a revolution. Instead, it urged the regime "to quickly implement the demanded reforms, abandon the policy of stubbornness, and address the people's legitimate demands." Most important, it made no mention of the Friday of Rage protests.[64]

The Brotherhood's tiptoeing, however, didn't reassure the regime. The January 25 demonstrations had far exceeded the Interior Ministry's own preparations. Meanwhile, riot police looked exhausted chasing a series of smaller protests the following day, and the ministry lacked sufficient reserves to replace its officers on the streets. The regime thus looked toward the Friday of Rage protests with great concern. So on January 26, State Security officers once again phoned the Brotherhood's provincial leaders and threatened to arrest them if the organization endorsed the demonstrations.[65]

According to Brotherhood leaders, this was the straw that broke the camel's back. The organization was angering many of its own members by calling for reform rather than revolution, and the regime was still threatening it. So that evening, the Brotherhood commanded its entire membership to participate in the Friday of Rage protests.[66] By Thursday morning, all Muslim Brothers had received the message that marching was "obligatory." Internally, the Brotherhood declared it *"thawrat al-masājid"*—"the revolution of the mosques"—since the uprising would start from the mosques after Friday prayers and press onward to the central squares all across the country.[67]

The regime apparently caught wind of these plans. On Thursday night, January 27, approximately half of the Guidance Office's leaders were arrested.[68] Meanwhile, hoping to stifle the protests, the regime shut down most Internet and cell phone networks throughout the country.

The regime's moves, however, smacked of desperation and came too late in any event. Thousands of Muslim Brothers and their family members, as well as many Egyptians from across the country's political spectrum, had already decided to protest. And the Friday of Rage strategy was so simple that a break in telecommunications had no perceptible impact. So from the moment that Friday prayers ended on January 28 at one in the afternoon, the streets were packed with protesters chanting for the fall of Mubarak's regime, and unprecedented street battles ensued.

For hours, security forces blanketed Cairo with tear gas and then tried to halt the protesters' advance with water cannons and birdshot. But it was to no avail. The activists on the front lines had studied the Tunisian revolutionaries' techniques and came prepared. They wore scarves to shield themselves from tear gas inhalation and distributed surgical masks among their fellow demonstrators. They sprayed the windshields of security vehicles with black paint, thereby rendering them too dangerous to drive. And they wore gloves so they could pick up tear gas canisters as soon as they were fired and throw them back toward the police.

Amid the chaos, police stations and prisons were attacked nationwide, with an estimated twenty thousand prisoners breaking free on January 28 and in the days that followed. The question of who initiated these attacks remains very controversial within Egypt and is the source of numerous conspiracy theories. At the time, revolutionary activists accused the Mubarak regime of releasing the prisoners to stoke chaos and create support for the police to return. However, the liberation of those Brotherhood leaders who were arrested on January 27 later fueled a different theory: The Brotherhood had directed the attacks on police stations and prisons.[69] Only the Brotherhood had the will and the nationwide organization to attack so many security installations, the theory goes. Still, the Brotherhood leaders' accounts of their prison breaks offer another explanation: As prisoners learned of the security forces' breakdown, they started resisting their prison guards, and structural damage to the prisons during the protests enabled them to flee.[70]

Either way, by late afternoon on January 28, Mubarak's police state had collapsed. Thoroughly overwhelmed, security forces withdrew from the streets, forcing the military to assert control within Cairo. It was the clearest signal that the regime was on the ropes and that its fate now lay firmly in the hands of the military. Would the generals side with Mubarak or respond to the protesters and topple him?

The military's internal deliberations during this critical moment are unknown. But two sets of considerations likely guided the generals' calculus. On one hand, they feared the prospect of political disorder if they removed Mubarak. Beyond the military's responsibility for Egypt's national security, it also controls a significant chunk of the Egyptian economy: It produces and sells consumer goods, builds infrastructure, and claims much of Egypt's uninhabited territory as its own. Political chaos would therefore threaten these interests.

But, at the same time, the military likely believed that it couldn't disperse the protests with force. The conscripts now stationed in Tahrir Square might refuse an order to shoot their countrymen, which would foment chaos within the military's ranks. And perhaps most important, the generals anticipated a political upside to the uprising. For over a year, the generals had signaled their opposition to Gamal Mubarak—a businessman with no military background—succeeding his father and likely saw the uprising as an opportunity to foreclose that possibility.

So, as the tanks rolled into downtown Cairo on the evening of January 28, Mubarak addressed the nation for the first time since the uprising began and played to the generals'—and the broader Egyptian public's—fear of instability. "The problems facing us and the goals sought by us cannot be achieved by violence or chaos," he said, adding that the demonstrations had left "the majority of the Egyptian people fearing . . . further mayhem, chaos, and destruction."[71] While Mubarak's words appealed to many Egyptians, Egypt's political momentum had shifted toward Tahrir Square, where the activists rejected Mubarak's promise to appoint a new cabinet as too little, too late. With hundreds of protesters injured and at least dozens killed, the activists would settle for nothing less than Mubarak's immediate ouster.[72]

• • • • • • • •

The revolutionaries had a very clear strategy for achieving a goal that appeared fantastical only a week earlier: They would occupy Tahrir Square indefinitely and thus force the military to side with them against Mubarak. And despite its initial hesitance to join the uprising, the Brotherhood's unparalleled mobilizing capabilities became vital to the Tahrir sit-in's success after the police state broke down on January 28.

The Brotherhood played three critical roles in supporting the uprising during this period. First, when armed thugs attacked Cairo's residential communities amid the breakdown of the police state, Muslim Brothers joined the "neighborhood watch" groups that local residents organized for protection. The Brotherhood was perfectly structured for contributing to these efforts. Its five- to ten-member cells existed in virtually every community, and in some cases local Brothers called meetings at nearby mosques to arrange shifts.[73] While the majority of those participating in neighborhood watch groups likely were non-Brothers, the Brotherhood's mobilizing prowess assisted local communities.

Second, within Tahrir Square, the Brotherhood worked to sustain the sit-in by ordering cadres from all over Egypt to set up camp there. On Sunday, January 30, Muslim Brothers from western Nile Delta governorates arrived in the square, and Brothers from Upper Egypt and Fayoum arrived shortly thereafter.[74] Along with other political groups and activists, the Brotherhood also worked to keep the square adequately supplied by bringing food and blankets.[75] These reinforcements helped ensure that Tahrir remained occupied even as the crowds typically waxed during the daytime and waned late at night.[76]

Third, the Brotherhood secured the square. On January 29, Brotherhood leaders began directing cadres to patrol the square's entrances, and they monitored activities within the square as well. The Guidance Office also set up an operations room in a former Brotherhood parliamentarian's law offices in downtown Cairo and appointed Osama Yassin to serve as the "general coordinator for Tahrir Square." Yassin initially answered to Guidance Office member Mohamed Ali Bishr, who was stationed in the square for much of the revolt. But starting on January 30, Yassin answered to Mohamed Morsi, who broke out of prison with other Brotherhood leaders the previous day and then assumed control of the organization's revolutionary activities.[77]

Within the square, Yassin organized the Brotherhood's cadres into twelve-hour shifts, which included four hours of providing security, four hours of interacting with the square and other political forces, and four hours of sleeping. He further stationed approximately fifty Brotherhood cadres at each Tahrir Square entrance to prevent intruders and check the identity cards of those entering. And to protect Cairo's neighborhoods from armed attacks, Yassin organized the cadres to spend half of the uprising's days in the square and the other half participating in the neighborhood watch groups. Throughout this period, the Brotherhood worked to "blend in with the individuals, people, and the [political] forces," apparently fearing that publicizing its role in the Tahrir sit-in would discredit the broader uprising. "Nobody knew that there was an organized leadership in the square," Yassin later said.[78]

The Brotherhood's activities in the square weren't purely defensive, however. On January 30, the Brotherhood directed its cadres to attack the Interior Ministry, which is located about a half mile southeast of Tahrir. "The regime had started to fall," Yassin later recalled in an interview with Al Jazeera. "And for the regime to fall, the Interior Ministry had to be targeted." The offensive, however, was unsuccessful. Snipers stationed atop the ministry successfully repelled the Brothers and their cocombatants, and the fighting ended when the military sent tanks to defend it.[79]

Yet despite the Brotherhood's full-fledged participation in the anti-Mubarak uprising from the January 28 Friday of Rage protests onward, it never adopted the other revolutionary forces' absolute refusal to negotiate with the regime. On February 1, two days after the failed siege of the Interior

Ministry, Brotherhood leaders Morsi and al-Katatny met secretly with former intelligence chief Omar Suleiman, whom Mubarak had appointed vice president only three days before. The precise details of this meeting are disputed. According to one version, Suleiman agreed that the regime would release Khairat al-Shater and businessman Hassan Malek, who had been imprisoned since 2007; dissolve Parliament; enact a variety of constitutional changes; and permit the Brotherhood to establish a political party for the next parliamentary elections.[80] According to another version, the Brotherhood's demands focused on al-Shater and Malek's release exclusively.[81]

Either way, on the night of February 1, the Brotherhood tried to enforce this agreement by calling on its members to leave Tahrir.[82] But al-Qassas and his fellow Brotherhood youths refused, and Brotherhood leaders feared that forcing Muslim Brothers to leave the square would create a substantial rift within the organization.[83] So the Brotherhood tabled the matter for the time being.

• • • • • • • •

At approximately eleven o'clock on the evening of February 1, Mubarak spoke to the Egyptian people for the second time since the uprising began. The speech came amid rising US pressure for him to respond to the protesters' demands and begin a political transition. In a conciliatory tone, Mubarak announced that he would not run for another presidential term and called for dialogue with the opposition. He also offered a wistful, nationalistic reflection on the forthcoming end to his political and military career: "Hosni Mubarak who speaks to you today is proud of the long years he spent in the service of Egypt and its people. This dear nation is my country, it is the country of all Egyptians, here I have lived and fought for its sake and I defended its land, its sovereignty and interests and on this land I will die and history will judge me and others for our merits and faults. The nation remains."[84]

While the Tahrir Square protesters rejected the speech and continued to demand Mubarak's ouster, his nationalistic appeal resonated with many Egyptians elsewhere. As journalist Ashraf Khalil noted, these Egyptians saw Mubarak "as a genuine war hero and father figure . . . and blamed his underlings for systemic problems like corruption and police brutality." Within hours, pro-Mubarak demonstrations emerged throughout the country, and clashes with the anti-Mubarak protesters broke out almost immediately in Alexandria.[85]

The following day, the violence hit Cairo.

At 1:40 p.m. on Wednesday, February 2, approximately a thousand pro-Mubarak demonstrators descended upon Tahrir Square, and intense fighting continued throughout the day. Initially the pro-Mubarak forces stormed deeply into the square, finding the anti-Mubarak protesters entirely unprepared. The Mubarakists smashed a podium and destroyed speakers, and the two sides threw rocks and bricks at each other furiously. The most iconic moment in the fighting came at around three o'clock, when a small group of horse- and camel-riding pro-Mubarak demonstrators dashed into the square, leading to even more severe fighting. February 2 became known as "the Battle of the Camel," a reference to a historic Islamic battle, and represented a turning point in the uprising.[86]

As pro-Mubarak forces descended from multiple directions and took control of Talaat Harb Square to the northeast, the Brotherhood scrambled to mobilize a response.[87] Amid the chaos, Muslim Brothers worked with other Tahrir activists to break bricks for use as projectiles, and Brotherhood activists deployed in lines to resist the Mubarakists' advance, with limited success during the battle's early hours.[88]

At approximately six in the evening, the tide started turning in the revolutionaries' favor, and the Brotherhood played a pivotal role. Brotherhood cadres helped organize protesters into an "improvised assembly line" for transporting broken bricks to the square's front lines, where revolutionaries, including many Muslim Brothers, engaged proregime forces in the most intense battles. Meanwhile, the Brotherhood worked with other forces in the square to detain and beat proregime thugs, before handing many of them over to military personnel stationed near the square. By eleven o'clock, the revolutionaries had resisted the proregime forces' assault and erected barricades to fortify the square.[89]

At two in the morning on February 3, however, pro-Mubarak forces mobilized a second attack. Tahrir's frontlines extended to just below the neighboring October 6 Bridge, which enabled approximately fifty pro-Mubarak thugs to seize the higher ground and rain rocks and Molotov cocktails on the protesters below. During the fighting, however, a group of anti-Mubarak protesters climbed one of the bridge's entrance ramps and confronted the Mubarakists, enabling more protesters to advance against the proregime forces. At this point, the military finally intervened, ensuring the protesters' victory.[90]

The protesters' success on the uprising's bloodiest day energized the revolution. Thirty-six hours later, a "million-man march" demanding Mubarak's ouster filled Tahrir Square.[91] Moreover, the Brotherhood's crucial role

during the Battle of the Camel won it respect among non-Islamist protesters. "If it wasn't for the Brotherhood, we would have gotten really screwed
that day," activist Mohamed El Dahshan told journalist Ashraf Khalil. "They
went to the front lines. Their people really shouldered a lot of the burden
on defense."[92]

• • • • • • • •

The Battle of the Camel was the regime's final attempt to clear Tahrir Square
violently, and the regime recognized its failure. So on February 5, Vice President Suleiman and newly appointed prime minister Ahmed Shafik invited
the Brotherhood and other political forces to participate in dialogue to end
the standoff.[93] After much internal deliberation, the Brotherhood accepted
the invitation and sent two leaders, Morsi and al-Katatny, to the February 6
meeting.[94]

The dialogue, however, was designed to protect the regime. Most of the
other participants hailed from legal opposition parties—political groups that
opposed the regime superficially because their very existence depended on
staying in the regime's good graces. Unsurprisingly, the meeting produced a
proposal that was very much at odds with the revolution's demands: Mubarak
would remain president while a committee drafted constitutional amendments, which would then be put to a referendum.[95] Initially al-Katatny defended this agreement. "We wanted the president to step down, but for now
we accept this arrangement," he told a press conference at the Brotherhood's
headquarters. "It's safer that the president stays until he makes these amendments to speed things up because of the constitutional powers he holds."[96]

The decision, however, garnered instant criticism from the revolutionary
camp, including many Muslim Brothers, who accused al-Katatny of selling
out the uprising. So the very next day, the Guidance Office backtracked. "This
popular revolution brought down the regime, so it inevitably must go," its
February 7 statement read. "And this exemplifies the need for the president
of the republic to step aside, which is the primary and greatest demand that
the masses advocate."[97]

The Brotherhood's unambiguous call for Mubarak's ouster meant that it
was—finally—fully aligned with the uprising's demands. That quelled the
criticism from within Egypt's revolutionary camp, but it also put the Brotherhood in a very uncomfortable position. After all, despite its pivotal work in
Tahrir Square, the Brotherhood desperately wanted to avoid becoming the
face of Egypt's uprising because it feared backlash from three sets of actors.

First, the Brotherhood knew that many Egyptians distrusted it. The Brotherhood thus wanted to dispel the notion that it would use the uprising to advance its theocratic political aims, and it consequently downplayed its longtime call for establishing an Islamic state in Egypt.[98] For example, in its first statement after the Battle of the Camel, the Brotherhood said that it "agreed fully with the clear, popular desire for Egypt to be a civil democratic state with an Islamic reference," in which "all citizens realize freedom, equality, and social justice." Most significantly, the Brotherhood minimized its political ambitions, promising that it "doesn't have any special agenda" and had "no aspiration to the presidency and no aspiration to rule or for any position." It affirmed this promise on February 10, when the Brotherhood's top legislative body convened and officially voted against running in the first presidential elections that would follow Mubarak's ouster.[99]

Second, the Brotherhood feared that the military would move against the uprising if it became too closely associated with the Brotherhood. The Brotherhood thus tried to reassure the military at every turn. In its February 5 statement, for example, the Brotherhood hailed "the proud Egyptian army for protecting the protesters peacefully against all forms of terrorism and thuggery."[100] Brotherhood leaders in the square also conferred with military officials who visited the protests, asking them to protect the demonstrations and advising them on the stationing of tanks around the square.[101] In this way, the Brotherhood's position was similar to most other political groups in the square, which tried to court the brass away from Mubarak.

Third, the Brotherhood feared that Western concerns of an "Islamist takeover" in Egypt would invite a foreign intervention, and it thus courted the international media vigorously. Brotherhood leader Abdel Moneim Abouel Fotouh wrote in a *Washington Post* op-ed that "contrary to fear-mongering reports, the West and the Muslim Brotherhood are not enemies" and said that the Brotherhood "embraced diversity and democratic values."[102] On CNN, Brotherhood leader Essam el-Erian similarly insisted that the Brotherhood was just one of many players that would play a role following Mubarak's departure. "This revolution is not led by one power," he said. "It is an Egyptian revolution, not colored by any color. It doesn't have any agenda except the demands of the protesters."[103] El-Erian also penned a *New York Times* op-ed, emphasizing the Brotherhood's acceptance of the uprising's prodemocratic demands and its promise not to pursue executive power. "We aim to achieve reform and rights for all: not just for the Muslim Brotherhood, not just for Muslims, but for all Egyptians," he wrote. "We do not intend to take a dominant role in the forthcoming political transition. We are not putting forward a candidate for the presidential elections scheduled for September."[104]

Of all the Brotherhood's fears, however, its concerns regarding the West were the most baseless. According to a Gallup poll taken in early February, 82 percent of American adults were "sympathetic to the protesters in Egypt who have called for a change in government," while only 11 percent were unsympathetic, and those numbers tilted 87–10 among those adults who followed the situation in Egypt "very or somewhat closely."[105] The inspiring images out of Tahrir Square, highlighting tech-savvy and mostly "liberal" protesters challenging an autocratic regime, fed substantial Arab Spring optimism in the West. Far from trying to stifle the uprising, many Western countries sought to ensure its success.

Still, Mubarak made one final appeal to exit on his own terms. On February 10, hours after Egypt's top generals met without him and promised to "safeguard the people and to protect the interests of the nation," Mubarak took the podium.[106] In a stubborn tone, Mubarak repeated the promises from his February 1 address, vowing to oversee a transition, implement various constitutional reforms, hold open parliamentary and presidential elections, and not run for reelection. He also delegated full presidential authority to Suleiman, rendering himself a virtual figurehead.[107] Yet these commitments still fell far short of the protesters' demands. The activists responded by threatening to march to the presidential palace, which risked a severe confrontation with the security forces protecting it.[108]

The following day, however, the military signaled that the protesters' demands would be answered. Shortly after six o'clock in the evening, Suleiman announced Mubarak's resignation in a thirty-second address, adding that the SCAF had assumed executive power.

Tahrir Square exploded in celebration, and the Brotherhood rejoiced with its non-Islamist corevolutionaries.[109] "Oh patient and steadfast masses of Egypt, oh heroes of freedom and partisans of truth, oh people of sacrifice and redemption, we greet you!" the Brotherhood declared in a statement, saluting the "great army of Egypt that protected the revolution."[110]

• • • • • • • •

The Brotherhood's decision making during the chaotic eighteen-day uprising was, it turned out, a smashing success. It mobilized its cadres during the pivotal January 28 Friday of Rage protests and defended Tahrir Square on February 2. At the same time, it avoided becoming the face of Egypt's revolution.

That title belonged to the mostly non-Islamist activists, who suddenly graced the covers of international news magazines and appeared frequently on Egyptian television programs that once shunned them. As a result, many observers, both within Egypt and elsewhere, underestimated the Brotherhood's post-Mubarak political prospects. "They will not win more than 10 percent, I think," one prominent activist told the *New York Times* a few days before Mubarak's ouster.[III]

The Brotherhood's leaders, however, knew better. With the fall of Mubarak's ruling party, the Brotherhood was now the only political organization in Egypt that possessed a significant nationwide structure. After many decades, its moment had finally arrived.

2   An Islamist Vanguard

On February 10, 2011, one day before Mubarak's ouster, US director of national intelligence James Clapper sat before the House of Representatives' Permanent Select Committee on Intelligence to testify on various international security threats. While the bulk of the hearing focused on al-Qaeda and other global terrorist organizations, it was only natural that the congressmen would turn their attention toward Egypt, where the dramatic uprising appeared to be reaching its fateful conclusion.

Washington had a great stake in Egypt's post-Mubarak political trajectory because it had sent Egypt approximately $1.3 billion in military aid annually since 1986.[1] And although the Washington foreign policy community largely shared the American public's broad sympathy for Egypt's protesters, it was somewhat divided on the uprising's ramifications. Was the uprising a long-awaited Arab Spring—the first step of a process that would finally bring democratic, inclusive rule to an autocratic region and thus promote greater stability? Or would the uprisings ultimately empower radical, theocratic forces, thereby catalyzing an "Islamist takeover" and a fundamental reorientation of Egypt's Western-aligned posture?

Congresswoman Sue Myrick fell into the latter, more skeptical camp. "Regarding the Muslim Brotherhood," the ninth-term North Carolina Republican told Clapper, "I'm very concerned that they're using the peaceful protests in Egypt for a power grab." Myrick proceeded to argue that the Brotherhood pushes "an extremist ideology that causes others to commit acts of terrorism" and cited court documents from a terrorism-financing trial alleging that the Brotherhood is engaged in a "civilizational jihadi process." She then asked the intelligence director whether he shared her view. "Do you consider the Muslim Brotherhood a danger based on their extremist ideology?"

He didn't.

"The term Muslim Brotherhood is an umbrella term for a variety of movements," Clapper said. "In the case of Egypt, a very heterogeneous group, largely secular, which has eschewed violence and has decried al-Qaeda as a perversion of Islam. They have pursued social ends, betterment of the political order in Egypt, et cetera."[2]

To be sure, parts of Clapper's description of the Brotherhood were accurate: The Brotherhood had renounced al-Qaeda, and it also focused much of its attention on providing social services to underserviced Egyptian communities. But two very badly chosen adjectives sunk his presentation: The Brotherhood's explicit call for an Islamic state in Egypt based on *sharī'ah*—Islamic legal principles—made it anything but "secular," and the fact that it was an all-male, all-Muslim organization made it anything but "heterogeneous." Within hours, his spokeswoman released a clarification, explaining that the intelligence director was "well aware that the Muslim Brotherhood is not a secular organization" but "makes efforts to work through a political system that has been, under Mubarak's rule, one that is largely secular in its orientation."[3]

Clapper's imprecision earned him a day of terrible press, and his description of the Brotherhood as "secular" and "heterogeneous" is often resurrected (including by this author) as a prime example of the Obama administration's various misjudgments in navigating the Arab Spring. Yet by emphasizing the Brotherhood's commitment to pursuing political change through formal political institutions rather than violence, Clapper was merely echoing what many analysts believed about the Brotherhood at that time—that the Brotherhood was a "moderate" Islamist organization that accepted democratic principles and rejected violent extremism.

● ● ● ● ● ● ● ●

The notion of a "moderate Muslim Brotherhood" had emerged most forcefully within Western policy and academic circles following the terrorist attacks of September 11, 2001. As the United States launched a "Global War on Terror" that focused primarily on al-Qaeda but also promised to defeat "every terrorist group of global reach,"[4] policymakers and scholars began looking for "moderate" Islamists who might assist US efforts in sidelining the violent forces within their own societies. This search for Islamist moderates was premised on a perfectly valid assumption: Islamists held significant political and ideological influence within many Muslim-majority countries, and moderate Islamists were thus viewed as necessary allies for discrediting the "extremists" who posed the greatest danger to Americans.

The Brotherhood emerged as the supposedly moderate Islamist group of choice for two reasons. First, the Brotherhood had renounced violence during the 1970s and rejected the violent ideologies of terrorist groups such as al-Qaeda. Second, it had participated in parliamentary elections for three decades, leading many analysts to view it as democratic.

Of course, the Brotherhood was not always a nonviolent organization. In the decade following its 1928 founding, its rapid expansion across Egypt made it a target for governmental repression, and it established a "secret apparatus" in 1943 (and possibly earlier) to serve as "defender of the movement against the police and the governments of Egypt." Yet the secret apparatus ultimately became an offensive tool: Two secret apparatus members were convicted of killing an Egyptian judge in November 1948; a young Muslim Brother assassinated Prime Minister Mahmoud al-Nuqrashi in December 1948; and secret apparatus volunteers participated in the 1948 Arab–Israeli War, much to Egyptian authorities' chagrin.[5] Five years later, a Muslim Brother allegedly attempted to assassinate President Gamal Abdel Nasser, and an extremely severe crackdown followed: Thousands of Muslim Brothers were arrested and tortured, eight members were sentenced to death, and the organization was legally dissolved.[6]

The crackdown persisted through the early 1970s, and during this period the Brotherhood's radicalism became most pronounced. In 1964, Brotherhood chief spokesman Sayyid Qutb wrote his infamous manifesto, *Milestones*, which advocated violent jihad against non-Islamic political systems.[7] Qutb argued that "the whole world is steeped in *jahiliyyah*," which refers to the period of "ignorance" that preceded the revelation of Islam according to Islamic theology, and he effectively accused contemporary Arab regimes of being non-Islamic. He called for a "movement struggling against the *jahili* environment while also trying to remove the influences of *jahili* society in its followers," after which this movement would confront non-Islamic influences globally. "Defense is not the ultimate objective of the Islamic movement of jihad," wrote Qutb, "but is a means of establishing the Divine authority" within Islamic lands, after which it "is then carried throughout the earth to the whole of mankind."[8]

Qutb's program was interpreted as a call for violent holy war within Egypt against infidels, which included the Egyptian government, after which the jihad would be extended worldwide. The Nasser regime immediately banned *Milestones*, and it then executed Qutb in 1966. As the 9/11 Commission Report noted, Qutb's writings later inspired the most dangerous global jihadis, including Osama bin Laden.[9]

While Qutb's execution made him a martyr within the Brotherhood, the organization publicly distanced itself from the ideas he expressed in *Milestones*. In 1969, top Brotherhood leaders in prison wrote *Preachers Not Judges*, which indirectly repudiated Qutb's puritanical interpretation of Islam, as well as the violence he embraced in promoting this interpretation. The book was initially distributed among Muslim Brothers and was later attributed to Supreme Guide Hassan al-Hudaybi when it was publicly released in 1977.[10]

In *Preachers Not Judges*, al-Hudaybi rejected the notion that society as a whole had fallen into a state of *jahiliyyah*. "Saying that society is *jahilli* is equivalent to saying that society is lost or that society is corrupt," wrote al-Hudaybi. "All of these formulations merely indicate that there is an explicit violation of Islamic precepts." Remedying these violations, argued al-Hudaybi, meant "returning to the precepts of *shari'ah* that are taken from the verses [of the Qur'an] and the *hadīth*."

Instead of advocating jihad, as Qutb did, al-Hudaybi emphasized that the Muslim Brotherhood's role was preaching: reciting "the laws of *shari'ah*, reading verses of the Holy Qur'an and the *hadīth* of the Prophet (peace be upon him) to the people, citing, if necessary, sayings of scholars of *fiqh*, language and *hadīth*." The interpretation of these laws should be left for the individual, wrote al-Hudaybi. "As we have said many times, we are preachers not judges."[11]

It is worth pointing out that *Preachers Not Judges* is only "moderate" relative to Qutb's jihadi tract. After all, *Preachers Not Judges* emphasizes the distinction between believer and infidel (*kāfir*) and argues implicitly that the latter should be excluded from the Islamic community. It also supported the application of Qur'anic *hudūd* punishments, which include cutting off the hands of thieves and stoning adulterers.[12] But al-Hudaybi's renunciation of Qutb's violent ideas was significant within the Brotherhood's Islamist context and created a rift between the Brotherhood and violent jihadi groups in the decades that followed.

Of course, this rift meant that the Brotherhood was moderate relative to violent jihadis—which isn't much of a standard for judging moderation. But many Western analysts found the Brotherhood's distance from the more violent Islamists encouraging nonetheless. In an influential 2007 *Foreign Affairs* article, Nixon Center fellows Robert S. Leiken and Steven Brooke wrote that the Muslim Brotherhood "presents a notable opportunity," touting the Brotherhood's "organizational discipline and a painstaking educational program" for "sifting radicalism out of its ranks." The United States could coop-

erate with the Brotherhood, they argued, "in specific areas of mutual interest—such as opposition to al Qaeda, the encouragement of democracy, and
resistance to expanding Iranian influence."[13]

George Washington University professor Marc Lynch took this argument
a step further. Not only could the Brotherhood act as an ally against al-Qaeda,
argued Lynch, but a strong Brotherhood could serve as a "firewall" against
al-Qaeda–style radicalism. "The [Muslim Brotherhood's] distinctive organization," he wrote, "allows it to effectively monitor and control social space—
through mosques, charities, organizational networks, and widespread networks," adding that the Brotherhood's presence in religious institutions made
it a more effective counter to jihadis than domestic intelligence agencies or
non-Islamists, neither of which could penetrate the religious sphere.[14] Lynch
was particularly bullish on the importance of empowering so-called moderates within the Brotherhood as a counter to Islamist extremists elsewhere.
"I'd reckon that seeing the moderate trends in the Brotherhood win out is
very much in the American interest—for promoting democracy and for fighting al-Qaeda and salafi-jihadist radicalism," he wrote, "and we should be upset
when we see allies undermining those interests."[15]

Within Western policy circles, these kinds of arguments amounted to a
call for pressuring the Mubarak regime to end its repression of the Brotherhood, as well as "engaging" the Brotherhood as an American partner against
violent extremism. "The Brotherhood hates Al Qaeda, and Al Qaeda hates the
Brotherhood," Shadi Hamid of the Brookings Doha Center told the *New York
Times* during the February 2011 uprising. "So if we're talking about counterterrorism, engaging with the Brotherhood will advance our interests in the
region."[16] The Brotherhood's sharp disagreements with jihadis, the thinking
went, made it a possible Western ally. "Many scholars of political Islam also
judge the Brotherhood [as] the most reasonable face of Islamic politics in the
Arab world today," wrote former CIA analyst Bruce Riedel, emphasizing that
the Brotherhood's "relative moderation has made it the target of extreme vil-
ification by more radical Islamists."[17]

There was, however, a major flaw with these arguments: The Brotherhood's commitment to nonviolence was hardly universal. And, more to the
point, the Brotherhood supported jihadis against the West in many cases.
"The Brotherhood does authorize jihad in countries and territories occupied
by a foreign power," Leiken and Brooke awkwardly admitted in their *Foreign
Affairs* essay. "Like in Afghanistan under the Soviets, the [Brotherhood] views
the struggles in Iraq and against Israel as 'defensive jihad' against invaders."[18]

Of course, the United States had troops in Iraq and Afghanistan during this time. So rather than being an ally against al-Qaeda, the Brotherhood's belief in "defensive jihad" meant that it supported al-Qaeda's attacks on American forces, at least ideologically.

Still, many analysts had a second reason for viewing the Brotherhood as a moderate Islamist group: For the past three decades, it had participated in elections. In the eyes of many Western observers, this signified the Brotherhood's acceptance of democratic institutions. "In most of the countries where it operates, the Brotherhood has embraced democracy," George Washington University professor Nathan Brown said in testifying before Congress in April 2011. "The Brotherhood's dedication to electoral politics, its acceptance of political parties, its rejection of Qutbism, and its full endorsement of rotation of power has become consistent and deeply engrained in the movement's appeals."[19]

The Brotherhood began its sustained involvement in Egyptian parliamentary politics in the 1984 elections, which was the first held under Mubarak. Aligning with the non-Islamist Wafd party, the joint list won 58 out of 448 elected seats, including eight Muslim Brothers.[20] Three years later, the Brotherhood unified with two other non-Islamist parties, and the combined list won 60 of 448 elected seats, including 38 Muslim Brothers.[21]

After joining most opposition parties in boycotting the 1990 elections, the Brotherhood ran again in 1995. Those elections were among the most violent in Egypt's history: 61 people were killed, 1,313 were injured, and 2,400 were detained. The Brotherhood was a special target of the crackdown: The regime sentenced fifty-four top Brotherhood leaders to multiyear prison terms one week before the election, and the Interior Ministry detained hundreds of the Brotherhood's poll watchers. Yet the Brotherhood continued its campaign, winning just one parliamentary seat out of the 150 races in which it competed.[22] Five years later, after a court order forced the regime to permit judicial monitoring of parliamentary elections, the Brotherhood won 17 seats, and it won a whopping 88 of 444 contested seats in the 2005 elections. And despite the severe repression it faced during the final years of Mubarak's reign, the Brotherhood continued nominating candidates for professional syndicate and parliamentary races, accepting defeat even in the most rigged of elections.

The Brotherhood's political behavior under Mubarak impressed Western analysts in a number of respects. Some argued that its political participation had transformed the Brotherhood into a responsive, capable political party.

"Brotherhood MPs take the [Parliament] more seriously than any other polit-ical force in the country—including the ruling party," professors Samer She-hata and Joshua Stacher wrote in their 2006 study of Brotherhood parliamen-tarians. "Their parliamentary bloc has demonstrated its seriousness through an unmatched record of attendance. . . . Brotherhood parliamentarians have committed themselves to learning about a range of important issues facing the nation, from maritime safety to avian flu and educational reform."[23]

Analysts further argued that electoral participation moderated the Brotherhood by forcing it to interact and compromise with other political forces. "Although the Brotherhood entered the political system in order to change it, it ended up being changed by the system," Emory University pro-fessor Carrie Rosefsky Wickham wrote in the February 2011 *Foreign Affairs*, just as Mubarak's demise appeared imminent. "Leaders who were elected to professional syndicates engaged in sustained dialogue and cooperation with members of other political movements, including secular Arab nationalists. Through such interactions, Islamists and Arabists found common ground in the call for an expansion of public freedoms, democracy, and respect for hu-man rights and the rule of law, all of which, they admitted, their movements had neglected in the past."[24]

Columbia University instructor Mona el-Ghobashy agreed. "The case of the [Brotherhood] confirms that it is the institutional rules of participation rather than the commandments of ideology that motivate political parties," she wrote in 2005. "Even the most ideologically committed and organiza-tionally stalwart parties are transformed in the process of interacting with competitors, citizens, and the state. Ideology and organization bow to the terms of participation."[25]

Hamid took this even further, claiming that the Brotherhood had re-thought some its core demands to widen its appeal. "In the past few years, instead of calling for an 'Islamic state,' . . . the Muslim Brotherhood began calling for a 'civil, democratic state with an Islamic reference,' suggesting a newfound commitment to the separation of mosque and state (although not of religion and politics)," he wrote just after the 2011 uprising.[26]

Finally, others argued that the Brotherhood's persistent electoral partic-ipation despite repression indicated its strong commitment to democracy. "The Egyptian Muslim Brotherhood . . . [has] done pretty much everything [it] could reasonably do to demonstrate [its] commitment to the democratic process, often paying heavy costs for [its] efforts," wrote Lynch in 2008, add-ing that while the Brotherhood hadn't necessarily "answered all the questions," its "demonstrated commitment to the democratic game is no small thing and should not be undervalued."[27]

Of course, as this book documents, the Brotherhood's autocratic behavior in power discredited the "moderate Muslim Brotherhood" argument to a great extent—and not because the Brotherhood's behavior or goals fundamentally changed once it became Egypt's ruling party, as some have argued.[28] Rather, those who touted the Brotherhood's "moderation" mistakenly privileged the group's political tactics, which have shifted over time, in their analysis, while downplaying the totalitarian and anti-Western goals that have defined the Brotherhood since its founding.

· · · · · · · ·

The Brotherhood's ideological roots date back to the so-called crisis of modernity that began with Napoleon's 1798 invasion of Egypt. France's occupation of Egypt was short-lived—it withdrew three years later—and few Egyptians interacted with the French scientists who came to Egypt during this period. But the speed and efficiency of Napoleon's conquest, in which only twenty-nine French soldiers died compared with over two thousand Mamluk fighters, highlighted Western technological and military superiority.[29] Then in the century that followed, European power expanded considerably within Muslim lands. By the time of Muslim Brotherhood founder Hassan al-Banna's birth in 1906, France had established colonies in Algeria, Tunisia, and Morocco, while Britain occupied Egypt, Sudan, and Yemen.

Europe's supremacy in Muslim lands greatly unnerved the Islamic thinkers of this era. Why, they asked, had the Islamic world fallen behind the West? Why was the Islamic world, which in the year 1000 controlled territory from as far west as present-day Morocco and Spain to the edge of the Indian subcontinent in the east, now dominated by European imperialists? And how could the Muslim world resist European encroachment and reemerge as a great global civilization?

For one set of Islamic thinkers, who became known as the "modernists," Western scientific advances fueled European supremacy. "The Europeans have now put their hand on every part of the world. The English have reached Afghanistan; the French have seized Tunisia," remarked Sayyid Jamal al-Din al-Afghani, one of the forerunners of Islamic modernism, during an 1882 address in India. "In reality, this usurpation, aggression, and conquest have come not from the French or the English. Rather it is science that manifests its greatness and power. . . . If we study the riches of the world, we learn that wealth is the result of commerce, industry, and agriculture. Agriculture is achieved only with agricultural science, botanical chemistry, and geometry. Industry is produced only with physics, chemistry, mechanics, geometry and mathematics; and commerce is based on agriculture and industry."[30]

Modernists such as Afghani argued that Islam embraced science and could therefore achieve the same advances that made the West powerful and prosperous. After all, they argued, Islam was a religion with scientific, rationalist underpinnings. The Qur'an, argued Afghani's protégé Muhammad 'Abduh, "does not require our acceptance of its contents simply on the ground of its own statement of them. On the contrary, it offers arguments and evidence. . . . It spoke to the rational mind and alerted the intelligence. It set out order in the universe, . . . and inspired a lively scrutiny of them that the mind must be sure of the validity of its claims and message."

So why had the Islamic world fallen behind the West? According to the modernists, the leading Islamic scholars, known as *ulema*, had abandoned science. Rather than interpreting *shari'ah* using reason, they simply applied traditional (*taqlīdī*) interpretations and then taught their students to memorize and apply the same rulings. This, 'Abduh argued, was contrary to the Prophet Muhammad's teachings. "In [the Prophet Muhammad's] preaching," 'Abduh wrote, "he took up the cudgels against the slaves of habit and traditionalists, calling on them to liberate themselves from bondage and throw off the chains withholding them from action and from hope."[31]

For the modernists, applying a scientific approach to *shari'ah* meant reinterpreting it for contemporary needs. The modernists therefore advocated the use of the Islamic jurisprudential tools known as *ijtihād*, or independent reasoning, and *istiṣlāḥ*, which means interpreting *shari'ah* for achieving social benefits. The answer to the Islamic world's decline, in other words, existed within Islam itself. Muslims could resist Western influence by reinterpreting *shari'ah* for modern times and then implementing it as law. This would engender prosperity and power.

Hassan al-Banna was an intellectual descendant of the modernists. Indeed, al-Banna's father, an imam, studied under 'Abduh at al-Azhar University, and al-Banna was steeped in 'Abduh's and Afghani's writings.[32] He was also an avid reader of the journal *Al-Manar*, whose publisher, Rashid Rida, was perhaps 'Abduh's most famous protégé.[33]

Al-Banna founded the Muslim Brotherhood in 1928 to address the same two problems that aroused the modernists: the Islamic world's decline and Western hegemony. Like the modernists, al-Banna believed that the keys to societal progress existed within traditional Islamic texts and that it was Muslims' duty to implement them. "The Qur'an is the comprehensive work which contains the fundamentals of this all-embracing social reformation," wrote al-Banna in one of his treatises. "It is demanded of the Muslim that he fulfill these obligations and put them into practice as the Qur'anic order has set them out."[34]

Al-Banna also shared the modernists' belief that *shari'ah* could be reinterpreted to satisfy changing societal circumstances. "The nature of Islam keeps pace with the times and the nations and responded to all purposes and demands," al-Banna told the Muslim Brotherhood's Fifth Conference in 1939, "and this is why Islam doesn't ever refuse to benefit from every good regime that doesn't conflict with its overall rules and general message."[35] And, in al-Banna's view, achieving prosperity meant implementing Islam to govern every matter because Islam is an "all-embracing concept which regulates every aspect of life, adjudicating on every one of its concerns and prescribing for it a solid and rigorous order."[36] This notion of Islam as an "all-embracing concept" is captured in the Brotherhood's motto: "Allah is our objective, the Prophet is our leader, the Qur'an is our constitution, jihad is our way, and death for the sake of God is our highest aspiration."[37]

What did implementing Islam as an "all-embracing concept" mean in practical terms? Al-Banna provided only a few hints. Islam, he wrote, was compatible with parliaments and constitutions so long as these institutions worked according to Islamic principles. Yet he was skeptical of political parties, seeing them as corrupt, as well as mechanisms for sowing divisions that benefitted foreign powers.[38] On economics, al-Banna's views were a mix of socialism and asceticism: He called for redistributing wealth and property and urged Muslims to reduce their luxury spending and focus on necessities.[39] But for the most part, al-Banna's writings emphasize those things that an Islamist order would ban: prostitution, alcohol, interest-based banking, and anything that contradicts *shari'ah*, including "every feature of the modern renaissance which is contrary to the principles of Islam."[40] In other words, al-Banna's Islamism was reactionary—it did not offer a positive vision of what an Islamic state would entail in any specific terms.

Who was responsible for the fact that the Muslim world was not governed according to these principles? Whereas the modernists typically blamed Islamic teachers and scholars, al-Banna blamed the West for introducing secularist ideas that stirred confusion and disunity among contemporary Muslims:

[Muslims] have been assailed on the political side by imperialist aggression on the part of their enemies, and by factionalism, rivalry, division, and disunity on the part of their sons. They have been assailed on the economic side by the propagation of usurious practices throughout all their social classes, and the exploitation of their resources and natural treasures by foreign companies. They have been afflicted on the intellectual side by anarchy, defection, and heresy which destroy their religious beliefs and overthrow the ideals within their sons' breasts.[41]

Remedying this, al-Banna argued, required "that the Islamic fatherland be freed from all foreign domination," after which "a free Islamic state may arise in this free fatherland, acting according to the precepts of Islam."[42]

How would this Islamic liberation be achieved? Here is where al-Banna made his most formidable contribution to Islamist thought, articulating a step-by-step, ground-up process for implementing Islam as an "all-embracing concept" in Egypt and beyond.

This process, al-Banna wrote, starts with the "reform of the individual" to ensure that he is physically fit, educated, organized, useful to others, "correct in his beliefs," and "prays properly." The reformed Muslim individual should then create a "Muslim home," which "maintains the ethics of Islam in manifestations of home life," including "the proper education of children" who should be "raised according to the principles of Islam." Next, the reformed Muslim should "guide the community" through preaching, "encouraging virtues . . . and the initiative to do good," with the ultimate goal of "winning public opinion to the side of the Islamic idea."

Thereafter, the Islamized society should "liberate the nation to rid it from all foreign—non-Islamic—domination, political, economic, and spiritual." Once this is accomplished, the society should "reform the government until it's truly Islamic," meaning that "its members are Muslims who perform the obligations of Islam" and that the government "executes the rulings of Islam and its teachings." Al-Banna clarified that non-Muslims would be permitted to serve in this Islamic government but only so long as they "agree with the general rules of an Islamic regime."

Finally, the Islamic state should seek to restore "the international entity for the Islamic nation, to liberate their countries," so that the caliphate, which ended following the fall of the Ottoman Empire in 1924, is reestablished. This, al-Banna asserted, would lead to *ustadhīyat al-'alam*—"mastery of the world"—as the call to implement Islam would spread further.[43] Indeed, al-Banna anticipated that Islam would ultimately govern everyone—Muslims and non-Muslims alike. "The Noble Qur'an," wrote al-Banna, "appoints the Muslims as guardians over humanity . . . and grants them the right of suzerainty and dominion over the world in order to carry out this sublime commission."[44]

In short, al-Banna sought to implement his interpretation of Islam as an "all-embracing concept" from the grass roots up. He would start by recruiting individuals to his Islamist cause, who would then build families around that cause. Those families would then promote that cause in the society, ultimately building support for establishing an "Islamic state," which would then be the building block of a new global Islamic order.

The Muslim Brotherhood was al-Banna's vehicle for achieving this Islamizing vision. Its members are fully indoctrinated according to al-Banna's understanding of Islam as an "all-embracing concept" and vetted for their commitment to promoting it. They are then organized in a rigid national hierarchy, which is designed to spread al-Banna's ideas within the society and build support for empowering the organization's ideas locally and globally.

• • • • • • • •

To ensure that every Muslim Brother is fully committed to the organization and its ideological goals, the Brotherhood subjects every prospective member to a five-to-eight-year indoctrination process known as *tarbīah*, meaning "education."

The *tarbīah* process begins at recruitment. On university campuses and in mosques throughout Egypt, specially designated local Brotherhood members scout for pious individuals, such as those who pray five times a day or have memorized parts of the Qur'an.[45] Initially, Brotherhood recruiters engage the prospective members in nonreligious social activities, such as soccer or tutoring, so that the Brotherhood can judge whether the prospect would be a good fit for the organization. Prospects are formally invited to join the Brotherhood only after their religiosity is confirmed, which can take as long as one year.[46] Muslim Brothers' children are typically introduced to the organization at a younger age through the organization's "cubs" (*ashbāl*) division, which runs activities for boys nine to thirteen years old.[47]

Once a recruit agrees to join the organization, he becomes a *muḥibb*, or a "lover." During this first stage in the five-stage promotional process, the recruiter continues monitoring the *muḥibb*'s personal piety, including whether he prays regularly and fasts on Ramadan, as well as whether he gets along with other Muslim Brothers.[48] The *muhibb* also participates in the Brotherhood's social activities, which include recreational activities with other Muslim Brothers as well as community work, and begins a rigorous study of Islamic and Brotherhood-sanctioned texts.[49]

The *muhibb* stage typically lasts from six months to one year. To advance to the next stage, the *muhibb*'s superiors must affirm that he avoids sins, prays with spirit, embraces al-Banna's notion of Islam as an "all-embracing concept," and is connected to a Brotherhood-approved preacher. The *muhibb* must also pass an exam that tests his religious knowledge and practices.[50]

At the second stage, the rising Muslim Brother becomes a *mu'ayyad*, or "supporter." At this stage, which lasts for one-and-a-half to three years, the *mu'ayyad* becomes more involved in the Brotherhood's political and social activities, such as preaching and teaching in mosques, as well as recruiting new Muslim Brothers. The *mu'ayyad* is also introduced to a more rigorous curriculum, which emphasizes memorization of parts of the Qur'an and al-Banna's teachings.

To advance to the next level, the *mu'ayyad* must participate in monthly "belief nights," during which Muslim Brothers fast while spending the night praying and reading the Qur'an. His superiors must also affirm that he lives an Islamic way of life, has memorized certain chapters of the Qur'an, knows Islamic purification practices, has studied al-Banna's biography, defends the Brotherhood from attacks against it, follows the organization's decisions, actively implements those decisions, and works to recruit people to Islam. Before moving to the next stage, the *mu'ayyad* is also administered a written or oral exam.[51]

Next, the rising Muslim Brother becomes a *muntasib*, or "affiliate," which lasts for approximately one year. As a *muntasib*, the Muslim Brother begins working in the Muslim Brotherhood's official divisions, such as those dedicated to serving workers, students, or youths, and he also begins paying membership dues, known as *ishtirak*, that range from 6 to 10 percent of his earnings. Whereas the earlier stages focus on indoctrination, the *muntasib* is effectively a professionalized Brother, and he is primarily judged on how he fulfills major tasks, such as organizing Brotherhood social services, recruitment, or preaching. To advance to the next level, the *muntasib*'s superiors must be satisfied with his work, and he is also tested on his knowledge of more advanced religious texts. Finally, his superiors must affirm that his political views are compatible with the organization's ideology.[52]

At the fourth level, the Muslim Brother is called a *muntazim*, or "orga-

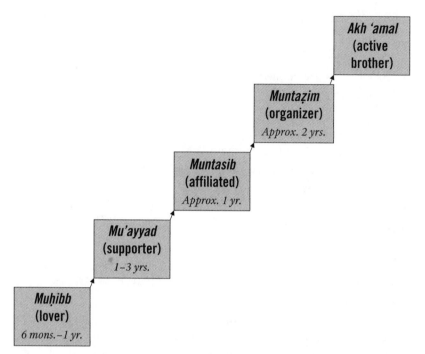

Figure 2.1 The Muslim Brotherhood's *Tarbīah* Process

nizer." At this stage, which often lasts two years, the Muslim Brother is expected to play an active role within the organization and can hold certain local leadership positions. The *muntaẓim* is also expected to memorize the Qur'an and sayings of the Prophet Muhammad,[53] and his superiors may test his loyalty to the organization by posing as security officials and monitoring whether he shares internal information. As before, his commitment to following orders—such as participating in demonstrations or organizing conferences—is also monitored.[54]

Finally, at the fifth stage, the candidate becomes an *akh 'amal*, or "active brother," at which point he is considered a full-fledged member with voting rights.[55] Upon becoming an *akh 'amal*, he takes the following oath (*bay'a*):

> I pledge allegiance in the name of God and swear to God and promise to be a loyal soldier in the Muslim Brotherhood and to listen and obey in hardship and ease, whether willingly or not, except in disobedience to God. And [I vow] to impact others and not to dispute commands and that I will expend my efforts, money, and blood in the path of God

and [will do] what I can for the sake of God, and God is who I call my advocate. "Whoever breaks his oath deviates from himself. And whoever fulfills his pledge to God will be offered great reward" [Qur'an 48:10].[56]

If a Muslim Brother violates this oath by disobeying the organization's directives, the organization may appoint a committee to investigate his activities and may dismiss him.[57]

The *tarbīah* process thus vets every Muslim Brother for his commitment to the organization's Islamizing principles and prepares him to carry on the Brotherhood's work of spreading and empowering those principles within the society. The *tarbīah* process also contributes to the Brotherhood's cohesiveness. After all, the sheer length of time that it takes to become a Muslim Brother means that defections are relatively rare. By the time the five-to-eight-year (and sometimes longer) process is completed, the Muslim Brother's social life revolves almost entirely around the organization, and leaving the organization would thus entail excommunication from his closest friends.

· · · · · · · ·

During the *tarbīah* process, every Muslim Brother is integrated into the organization's nationwide chain of command, which is structured for spreading al-Banna's Islamizing message throughout the society, so that the organization can ultimately win power and establish an Islamic state. This chain of command has two components: the "field apparatus," which is designed to penetrate each geographic region of Egypt, and the "professional operations" unit, which is designed to attract adherents from within various societal and vocational sectors.[58]

The lowest level of the field apparatus comprises thousands of Brotherhood cells known as *usar*, meaning "families." Consisting of five to ten members, the *usar* are scattered throughout virtually every town and neighborhood in Egypt, and they are tasked with executing commands from superior tiers of the Brotherhood's leadership at the local level. Each *usrah* (singular of *usar*) is headed by a *naqīb*, or chief, and it meets weekly for approximately three hours. In these meetings, Muslim Brothers recite the Qur'an, present sections of Brotherhood's curriculum to each other, and study Islamic legal texts. They also discuss current events, share matters from their personal lives, and organize the administration of their local activities.[59] Finally, Muslim Brothers pay their membership dues during the *usrah* meetings.

The *usrah* meetings serve two essential purposes for the organization. First, the doctrinal discussions enable local Brotherhood leaders to ensure that their cadres are unified behind the organization's goals, so they can intervene with any member who appears to be diverging. Second, the regularity of these meetings strengthens the social bonds among members and thereby ensures a unity of action. Indeed, the members of a Muslim Brother's *usrah* become his closest friends—the kinds of people who will loan him money if he faces financial troubles or who will take care of his family if he becomes ill or incapacitated. He therefore faces a type of peer pressure that prevents him from shirking his responsibilities to the organization.

Approximately six to twelve *usar* comprise a *shu'abah*, or "branch," which is the next level up in the Brotherhood's chain of command. A *mas'ul*, or official, chairs the *shu'abah*, and an administrative board of five to seven members, which meets every two weeks, manages the Brotherhood's activities within the *shu'abah*. Broader questions of local strategy are discussed in the *shura* (consultative) committee, which can include up to forty local members and meets semiannually. All of the individuals in these positions are elected every four years.[60]

The *shu'abah* leadership has two primary responsibilities: spreading the Brotherhood's ideology and recruiting talented individuals within its geographic domain. But it plays two additional roles. First, it composes semiannual reports about local conditions that are sent to higher tiers of Brotherhood leadership, thereby informing those leaders' regional and national strategies. Second, the *shu'abah* ensures that commands from the top of the Brotherhood's hierarchy are implemented on the ground by the *usar*. For this reason, every *shu'abah* official must take the following oath: "I swear by Almighty God that I will be a faithful guard to the principles of the Muslim Brothers and their foundational organization and trust their leaders, executing the decisions of the Guidance Office and the decisions of the administrative office, even if I have a different opinion, struggling for God's will, and I promise God this, God is my agent."[61]

Every successive layer of the Brotherhood's pyramidal chain of command is organized in a similar fashion: An administrative board manages its day-to-day affairs, and a larger *shura* committee meets a few times a year to provide feedback and advice on broader strategic questions.[62] The remainder of the Brotherhood's hierarchy is as follows: Three to five *shu'ab* constitute a *minṭaqah*, or "area"; all of the *manaṭiq* in a given province are organized under the administrative office of the *muḥāfaẓah*, or "governorate."

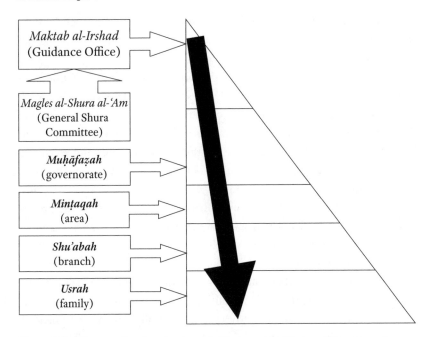

Figure 2.2 The Muslim Brotherhood's Nationwide Chain of Command

The Guidance Office (*maktab al-irshad*), the Muslim Brotherhood's executive bureau, stands at the very top of this nationwide chain of command. According to the Brotherhood's internal bylaws, it "oversees the progress of outreach (*da'wah*) and guides its policy and administration." It has approximately fifteen to twenty members (the number historically fluctuated due to repression and other political developments), and a Muslim Brother must have held the highest rank of *akh 'amal* for at least three years in order to be elected to the Guidance Office.[63] In theory, Guidance Office members are elected to four-year terms, but in practice the threat of repression and the Brotherhood's culture of political obedience meant that Guidance Office members were effectively selected through consensus and in many cases enjoyed life terms.

The Guidance Office is advised by the General Shura Committee (not to be confused with the Shura Council, Egypt's upper parliamentary house until 2014), which includes approximately 110 members and effectively serves as the Brotherhood's national legislative branch. All Guidance Office members are also members of the General Shura Committee. Finally, this entire hierarchy is chaired by a Supreme Guide, who must be at least forty years old and have been a Brother for at least fifteen years. The Supreme Guide is elected by the General Shura Committee and serves a six-year term that can be renewed.[64]

The second component of the Muslim Brotherhood's nationwide hierarchy is its "professional operations" infrastructure. This comprises various thematic "divisions" (*aqsām*), each of which handles a different type of task within the organization. These include divisions dedicated to preaching, which focuses on spreading the Brotherhood's message and recruiting in mosques; education, which administers the Brotherhood's curriculum; workers, which seeks to recruit Muslim Brothers from within labor unions; professionals, which seeks to organize Brotherhood activities in the professional syndicates; students, which oversees Brotherhood university activities and campus recruitment; media, which focuses on the Brotherhood's external messaging; politics, which focuses on the Brotherhood's political work and coordination with other political organizations; religious, which prepares Brotherhood statements on doctrinal matters; sisters, which oversees the work of the Muslim Sisters, the Brotherhood's female division; and financial, which handles the Brotherhood's expenses and collects dues.[65] These portfolios have shifted and been renamed at various points during the Brotherhood's history, but the basic structure has not changed.

Each Guidance Office leader oversees a different portfolio and is thus responsible for executing a section of the Brotherhood's work on a national level. The administrative offices of each subsidiary level in the Brotherhood's chain of command—from the governorate level down to the *shu'abah*—are similarly organized, with individual leaders overseeing various portfolios. Ground-level members are also tasked with specific responsibilities within their "usar." This ensures that virtually every Muslim Brother, from the very top of its chain of command to the very bottom, knows his role, whether that entails managing new Muslim Brothers' *tarbiah* process, preaching at the local mosque, administering local finances, or running student programs.

In other words, the Brotherhood's chain of command isn't just bureaucratic trivia. It is an essential part of what it means to be a Muslim Brother. It defines every Muslim Brother's precise task, which he has taken an oath to fulfill, even if he has misgivings. And the *tarbiah* process teaches every Muslim Brother that working through the organization and following its leaders' directives are essential to implementing al-Banna's vision of Islamizing society, building an Islamic state, and erecting a neocaliphate that will challenge the West in the long run. Most important, the Muslim Brother is taught that this political mission *is* "the true Islam."

• • • • • • • •

In short, the Muslim Brotherhood was never a moderate organization or a democratic one in any sense of that word. It is a rigidly hierarchical, purpose-driven vanguard that seeks total control over its members so that it can mobilize them for empowering Hassan al-Banna's deeply politicized interpretation of Islam as an "all-embracing concept." It accepts electoral institutions as a mechanism for winning power, but its ultimate goal is theocratic: It seeks to establish an Islamic state and ultimately establish a global Islamic state that will challenge the West. And following Mubarak's ouster, it was the only political group in Egypt with a nationwide machine. The Brotherhood therefore had an unprecedented opportunity to finally transition from spreading its message within Egyptian society to pursuing power outright.

But would it?

3 Postrevolutionary Posturing

Hosni Mubarak's February 2011 ouster brought forth a patriotic pride that Egypt hadn't experienced in decades. For many Egyptians, the eighteen-day uprising had restored the country's dignity, toppling an aging and corrupt dictator and preventing him from bequeathing power to his son. Egyptian flags were suddenly ubiquitous, radio stations played patriotic songs on loop, and seemingly every commercial advertising campaign tapped into the postrevolutionary spirit.

Yet the political reality was hardly revolutionary. The cabinet that Mubarak appointed in late January, headed by Prime Minister Ahmed Shafik, largely remained in place. The Interior Ministry, whose brutal police had been the uprising's initial target, was weakened but not reformed. And the Egyptian military now controlled the country, meaning that the octogenarian Mubarak was replaced by his septuagenarian defense minister, Field Marshal Mohamed Hussein Tantawi.

The military formalized its rule through a constitutional declaration, which it released on February 13. The declaration dissolved both houses of Parliament, suspended the constitution, and put total authority in the hands of the SCAF. It further outlined a vague transition process in which the SCAF would convene a committee to amend the constitution and then hold parliamentary and presidential elections. The SCAF would "administer the affairs of state temporarily, for a period of six months or when the elections for the People's Assembly, Shura Council, and President of the Republic conclude."[1]

But which of these elections would come first? When would a new constitution actually be written, if at all? And would this transition occur within six months, as suggested, or would the SCAF end up ruling for much longer?

Each of the major stakeholders in this fluid post-Mubarak period—the mil-

itary, the revolutionaries, and the Muslim Brotherhood—had different prefer-
ences and therefore different strategies.

· · · · · · · ·

While the military's internal deliberations during the January uprising are unknown, its response to the protests suggested ambivalence. It assumed control of Egypt's major cities on January 28, after the massive Friday of Rage
protests overwhelmed the Interior Ministry, but then remained on the sidelines when Mubarakists attacked Tahrir Square during the Battle of the Camel
on February 2, seemingly giving the regime one last chance to regain control.
The military removed Mubarak only after these efforts failed, and the generals now signaled that they wanted a return to normalcy—for roads to remain
open, for Egyptians to return to work, and for tourists to return to Egypt. To
encourage this calm, the SCAF seized control of Egypt's state-run media, air-
ing programs that urged Egyptians to get on with their lives and warning that
more revolutionary activity would wreak havoc on Egypt's already delicate
economy.[2]

   The SCAF was uncomfortable in power for two reasons. First, it was not
accustomed to wielding direct political control. While the military had been
the backbone of Egypt's regime since the 1952 Free Officers Revolution, in
which a small group of officers toppled King Farouk, its direct political involvement diminished after the 1967 Six-Day War, when Egypt's humiliating
defeat catalyzed a popular backlash against the brass. As Steven Cook of the
Council on Foreign Relations notes, the military "relinquished its significant
role in day-to-day governance of Egypt in favor of a mission that focused almost exclusively on preparing for another round of warfare with Israel." The
military regained its stature after its successful opening campaign during
the 1973 Arab–Israeli War, when the Egyptian army surprised the Israelis
by crossing the Suez Canal and inflicting heavy casualties, and the Egyptian
government insulated the military from political criticism thereafter.[3] With
Mubarak's fall, however, nothing stood between the armed forces and the
public—and that meant that the generals could become the target of any subsequent protests.

   Second, the SCAF feared that the political environment of post-Mubarak
Egypt might threaten the extensive economic empire that it built during the
peaceful decades that followed the 1973 war. This empire includes a wide
range of business ventures, with military companies producing kitchen appliances, televisions, bottled water, and clothing, among many other consumer

products. Moreover, under a 1997 presidential decree, the Egyptian military gained management rights to all of Egypt's unused land.[4] So long as the military remained in the political background, these holdings were safe from scrutiny. But after Mubarak's ouster, the military's wealth risked becoming a target of either protesters' ire or an elected civilian government's oversight.

The SCAF thus wanted to extricate itself from direct governance as soon as possible—but only so long as its perquisites were protected. So it used its February 13 constitutional declaration to give itself wide latitude for managing the post-Mubarak transition: It could wrap the whole transition up within six months if it felt sufficiently comfortable, or it could stay longer if it didn't. Meanwhile, the SCAF maintained a variety of tools at its disposal for restoring calm, including the Mubarak-era emergency laws, which granted the junta far-reaching arrest powers.[5]

• • • • • • • •

The revolutionary activists had a very different mindset following Mubarak's ouster. On the heels of the uprising's success, the activists had suddenly become media darlings. They were celebrated guests on Egyptian television shows that once shunned them, and international correspondents hung on their every word at their standing-room-only press conferences. They were lauded on the cover of *Time* as "the generation changing the world,"[6] and they vowed to continue fighting for change. Mubarak might be gone, they argued, but he was merely the chief executive of a thoroughly corrupt and repressive regime that was still largely in place. That regime had to be uprooted in its entirety before the country could move forward. Whereas the SCAF wanted the revolution to cool off, the activists insisted that the revolution should continue "until victory."

The revolutionaries had three demands. First, they wanted justice for the approximately eight hundred people who were killed during the eighteen-day uprising, as well as the release of remaining detainees, including Brotherhood leaders.[7] Second, they wanted "the fall of the whole regime." This meant removing the Mubarak-appointed Shafik government, trying Mubarak and his former colleagues, and reforming the state's repressive apparatuses. They also wanted the SCAF to appoint a new civilian-led government to oversee the transitional period, rather than leaving governance in the junta's hands, and demanded the cancellation of the emergency laws that the Mubarak regime had routinely used to repress their activities.[8]

Third and perhaps most important, the revolutionaries demanded that a

new constitution be drafted before any elections—parliamentary or presidential—took place. The revolutionaries rejected the SCAF's call for amending
only a few articles of the constitution, arguing that electing a new government
under a slightly amended Mubarak-era constitution risked resurrecting the
very regime that the revolution sought to dismantle.[9]

How did the revolutionaries intend to achieve these demands? Through
the same tactic that compelled the military to topple Mubarak: ongoing mass
protests. "We need the army to recognize that this is a revolution, and they
can't implement all these changes on their own," revolutionary activist Alaa
Abd el-Fattah told the *Guardian*. "The [generals] are the custodians of this
particular stage in the process, and we're fine with that, but it has to be temporary."[10] The revolutionaries thus called for a new "million-man march" almost
every Friday after Mubarak's ouster to exert more pressure on the military.

• • • • • • • •

The Muslim Brotherhood firmly rejected the revolutionaries' attempt to
drive the post-Mubarak political momentum. As Brotherhood leaders saw
it, the revolutionaries were ragtag youths with no political experience, no
base beyond the major cities, and no coherent strategy. Sure, the activists
had mobilized tens of thousands into the streets on January 25 to get the uprising started. But it was the Brotherhood's *hundreds of thousands of cadres*
that overwhelmed security forces on January 28, kept Tahrir Square occupied, and successfully defended the square from the regime's assault during
the Battle of the Camel on February 2.[11] Moreover, the revolutionaries were
largely non-Islamist and therefore out of touch with Egypt's religious, and
overwhelmingly Muslim, society. So what right did the revolutionaries have
to set the agenda?

To be sure, the Brotherhood and the revolutionaries converged on certain points. Like the revolutionaries, the Brotherhood wanted to use the
Arab Spring's momentum to ensure that the old regime couldn't return and
joined the revolutionaries in calling for the fall of the Shafik government. The
Brotherhood similarly demanded that the SCAF lift the Mubarak-era state of
emergency, which was often used as legal cover for arresting Muslim Brothers. And, like the revolutionaries, the Brotherhood had significant objections
to the existing constitution. It particularly objected to the 2007 amendments
that prevented the establishment of any political party "on the basis of religion," which undermined the Brotherhood's political participation moving
forward.[12]

At the same time, however, the Brotherhood feared that if it looked too politically aggressive, it would invite a popular blowback. It frequently invoked the Algerian experience—in which the Algerian military ousted an elected Islamist parliament in 1991 and plunged the country into an eight-year civil war—as something it desperately wanted to avoid. So on February 10— one day before Mubarak's ouster—the Brotherhood announced that it would not run a presidential candidate, and its top leaders insisted thereafter that it wouldn't pursue a parliamentary majority either.[13]

Yet the Brotherhood's biggest concern was the SCAF itself. For nearly six decades, Egypt's military had been the Brotherhood's foremost adversary. Following the Free Officers Revolution, the emerging junta outlawed the Brotherhood, jailed many of its leaders for decades, and executed those whom it accused of trying to overthrow the state. And under the Mubarak regime, military courts sentenced dozens of Brotherhood leaders to lengthy prison terms.

The Brotherhood therefore wanted the SCAF to retreat from politics as soon as possible. But how could this be achieved? The revolutionaries' insistence on drafting a new constitution before elections meant an indefinite transition that would prolong military rule. By contrast, the SCAF's own transition plan provided a relatively clear road map toward its own exit from power: It called for a referendum on a few constitutional amendments, followed by parliamentary and presidential elections, after which the SCAF promised to return to the barracks. For the Brotherhood, that transition plan was workable and couldn't start soon enough.

But the SCAF's transition plan provided an additional bonus for the Brotherhood. By merely calling for amendments to the existing constitution, it effectively postponed the drafting of a new constitution until *after* parliamentary elections were held. This provided the Brotherhood with its best shot at influencing the constitution-drafting process, since it anticipated winning many seats in the next Parliament.

The prospect of influencing Egypt's next constitution was particularly important to the Brotherhood. It saw the constitution-writing process as an opportunity to expand the use of *shari'ah* in Egyptian legislation and thus advance Hassan al-Banna's vision of Islamizing the Egyptian state. Alternatively, if the SCAF acceded to the revolutionaries' "constitution first" demand, the Brotherhood would have little influence over the constitutional process, since a SCAF-appointed constitution-drafting committee would likely feature few, if any, Muslim Brothers.[14]

The Brotherhood outlined these positions in its February 13 statement.

While the Brotherhood echoed the revolutionaries' call for freeing political prisoners, ending the state of emergency, and firing the Shafik government, it responded favorably to the transition plan that the SCAF outlined in its constitutional declaration. The Brotherhood's statement further called for expediting the transition process to "deepen the trust between the military and the people" and saluted the SCAF's leadership over the post-Mubarak transition. "We are confident in our great military," the Brotherhood's statement read, "and its commitment . . . to the promises that it made on its own."[15]

One day later, the Brotherhood took an unprecedented measure. In a press statement, Mohamed Morsi, who oversaw the Guidance Office's "political file," announced that the Brotherhood would soon form a political party.[16] The Brotherhood had briefly considered forming a political party during the 1980s, but the fear of regime repression ultimately prevented it from doing so. By declaring its intention to establish a party now, the Brotherhood was sending the SCAF yet another signal that it would accept the junta's transition process so long as it could participate fully.

The SCAF seemingly got the message. On February 15, the SCAF-backed government appointed the ten-person committee that would draft amendments to the existing constitution, naming Islamist judge Tarek el-Bishry as its chairman and Sobhi Saleh, a former Brotherhood parliamentarian, as a member. "This is a good thing," Rashad al-Bayoumi, one of the Brotherhood's deputy supreme guides, told the Egyptian daily *Al-Wafd* after el-Bishry and Saleh were appointed, adding that the generals were "dealing with reality."[17]

For the next few weeks, the Brotherhood managed a difficult balancing act. It joined the revolutionaries in weekly demonstrations to demand that the SCAF release all political prisoners, arrest top Mubarak regime officials, fire the Shafik government, and dissolve the domestic intelligence service State Security.[18] But at the same time, the Brotherhood repeatedly signaled its desire to avoid a confrontation with the SCAF.

The uncertainty of Egypt's Arab Spring atmosphere, however, made the SCAF hesitant to lift the emergency laws or shutter the State Security apparatus. But on March 2, the SCAF-backed government acceded to one of the Brotherhood's most pressing demands when it released the Brotherhood's most prominent prisoner: Deputy Supreme Guide Khairat al-Shater.[19]

• • • • • • • •

Until his imprisonment in late 2006, al-Shater had been the Brotherhood's "organization man." He was a towering presence within the organization, both literally and figuratively. The hefty, six-foot-four leader managed the Brotherhood's finances, handled its relations with the Mubarak regime's security services, developed its policy agenda, and spearheaded the construction of its Internet portals. Brotherhood leaders and cadres alike revered al-Shater, regarding him as their most capable administrator.

Al-Shater was from the generation of Brotherhood figures who revived the organization during the mid-1970s, when President Anwar Sadat, who took power following Nasser's death in 1970, granted Islamists greater freedom. Al-Shater joined the Brotherhood in 1974 while studying engineering at Alexandria University and fled abroad in 1981 to avoid the crackdown that preceded Sadat's assassination. After five years spent working in the Persian Gulf region and Europe, al-Shater returned to Egypt in 1986 and founded a computer information systems company, Salsabeel, with his business partner Hassan Malek. Al-Shater soon became a millionaire and grew his wealth through additional investments in the agriculture and services industries. Meanwhile, al-Shater's profile within the Brotherhood continued to rise, and in 1995 at the relatively young age of forty-five he was named to the Brotherhood's executive Guidance Office.[20]

Yet al-Shater's success in the worlds of business and Islamism came at a steep price. In 1992, the Mubarak regime raided Salsabeel and imprisoned him for a year. In 1995, the regime arrested dozens of top Brotherhood leaders, and al-Shater was sentenced to five years in prison for his involvement in the legally banned organization. After his release in 2000, he was again arrested in 2001 and spent another year behind bars.

Al-Shater's power within the organization peaked when Mehdi Akef became the Brotherhood's seventh supreme guide in 2004. Al-Shater assumed responsibility for the organization's finances, successfully investing its funds while devising mechanisms for avoiding the Mubarak regime's security monitoring.[21] He also founded the Brotherhood's Arabic- and English-language websites, began developing a Brotherhood policy program, and pushed the Brotherhood to run more assertively in Egypt's parliamentary elections.[22] Perhaps most important, al-Shater became one of the Brotherhood's key intermediaries with the Mubarak regime's security services and communicated with State Security officials to coordinate the Brotherhood's various political activities.[23]

Yet the Brotherhood's impressive performance during the November 2005 parliamentary elections, during which it won an unprecedented 88 of 444 elected seats, greatly unnerved the Mubarak regime. It responded with a new crackdown on the organization, detaining hundreds of Muslim Brothers during the next eight months.[24] The repression worsened in December 2006, when dozens of masked Muslim Brotherhood–affiliated students staged a martial arts demonstration at al-Azhar University that mimicked militant demonstrations held by Hamas and Hezbollah. The regime responded to the implicit threat by arresting al-Shater and his business partner Malek. A military tribunal sentenced both men to seven years in prison and seized assets totaling approximately $14 million from al-Shater and $21 million from Malek.[25]

Even from prison, however, al-Shater remained a highly influential player within the Brotherhood. As the *New York Times* later reported, Brotherhood youths visited him weekly to deliver files on the organization's activities that were sometimes as long as two hundred pages.[26] Moreover, the sheer length of time that he spent in prison—ultimately twelve years altogether, more than any of the Brotherhood leaders from his generation—made him a hero to many Muslim Brothers who admired his willingness to suffer for the cause.

The SCAF's decision to release al-Shater in early March 2011 was thus highly significant: The Brotherhood's most central decision maker was now back in action at the very moment that the Brotherhood was developing its strategy for the more open political environment.

As al-Shater headed back to his apartment following his release, supporters and journalists swarmed him. "Our slogan . . . in this stage would be to rise up and resist—to rise up and resist," al-Shater declared.

> To build [our] nation and resist the Zionist–American project that aims to control the Muslim countries and our region, we need to . . . build, in all sectors, in our schools, our education, our fields, our production, our companies, our interior and exterior, our social and economic affairs. Build ourselves up and build our nation based on our Islamist agenda in a comprehensive way and at the same time pay attention to the revolution's enemies internally and externally.[27]

It was a perfect distillation of al-Banna's ideology: The Brotherhood would fight the West by Islamizing Egypt.

• • • • • • • •

One day after releasing al-Shater, the SCAF made an additional concession. On March 3, Prime Minister Shafik resigned, and the SCAF appointed Essam Sharaf in his place. Although Sharaf previously served as transportation minister under Mubarak from 2004 to 2005, his participation in the January uprising made him a prorevolutionary choice in many activists' eyes.[28] The following day, Sharaf addressed the now-weekly Friday demonstration in Tahrir Square. "I've come here with a promise that I took from the SCAF, which sponsored this revolution," Sharaf said. "And it's also incumbent upon me that I receive my legitimacy from you, because you alone hold legitimacy." At that point, Brotherhood leader Mohamed al-Beltagy, who was standing next to Sharaf, took the microphone from the prime minister and began leading the square in chants. "Legitimacy comes from Tahrir! It doesn't come from forgery!"[29] It was a striking image: After decades as a banned opposition organization, the Muslim Brotherhood was now sharing a stage with Egypt's head of government.[30]

The SCAF's firing of Shafik undercut the revolutionaries' rationale for continuing their weekly protests. Mubarak and the last government that he appointed were now history, and leading revolutionaries argued that the Sharaf government deserved a chance to work without the specter of demonstrations.[31] On March 9, security forces took advantage of this opening: They violently cleared the handful of tents that remained in Tahrir Square, arrested dozens of protesters, and subjected female protesters to invasive "virginity tests."[32] The revolutionaries cried foul and considered mobilizing a response. But barely a month after Mubarak's ouster, there was little public outcry against these new police abuses.

The country was now focused on the national referendum on the proposed constitutional amendments, scheduled for Saturday, March 19. The proposed amendments affected nine of the 211 Mubarak era constitutional articles. For the most part, the amendments sought to prevent the emergence of another dictator, such as by easing the procedures for getting on a presidential ballot, shortening the presidential term from six to four years, establishing a presidential two-term limit, expanding judicial supervision of elections, mandating that the president appoint at least one vice president within sixty days of being elected, and restricting the president's ability to impose states of emergency by forcing him to receive approval from Parliament within seven days. The proposed amendments also barred dual nationals or those married to non-Egyptians from running for president, empowered the Supreme Constitutional Court (SCC) to rule on challenges to parliamentary race, and eliminated a previous article that waived constitutionally mandated human rights provisions in terrorism cases.[33]

The proposed amendments were also noteworthy for what they didn't change. They essentially maintained Egypt's presidential system, which implied a relatively weak Parliament. The amendments also preserved Article II of the constitution, under which *sharī'ah* is the "principal source of all law." This made the amendments especially appealing to Egypt's Salafists—Islamist fundamentalists who seek to implement Islamic legal texts literally—who feared that non-Islamists would try to water down the constitution's *sharī'ah* content. Indeed, the Alexandria-based Salafist Call, Egypt's most prominent Salafist organization, was among the first groups to endorse the amendments.[34]

But in many respects, the content was beside the point. The referendum's ultimate significance was the procedural clarity that it provided regarding Egypt's next steps. If the referendum passed, Egypt would hold parliamentary elections and the transition would move forward. Alternatively, a "no" vote would tarnish the SCAF's authority, create a constitutional vacuum, and leave Egypt's political future completely up in the air. For this reason, the SCAF and its government worked to ensure the referendum's success by ordering state-run television stations to stop featuring critics of the proposed constitutional amendments as the referendum approached.[35] Remnants of Mubarak's former National Democratic Party (NDP) also supported the referendum, worrying that its failure would catalyze even greater instability. History was also on the referendum's side: All of the fifteen referenda that Egypt had held since 1956 produced an overwhelming "yes" vote.

The Brotherhood, however, was quite focused on the amendments' content. It especially prized newly amended Article 189, which provided a formal road map for drafting a new constitution once parliamentary and presidential elections had taken place. According to the amended article, a joint session of Egypt's bicameral Parliament would elect a hundred-member Constituent Assembly to "prepare a draft constitution no later than six months from the date of its formation and present it to the president of the republic," after which the public would vote on the new constitution draft via national referendum.[36] The passage of the referendum would thus close the door on the revolutionaries' call for a new constitution to precede the parliamentary elections. And since the Brotherhood anticipated winning many parliamentary seats, an amended Article 189 represented its best chance for influencing the constitution-drafting process and Islamizing the Egyptian polity.

The Brotherhood officially declared its support for the amendments at a press conference on March 12, one week before the referendum. "When we say that we accept the constitutional changes, and we vote 'yes,' then this is a clear message to the entire Brotherhood front, which is to vote 'yes,'" said Brotherhood Guidance Office leader Essam el-Erian. The referendum's passage, el-Erian noted, would pave the way for parliamentary and presidential elections, thereby ending the SCAF's control of the country and enabling it to focus on other threats, such as "the Zionist enemy, which is the biggest loser of the Egyptian revolution."[37]

Of course, amended Article 189 was a nonstarter for the revolutionaries. They had been calling for a new constitution from practically the moment that Mubarak fell, arguing that holding parliamentary and presidential elections under a slightly amended form of the constitution was a recipe for restoring autocracy. So on March 14, the Coalition of Revolutionary Youth issued a statement rejecting the proposed amendments and advocating the formation of a civilian-led presidential council to administer the transition. The statement also called for appointing a constituent assembly to draft a new constitution before any elections took place.[38]

The revolutionaries weren't alone in rejecting the amendments. The socialist Tagammu party argued that the amended constitution left too many powers in the hands of the president, and the nationalist Wafd party also called on its members to vote against the referendum.[39] Arab League secretary-general Amr Moussa, viewed as a leading presidential contender, participated in a YouTube video calling on Egyptians to vote "no" and argued—rather self-servingly—for presidential elections to be held first, after which the newly elected president would appoint a constitution-drafting committee.[40] Meanwhile, early polls suggested that a "no" vote would carry the day by a twenty-point margin.[41]

When the March 19 referendum arrived, the turnout was unprecedented. In polling stations nationwide, voters waited for hours to cast their ballots, often basking in the novelty of participating in an open and competitive referendum. Meanwhile, the Brotherhood and revolutionaries declared their acceptance of the referendum's result, win or lose.

The result, however, floored the revolutionaries: The referendum passed by a whopping margin of 77 percent "yes" to 23 percent "no," with a turnout of 41 percent. "Yes" carried every single governorate, including 60.5 percent of the votes in Cairo, ground zero of Egypt's revolution.[42] The Brotherhood was not the only force that had mobilized for "yes"—but it was the most prominent in its support for the motion and thus was viewed as the referendum's big winner.

• • • • • • • •

The referendum's passage added new urgency to the Brotherhood's creation of a political party, since parliamentary elections were now supposed to take place within six months.

While the Brotherhood had considered forming a party at various points in its history, it was always a controversial matter within the organization. Brotherhood founder Hassan al-Banna decried *hizbiyya*, or party factionalism, viewing it as a source of disunity and thus social weakness, but never ruled it out entirely. The Brotherhood first considered forming a party following its successful alliance with the Wafd in the 1984 elections, when the supreme guide formed a committee to study the matter.[43] The Brotherhood revisited the matter every few years thereafter but repeatedly decided against it.[44] So long as Mubarak was in power, Brotherhood leaders concluded, real political competition was impossible, and forming a political party was thus a waste of time. So the Brotherhood focused instead on its outreach work, preparing Egyptian society for embracing Islamist rule at some point in the future.[45]

The fall of Mubarak, however, fundamentally altered the Brotherhood's internal debate on this issue. While a small but vocal minority of Brotherhood leaders still believed that the Brotherhood should stay focused on outreach work,[46] most viewed Egypt's Arab Spring as a prime opportunity for the organization to transition from spreading al-Banna's ideas within the society to establishing an Islamic state in Egypt. This required forming a political party that could compete in elections and then using the Brotherhood's chain of command for getting out the vote. And to ensure that the Brotherhood's hundreds of thousands of cadres supported the new party, the Brotherhood's supreme guide mandated in a March 15 statement that "members of the [Brotherhood] cannot establish, participate, or join any other parties."[47] The Brotherhood called its new party the Freedom and Justice Party (FJP).

The overwhelming majority of Muslim Brothers seemed to accept the Brotherhood's pivot toward seeking power. After all, becoming a Muslim Brother entails taking an oath to abide by the leadership's decisions. Moreover, the transition from societal outreach to power-seeking is a central theme of al-Banna's writings, which every Muslim Brother studies through the organization's five-to-eight-year *tarbiah* process. This broad acceptance of the Brotherhood's new political activity was reflected on the ground, as the Brotherhood's rank-and-file members began establishing party headquarters in every governorate at a furious pace.

These decisions, however, outraged the vocal segment of Brotherhood youths who were closely aligned with the revolutionaries. This included cadres such as Mohamed al-Qassas, who had participated actively in the January uprising from its first day while the Brotherhood's leadership cautiously kept the organization on the sidelines. From these Brotherhood youths' perspective, the organization's top-down decision making was an artifact of the autocratic Mubarak era. In the freer environment of post-Mubarak Egypt, the youths argued, the Brotherhood should stay focused on its societal work and allow its members to join whatever party they wanted, rather than demanding that every Muslim Brother support the FJP.[48]

So on March 26, the Brotherhood youth activists took a bold step. Against the Guidance Office's explicit orders, they organized a public conference at Giza's Safir Hotel titled "A New Vision from Within" and publicly criticized the Brotherhood leadership's post-Mubarak approach with hundreds of their colleagues in attendance.[49] For these Brotherhood youths, the move was gut-wrenching: They had invested many years of their young lives in the Brotherhood and knew that their public battle with the Guidance Office risked banishment.

The youths concluded their "new vision" conference by releasing an open letter to the Brotherhood that contained twelve demands. It called on the Guidance Office to guarantee youth representation on the FJP's leadership board, to ensure the FJP's independence from the Guidance Office, to consult with specialists from outside the Brotherhood in establishing the FJP's vision, and to allow Muslim Brothers to join parties other than the FJP, so long as those parties "do not conflict with the fundamental principles of Islam." In addition, the letter advocated the creation of youth-led "decision-making centers" within the Brotherhood for promoting younger leaders.[50] A copy of the letter was immediately sent to the supreme guide.

The conference outraged the Brotherhood's leadership. In an exceedingly rare interview with the Brotherhood's news portal, Mahmoud Abuzeid, the Guidance Office leader who oversaw the organization's students division, lambasted the insurgent youths for gathering without the Brotherhood leadership's permission, as well as for publicizing the typically secretive organization's internal disagreements.[51]

Among the Brotherhood youths' revolutionary peers, however, the response was quite different. Non-Islamist activists hailed the Brotherhood youths for standing up to the Guidance Office and saw the conference as the first sign of a possible split within the organization that would weaken it and prevent it from seizing the post-Mubarak political momentum. That split, however, never came: While the Brotherhood's dissidents were among the organization's most prominent young members, they were not representative of the organization's cadres more broadly. Indeed, most Brotherhood youths remained loyal to the Guidance Office, in accordance with the oath they had taken upon joining the organization.

"A revolution [inside the MB] is not realistic because the leadership has too much consensus around it," Anas al-Qassas, a Brotherhood youth, said as the tensions started to emerge in early March. "And any minority that wants to [impose] their hopes and wishes on all the Muslim Brothers—this is not logical."[52]

· · · · · · · ·

Six weeks after Mubarak's ouster, the SCAF's transition plan was right on track. A ten-person committee had drafted constitutional amendments, voters had approved the amendments overwhelmingly in a successful referendum, and elections were set to conclude within roughly six months—exactly as the SCAF outlined in its February 13 constitutional declaration.

Yet on March 30, the SCAF suddenly issued a second constitutional declaration that entirely supplanted the newly amended constitution. Among other stipulations, the sixty-three-article document loosened previous restrictions on religious parties. Whereas the amended version of the constitution banned parties established "on any religious reference or basis," the SCAF's declaration merely banned parties founded "on a religious basis," thereby legalizing parties with a "religious reference."

The new constitutional declaration also broadened the SCAF's authority to include legislation, public policymaking, and political appointments and mandated that the SCAF would continue to hold these powers until a new president was elected. Finally, the declaration directly contradicted one of the key constitutional amendments that millions of Egyptians had approved via referendum only eleven days earlier: Rather than authorizing Egypt's next president to request the drafting of a new constitution, the SCAF empowered itself to invite the two houses of Parliament to choose the constitution-writing committee in a joint session within six months of the parliamentary elections. In other words, a new constitution could be written *before* the new president was elected, and Parliament was thus given greater and more immediate control over the process.[53]

For the most part, this was quite palatable for the Muslim Brotherhood. After all, the Brotherhood said that it wanted the state to have a "religious refer-ence"—"*marga'iya diniya*"—and the SCAF's new declaration legalized parties established on this precise basis.[54] Moreover, the Brotherhood strongly pre-ferred writing the new constitution between the parliamentary and presiden-tial elections because it had promised not to run a presidential candidate and thus feared losing influence over the process once a non-Brotherhood pres-ident was elected. Indeed, even while supporting the March 19 referendum, Brotherhood leaders expressed misgivings about writing a constitution after presidential elections. "If we bring a president before the institutions [are established], then we will have created a dictator and will have inaugurated a God," Sobhi Saleh, the Brotherhood leader on the constitution-amending committee, said in early March.[55] That concern was now addressed.

The revolutionaries, however, overwhelmingly rejected the SCAF's lat-est declaration. Substantively, they objected to the declaration's articles that preserved an aspect of the Mubarak-era elections, under which workers and farmers made up 50 percent of Parliament. The revolutionaries feared that Mubarakist former parliamentarians would exploit this provision to return to power.

But more important, the declaration coincided with the activists' growing realization that they were losing the revolution that they started only two months earlier. Their call for a "no" vote during the March 19 referendum garnered a paltry 23 percent, and they now worried that the convergence between SCAF and Brotherhood prerogatives was squeezing them out of the picture. Adding to their weakness, the revolutionaries were increasingly di-vided on how to push their revolution forward. The Islamists, communists, socialists, and Nasserists that dominated the revolutionaries' ranks could not agree on what kind of republic they hoped to establish and who their partners should be for achieving it. As a result of their internal disputes, Tahrir Square lay empty for weeks, giving the SCAF a low-pressure environment for push-ing a transition plan that the revolutionaries increasingly rejected.[56]

The revolutionaries thus changed their strategy. Since they could not agree on the path forward, they decided instead to focus on the one thing that unified them in the past: opposition to the Mubarak regime. So on Friday, April 1, they called for demonstrations to "protect the revolution," demanding that the SCAF arrest top Mubarak regime officials, put corrupt businessmen on trial, and replace all governors whom Mubarak appointed. Thousands of Egyptians filled Tahrir Square, and the chants included calls for the fall of the SCAF's top official, Field Marshal Tantawi.[57] Six days later, the SCAF granted one of the revolutionaries' key demands: It arrested Mubarak's former chief of staff, Zakaria Azmi.[58] Suddenly the revolutionaries' momentum was back, which encouraged them to keep pressing.

The following week, the Brotherhood joined the revolutionaries in Tahrir Square, where even larger crowds called for more Mubarak regime officials to be arrested, including the deposed president himself. "We don't only want to try him for the millions [of dollars] but also for the blood," Islamist preacher Safwat Hegazy, a prominent Brotherhood supporter, said while addressing the crowd. "We want to try him just as he tried the people in state security courts, but we want a popular trial."[59] The revolutionaries also called for the appointment of a civilian-led presidential council. Meanwhile, approximately fifteen army officers broke ranks and joined the protesters in the square, embarrassing the SCAF.[60]

Once again, the demonstrations yielded immediate results. Three days later, former NDP Shura Council leader Safwat Sherif was arrested. Then, later that week, the once unthinkable happened: Mubarak and his two sons were detained, and the authorities opened investigations into their activities.[61]

It was a smart move by the SCAF. Mubarak was the revolutionaries' trump card, and now that he and his would-be heirs were behind bars, the revolutionaries had no way of rallying the masses behind their other demands. So once again protest activity fizzled, and the revolutionaries returned to the drawing board.

Meanwhile, the Brotherhood leadership turned its attention inward, preparing its rank and file for the next step.

• • • • • • • •

From the moment he left prison in early March 2011, Brotherhood Deputy Supreme Guide Khairat al-Shater touted something that he referred to as the "Renaissance Project." During an extemporaneous interview upon his release, al-Shater warned that Egyptians must resist the Renaissance Project's enemies.[62] He repeated this term four days later during an in-depth television interview, explaining that the Renaissance Project is a "comprehensive concept that doesn't conform to the idea of separation of religion, as defined by the West and the churches."[63] And in a subsequent interview with Hamas's Al-Aqsa satellite network, al-Shater denied any interest in running for president, vowing to work "in the trenches" for the Renaissance Project instead.[64]

But what exactly was the Renaissance Project?

On April 24, during a ninety-two-minute address to Muslim Brothers in Alexandria, al-Shater finally elaborated. "You all know that our main and overall mission as Muslim Brothers is to empower God's religion on earth," he told his audience, "to organize our life and the lives of people on the basis of Islam, to establish the renaissance of the Islamic nation and its civilization on the basis of Islam and subjugation of people to God on Earth." In other words, the Renaissance Project was the Brotherhood's longtime agenda: a program for implementing al-Banna's interpretation of Islam as an "all-embracing concept" through societal and political work. And in the freer environment of post-Mubarak Egypt, the Brotherhood now had a tremendous opportunity to advance this project as never before.

The Brotherhood was responsible for implementing this "renaissance," al-Shater explained, because it was designed as "an instrument or means to Islamize life in its entirety." The organization's hierarchical chain of command, which "needs to be obeyed and committed to," drew from the structure of the Prophet Muhammad's own society and sought the exact same ends: instituting "the religion of God Almighty." Al-Shater thus equated the Brotherhood's political mission with Islam itself and argued that the Brotherhood's agenda and hierarchical decision-making processes were nonnegotiable:

No one can come and say, "Let's change the overall mission." No one can say, "Let's remove one of these objectives." No one can say, "instead of the [Brotherhood] let's make a party or two." No one can say, "We'll work along three lines other than definition, formation and execution." No one can say, "Forget about obedience, discipline and structures of the [Brotherhood]," claiming that we can call any gathering a [Brotherhood]. No. All of these are constants that represent the fundamental framework for our method, the method of the Muslim Brotherhood. It is not open to developing or change.

Al-Shater's explication of the Brotherhood's agenda was nothing short of totalitarian: The Muslim Brotherhood was now going to intensify its efforts to "organize" the "lives of people" according to its own interpretation of Islam. And, moving forward, it would tolerate no dissenters within its ranks.

In turn, those who disagreed with the Brotherhood's decisions, said al-Shater, had a choice: either comply or leave the organization. The Brotherhood would remain strong either way. "Hundreds join the [Brotherhood] daily," al-Shater said. "So there's no problem for us in numbers, even if we feel badly if any human being leaves us or walks away from us." It was a clear message to the dissident Brotherhood youths demanding greater participation in the organization's decision making: Forget about it.

Still, al-Shater explained, many of the Brotherhood's normal activities would continue in the post-Mubarak era. "We are now developing the Muslim individual, and, God willing, we will continue," al-Shater said. "We are developing the Muslim household, and, God willing, we will continue. We are developing the Muslim society, and, God willing, we will continue." And this Islamizing work had the exact same goal that al-Banna articulated many decades earlier. "We are preparing this society for the stage of Islamic government," said al-Shater, "which is what organizes the remaining aspects of people's lives outside the scope of society such as economics, politics, and all other fields, on the basis of Islamic reference."

But there would be one major difference: The Brotherhood would now prepare for the "stage of Islamic government" by drafting a wide-ranging policy agenda. "This 'renaissance' is big talk," he said. "But in the end we need to have a number of tracks in social, economic, health, education, and moral development in many fields. Each of these tracks comprises subtracks, and these subtracks comprise projects." Al-Shater thus committed the Brotherhood to developing and administering policies for achieving an Islamist "renaissance" in Egypt.

Pursuing this "renaissance," al-Shater repeatedly insisted, didn't mean that the Brotherhood sought to "reach the seat of government." But the deputy supreme guide nevertheless anticipated a significant political role for the organization in the coming period. "We will think and plan, while at the same time we want to arrange for how the work will go," al-Shater told his Brotherhood audience, "because we are the biggest faction currently present in the [Islamic nation]—present, organized, and aware of the issues management." In this vein, al-Shater announced that the Brotherhood was "preparing a media strategy," which included acquiring media outlets, and he further charged Muslim Brothers to act as advocates for the organization's political vision. "The biggest independent newspaper in Egypt distributes 400,000 copies," he said. "You all participate in society and can reach millions of people, not 400,000. Therefore our ability to influence and communicate directly is, God willing, important and effective."[65]

In short, the Brotherhood's Renaissance Project was a call to action. In the freer political environment of post-Mubarak Egypt, the Brotherhood would intensify its outreach work. At the same time, its chain of command would be repurposed for new activities: promoting its agenda in the media, pursuing a share of power, and implementing Islamist public policies.

But what, exactly, were those policies? What did it mean to "implement *shari'ah*" in government? Al-Shater never said. He was focused primarily on the organizational process for implementing al-Banna's ideological vision and anticipated filling in the details later.

The vagueness of the Brotherhood's policy vision would be a major shortcoming once it achieved power. But, at the time, it made no difference. Three months after Mubarak's ouster, the Brotherhood was the only political player with a clear set of political goals, as well as the organizational infrastructure for achieving them. It was also aligned with the country's ultimate power holder, the SCAF, and supported its transition program. The revolutionaries, by contrast, were in total disarray, desperately seeking a new rallying cry to recapture their Arab Spring glory.

4 Preparing for Power

*Mohamed Morsi was one of the Guidance Office's most notoriously hardline fig-*ures—"an icon of the extremists in the Muslim Brotherhood," a former Brotherhood youth told me years before Morsi became a household name.[1] Within the organization, he was known for his strict adherence to the Brotherhood's hierarchical processes and was often the Guidance Office leader responsible for punishing internal dissenters. "There are people who think they're the temple guards, and he's one of them," said Islam Lotfy, a prominent Brotherhood youth who later left the organization. "He cares a lot about the system, more than the people."[2]

Born in 1951 in Al-Adwa, an impoverished village in the Nile Delta governorate of Sharkiya, Morsi earned his master's degree from Cairo University's engineering faculty in 1978 and then moved to Los Angeles for doctoral studies at the University of Southern California. Newly married and uncomfortable in libertine American society, Morsi found his community among Muslim Brothers in California and joined the organization while still in the United States. Upon returning to Egypt in 1985, he landed a professorship at the University of Zaqaziq in Sharkiya's provincial capital and became a prominent Brotherhood figure through his membership in the university's faculty club, as well as his participation in the governorate's Committee to Resist Zionism.[3] He was elected to Parliament in 2000, joining sixteen other Brotherhood parliamentarians in constituting the legislature's largest opposition bloc.

At the urging of Mohamed Ali Bishr, a Brotherhood leader who knew Morsi from their time in America, the Guidance Office selected Morsi as its parliamentary bloc chair.[4] In this capacity, Morsi effectively served as liaison between the other Brotherhood parliamentarians and the Guidance Office and emerged as both a fierce critic of the Mubarak regime and a reliable exponent of the Brotherhood's theocratic ideology. (His first parliamentary speech attacked interest-based banking, which Islam forbids.) This apparently pleased the Brotherhood leadership, which inducted him into the Guidance Office in 2002. But Morsi's behavior in Parliament also angered the Mubarak regime. While the Brotherhood won a whopping eighty-eight seats in the 2005 parliamentary elections, the regime forced a Zaqaziq elections judge to forge the results against Morsi, thereby ending his legislative career.[5]

The Guidance Office, however, offered Morsi a consolation prize: It appointed him to oversee the Brotherhood parliamentary bloc's work. His responsibilities within the Brotherhood expanded further following the arrest of Deputy Supreme Guide Khairat al-Shater in late 2006. The Guidance Office appointed Morsi to replace al-Shater as its primary liaison to the Mubarak regime's State Security apparatus, viewing Morsi as ideologically rigid and therefore unlikely to concede too much to the authorities.[6] Meanwhile, Morsi used his growing influence within the organization to promote and enforce hardline positions. He oversaw the drafting of the Brotherhood's 2007 political platform, which called for restricting the presidency to Muslim men and appointing a council of Islamic scholars to advise Parliament on the shari'ah-compliance of legislation.[7] Two years later, Morsi led the push to oust two top Guidance Office leaders who had voiced their disagreement with the platform, seeing them as threats to the organization's internal unity.[8]

Within the Brotherhood, Morsi was considered one of the foremost "Qutbists," meaning that he embraced Sayyid Qutb's belief that the Brotherhood should separate itself from society until it was strong enough to transform it.[9] While some Brotherhood figures advocated cooperating with other political groups to build a broad coalition that could challenge the Mubarak regime, Morsi—like most Guidance Office members—worried that this would undermine the Brotherhood's ideological integrity. He therefore believed that the Brotherhood should focus on societal outreach and only pursue political power once its theocratic agenda was broadly supported.

For this reason, when I asked Morsi in August 2010 whether the Brotherhood would nominate a presidential candidate "if Mubarak died tomorrow," he said it wouldn't. "Our program is a long-term one, not a short-term one," he told me. "Our goal is not to become governors. Our country should be governed by these kinds of principles—by Islam." He additionally said that the Brotherhood wouldn't get involved in "randomness movements," by which he meant mass protest activities.[10] Participating in demonstrations, after all, meant working with non-Islamists, which would force the Brotherhood to compromise on its Islamist mission. It was thus unsurprising when Morsi rejected Brotherhood youths' call for mobilizing the organization to support the January 25, 2011, protests. Morsi didn't want the Brotherhood to simply be one group among many—he wanted it to act only when it could dominate.

The success of the January uprising, however, fundamentally changed the Guidance Office's strategy. The suddenly open political field represented an unprecedented opportunity for the Brotherhood to promote its agenda and pursue political power at the same time. The Guidance Office also feared that *failing* to intensify its political work would enable other forces—perhaps even those tied to the Mubarak regime—to seize the momentum and create new barriers to the Brotherhood's Islamizing agenda.

So the Brotherhood leadership turned to its most reliable hardliner to manage the organization's political work during this transitional period. On April 30, 2011, it named Morsi the first chairman of its nascent FJP. Two more Guidance Office members were appointed to the party's other top positions: Essam el-Erian, a former Brotherhood parliamentarian and one of its most prolific political networkers, was named vice-chair, and Saad al-Katatny, a former parliamentarian who succeeded Morsi as the Brotherhood's parliamentary bloc chair from 2005 to 2010, was named the FJP's secretary-general.

• • • • • • • •

From the moment it established the FJP, the Brotherhood insisted that the new party would function separately from the organization, which is why the Brotherhood formally relieved the three top FJP leaders—Morsi, el-Erian, and al-Katatny—of their Guidance Office duties and later appointed replacements.[11] But this Brotherhood–FJP separation was a badly executed ruse. The three leaders, after all, remained members in the Brotherhood's General Shura Committee, which is the organization's legislative arm. That meant that they were still directly involved in the Brotherhood's leadership and bound by oath to follow its decisions, rendering the FJP an appendage of the Brotherhood rather than a separate entity.

Morsi acknowledged his obedience to Brotherhood dictates during one of his first interviews as FJP chair, when he explained that the Brotherhood's leadership had ordered him to resign from the Guidance Office and become FJP chair. "This decision could have been emotional for me in various ways, thus uncomfortable," Morsi told ONTV's Yosri Fouda. "But there is a difference between emotions and the commitment to the principles that we have all embraced. . . . Whenever the [Brotherhood] decides something, it is my duty to respect this decision."[12]

The Brotherhood's nationwide structure was also vital to the FJP's rapid expansion throughout Egypt. In the months that followed Morsi's appointment as FJP chairman, Muslim Brothers opened new FJP headquarters in every governorate, as well as in numerous towns and villages. While FJP offices were kept separate from local Brotherhood headquarters to bolster the impression that the FJP was distinct from the Brotherhood, the FJP performed many of the same functions. FJP offices thus organized medical clinics, educational programs, vocational trainings, and food-distribution efforts—the very same social services that the Brotherhood had provided to win popular support throughout its history.[13] Local FJP offices also hosted political conferences featuring top Brotherhood figures that sometimes drew thousands of supporters. The key difference between the Brotherhood and the FJP was ultimately legal: The Brotherhood never registered itself with the Egyptian government and thus remained an illegal organization, while the FJP was licensed as a legal political party on June 6.[14]

More to the point, by FJP leaders' own admission, the FJP was ideologically indistinct from the Brotherhood. The party and organization "start from the same principles," Morsi declared during a ribbon-cutting ceremony at the FJP's new headquarters in the Nile Delta governorate of Dakhaliya in July.[15] Morsi made it quite clear, for example, that the FJP was working toward the Brotherhood's long-term goal of establishing a caliphate. "If Muslim countries in the future create a union based on their Islamic identity, just like [the European Union], then what is wrong with that?" Morsi said during an interview in June, when asked about this element of the Brotherhood's agenda. Morsi further echoed the Brotherhood's call for a system in which the "principles of Islamic *sharī'ah* are the envelope and the reference for the laws of this state."[16] To emphasize the continuity between the Brotherhood and the FJP for the organization's supporters, many of the party's early banners and posters contained both logos.

The FJP's direct link to the Brotherhood facilitated the organization's swift transition from underground Islamist society to prominent political actor. After all, the Brotherhood was already a well-established national organization, with administrative offices in every governorate and hundreds of thousands of deeply committed cadres eager to advance the Brotherhood's political mission through its new political vehicle. When a German parliamentary delegation asked Morsi how the FJP would campaign during the parliamentary elections, Morsi made the link between the Brotherhood's organization and the

FJP quite explicit. "The popular movement on which the party was founded has been working for eighty years," he said.[17]

So when it founded the FJP, the Brotherhood moved personnel from its various governorate offices over to the newly founded FJP offices, where they often performed similar functions under different titles. Local Brotherhood officials responsible for recruiting students, for example, became the local FJP officials responsible for campaigning among students. Building the FJP was thus a relatively seamless operation. On the evening that he was appointed the FJP's first chair, Morsi boasted on Al Jazeera that the FJP already had an impressive seven thousand founding members,[18] and many more Muslim Brothers joined thereafter.

In all of these ways, the Brotherhood was far ahead of every other legal political party, none of which possessed the FJP's instant nationwide organization, legions of cadres, well-developed ideology, or strong brand name. Indeed, despite enjoying greater freedom under Mubarak than the Brotherhood, these other parties were overwhelmingly small, weak, and unpopular— yet, ironically, quite prominent, which made them hard for the Brotherhood to ignore entirely.

· · · · · · · ·

The approximately two dozen legal opposition parties that existed under Mubarak were, in a certain sense, extensions of the regime itself. The Egyptian government founded the two original opposition parties, leftist al-Tagammu and nominally rightist al-Ahrar, in 1976, when President Sadat sought to signal Egypt's liberalization by creating opposition parties that would run against his own ruling Egypt Party.[19] Two years later, when both al-Tagammu and al-Ahrar opposed his peace efforts with Israel, Sadat encouraged his agriculture minister to establish the Socialist Labor Party.[20] Mubarak, who took power following Sadat's assassination in 1981, permitted the establishment of many more opposition parties, though the regime maintained total control over the process: Parties had to receive licenses from the upper parliamentary house's Political Parties Committee, which the ruling NDP controlled.

The opposition parties, in other words, existed entirely at the regime's pleasure, since the regime only granted licenses to those parties that it saw as nonthreatening. To be sure, the most prominent legal parties—al-Tagammu, the nationalist Wafd, and the pan-Arabist Nasserist Party—contained genuine critics of the regime and its policies. Many of their members were, at one time, strident oppositionists who envisioned their parties as vehicles for challenging Mubarak politically. But throughout Mubarak's thirty-year rule, Egypt's security state effectively kept these parties in check by offering them a deal they couldn't refuse: If they wanted to continue existing, they couldn't cross the regime's "red lines."

The red lines represented the upper bounds of oppositional activity that the regime was willing to tolerate, and the punishments for crossing them could be substantial. Rogue oppositionists risked sanctions on their businesses, disclosures of their private lives in Egypt's sensationalist press, harassment by authorities, and, of course, imprisonment. And to induce the opposition parties' caution, the regime kept these red lines somewhat ambiguous, such as by permitting intense criticism at certain times but punishing critics quite harshly at other times.

Yet opposition party leaders understood that three topics were off-limits: They could not criticize President Mubarak, the Mubarak family, or the Egyptian military. They also understood that two specific activities represented clear violations of the red lines. First, parties could not participate in mass protest activities because the regime viewed this as an act of insurrection. For this reason, the legal opposition parties steered clear of the various opposition movements, such as Kefaya and the April 6 Youth movement, that emerged during the final decade of Mubarak's rule. Second, particularly during the latter years of Mubarak's rule, parties could not align with the Brotherhood because the regime viewed the mass appeal of the Brotherhood's Islamist ideology as uniquely threatening.[21]

In exchange for abiding by the red lines, the regime granted the parties certain privileges. Legal opposition parties were permitted to maintain headquarters where they could organize large events with relatively little interference from the regime.[22] The parties were also permitted to print newspapers, which enabled them to send correspondents to various governmental ministries and institutions for collecting information.[23] Finally, parties could run in parliamentary elections, and the regime often awarded a few seats to quiescent parties. While Parliament largely served as a rubber stamp for the Mubarak regime's policies, participation in Parliament carried key benefits, including a boost in a party's public profile. Parliamentarians also enjoyed parliamentary immunity, which enabled them and their partners to pursue lucrative business deals extralegally.[24]

Given the autocratic context in which the legal opposition parties operated, this wasn't such a bad deal. So long as they kept their critiques of the regime within certain boundaries, they were granted a platform. Opposition leaders thus graced the pages of the major newspapers and appeared frequently on television, sometimes as counterparts to ruling party shills. They were, in other words, prominent figures from recognized organizations.

Yet the legal opposition parties' adherence to the regime's red lines meant that they had little support in the streets. Confined to their headquarters, these parties rarely interacted with citizens and had only a skeletal presence in most governorates outside of Cairo. They also lacked coherent political principles or agendas. Perhaps most important, as these parties quietly adhered to the regime's red lines for decades, they alienated younger oppositionists, many of whom preferred the more stridently antiregime activism of groups such as Kefaya and April 6.

Of course, the Muslim Brotherhood also adhered to the Mubarak regime's red lines to a great extent: The organization rarely criticized Mubarak or his family personally and often avoided mass protest activity, including on January 25, 2011. But this didn't hurt the Brotherhood's growth as it stunted the legal opposition parties' development, for two reasons. First, unlike the political parties, the Brotherhood was not primarily interested in winning parliamentary seats under Mubarak. Its foremost goal was Islamizing society through nonpolitical work, and the regime put fewer constraints on these activities.

Second, the Brotherhood's internal dynamics made it less susceptible to regime pressure. Joining a legal political party under Mubarak was relatively easy: Prospective members submitted written applications to internal party committees through an open process. The legal opposition parties' members were therefore politically interested Egyptians but hardly diehards—and thus unwilling to sacrifice greatly for their party's cause. By contrast, as discussed in chapter 2, every Muslim Brother went through a multiyear *tarbiah* process that ensured his total commitment to the Brotherhood's cause. The Brotherhood therefore comprised individuals who were selected for their willingness to withstand regime pressure.

So when Mubarak fell in February 2011, the legal opposition parties had few illusions about the Brotherhood's strength. Indeed, the opposition parties' early attempt at flexing their muscles was a tremendous embarrassment. While the Brotherhood strongly supported the March 19 referendum on proposed constitutional amendments, most of the prominent Mubarak-era opposition parties campaigned for "no," and "yes" carried the day with an overwhelming 77 percent of the vote.

Unable to beat the Brotherhood, the opposition parties sought to partner with it. On June 14, eleven parties met with the FJP to discuss the formation of an electoral coalition. In their first joint press statement, the parties declared their objectives: They would draft a proposed parliamentary elections law, which they would submit to the SCAF and then coordinate during the upcoming parliamentary elections with the aim of building a "national unity government."[25]

One week later, the Democratic Alliance for Egypt was announced. The Alliance committed itself to protecting "freedom of thought and expression," the "devolution of power through universal, free, and impartial suffrage," the "right of peaceful assembly of political parties, NGOs, and trade unions," and the "independence of the judiciary," as well as the establishment of "an economic system based on freedom and social justice." The statement also hinted toward a reorientation of Egypt's foreign policy, calling for a "strategic dialogue with Iran" and revising the peace treaty with Israel. Eighteen parties signed onto the Alliance, representing a wide (and unwieldy) range of ideologies: leftists, Nasserists, and Salafists.[26]

The FJP's primary partner in this effort, however, was the Wafd, which was the most prominent Mubarak-era legal opposition party, as well as the only party whose name truly resonated with the Egyptian public. Founded in 1918 to represent Egyptian interests at the Paris Peace Conference, the Wafd—which means "delegation"—was the major Egyptian nationalist party of its era, leading the struggle for Egyptian independence and then serving as the ruling party at various points until the early 1950s. Like the Brotherhood, it was outlawed following the 1952 Free Officers Revolution but reorganized and returned to parliamentary politics—albeit in significantly weakened form—under Mubarak.[27] At the time of Mubarak's ouster, it was one of the few parties with headquarters in every governorate, and it was the only opposition party that printed a daily newspaper, *Al-Wafd*.

Despite considering itself an ecumenical "liberal" party whose symbol is an interlocking cross and crescent, the Wafd had aligned with the Brotherhood previously and quite successfully. During the 1984 elections, a joint Brotherhood–Wafd list won an impressive 58 of 448 contested seats.[28] The Wafd never came close to achieving this seat total in the elections that followed. Running without the Brotherhood in 1987, it won only thirty-five seats to the Brotherhood-dominated Islamist Bloc's sixty seats, and by the 2005 elections the Wafd could muster only five seats to the Brotherhood's eighty-eight. The Wafd thus viewed an alliance with the Brotherhood as its best strategy for vastly increasing its representation within the post-Mubarak Parliament, given the Brotherhood's unparalleled nationwide mobilizing network. Indeed, the Wafd anticipated riding the Brotherhood's coattails to victory.

But the Brotherhood also benefited from its participation in the Democratic Alliance. By building a coalition with Egypt's most recognizable "liberal" party, the Brotherhood was able to position itself toward the political center, thereby reassuring those Egyptians who feared an "Islamist takeover."

More important, the Brotherhood envisioned the Alliance as a mechanism for quietly dominating Egypt's next Parliament. After all, the Brotherhood had promised to run for fewer than half of all parliamentary seats. But since the other coalition partners in the Alliance would depend on the Brotherhood's mobilizing capabilities to win the remaining seats, those parties' parliamentarians would ultimately follow the Brotherhood's lead. The Alliance would enable the Brotherhood to dominate Parliament without holding a majority of the seats. The Brotherhood sought power but feared looking power-hungry.[29]

The Brotherhood was still quite worried about appearances. "We won't compete for a parliamentary majority, meaning we don't want to be more than 50 percent in Parliament," Deputy Supreme Guide al-Shater said during a mid-June television interview. "Why? . . . If a country comes and says 'I won't do business with this government if it's controlled by the Muslim Brotherhood,' then I've exposed the interests of the Egyptian people to risk, as has happened in other places."[30]

Yet the Brotherhood's fear that foreign powers would intervene in Egypt to prevent its emergence was completely unfounded. In fact, the very opposite was happening: Western powers, recognizing the Brotherhood was Egypt's preeminent political force, were eagerly courting it.

• • • • • • • •

The great irony of the Brotherhood's post-Mubarak behavior is that despite believing that foreign powers sought to stymie its rise, it never toned down its virulently anti-Western rhetoric. Brotherhood leaders took great pains to reassure the international community that they wouldn't rush to power and repeatedly professed their commitment to democracy to every foreign journalist, pundit, researcher, and official willing to hear them out. But like addicts hooked on heroin, they couldn't avoid the types of provocative statements that most centrally contributed to Western distrust of the organization in the first place.

When US forces killed Osama bin Laden in Pakistan on May 2, the Brother-hood issued a mournful statement. Referring to the offed al-Qaeda leader as a "sheikh," the Brotherhood made no mention of bin Laden's crimes. Instead, it lambasted Washington for killing him without putting him on trial and ac-cused the United States of "linking Islam with terrorism." Perhaps most offen-sively, the Brotherhood validated al-Qaeda's ongoing fight against the West: "So long as the occupation remains, resistance will remain legitimate," the statement read, "and it's incumbent upon America, NATO, and the European Union to announce quickly the end of the occupation of Iraq and Afghanistan and to recognize the legitimate rights of the Palestinian people."[31]

Meanwhile, the Brotherhood repeatedly declared its intention to end Egypt's 1979 peace accord with Israel. "The Egyptian revolution wasn't just a revolution against the regime," the supreme guide wrote in his weekly state-ment on May 6, "but an internal revolution against repression, humiliation, intimidation, starvation, and despair, and an external revolution in a lead-ing position, joining the Arab fold and performing a national role after thirty years of being subject to the policies of the American–Zionist project and the capitulary Camp David [Accords]."[32] Two weeks later, the supreme guide called for Israel's destruction. "These blessed revolutions are a prelude to ending injustice and the Zionist peak, liberating the holy sites, and ending Zi-onist arrogance in all its forms and manifestations," the supreme guide wrote to mark the anniversary of Israel's founding.[33]

Yet even as the Brotherhood emerged as Egypt's preeminent political force, US officials and analysts often brushed off these types of statements. Within Washington, it was broadly accepted that postauthoritarian Arab states would pursue more populist foreign policies, including in ways that ran counter to US interests. And those who expressed concerns regarding Egypt's post-Mubarak foreign policy trajectory were roundly dismissed as disrespectful of Arabs' democratic aspirations. Arab Spring enthusiasm reigned supreme, and previous debates about *whether* the United States should promote democracy in the Middle East suddenly became moot. The overwhelming consensus held that democratization *was* happening, and, with the situation framed in this way, the Obama administration faced a stark choice: It could either be on the "right side of history" or get left behind.

The administration thus channeled great enthusiasm for the Arab world's political transitions. President Obama reportedly ordered his staffers to study transitions in fifty to sixty countries for policy guidance, and, based on this comparative analysis, the administration viewed the Arab world's prognosis very positively. An unnamed administration official told the *New York Times* that "Egypt is analogous to South Korea, the Philippines and Chile, while a revolution in Syria might end up looking like Romania's."[34] If the administration had any concern that ideology—such as Islamism—might interfere with these countries' ultimate progress toward democracy and prosperity, it kept silent. And it similarly sidestepped the question of what might happen to these countries' foreign policies if anti-Western forces won elections.

The president declared his full embrace of the Arab Spring on May 19, during a major address on the Middle East at the State Department. "It will be the policy of the United States to promote reform across the region, and to support transitions to democracy," he said. "That effort begins in Egypt and Tunisia. . . . Both nations can set a strong example through free and fair elections, a vibrant civil society, accountable and effective democratic institutions, and responsible regional leadership." Those countries that "take the risks that reform entails," the president emphasized, would "have the full support of the United States." The president's speech presaged a policy of "engagement" with the region's emerging political forces, irrespective of their ideologies or foreign policy views. "We look forward to working with all who embrace genuine and inclusive democracy," the president said.[35]

That was good news for the Brotherhood. After all, the bar for achieving American support was embracing procedural democracy, and the Brotherhood had been doing exactly that since Mubarak's ouster: It established a political party, built an electoral coalition, and was now preparing for the ballot box. Perhaps most important, the Brotherhood was doing these things more enthusiastically than the revolutionary youths who had catalyzed the January uprising, many of whom still wanted to defer elections indefinitely, until after a new constitution had been written.

So on June 30, the administration officially announced that it was open to "dialogue" with the Brotherhood. "We believe, given the changing political landscape in Egypt, that it is in the interests of the United States to engage with all parties that are peaceful and committed to nonviolence, that intend to compete for the parliament and the presidency," Secretary of State Hillary Clinton told reporters in Budapest. Clinton added that the administration would use its dialogue with the Brotherhood "to emphasize the importance of and support for democratic principles, and especially a commitment to nonviolence, respect for minority rights, and the full inclusion of women in any democracy."

Clinton's statement caught the Brotherhood by surprise, but the organization stayed firmly on message. "The U.S. is hated in the Middle East region more than any other country according to polls published in the U.S.," Brotherhood spokesman Mahmoud Ghozlan told CNN. "If the U.S. is serious in opening a dialogue, they must first respect the people's choices for a true democracy, independence and respect their choice of leaders."[36]

A few days later, at an FJP rally in Dakhaliya, Morsi accused the United States of financing conspiracies in Egypt. "The Zionists and the Americans have spent in five months 240 million Egyptian pounds, 40 million dollars, given to 60 institutions," he declared, referring to US support for prodemocratic nongovernmental organizations (NGOs). "Every one of the institutions got 4 million Egyptian pounds in 5 months. What do they do with this money? . . . It is so [people] move to implement the American people's interests, and the [interests of the] criminal Zionist people!"[37]

Yet despite the Brotherhood's unflinching anti-Americanism, Washington persisted in its outreach. In early October, President Obama sent National Security Council (NSC) official Prem Kumar to meet with FJP secretary-general Saad al-Katatny. The White House wasn't leaving "engagement" with the Brotherhood to its ambassador, as other countries were doing, but instead was granting the Brotherhood recognition straight from the president's office. And since the meeting came without any conditions, al-Katatny used the encounter to harangue Kumar on supposed "U.S. interference in internal Egyptian affairs," which the Brotherhood proudly highlighted in its subsequent press release.[38] Of course, the Brotherhood's behavior came at no cost: Kumar was the first of many high-level American officials who passed through the FJP's headquarters in the months that followed.

Slowly but surely, the Brotherhood got the message: The international community was far less averse to its emergence than it anticipated. Foreign officials routinely encouraged the Brotherhood to respect the peace treaty with Israel and embrace pluralism but exerted no significant pressure toward those ends. When the French ambassador asked the Brotherhood's party about the future of Egyptian–Israeli relations, he endured a lecture from Morsi. "We see Palestinian blood being shed everyday by the Israelis," Morsi exclaimed, according to a statement that the FJP issued after the meeting. "And despite this you ask us about our support and backing for the Palestinians and our position with them, despite the presence of European activists who are sympathetic with them like us."[39]

Still, more French delegations followed. When a French senator visited the FJP following an outbreak in anti-Christian violence in October, FJP leader

Saad al-Husseini insisted that "applying the principles of Islamic *sharī'ah* is the best guarantee for the rights of Copts in Egypt."[40] The Brotherhood was doubling down on its ideology because, in the presence of its foreign guests, there was no cost for doing so. As Western governments' unconditional "engagement" with the Brotherhood continued, one factor that might have compelled the Brotherhood's moderation—its paranoid, but exploitable, fears of the West—gradually dissipated.

• • • • • • • •

While the Brotherhood was preparing for elections and power, the SCAF seemed to be losing control. Fearing that any false move might incite another uprising, the military and police largely stood to the side as crime and civil strife rose dramatically during the months that followed Mubarak's ouster. Mid-May witnessed deadly sectarian clashes, multiple jailbreaks, the ransacking of an upscale Cairo neighborhood, and a violent standoff in front of the Israeli embassy in Giza, among other incidents. In an attempt to restore order, the SCAF referred suspects to military courts, but this only intensified the backlash.[41] Suddenly, the revolutionary activists sensed an opportunity to revive their calls for further and faster political change. They declared that May 27 would be Egypt's "second Friday of Rage"—in other words, a repeat of the pivotal January 28 mass protests against the Mubarak regime, except that the SCAF was now the target.

Among other demands, the revolutionaries called for the immediate election of a constitution-writing committee that would include representatives from a range of institutions (such as al-Azhar University, the Coptic Orthodox Church, and the police) and professors from a range of subject areas (such as medicine, law, and engineering).[42] This was, in other words, a restart of the revolutionaries' "constitution-first" campaign—and an attempt to disregard the March 19 referendum and the SCAF's March 30 declaration, which empowered the next Parliament to steer the constitution-drafting process.

The Brotherhood viewed the new protest calls as threatening its post-Mubarak political strategy. After all, it anticipated dominating the first Parliament so that it could control the constitution-drafting process and therefore opposed writing a constitution before the parliamentary elections. With the revolutionaries once again organizing mass protests to advance their constitution-first agenda, the Brotherhood now feared that the SCAF might concede to the activists—as it had done when it arrested Mubarak and his cronies following the early April Tahrir protests.

So, for the first time, the Brotherhood aggressively denounced the demonstrations and declared its support for the SCAF. "The call for new activism in the name of an anger revolution or second revolution means nothing but two things," it said in a statement. "First, that this revolution is against the people or a clear majority of them. Second, that it's driving a wedge between the people and their armed forces and the SCAF leaders."[43]

Ultimately, the May 27 demonstrations didn't force major concessions from the SCAF. But as tens of thousands of Egyptians filled Tahrir Square, focusing their chants against both the SCAF and the Brotherhood simultaneously, the revolutionaries suddenly felt reempowered.[44] Yet their attempts to organize follow-up demonstrations failed. Only a few hundred protesters filled the square in the weeks that followed, and the activists went back to the drawing board.

Then on June 28, Egypt's police gave the revolutionaries a new rallying cry. As families of those who died during the January uprising marched near Cairo's Balloon Theater, thugs attacked the procession, catalyzing clashes between protesters and security forces. Over one thousand were injured, and police blanketed the area with tear gas.[45] As news of the assault spread over social media, activists flocked to Tahrir Square and briefly declared a sit-in.[46] The revolutionaries used the incident to declare another round of mass protests against the SCAF, and a wide variety of groups agreed to participate on Friday, July 8, which they dubbed "Determination Friday."

The Brotherhood was inclined to reject the protest call, as it had done on May 27. From its perspective, the protest was a thin veneer for the revolutionaries' constitution-first agenda, and the Brotherhood absolutely refused to entertain a revision of the elections-first road map that the March 19 referendum ordained. But with many of its partners in the Democratic Alliance for Egypt, including the Wafd, declaring their participation in the July 8 demonstrations, the Brotherhood worried that the scales might tip against it—that large crowds might converge on Tahrir Square and force the SCAF to make some major concessions. So two days before the protests, the Brotherhood made the revolutionaries an offer: It would participate in the July 8 demonstrations so long as the activists dropped their "constitution-first" demand.[47] The activists saw an opportunity to unify the country's political forces for the first time since Mubarak's ouster and agreed.

The Brotherhood played its hand brilliantly. On Determination Friday, Egyptians filled public squares across the country, and tens of thousands of demonstrators packed Tahrir Square. The Brotherhood, however, assembled the largest and tallest podium, from which it broadcast its support for the military and its demand that parliamentary elections take place by September. Then at six in the evening, the Brotherhood's cadres withdrew from the square en masse, leaving behind a few thousand revolutionary activists who declared an open-ended sit-in against the SCAF.[48]

The Brotherhood's message to the SCAF was clear: *We are the best-organized and most capable force of the Egyptian street—not the revolutionaries. Make concessions to them, and you'll face us.*

By contrast, the revolutionaries, who continued occupying Tahrir Square through the end of July, played their hand miserably. Having already agreed to drop their constitution-first demand, they now called for "supraconstitutional principles"—a set of guaranteed political rights that would supersede Egypt's next constitution. These principles, the revolutionaries argued, would prevent Islamists from using their anticipated victory in the next parliamentary elections to draft a restrictive, theocratic constitution.

Of course, the Islamists viewed supraconstitutional principles as a threat for precisely this reason: It would handcuff their ability to establish an Islamic state in Egypt. So on Friday, July 29, the Brotherhood and top Salafist groups mobilized a massive demonstration against the supraconstitutional principles. Decrying secularism and liberalism, tens of thousands of Islamists overwhelmed the revolutionaries in Tahrir Square.[49] The revolutionaries derided the heavily bearded demonstration as "Kandahar Friday," referring to the Taliban's former Afghan capital, but the Islamists' impressive turnout again signaled to the SCAF that they—and not the revolutionaries—were Egypt's true street power.

Meanwhile, the revolutionaries' open-ended sit-in rapidly alienated the broader Egyptian public. The weeks-long shutdown of Tahrir Square outraged local residents and shopkeepers, who resented the revolutionaries for blocking traffic and turning the heart of downtown Cairo into a filthy encampment. The revolutionaries' sit-in also became a ripe target for the Egyptian media, which accused the revolutionaries of conducting all sorts of nefarious acts within their tent city. When security forces cleared the sit-in on August 1, local residents and shopkeepers cheered and in some cases even lent a hand.[50]

Six months after the fall of Mubarak, popular support for the revolutionaries had bottomed out. The once-lauded freedom fighters were now widely viewed as directionless agents of upheaval.

5 The Road to Parliament

While the revolutionaries spent July 2011 fruitlessly occupying Tahrir Square, the Muslim Brotherhood turned toward the next phase. Parliamentary elections were expected in September, and the Brotherhood prepared its cadres for campaign work through camping trips known as *mua'skarat*.

The Brotherhood's *mua'skarat* are part of the organization's *tarbīah*—educational—program. The goal of these excursions is to improve Muslim Brothers' physical fitness, ensure their commitment to the Brotherhood's ideological agenda, and cultivate unity.[1] During *mua'skarat*, Muslim Brothers cook for each other, engage in intensified study and prayer, listen to lectures from Brotherhood leaders, and perform physical training drills. The physical component of the *mua'skarat* is the most controversial: YouTube videos, posted by Muslim Brothers, depict cadres running in formation and performing directed group exercises, which raised suspicions that the Brotherhood was training militias.[2] For this reason, the Brotherhood kept its *mua'skarat* low profile during the Mubarak era, sometimes operating them at members' homes.[3]

In the much freer post-Mubarak environment, however, the Brotherhood saw little need for discretion. In virtually every governorate, Brotherhood administrative offices organized the largest and most public *mua'skarat* in decades. They bused cadres by the hundreds to dozens of encampments around the country, and young Muslim Brothers posted photos, videos, and written accounts of their *mua'skarat*'s activities online.

Meanwhile, the Brotherhood dispatched its top leaders to the *mua'skarat* to rally the base behind the organization's aggressive political approach. In speech after speech, Brotherhood leaders reminded their cadres that the organization's very purpose *was political:* The Brotherhood's raison d'être was spreading Islam in the society to establish an "Islamic state" in Egypt and, thereafter, a "global Islamic state" that would challenge Western hegemony. And the time to advance that agenda, the Brotherhood leaders argued, was now.

"The Muslim Brothers need to be leaders, leaders of this [Islamic nation]," Deputy Supreme Guide Mahmoud Ezzat told a *mua'skar* in Matrouh in late July 2011. "Yes, that is what God has entrusted within us. Every Muslim is called in this. This [Islamic nation] as a whole, from the east of the land to its west, is also entrusted in embracing this message."

In the years before the uprising, Ezzat reminded his audience, the Mubarak regime's repression forced the Brotherhood to act "patiently" and focus on spreading their ideas within the society rather than pursuing power. "God has set [Muslim Brothers] on this road," said Ezzat.

> So some of them have passed through jail, some of them injured, some of them displaced, and some of them martyred. . . . Yes, during all these years, we could have been on the road that the Prophet, peace be upon him, set for us. And we were confident that educating the [Islamic nation], fashioning the people, strengthening the desire, and introducing the principle and belief in [God] and the value of him—this would prevent straying [from God's path].

So in lieu of pursuing political power, Ezzat said, the Brotherhood worked under Mubarak to unify the people "around Islam, as a religion for Muslims and civilization for non-Muslims."

Mubarak's ouster, Ezzat explained, enabled the Brotherhood to accelerate its Islamizing project by establishing a political party and new offices nationwide, which would enhance the organization's preaching and outreach work. "People still do not know us," Ezzat acknowledged, so the Brotherhood would work to "clarify the greatness of this religion." Ezzat added that improving the Brotherhood's international image might require holding dialogue with the United States, among other nations, but reassured his audience that the Brotherhood's struggle against Israel would continue. "This battle between us and Zionism . . . will improve the future of civilization."[4]

Speaking at the same encampment in Matrouh, Deputy Supreme Guide Khairat al-Shater rallied the cadres around the Brotherhood's ultimate ambition: creating a global Islamist order that could resist the West.

"Today, the leadership of humanity is of the West, the Americans," al-Shater said. "Western civilization is now the dominant leader. . . . As for us,

now, we are not the masters of the world as Muslims, we don't have a caliphate, and we don't have governments at the state level or our own country."
Islam, al-Shater lamented, existed only in "the souls of individuals and groups
at the societal level." The Brotherhood's task in the post-Mubarak era was to
enact Islam in its "comprehensive role: Islam as a religion and state, Islam as
a system [that] organizes all matters in our lives, at all levels."

How would the Brotherhood achieve this? Al-Shater pointed to Brotherhood founder Hassan al-Banna's bottom-up approach for implementing Islam
as an "all-embracing concept":

> We start by bringing Islam back to our lives as individuals; this com-
> prehensive understanding of Islam in which we believe, are convinced
> of, raise ourselves according to—this is what engraining, establishing,
> and organizing it means—as individuals. That's why Imam al-Banna said
> that the first stage is . . . the Muslim individual. The individuals then
> mobilize within their family, which in turn gives way to the stage of the
> Muslim family; then, the individuals, families, and households mobilize
> on the level of society. And once we return comprehensive Islam to the
> level of the society, then we can say we have a Muslim society. Then,
> when we transform Egypt into a government that manages the affairs
> of the people according to an Islamic reference, that's what we call the
> stage of the "Muslim State." Then the governments in Egypt, Malaysia,
> Saudi Arabia, and everywhere else, having been enabled to establish
> Islamist rule, coordinate, unite, and cooperate in every conceivable
> sense, and form a unified Islamic state, or a global Islamic union, . . .
> like the European Union today.

"The Muslim Brotherhood was founded to bring out the reestablishment
of this understanding [of comprehensive Islam]," al-Shater reminded the
group. He then launched into a rousing pep talk, calling on the cadres to focus
on establishing an Islamic state in Egypt and, thereafter, a global Islamic state.
"You have to discipline yourself, educate yourself, and prepare yourself," al-
Shater said, "because you are in charge of a grand mission that won't end
except with the strengthening of the Almighty God's religion on earth."[5]

What exactly did it mean to "strengthen Almighty God's religion on
earth?" What policies might change if the Brotherhood achieved its vision
of an Islamic state in Egypt? The Brotherhood's leaders offered no specifics.
Their vagueness reflected the fact that, for many decades, the Brotherhood

was the only Islamist group participating in Egypt's electoral politics. It didn't need to explain its interpretation of *sharī'ah* because merely promising to "implement" *sharī'ah* was sufficient for distinguishing the Brotherhood from its non-Islamist competitors.

Yet as Muslim Brothers gathered at the summer 2011 *mua'skarat*, Egypt's political landscape was rapidly changing. A new Islamist political force was emerging, promising to mobilize millions of Egyptians who had never participated in politics previously. And its political vision was far more specific than the Brotherhood's and also more authentic in the eyes of many Egyptians.

• • • • • • • •

The term "Salafist" refers to Islamists who seek to implement the literalist interpretation of *sharī'ah* that the companions of the Prophet Muhammad, known as the *salaf*, practiced during the AD 600s. In contrast to the Brotherhood's vagueness regarding how it would interpret *sharī'ah*, Salafists offered a concrete, albeit radical, argument: Islam's reemergence required "returning to the purest roots of Islam and the strict emulation of its prophet."[6] For example, whereas the Brotherhood hemmed and hawed as to whether it would ban alcohol in Egypt, Salafists left no doubt: They would. Whereas the Muslim Brotherhood indicated that it might permit interest-based lending practices, which contravene Islamic law, many Salafists stated quite clearly that they sought to prohibit them as soon as possible. And whereas the Brotherhood showed some openness to Shiite *sharī'ah* concepts, Salafists typically regarded Shiites as infidels and enemies.

Like the Brotherhood, Salafism emerged within Egypt most forcefully during the 1970s, when then-president Sadat lifted Nasser's repression of Islamists. On campuses nationwide, the two competing trends battled over *sharī'ah* interpretations, as well as over the method for implementing *sharī'ah*.

In the years that followed, a variety of Salafist-oriented organizations arose, including jihadi groups such as the US-designated terrorist organization al-Gamaa al-Islamiya, and nonviolent preaching organizations such as the Alexandria-based Salafist Call, which was founded in 1982.[7] The proliferation of Salafist groups encapsulates the most basic difference between the Brotherhood and Salafists: Whereas the Brotherhood is a unified organization, Salafism is ultimately an ideology to which many competing groups and scholars adhere. Unlike the rigorous process through which one joins the Brotherhood, one becomes a Salafist simply by declaring his commitment (*iltizām*) to emulating the practices of the Prophet Muhammad and his companions.

And unlike the Brotherhood's rigid chain of command, Salafists may follow any sheikh or movement they prefer—or, if they are quietists, no movement at all.[8] So it is much easier to become a Salafist, which is why Salafists are believed to outnumber Muslim Brothers in Egypt by a considerable margin.

During the Mubarak era, the Brotherhood and Salafists experienced very different treatment. While the regime permitted the Brotherhood to participate in parliamentary elections, it prohibited the Salafists from political work entirely. Under the watchful eye of Egypt's State Security apparatus, Salafists focused on preaching and outreach activities exclusively: They operated mosques, ran social services, established religious schools, and—toward the end of the Mubarak era—built satellite television networks for promoting their ideology. Always fearful of a severe regime crackdown, nonviolent Salafist groups such as Salafist Call preached loyalty to the state, including at the height of the January 2011 uprising.[9]

In the immediate aftermath of Mubarak's ouster, however, Salafists saw an unprecedented political opportunity. While some prominent sheikhs decried electoral politics as being forbidden in Islam, the Salafist Call—by far the largest Salafist organization—announced in mid-May that it would establish the Nour Party and named Emad Abdel Ghafour as its first chairman. In the months that followed, three other major Salafist parties emerged: Cairo-based Salafists formed the Fadila and Asala parties, while al-Gamaa al-Islamiya formed the Building and Development Party.

Initially, the Brotherhood took a dim view of the Salafists' political prospects. From its perspective, the Salafists were political newcomers whose lack of experience and radical ideas would make them, at best, bit players in Egypt's post-Mubarak political order. Nour Party leaders felt the snub. At the first meeting of the Democratic Alliance for Egypt, which convened in June at the Brotherhood's FJP headquarters, the Salafists were seated at the end of the table, and the FJP had declined to print nameplates for them.

A few weeks later, Nour Party leader Abdel Ghafour met FJP chairman Mohamed Morsi at a meeting of political party leaders that the SCAF convened to discuss the upcoming parliamentary elections. "Who are you?" Morsi dismissively asked Abdel Ghafour. When Abdel Ghafour introduced himself, Morsi asked the question a second time: "Who are you?"

Morsi, however, wasn't the only one who considered the Nour Party irrelevant. At the meeting, the SCAF seated its top generals directly across from Morsi and placed Abdel Ghafour at the far end of the table.[10]

On July 29, however, the Brotherhood suddenly realized that the Salafists would be an electoral force to be reckoned with. During the massive Islamist protest in Tahrir Square against "supraconstitutional principles," Salafists outmobilized the Brotherhood by a substantial margin, demonstrating that they had both the numbers and resources to mount a significant challenge on election day. By that point, however, the Nour Party had already decided that it would leave the Democratic Alliance for Egypt.[11] When it made this decision official in early September, it emphasized its objection to the Alliance's inclusion of secular parties. This was a jab at the Brotherhood, which Salafists cast as a sellout for cooperating with non-Islamists.[12]

· · · · · · · ·

When it first took power after Mubarak's ouster on February 11, the SCAF had promised to complete a political transition process within six months. But by early September, parliamentary and presidential elections had not been scheduled, and a new constitution was nowhere in sight. Meanwhile, sectarian clashes exploded in Upper Egypt, workers' strikes spread to seemingly every profession, and anti-SCAF demonstrations proliferated. The SCAF responded to these incidents repressively: It cracked down on protests, referred over twelve thousand civilians to military courts, and arrested prominent activists. But its brutality didn't quell the instability. As a result, the SCAF suddenly appeared eager to move the country toward elections and remove itself from day-to-day governance.

On September 18, the SCAF called a meeting with political party leaders to discuss the parliamentary elections law. Since 1990, Egypt had been divided into 222 two-member districts, with each district electing one professional and one farmer or worker in a winner-take-all system. But many of the political parties feared that this format would enable members from Mubarak's old ruling party to return to Parliament in their old seats and therefore pressed the SCAF to institute a party-list voting system, in which seats would be awarded proportionally. Such a system, the thinking went, would work to the advantage of parties that had strong name recognition—such as the Wafd—but insufficient resources to mount a successful campaign effort in every district. The Brotherhood preferred a mixed system but anticipated winning no matter which system was used and thus went along with the other parties' demand.

Six days later, the SCAF released a system that pleased nobody: Two-thirds of the seats would be elected through a proportional party-list system, and one-third of the seats would be reserved for political independents, who would run in winner-take-all, individual-candidacy races.[13] The Brotherhood was furious. By reserving one-third of Parliament for political independents, it argued, the SCAF was enabling the return of former parliamentarians from Mubarak's old ruling party, known as *feloul*. Immediately, the Democratic Alliance for Egypt threatened to boycott the elections, now scheduled for late November.[14]

To defuse the crisis, the SCAF called another meeting with political party leaders on October 1 at the Ministry of Defense. At the meeting, FJP secretary-general Saad al-Katatny pressed the SCAF to allow party-affiliated candidates to run for every seat in Parliament—including the one-third of the seats that the new elections law reserved for political independents. The other party representatives in attendance echoed al-Katatny's demand.

An SCC judge in attendance, however, warned that this system would put political independents at an unconstitutional disadvantage. Indeed, the judge noted, the court ruled to dissolve two Mubarak-era Parliaments—in 1987 and 1990—on this very basis. And since the court ruled on the basis of precedent, it would have no choice but to dissolve the next Parliament if it failed to reserve seats for political independents.

The party representatives, however, didn't take the judge seriously, and al-Katatny persisted with the demand that party-affiliated candidates be permitted to run for every seat. Seeming exhausted, a SCAF general relented. "Do what they want," he told the judge. "I don't want a headache."[15]

The political parties greeted the SCAF's concession in unified relief. But trouble was already brewing within the Democratic Alliance for Egypt. Many of the Alliance's non-Islamist parties were internally divided over their alignment with the Brotherhood, and those divisions were starting to spill out into the open. These internal fights were particularly pronounced within the Wafd, which projected itself as Egypt's historic "liberal" party, and a dissident faction of Wafdists accused their party chairman of being a closeted Islamist.

There were also substantial disagreements within the Alliance over the apportionment of parliamentary candidacies. The FJP insisted that its candidates would run for 40 percent of the seats.[16] This would enable the Brotherhood to seek fewer than half of all seats as it promised, while at the same time giving it a shot at a parliamentary plurality. Meanwhile, seeing itself as the Brotherhood's equal partner, the Wafd similarly demanded 40 percent of the total candidacies. And that left only 20 percent of the candidacies for the remaining three-dozen or so parties.[17]

These tensions exploded in the immediate aftermath of the October 1

SCAF meeting, as the new elections law was finalized. The Wafd indicated the following day that it was withdrawing from the Alliance, and subsequent negotiations aimed at saving the Alliance failed.[18] Within weeks, most of the Alliance's original parties followed the Wafd out the door.[19]

In the wake of these mass defections, two new electoral coalitions suddenly emerged. Three prominent non-Islamist parties—the right-of-center Free Egyptians, the left-of-center Egyptian Social Democratic Party, and the socialist al-Tagammu—formed the Egyptian Bloc as the secularist alternative to the Brotherhood. Meanwhile, the Nour Party aligned with two smaller Salafist parties to form the Islamist Bloc. This effectively made the Brotherhood-dominated Alliance the centrist choice for Egyptian voters—a prized position that bolstered the Brotherhood's optimism.

By the end of October, only eleven parties remained in the Democratic Alliance: the FJP and ten small, mostly non-Islamist parties that utterly depended on the Brotherhood's mobilizing capabilities and resources for winning any seats at all. These parties benefited tremendously from their association with the FJP, which agreed to fund their campaign materials and media advertisements.[20]

· · · · · · · ·

Yet the Brotherhood suddenly faced a dilemma. Ever since February 10, one day before Mubarak resigned, the Brotherhood had promised not to seek outright power, announcing that it would neither run for the presidency nor seek majority-control of Parliament, and it touted these promises repeatedly in the months that followed. But the mass defections from the Democratic Alliance meant that the FJP was now its only party with any significant support and resources. It was therefore no longer practical for the FJP to field only 40 percent of the Alliance's candidates, since this meant leaving the remaining 60 percent to the Alliance's ten other political parties, all of which were quite weak.

So the Brotherhood had a choice: It would either break its promise and run FJP candidates for the vast majority of Parliament's seats or keep its promise and thus force the Alliance to run for a small percentage of the entire Parliament.

Two factors seemingly shaped the Brotherhood's resolution of this dilemma. First, within the Brotherhood's administrative districts, cadres increasingly demanded that the organization compete for seats more aggressively. *All of the other parties and coalitions are trying to run for 100 percent of the seats*, the Brotherhood's cadres observed. *Why aren't we?* For months the Brotherhood's leaders had told the cadres that the Brotherhood's moment was now. So with new competitors emerging as the Democratic Alliance narrowed, how could the Brotherhood let other parties steal the show?

Second, after initially doubting the Salafists' seriousness, the Brotherhood now saw its more fundamentalist Islamist counterparts as significant threats. Indeed, the Salafists had proven far more politically adept—as well as much more popular—than the Brotherhood expected. Drawing on the Salafist Call's social services and mosque networks in Alexandria and the countryside, the Islamist Bloc was fielding a full slate of candidates. Moreover, by unifying all Salafist parties in one coalition, the Islamist Bloc had given Egyptian Salafists—a previously untapped electoral constituency—a single ticket to support. The Brotherhood feared that if it didn't field a full slate of candidates, the Salafists might emerge as Egypt's preeminent Islamist force—which would be a disaster for the Brotherhood, given its pretension to represent the "true Islam."

So the Brotherhood backtracked on its promise. It ran FJP members in 70 percent of the party-list candidacies and 90 percent of the individual candidacies, meaning that Muslim Brothers were candidates for approximately 77 percent of all seats.[21] That left the remaining 23 percent of the Democratic Alliance's candidacies to the coalition's other ten parties.

Meanwhile, in picking its candidates, the FJP relied heavily on the Brotherhood's chain of command. The candidate selection process began a few months earlier, when the Brotherhood's Guidance Office informed the governorate-level Brotherhood offices that the FJP would participate in the parliamentary elections and ordered them to select candidates. The governorate offices then passed this message down the Brotherhood's hierarchy, ordering cadres who wanted to run for office to notify their local Brotherhood *usrah* leaders. After receiving their *usrah* leaders' approval, prospective Brotherhood parliamentary candidates then passed their application upward through the organization's hierarchy, with candidates requiring approval from each tier up through the governorate leadership. Finally, the governorate offices passed the proposed candidates onto the FJP leadership, which was headed by three former Guidance Office members—Morsi, el-Erian, and al-Katatny.[22]

Of course, the FJP's reliance on the Brotherhood's nationwide structure for selecting its members made sense. Local Brotherhood *usar* knew which of its members were the most active and popular in their respective electoral districts. So in many cases, the FJP's nominees were established local Brotherhood leaders—former parliamentarians, professional syndicate officials, and social services managers.

But the fact that multiple tiers of Brotherhood leaders vetted FJP candidates before nominating them also meant that FJP candidates were, for the most part, committed Muslim Brothers who could be expected to follow Guidance Office orders. Indeed, most of the FJP's candidates were Muslim Brothers who had achieved the top rank of *akh 'amal*, meaning they had sworn to obey the orders of Brotherhood leaders. These were, in other words, ideologues who could be trusted to implement the organization's Islamizing agenda in Parliament—not compromisers who would moderate in power, as some Western analysts expected.

· · · · · · · ·

Even as the Brotherhood ditched its promise to run for fewer than half of Parliament's seats, it tried to deflect accusations of power hunger by insisting that its ultimate goal was to win 40 percent of Parliament—still less than a majority. But the SCAF wasn't so reassured. The Brotherhood now appeared destined to have a plurality in Parliament at the very least, which would give it tremendous influence over the drafting of Egypt's next constitution. And that would empower the Brotherhood to take a sharp stab at the military's perquisites, including its economic empire and its autonomy over its own affairs.

So on November 1, SCAF-appointed vice–prime minister Ali el-Salmi released a twenty-two-point document asserting the "basic principles of the constitution of the modern Egyptian state." The "el-Salmi Document," as it came to be known, was in many respects the supraconstitutional principles that the revolutionaries had been demanding since July. It contained a series of political rights and principles that would be enshrined in the constitution irrespective of who wrote it. These included "equal opportunities for all citizens without any discrimination or distinction," "independence of the judiciary," guaranteed "freedom of opinion, expression, press, and media," the universal "right to know, transmit, and publish information," and the right to "participate in cultural life," among others.

The el-Salmi Document, however, didn't stop at these principles. First, in Article 9, it shielded the military's budgets, legal status, and war-making decisions from any future parliamentary or presidential oversight:

> And the Supreme Council of the Armed Forces specializes, without any other, in all matters relating to affairs for the armed forces and discusses

the terms of its budget such that [its allotment] is inserted as one number in the state's budget. It also has exclusive purview to approve any legislation relating to the armed forces before issuance. The president is the supreme commander of the armed forces, and the defense minister is the general commander of the armed forces. The president of the republic declares war after the approval of the Supreme Council of the Armed Forces and People's Assembly.

Second, the el-Salmi Document substantially diminished the next parliament's power to choose the constitution-writing assembly. It mandated that only twenty of the assembly's one hundred members could be partisan parliamentarians, while the other eighty had to be individuals "representing all sectors of Egyptian society." The document then specified the exact number of members who should come from each sector: fifteen judges, fifteen professors, fifteen professional syndicate members, five workers syndicate members, five farmers, five civil society members, ten individuals nominated by the government, and representatives from the Chamber of Commerce, production unions, workers societies, the National Human Rights Council, the armed forces, the police, sports unions, students unions, al-Azhar University, and the Coptic Orthodox Church.

Finally, the el-Salmi Document placed significant restrictions on the future constitution-writing body. It held that the next constitution could not contravene the SCAF's March 30 constitutional declaration. And if the constitution-writing assembly failed to draft a new constitution within six months, the el-Salmi Document empowered the SCAF to dissolve the assembly and appoint a new one.[23]

The Brotherhood was outraged. It opposed supraconstitutional principles from the moment that the revolutionaries demanded them, arguing that the elected Parliament—which it anticipated controlling—should determine the next constitution without any preconditions. And the Brotherhood especially objected to the significant constraints that the document placed on the next Parliament's ability to pick the constitution-writing assembly.

So in its first statement responding to the el-Salmi Document, the Brotherhood called it "a coup" against the March referendum and "a rape of the right of the people to elect the constitutional assembly" and demanded the resignation of the entire government.[24] Then, two days after the document was released, the Brotherhood presented the government with an ultimatum: Either withdraw the el-Salmi Document or face a "second revolution" on November 18.[25]

The crisis continued for two weeks. The Brotherhood's call for November 18 protests drew the support of revolutionary groups such as the April 6 Youth movement, as well as Salafist organizations such as al-Gamaa al-Islamiya.[26] In multiple rounds of negotiations, however, the SCAF-backed government refused to withdraw the document.[27] Meanwhile, the Brotherhood pressed ahead with preparations for the elections, which were set to begin on November 28.

On Friday, November 18, tens of thousands of Egyptians—mainly Islamists—packed Tahrir Square to protest SCAF rule, and similar protests were held in cities across the country. It was one of the largest antimilitary demonstrations since the January uprising. Meanwhile, the Brotherhood used the mass turnout to reinforce its demand for the el-Salmi Document to be withdrawn. It also added a new demand: that presidential elections be held by April 2012, at which point the SCAF-led transition would end.[28]

When evening came, the Brotherhood withdrew its protesters, and the other political forces followed suit. Only a few hundred protesters, many of whom were relatives of protesters who had been killed or injured during the January uprising, remained in Tahrir Square. The following morning, the SCAF acceded to the protesters' core demand, announcing that the el-Salmi Document would only be advisory rather than binding.[29]

But that same morning, the Interior Ministry went on the offensive. At approximately ten o'clock, Central Security Forces police attacked the small Tahrir Square sit-in, tearing down the tents, wounding two people, and arresting four.[30] Within hours, thousands of demonstrators filled Tahrir Square to protest the crackdown, and intense street battles raged in downtown Cairo for days.

Security forces blanketed the area with tear gas and used live fire on the protesters, which only encouraged more revolutionary activists to enter the fray. The most intense fighting broke out on Mohamed Mahmoud Street, where police aimed birdshot at protesters' eyes, leaving some demonstrators fully or partially blind. Over the next five days, over three thousand were injured and thirty-eight killed, according to the Ministry of Health.[31]

The Mohamed Mahmoud protests, as the crisis came to be known, represented the most significant challenge that the SCAF faced during its nine-plus months of ruling the country. Security forces' violent repression of the protests garnered unprecedented international condemnation, including from Washington, which lambasted the use of "excessive force" and expressed support for "the Egyptian people and their goal of having a democratically elected civilian government."[32] Meanwhile dozens of flights to Egypt were canceled, and downtown Cairo became a veritable war zone.[33]

While protesters battled security forces, however, the Muslim Brotherhood stood aside. The longer the fighting raged, the Brotherhood feared, the more likely that the SCAF would delay the parliamentary elections.[34] Indeed, on November 22, the Wafd called for the SCAF to postpone the elections for at least two weeks, and the protesters—who had argued all along that Egypt should not hold elections until a new constitution was drafted— agreed that elections could not take place under the current conditions.[35] Meanwhile, the revolutionaries added new demands, such as the immediate appointment of a civilian presidential council that would include Mohamed ElBaradei, and rumors swirled that the SCAF was considering ElBaradei for prime minister.[36]

This greatly unnerved the Brotherhood. It feared that the ongoing chaos might scuttle its plan for winning the parliamentary elections and controlling the process of drafting Egypt's next constitution. So it urged its supporters to continue their parliamentary campaign work, arguing that electing a new Parliament was the best mechanism for "completing the revolution."[37] Meanwhile, the Brotherhood negotiated with the SCAF. On November 22, the fourth day of fighting, Morsi announced that the FJP and other political forces had reached an agreement with the junta: Parliamentary elections would proceed as scheduled, the Sharaf government would resign, and the SCAF would hand over power to an elected president by July 2012.[38] That evening, Field Marshal Tantawi addressed the nation to announce these provisions, and former prime minister Kamal al-Ganzoury was later named as Sharaf's replacement.[39]

Tantawi's announcement, however, did not appease the many thousands of protesters in Tahrir Square. After days of deadly street battles, in which dozens had been killed and thousands injured, they wanted the military out of power immediately—not after seven months.[40] And so the street battles continued, with the activists calling for a boycott of the elections and demanding the appointment of a civilian presidential council.

But, once again, the revolutionaries overplayed their hand. The mood of the country had shifted decisively against street activity and strongly favored the turn toward the ballot box that the Brotherhood–SCAF deal entailed. The activists' hopes for ousting the junta faded away, and they privately acknowledged what had been obvious for months: They had lost the very revolution that they'd started.

Indeed, by the end of the week, some of the most prominent revolutionaries had reversed their calls for boycotting the elections and jump-started their own parliamentary campaigns. But they were poorly organized, underfunded, and just too late.

· · · · · · · ·

The Brotherhood won the 2011–12 parliamentary elections for one basic reason: Its unique nationwide chain of command was perfectly organized for mobilizing an unparalleled get-out-the-vote effort. Indeed, the Brotherhood wasn't the only party with strong brand-name recognition—the Wafd also possessed this quality. Nor was the Brotherhood the only political force with strong ideological resonance for certain subsections of Egyptians—the Salafist Islamist Bloc and the non-Islamist Egyptian Bloc also had this advantage. But only the Brotherhood could match these qualities with the organizational machinery for conducting retail politics all across Egypt.

The Brotherhood's internal unity was a key component of this machinery. As part of the *tarbīah* process, all of the Brotherhood's members had taken an oath to obey the Guidance Office's edicts. And through its rigid chain of command, the Guidance Office directed its followers to campaign aggressively and vote for FJP candidates.[41] The Brotherhood's five-to-ten-member *usar* operationalized these orders, working locally to distribute campaign literature, knock on doors, hang banners, and organize political rallies all over the country.

To ensure sufficient judicial monitoring, the SCAF held the parliamentary elections in three rounds, and, when the first round began on November 28, the Brotherhood was the most visible party. Brotherhood *usar* established voter kiosks at virtually every local polling station, with at least two cadres manning laptops to direct voters toward the correct stations. Of course, the Brotherhood's FJP wasn't the only political force doing this—but it was the only party that was able to do it practically everywhere. And many Egyptians believed that the Brotherhood's organizational prowess meant it was qualified for governing.[42]

Still, the Brotherhood's massive campaign operation was only one component of its appeal. Its Islamist ideology mattered as well.[43] While religious sloganeering was prohibited, the Brotherhood circumvented this injunction by affixing "Islam Is the Solution" posters with the Brotherhood's insignia next to FJP campaign posters, which had no religious messages. The Brotherhood also accused its non-Islamist opponents of a variety of religious offenses, such as not respecting *sharī'ah* or converting away from Islam—although, in a few notable cases, these ugly campaign tactics failed.[44]

When the first round of voting concluded, the outcome was no surprise: The FJP-led Democratic Alliance for Egypt won 49 percent of the seats. The Nour Party–led Islamist Bloc came in a distant second with 20 percent, and the non-Islamist Egyptian Bloc won 10 percent of the seats for third place. The FJP did especially well in the individual candidacy races: It won 33 of 48 seats. In many cases, FJP candidates faced Salafist opponents in runoff elections for those seats and won by touting the Brotherhood's "moderation" relative to the Salafists' fundamentalism.[45]

The Brotherhood's massive victory in the first round encouraged it to back off its more aggressive tactics during the second and third rounds. But this had little impact on its momentum. By the time parliamentary elections wrapped up in early January, the Democratic Alliance had won a commanding 47 percent of the parliamentary seats, and 213 of the Alliance's 235 seats belonged to FJP members. The Salafist Islamist Bloc finished a strong second, winning approximately a quarter of the parliamentary seats, while the Wafd finished third with 7.5 percent. Of all the electoral coalitions, the Revolution Continues Alliance performed the worst, winning just seven seats, or 1.4 percent of Parliament.[46]

• • • • • • • •

This wasn't how the Brotherhood had anticipated its rise to power twelve months earlier. At the time of Mubarak's ouster, the Brotherhood sought a subtler, and perhaps slower, emergence. Hoping to prevent domestic and foreign blowback for demonstrating its political ambitions too aggressively, the Brotherhood wanted to situate itself within a coalition of much weaker parties—an electoral alliance that the Brotherhood could effectively control without numerically dominating. That plan had fallen apart, but the Brotherhood achieved its ultimate ambition nonetheless: It was now—without question—the leading force in Egyptian politics. For the first time in its eight-decade history, the Brotherhood held actual power.

Or so it thought.

6 Powerless Parliamentarians

Saad al-Katatny was the mild-mannered face of the Muslim Brotherhood's lead-ership—a "soft man" in the eyes of his typically rigid colleagues.[1] Doughy, short, and clean-shaven, with a shock of gray, curly hair framing his balding scalp, the low-pitched al-Katatny struck an entirely different image from scowling firebrands such as Khairat al-Shater and Mohamed Morsi. Yet he was the product of the same hierarchical organization and just as committed to obeying the Brotherhood's edicts in pursuit of its theocratic vision.

Born in the Upper Egyptian governorate of Sohag in 1952, al-Katatny be-came politically active as a student at Asyut University in the early 1970s and joined the Muslim Brotherhood while studying for his PhD in botany in 1981. Like many Brotherhood leaders of his generation, al-Katatny rose to local prominence through the professional syndicates, which were relatively open to Brotherhood participation even while political life was tightly controlled. After joining the botany faculty of Minya University in 1984, al-Katatny was elected secretary-general of the Minya Scientists Syndicate, and in 1993 he was elected chair. As a result, the Brotherhood tasked al-Katatny with over-seeing the organization's syndicate work within Minya, and he quickly as-cended the Brotherhood's ranks. By the early 2000s, he was the top Brother-hood official in Minya.[2]

Al-Katatny's first brush with national attention came in 2005 when he was one of an unprecedented eighty-eight Muslim Brothers elected to Parliament. The Brotherhood's parliamentarians elected al-Katatny as their parliamen-tary bloc chair, and his calm demeanor contrasted sharply with that of the previous bloc chair, Morsi, who lost his seat that year.

In this capacity, al-Katatny served as the Brotherhood's spokesman when-ever the organization wanted to reassure its skeptics that its rising visibil-ity didn't presage an "Islamist takeover." Whenever he was asked about the

Brotherhood's political ambitions, al-Katatny softly intoned that the Brotherhood only sought "political participation" and had no intention of ousting
the Mubarak regime.[3] Al-Katatny was also among a handful of Brotherhood
leaders who maintained good relations with Egypt's other opposition forces,
which bolstered his reputation as a Brotherhood "moderate."[4] Meanwhile,
when Washington sought to engage the Brotherhood in 2007, the Guidance Office dispatched al-Katatny to meet US House Majority Leader Steny
Hoyer.[5] Al-Katatny later represented the Brotherhood at a cocktail party at
the US ambassador's residence in 2007 and headed the Brotherhood delegation that attended President Obama's June 2009 speech at Cairo University.[6]

Yet within Parliament, al-Katatny was the Guidance Office's loyal foot
soldier and answered directly to Morsi, who handled the Guidance Office's
political portfolio during this period. In turn, al-Katatny pushed the Brotherhood's hardline agenda whenever an opportunity arose. For example, when
the Mubarak regime passed a law in 2008 designed to protect the rights of
children, al-Katatny led the Brotherhood's parliamentarians in voting against
it, decrying provisions that banned female genital mutilation and prohibited
marriages before the age of eighteen. "It does not reflect the norms of our society," al-Katatny told journalist Liam Stack. "It reflects international norms."[7]
Al-Katatny also led the Brotherhood's opposition to television programs
during Ramadan that the organization deemed "immoral."[8]

At other times, al-Katatny led the Brotherhood bloc in opposing the regime's repressive emergency laws, criticizing its torture of prisoners, and
boycotting certain parliamentary votes.[9] And thanks to his political stature
and parliamentary immunity, al-Katatny was able to undertake missions that
other Brotherhood leaders—who often faced travel bans—could not, such as
heading a January 2009 delegation to meet top Hamas leaders in Damascus.[10]

By this point, the Brotherhood had already rewarded al-Katatny's obedience by electing him to the Guidance Office in mid-2008, where he served
as Morsi's deputy in managing the Brotherhood's political file.[11] In early 2011,
when youth activists called on the Brotherhood to join the January 25 protests, al-Katatny enforced the Guidance Office's decision to limit Brotherhood
involvement.[12] A few months later, when the Brotherhood's General Shura
Committee voted to establish the Freedom and Justice Party, it appointed al-
Katatny secretary-general. In this capacity, he once again answered directly
to Morsi, the FJP chair, and dutifully implemented the Brotherhood leadership's decisions as the Brotherhood's political strategy became more aggressive during the year that followed Mubarak's ouster.

To be sure, the Brotherhood often insisted that it was separate from the FJP—that the organization focused on preaching and outreach, while the party focused on politics. But in practice, this was never the case. The Brotherhood viewed the FJP as its political arm—a mechanism for advancing its Islamizing agenda in the political sphere, much as its students division advanced its agenda within the universities. And as it became clear that the FJP would dominate Egypt's first post-Mubarak Parliament, the Brotherhood's leadership moved to establish its ultimate authority over the FJP's legislative work.

So on January 14, during its first meeting following the parliamentary elections, the Brotherhood's General Shura Committee "authorized the Guidance Office, in consultation with the FJP, to do what it deems appropriate regarding Parliament and the government, with an emphasis on the necessity to take responsibility and translate the people's trust in them."[13] Two days later, the FJP announced that al-Katatny would be its pick for parliamentary speaker.

In the months that followed, the Guidance Office established a formal mechanism for monitoring the FJP's parliamentary work and political strategy. Every week, the FJP's top three leaders—Morsi, el-Erian and al-Katatny—held "coordination" meetings with four of the Brotherhood's top leaders—deputy supreme guides al-Shater and Mahmoud Ezzat, Secretary-General Mahmoud Hussein, and spokesman Mahmoud Ghozlan.[14] By contrast, the FJP's own high committee met only a handful of times during the first half of 2012 and was expected to rubber-stamp the decisions that the smaller Brotherhood–FJP "coordinating" body had taken.[15] While the Guidance Office ultimately left many, and perhaps most, day-to-day political decisions to the FJP leadership's discretion, the "coordination" process ensured that the FJP ultimately answered to its mother ship.

· · · · · · · ·

Even as the Guidance Office signaled that it would retain control over the FJP's parliamentary bloc, the FJP expressed its commitment to work across the aisle.[16] On January 16, 2012, one week before the new Parliament's first session, the FJP announced that its parliamentary coalition would include five other parties. Three of these were small non-Islamist parties: the Reform and Development Party (RDP), the Karama Party, and the Egyptian Social Democratic Party (ESDP). The other two were Salafist parties: the Salafist Nour Party and the Building and Development Party (BDP), which was the political wing of al-Gamaa al-Islamiya.

In their joint statement announcing the coalition, the six parties called for political inclusiveness. They vowed "to distance the Parliament of the revolution from all appearances of domination, acquisition, exclusion, marginalization, conflict, or polarization," adding that the new Parliament would "express national consensus among all factions."[17] In keeping with this spirit, the FJP signaled that it would work to broaden its coalition further.[18]

Behind closed doors, however, the Brotherhood's political party worked to consolidate power for itself. As non-Islamist party leaders negotiated with Morsi over the distribution of committee chairs and jockeyed for some of the more significant posts, Morsi held firm. He refused the RDP's request to chair the Foreign Affairs Committee, and when the ESDP responded to the initial offer of chairing the Economics Committee by demanding an additional few chairs, Morsi declined this request as well.[19] The ESDP ultimately walked away.[20]

The FJP released its list of proposed committee chairs on January 22, the day before Parliament was set to convene, and it was far from inclusive. The FJP proposed that its own parliamentarians chair twelve of nineteen committees and granted another three committee chairs to independents aligned with the FJP. Only four committee chairs went to other parties: The Salafist Nour Party was awarded the Agriculture, Education, and Suggestions and Complaints Committees, and RDP chair Mohamed Anwar Esmat Sadat was offered the chair of the Human Rights Committee. Finally, the FJP offered deputy committee chairs to some of the other parties that had been part of the Democratic Alliance for Egypt, as well as the Wafd and the BDP.[21]

The FJP presented this proposal in Parliament two days later during a tense session. MP Mohamed Abu Hamed of the non-Islamist Free Egyptians Party accused the FJP of behaving like Mubarak's old ruling party, and the Wafd's parliamentary delegation withdrew in protest.[22] But given its alignment with the Nour Party, the FJP had the votes, and its proposed committee chairs passed overwhelmingly.

The FJP's aggressive behavior wasn't surprising. From its perspective, the massive plurality that it won during the parliamentary elections was a mandate—for its own political empowerment first and foremost, since it had captured 47 percent of the seats, but for Islamism more broadly, since Islamists had won nearly three-quarters of Parliament. By contrast, the non-Islamists had performed quite poorly and yet had the temerity to demand a greater share of the committee chair positions than their parliamentary power justified. The non-Islamist parties could grab headlines with their whining,

Brotherhood leaders seemingly reasoned, but ultimately this was just noise. The people had spoken.

Nevertheless, the FJP's pattern of appointments was interesting because it reflected the Brotherhood's attempt to reinforce its authority over Parliament's work via the FJP. Of the twelve FJP members appointed to committee chairs, eleven were fully committed Muslim Brothers, some of whom simultaneously held high ranks within other Brotherhood bodies. At least four of the eleven were members of the Brotherhood's General Shura Committee: Essam el-Erian (Foreign Affairs), Saad al-Husseini (Budget and Planning), Al-Sayyid Askar (Religious Affairs), and Akram al-Sha'ir (Health). At least two other General Shura Committee members were appointed as committee vice-chairs—Farid Ismail (Defense and National Security) and Sobhi Saleh (Legislation). And the parliamentary majority leader, Hussein Ibrahim, was also a member of the Brotherhood's General Shura Committee.[23]

The other FJP committee chairs previously served as high-ranking figures within their governorate-level Brotherhood organizations, and Workforce Committee chair Saber Abouel Fotouh had previously chaired a Brotherhood administrative unit that encompassed three governorates.[24] The FJP further ensured that it had deputy chairs on every committee that wasn't chaired by a Muslim Brother, with one exception: the Human Rights Committee, to which the FJP appointed a deputy from al-Gamaa al-Islamiya's party, the BDP.[25]

Only one of the FJP's twelve committee chairs was given to a non-Brotherhood FJP member: Abbas Mukhaymer, a former military intelligence general with no prior Brotherhood affiliation, was appointed to lead the Defense and National Security Committee, which oversees two of the most politically sensitive Egyptian governmental institutions, the military and the Interior Ministry. The FJP had promised Mukhaymer this position when it approached him about running prior to the parliamentary elections, and it placed him near the top of one of its party lists in Sharkiya, a Brotherhood stronghold where Mukhaymer was virtually guaranteed to win.[26] By appointing Mukhaymer to lead this committee, the Brotherhood was apparently trying to reassure the SCAF that it would not mess with the military's perquisites. A military man, after all, was in charge of the committee that dealt with the military.

During the opening session of the new Parliament on January 23, newly inaugurated speaker al-Katatny made the Brotherhood's conciliatory message toward the SCAF even clearer. "On behalf of everyone, I would like to once again thank the personnel, soldiers, and officers of the great army of Egypt, which, along with the loyal policemen, held the responsibility for safeguarding the electoral process, until it became an exemplified [process] praised by everyone," al-Katatny said.[27]

Al-Katatny's paean to Egypt's junta, which the Nour Party echoed thereafter, outraged a small coterie of revolutionary-oriented parliamentarians, who called on Parliament to hold the SCAF accountable for the deadly repression that had occurred since Mubarak's ouster.[28] "It was incumbent upon us, before we began the first session yesterday, to call for the presence of some of the families of the martyrs and some of those injured in the revolution, to recognize that without them, the revolution wouldn't have succeeded and we wouldn't have this Parliament," non-Islamist MP Amr Hamzawy declared on the second day of Parliament's session.[29]

But the FJP had no interest in fulfilling these demands. In the twelve months since Mubarak's ouster, the Brotherhood had gone from outlawed opposition movement to leading parliamentary party—and it wasn't about to sacrifice its newfound power by angering the SCAF with these kinds of pronouncements.

"Our hearts bleed and our eyes gush with tears for the martyrs and the injured and their families," FJP MP Essam el-Erian said in a speech from the floor. "However, in order for us to make decisions that are objective, can be carried out, and are obeyed by all those who must obey them, all our recommendations and decisions must be made in line with the oath we took yesterday, the rulings of the [SCAF's] constitutional declaration, and the law, until we ourselves change the law."[30]

The Brotherhood, in other words, was signaling its respect for the junta's executive authority, as per the deal that the two sides had struck in November just prior to the parliamentary elections. And the SCAF similarly signaled its commitment to that bargain. In a congratulatory letter marking Parliament's opening, Field Marshal Tantawi ceded legislative and oversight authority to the legislature and affirmed the junta's commitment to relinquish executive power to an elected president by the end of June.[31]

• • • • • • • •

When the SCAF responded to mass protests by ousting Mubarak from power in February 2011, the Obama administration welcomed the military's administration of the subsequent transition. But nearly a year later, Washington had soured on the SCAF and blamed its repressive rule for making Egypt even less stable.

The previous three months had been especially violent. In October 2011, Washington watched in horror as armored military vehicles ran over Coptic protesters outside the state media building in Cairo, killing twenty-eight and wounding more than two hundred.[32] During the onslaught, Egypt's state-run media ramped up anti-Christian sentiments by calling citizens into the streets to "defend the soldiers who protected the Egyptian revolution" against "armed Copts," and soldiers raided the Cairo offices of the US-funded satellite network Alhurra.[33] The following month, the SCAF-backed government had responded even more repressively to the preelections Mohamed Mahmoud protests, killing dozens and wounding thousands more, while blanketing large sections of downtown Cairo with US-made tear gas. And in mid-December, the government once again used excessive force against protesters during demonstrations outside the prime minister's office, killing ten and wounding over four hundred.[34]

As the SCAF's abuses mounted, the Obama administration resisted calls for withholding the $1.3 billion in annual US military aid to Egypt, fearing that this would jeopardize Washington's strategic relationship with Cairo. Instead, it urged the SCAF to move forward with the transition process. An elected government, the administration believed, would have greater popular legitimacy than the military and would therefore yield greater political stability.

So as it became clear that the Muslim Brotherhood would win Egypt's first post-Mubarak parliamentary elections, the Obama administration shifted its approach. Rather than seeking "limited contacts" with the Brotherhood, as Secretary of State Hillary Clinton had announced in June, American officials suddenly started beating a path to the Brotherhood's door. Through "engagement," as the policy became known, the administration hoped to win the Brotherhood's cooperation on core American interests in Egypt, such as maintaining the 1979 peace treaty with Israel and partnering on counterterrorism. And that often meant papering over long-standing American concerns about the Brotherhood's goals and ideology, in pursuit of establishing goodwill.

On December 10, Senate Foreign Relations Committee chair John Kerry and US ambassador to Egypt Anne Patterson visited the FJP's headquarters in Manial, where they met with four top FJP leaders, including Morsi and al-Katatny. Only one of Egypt's three rounds of elections had been completed, but Kerry addressed the FJP as if it had already won, reportedly telling Morsi that he wasn't surprised by the Brotherhood's success in the elections.

Meanwhile, Morsi told Kerry that the Brotherhood would "respect the treaties and conventions" that Egypt had signed, which naturally soothed American concerns about the future of regional peace.[35] Yet it was classic Brotherhood double-talk. Three months earlier, the Brotherhood Guidance Office's official spokesman had called for a referendum on the Egyptian–Israeli treaty, which, given Israel's unpopularity within Egypt, would have sunk it.[36] On the same day that Kerry met the FJP's leadership, one of the FJP's top leaders affirmed to me in an interview that the FJP intended to put the treaty to a referendum. This seemed to be the Brotherhood's strategy for destroying the treaty without being blamed for it, since it could plausibly claim that the Egyptian people—not it—had rejected the agreement.[37]

One month later, Deputy Secretary of State William Burns met with Morsi and other top FJP leaders at the party's headquarters. Despite the fact that the final round of the parliamentary elections was still ongoing, Burns congratulated the FJP on its forthcoming victory and vowed that Washington would support Egypt economically and encourage investment. Morsi thanked Burns and then proceeded to harangue him about previous American administrations' "bias . . . against Arab issues" and called on Washington to "rethink its policies."[38] The FJP published Morsi's rebuke of Burns in a press release. Yet this insult didn't stop Burns from once again praising the Brotherhood in a subsequent interview on Egyptian television. When asked about Washington's communication with the Brotherhood, Burns referred to the FJP as a "democratic party that is committed to democratic principles."[39]

Then on January 18, Ambassador Patterson visited Brotherhood Supreme Guide Mohamed Badie and congratulated him on the FJP's victory in the parliamentary elections. It was a controversial choice. On one hand, Patterson was merely recognizing reality: The FJP was entirely subservient to the Brotherhood's hierarchy, and it thus made sense to communicate with the Brotherhood at its highest level. But at the same time, the United States was touting the importance of democracy—and what could be less democratic than having an unelected, and technically illegal, organization controlling an elected party from behind the scenes?

Still, the goal was friendly "engagement," and Patterson handled the supreme guide quite graciously, according to the Brotherhood's subsequent account. When Badie told Patterson that Washington was unpopular because "successive American administrations would rule peoples through dictators," Patterson admitted that Washington had made mistakes. When Badie touted shari'ah as the "greatest guarantor of private and public freedoms," Patterson urged the supreme guide to focus on the economy. And when it came time to pose for a photo, Patterson stood between Badie and one of his deputies and grinned.[40]

The Brotherhood was stunned. According to Hassan al-Banna's teachings, the West was supposed to be the ultimate barrier to its Islamizing agenda—yet here was Washington reaching out warmly, aggressively, and without any conditions. "The world is now more amenable than it was before to the presence of the Muslim Brotherhood in the public sphere," Morsi told the Brotherhood's General Shura Committee during an early 2012 meeting, specifically recounting his meetings with Kerry and Burns. "It's very clear from what they're saying, and from what the situation looks like, that they want to work with the Muslim Brotherhood in power."[41]

One of the primary barriers that the Brotherhood anticipated to its emergence simply didn't exist, and that bolstered its confidence as it took control of Egypt's Parliament.

• • • • • • • •

It didn't take long for the two-month-old Brotherhood–SCAF détente to unravel. Despite achieving an overwhelming plurality in the parliamentary elections, the Brotherhood realized very quickly that it had actually won very little power. The SCAF still held executive authority, and, even despite Tantawi's letter ceding legislative and oversight power to the new Parliament, the junta continued to legislate.

The first tensions erupted on January 27, only four days after Parliament's opening session, when the SCAF signaled that it would ratify a law granting institutional independence to al-Azhar, Egypt's most prominent Islamic university. Under the previous law, which Nasser enacted in 1961, the Egyptian president appointed the sheikh of al-Azhar. But in the aftermath of Mubarak's ouster, al-Azhar's leadership feared Brotherhood domination and thus advocated changing the law to empower its own scholars to choose al-Azhar's senior officials.[42] The SCAF's ratification of the "al-Azhar independence" law thus antagonized the Brotherhood in two respects: It undercut the FJP-controlled Parliament's legislative authority and blocked the Brotherhood from influencing appointments within Egypt's religious establishment. On Twitter, Deputy Supreme Guide al-Shater blasted the SCAF's announcement, calling it "flagrant aggression against the new Parliament."[43]

Then on January 31, Tantawi and the Cabinet of Ministers voted to amend the presidential elections law and sent the new draft to the SCC without consulting Parliament.[44] Once again, the Brotherhood was incensed. "The Parliament has become the authentic representative of the Egyptian people," the Brotherhood said in a statement. "And so it stops emphatically in the face of an attempt to usurp its legislative powers by issuing laws regarding the noble al-Azhar and the presidential elections." The Brotherhood further accused the Interior Ministry of doing too little to protect Parliament from demonstrators, who protested the new Parliament during its first week, and claimed that "businessmen with links to the former regime" were funding a negative media campaign against it.[45]

The Brotherhood–SCAF standoff intensified following a devastating soccer riot in Port Said on February 1. The riot began when ultras supporting Port Said's al-Masry team attacked supporters of Cairo's al-Ahly club with clubs, knives, and stones. Over seventy fans were killed in the melee, and eyewitnesses alleged that police officers stood to the side and refused to open the stadium gates to allow al-Ahly's fans to escape.[46] As news of the carnage spread, clashes erupted between revolutionary activists and security forces in downtown Cairo, during which at least ten were killed and over two hundred wounded. The Brotherhood attempted to mediate a truce, but the revolutionaries accused the Brotherhood of colluding with the SCAF and refused.[47]

The Port Said Massacre, as it became known, was among the deadliest sports-related riots in world history and ignited widespread calls for investigations. At first, the Brotherhood responded by holding the Interior Ministry accountable. The following day in Parliament, FJP vice-chair el-Erian proposed a measure to indict the interior minister for negligence; the measure received 143 cosponsors and passed overwhelmingly.[48] "The events of Port Said were premeditated and are a message from the remnants of the former regime," el-Erian said. "The collapse wasn't in any athletic institutions, but in the security apparatus, as vengeance against us for calling for an end to the state of emergency and as a premeditated act of sabotage on the anniversary of the revolution."[49]

Then on February 5, Defense and National Security Committee chair Mukhaymer discussed a plan for "cleansing" the Interior Ministry of "remnants" from the previous regime.[50] The following day, the committee compiled a report demanding the right to investigate the intelligence services, the CSF, and—most sensitively—the military police. The committee further recommended placing cameras around Tahrir Square and Parliament, a measure that appeared to be aimed at monitoring the revolutionaries, who now opposed the SCAF and Brotherhood equally.[51]

At the same time, the Brotherhood used the Port Said incident to chip away at the SCAF's political legitimacy. In the immediate aftermath of the carnage, Supreme Guide Badie held the SCAF partially responsible and accused the junta of possessing "evidence and documents" regarding plans to "create chaos and sabotage."[52] Later that week, as violent protests against security forces continued in downtown Cairo, the FJP tried to use the furor to abridge the SCAF-led transition. "We want presidential elections that could start after February 28, meaning in less than twenty or so days, so that at least fifty million Egyptians could participate in choosing a president," prominent FJP parliamentarian Mohamed al-Beltagy said during coverage of the protests.[53] The following day, Brotherhood spokesman Mahmoud Ghozlan doubled down on al-Beltagy's remark, announcing that the Brotherhood would accept early presidential elections—a move that would return the SCAF to the barracks long before the deadline of June 30.[54]

But when it became clear that the SCAF would not agree to early presidential elections, the Brotherhood sought to leverage the mounting anti-SCAF anger for a different political gain: It called on the SCAF to include Muslim Brothers in a coalition government.

"We call on the military council to sack this government that has failed to handle this big event and to form another government," Brotherhood spokesman Ghozlan told the Associated Press one week after the Port Said stadium massacre. "If there is a government in place that is really backed by the choice of the people, it will act without regard for any pressure from anyone. It will seek to reassure the people and provide it with security." On Al Jazeera, al-Shater suggested that the new government would include the various parties elected to Parliament according to their strength and that the prime minister would come from the FJP, though he denied rumors that he would personally head the government.[55]

The following day, pro-Brotherhood media sites reported that the FJP was working on a parliamentary measure to withdraw confidence from Prime Minister Kamal al-Ganzoury's government and appoint a new one. According to the plan, Morsi would serve as prime minister. The FJP also sought half of the ministerial portfolios, particularly those that emphasized the provision of services, such as Health and Education, but signaled that it wouldn't touch the more politically sensitive ministries, such as Defense and Foreign Affairs, and would leave the Interior Ministry to a non-FJP civilian. Finally, the FJP called on the Nour Party to join the government, and the Salafists confirmed that they were studying the matter.[56]

The SCAF, however, was not amused. During a February 14 meeting with al-Katatny and other parliamentary leaders, Tantawi refused to dismiss al-Ganzoury's government.[57] The Brotherhood ultimately backed down, reasoning that its parliamentary plurality would enable it to form the government once the SCAF ended its reign on June 30, which was only four months away. So in preparation for that period, the Brotherhood's Guidance Office ordered the organization's provincial offices to send nominations for appointing ministers.[58]

· · · · · · · ·

The Brotherhood soon found another pretext for chipping away at the SCAF's legitimacy.

Two months earlier, in late December 2011, Egyptian commandos had raided the offices of ten prodemocratic nongovernmental organizations (NGOs), including three prominent US-funded organizations—Freedom House, the National Democratic Institute (NDI), and the International Republican Institute (IRI). In a blatant attempt to displace blame for the country's problems, the SCAF-backed government accused the NGOs of using foreign funding to destabilize and divide the country. In late January, the government enforced travel bans on the NGOs' American employees, including the son of an Obama administration cabinet secretary.[59]

As Washington scrambled to resolve the crisis, US officials actively engaged the Brotherhood as a potential ally. These efforts were based on the fanciful premise that the Brotherhood would be sympathetic to the NGO workers, when in fact the Brotherhood had eagerly supported the raids on their offices. Indeed, back in August 2011, three months before the raids, the Brotherhood called on the SCAF-backed government to investigate American funding of NGOs.[60] And as the crisis between Washington and Cairo escalated, the Brotherhood hyped conspiracy theories accusing the United States of funding NGOs for "the demolition of Egypt and the destruction of society."[61] But as relations between the SCAF and Washington deteriorated, the Brotherhood sensed an opportunity to undermine the SCAF and tried to appear helpful to US officials.

In late January, FJP foreign policy chief Essam el-Haddad met with Assistant Secretary of State Michael Posner, and top Brotherhood leaders offered reassuring messages to a Senate delegation that visited Cairo in February.[62] "After talking with the Muslim Brotherhood, I was struck with their commitment to change the law because they believe it's unfair," Sen. Lindsey Graham told the *Wall Street Journal* after a meeting in Cairo, referring to the law under which the NGO workers were being prosecuted.[63] The standoff finally ended on February 28, when the SCAF-backed government responded to the Obama administration's threat to cut military aid and permitted the NGO workers to leave the country.

At the time, Sen. John McCain, the IRI chair, credited the Brotherhood for playing a "constructive role" in resolving the crisis.[64] But as soon as the NGO workers left, the Brotherhood reversed course and used the incident against the SCAF. In a statement, Brotherhood spokesman Ghozlan lambasted the SCAF for "bartering [Egypt's] national dignity" and succumbing to US pressure.[65] In Parliament, Speaker al-Katatny called for summoning governmental officials to "hold accountable those responsible for this crime, which represented a blatant intervention in the affairs of Egypt's judiciary." The FJP further squeezed the SCAF by threatening a parliamentary vote on ending Egypt's acceptance of US aid to Egypt, including the $1.3 billion in annual military aid. "I wish members of the U.S. Congress could listen to you now to realize that this is the parliament of the revolution, which does not allow a breach of the nation's sovereignty or interference in its affairs," al-Katatny declared during a mid-March parliamentary session.[66] During another session, he accused the NGOs of working to "infiltrate Egypt and threaten national security."[67]

None of this anti-American grandstanding affected the Brotherhood's reception in Washington, however, where the Brotherhood's behavior was brushed aside. "This is a sensitive and difficult time for Egypt, and we've pledged to work with the Egyptian people," deputy State Department spokesman Mark Toner said at the time.[68] And in early April, when the FJP sent its first-ever official delegation to the American capital, the delegates received top-level treatment, including meetings with NSC officials Samantha Power and Steve Simon and with Deputy Secretary of State Burns.[69]

• • • • • • • •

Throughout February, while the FJP-led People's Assembly found its bearings vis-à-vis the SCAF, the Brotherhood's political party was consolidating its control over yet another legislative body.

In the elections for the Shura Council, Egypt's upper parliamentary house, the FJP won an outright majority, with 58 percent of the chamber's 180 elected seats, while the Nour Party again finished second with approximately 25 percent. Historically, the Shura Council had few responsibilities, and, because the president appointed one-third of the chamber, it was typically seen as a haven for autocratic cronyism. For this reason, the first post-Mubarak Shura Council elections received minimal attention: Non-Islamist parties participated weakly or not at all, and the ultimate turnout rates were 15 percent in the first round and 12.2 percent in the second—a sharp contrast to the 62 percent turnout rate of the People's Assembly elections.[70]

But the Brotherhood took the Shura Council elections seriously for one reason: According to the SCAF's March 2011 constitutional declaration, the hundred-member constitution-writing committee, known as the Constituent Assembly, would be chosen by the People's Assembly *and* the Shura Council together. The FJP's success in the Shura Council elections thus bolstered its prospective influence over the Constituent Assembly's selection.

A week after the Shura Council elections concluded, the two bodies of Parliament met for a joint session to discuss the formation of the Constituent Assembly. "We seek a constitution, and a Constituent Assembly, comprising all components of the nation without exclusion, marginalization, or exception," FJP leader Beltagy declared during the joint session's first meeting on March 3.[71] But the FJP's behavior in the Constituent Assembly fell far short of this promise.

The first matter before the joint parliamentary session was determining the Constituent Assembly's composition. The FJP proposed that 40 percent would consist of parliamentarians and 60 percent would be nonparliamentarians, most of whom would represent various sectors of society. The Nour Party, by contrast, proposed the reverse formula of 60 percent parliamentarians and 40 percent nonparliamentarians. Non-Islamist parties, however, wanted the Constituent Assembly to include a much lower percentage of sitting parliamentarians, believing that a higher percentage of nonparliamentarians would reduce the likelihood of outright Islamist domination.

Yet the FJP's goal was "implementing *shari'ah*" through an Islamist constitution and that made the Nour Party a necessary bedfellow. So the FJP ignored the non-Islamists completely and reached an even compromise with the Salafists, agreeing to a 50/50 parliamentarian/nonparliamentarian split, which a joint session of Parliament passed on March 24.[72]

The FJP and Salafists then selected an overwhelmingly Islamist Constituent Assembly. Of its fifty parliamentarians, twenty-five came from the FJP and eleven from the Nour Party, while the non-Islamists included many of the FJP's parliamentary allies. The fifty nonparliamentarian members of the Constituent Assembly similarly contained many Islamists, including a Brotherhood writer, a pro-Islamist diplomat, a pro-Islamist jurist, and two advocates of Islamic banking. The only student representative just so happened to be Morsi's nephew. Meanwhile, the Constituent Assembly included only six women—two of whom were FJP members—and six Christians. By *Al-Ahram*'s tally, at least sixty-four of the Constituent Assembly's one hundred members were connected in one way or another to Islamist movements.[73] Perhaps most glaringly, it included few actual constitutional scholars—which just reinforced the extent to which the FJP and Nour had engineered the body for their narrow ideological interests.

The non-Islamists were outraged. The Constituent Assembly's composition rendered them wallflowers in a process destined to produce a theocratic document. The Islamists countered that they were elected to ensure that Egypt's next constitution reflected the popular will, which—based on the parliamentary elections—favored Islamism overwhelmingly. But the non-Islamists would have none of it: Twenty-five of the hundred members declared a boycott of the Constituent Assembly's first session. The Islamists responded by pushing forward without them. The Constituent Assembly elected al-Katatny its chair by a 71–1 vote and immediately threatened to choose from the forty reserve members if the non-Islamists continued their boycott.[74]

But the non-Islamists' boycott quickly picked up steam. The SCC's representative withdrew after the Brotherhood released a statement accusing the court of cooperating with the SCAF to rig the forthcoming presidential elections. Al-Azhar's representative withdrew after the Constituent Assembly dismissed its widely praised 2011 document calling for a "democratic and constitutional" state.[75] The chairs of the lawyers, actors, and media syndicates similarly walked out. And on April 2, the Coptic Orthodox Church withdrew its two representatives. The FJP scrambled to stop the hemorrhaging, agreeing at one point to give up ten of its seats, with one stipulation: The replacements would have to be approved by the FJP-dominated People's Assembly. The non-Islamist parties, however, rejected this offer.[76]

Al-Katatny reiterated his threat, warning boycotting members that "if they withdraw they will be replaced." But the judiciary soon intervened. On April 10, Egypt's Supreme Administrative Court suspended the Constituent Assembly, ruling that its composition violated an earlier judicial ruling that prevented parliamentarians from electing themselves. Non-Islamists hailed the ruling, which the FJP denounced as "a horrendous error," yet it would ultimately stand, putting the Brotherhood's constitutional ambitions on hold for the time being.[77]

Once again, despite its parliamentary dominance, the Brotherhood found itself entirely powerless, as well as increasingly isolated.

• • • • • • • •

Still, the Brotherhood did not expect to be powerless for long. In late February, the FJP-led Parliament started working on amendments to the SCAF's presidential elections law, which paved the way for the opening of the nominations period in early April.[78] And as the June 30 deadline for the SCAF to hand executive power to an elected civilian president approached, the FJP anticipated that its parliamentary plurality would finally enable it to appoint the government.

Yet the Brotherhood saw one major problem on the horizon: The forthcoming FJP-dominated cabinet would inherit a severely broken country.

Indeed, more than a year after Mubarak's ouster, Egypt was struggling. The country's cash reserves, which stood at $33.3 billion in February 2011, had dwindled to just $15.1 billion by March 2012. Lingering instability deterred tourism and foreign investment, and new challenges—including domestic security and sustaining Egypt's costly food- and fuel-subsidy programs—forced the government to increase spending.[79] By early 2012, ordinary Egyptians were already feeling the effects, including a gasoline shortage and an emerging wheat crisis.[80] And before long, all fingers were pointed at the government of Kamal al-Ganzoury.

To be sure, al-Ganzoury's government faced many challenges when the SCAF installed it at the height of the November 2011 Mohamed Mahmoud incidents. But al-Ganzoury had failed to address these challenges, and his government's mad-dash spending habits often made these problems worse. Yet the Brotherhood didn't see al-Ganzoury's government as either hapless or inept—it saw it as downright evil. Indeed, during a session of Parliament, al-Katatny alleged that the government was "fabricating" the crises.[81] "When the problems faced us [. . .] —gas crisis, bread crisis, petrol crisis—I guess that these crises were attended to, put in front of the Parliament to make the Parliament lose its concentration," FJP parliamentarian Helmy al-Gazzar told me during a July 2012 interview, looking back.[82]

So on March 1—only two weeks after abandoning its first call for forming a new government—the FJP once again called for replacing al-Ganzoury and his cabinet. "The FJP watches with great worry the deteriorating performance of the government, especially in terms of the economy, security, and the fight against corruption," the Brotherhood's party wrote in a statement.

"So for these reasons and others, the party sees expediting the formation of a new government that enjoys the support of a parliamentary majority as an urgent matter."[83]

A week later, after the travel ban on the American NGO workers was lifted, the FJP's executive office reiterated its call for a new government, and the FJP-dominated Parliament started gathering votes for a no-confidence measure against al-Ganzoury.[84] While a no-confidence vote wouldn't have any legal effect—the SCAF still held the power to appoint the government, not Parliament—it would have been a tremendous embarrassment for al-Ganzoury's government and the SCAF. More important, a no-confidence vote threatened to undermine the government's negotiations with the International Monetary Fund (IMF) over a $3.2 billion loan, which Cairo sought to address Egypt's looming financial crisis.[85]

Hoping to defuse the tension, Nour Party chair Emad Abdel Ghafour met with military chief of staff Sami Anan, the SCAF's number two official, and urged him to fire al-Ganzoury. Anan, however, refused, arguing that al-Ganzoury's premiership would end when the SCAF handed power to the next president at the end of June and that there was no need to insult al-Ganzoury by removing him earlier. But Anan floated a counteroffer: Al-Ganzoury would stay, but the FJP-controlled Parliament could appoint ten ministers, as well as assistants in many of the other ministries.

When Abdel Ghafour brought this offer to al-Shater, however, the Brotherhood's deputy supreme guide refused, accusing the SCAF of subterfuge. "We'll hire the ministers and they'll burn them," Abdel Ghafour recalled al-Shater saying.[86] At another point during this period, the SCAF made a similar offer directly to Morsi, but the FJP chair also refused. If the FJP-controlled Parliament couldn't appoint the entire government, the Brotherhood reasoned, then the party would be held responsible for Egypt's failures despite lacking complete control.[87]

So the Brotherhood continued to push for al-Ganzoury's ouster. In a harsh March 18 statement, the Brotherhood declared that "the SCAF's insistence on keeping the current government headed by Kamal al-Ganzoury, and not withdrawing confidence in it despite its failure, is an attempt to make the Parliament fail so that it remains a [parliament] of words that can't achieve anything."[88] Six days later, the Brotherhood pounced again, enumerating the al-Ganzoury government's failures and asking whether the SCAF's refusal to replace it reflected "a desire to abort the revolution and make the people give up on their ability to achieve their goals." Most explosively, the Brotherhood alleged that the SCC had already written a decision declaring the FJP-controlled Parliament unconstitutional and implied that the SCAF was trying to manipulate Parliament by threatening to enforce this decision.[89]

The SCAF responded immediately and furiously. Referring to the Brotherhood's accusations as "baseless slander," the SCAF touted its role in administering the very parliamentary elections that "allowed the current political forces"—meaning the Brotherhood—"to feature in the People's Assembly and the Shura Council." The junta added that it "always put the people's best interest before anything else" and accused the Brotherhood of trying to "pressure the armed forces and its Supreme Council with the intention of making them abandon their national mission to rule the country during the transitional period." The SCAF closed its statement with a not-so-veiled threat: "We ask everyone to be aware of the lessons of history to avoid mistakes from a past that we do not want to return to, and to look towards the future."[90]

The Brotherhood understood this last comment quite well: The junta was threatening that further Brotherhood agitation risked a repeat of 1954, when the Nasser regime crushed the organization after initially cooperating with it.[91]

While Brotherhood leaders dismissed the SCAF's threat, the episode unnerved them. The FJP was powerless despite controlling both houses of Parliament, and the Brotherhood was still vulnerable to the whims of whoever held executive power. And this was one reason why the Brotherhood started seriously rethinking its oft-repeated promise that it would not nominate a presidential candidate.

It was not the only reason, however. In fact, the Brotherhood had been struggling with this promise from nearly the moment it made it.

7 The Road to Ittahidiya Palace

When the Brotherhood's General Shura Committee voted on February 10, 2011, not to run a presidential candidate in the first post-Mubarak elections, it sought to reassure the Egyptian public and the international community that Mubarak's imminent ouster wouldn't give way to an "Islamist takeover." But the decision created a host of new complications—especially when one of the Brotherhood's most prominent leaders declared that he was considering running for president shortly thereafter.

Abdel Moneim Abouel Fotouh was a longtime Brotherhood icon. Born in 1951 in the Nile Delta governorate of Al-Gharbiya, Abouel Fotouh began his Islamist activism at Cairo's Qasr el-Eini Medical School in the 1970s, where he cofounded a militant Islamist society. After being elected president of Cairo University's student union in 1975, however, Abouel Fotouh became disenchanted with his group's radicalism, objecting in particular to its embrace of violence and "putschist" aims against the Sadat regime. This period coincided with many Brotherhood leaders' liberation after two decades of imprisonment under Nasser, and in the late 1970s Abouel Fotouh joined the Brotherhood, which had renounced violence by that time.[1]

Abouel Fotouh was from the generation of young Muslim Brothers who helped resurrect the organization in the late 1970s and 1980s. He also helped spearhead the Brotherhood's international efforts, including the provision of aid to the mujahedeen in Afghanistan during their war against the Soviet Union, and he became a member of the Guidance Office at the relatively young age of thirty-six in 1987.

Years later, after his imprisonment from 1995 to 2000 along with many of the Brotherhood's other top figures, Abouel Fotouh developed his reputation as one of the organization's so-called moderates. Whereas the organization's Qutbists, such as Morsi, focused on maintaining ideological purity and reinforcing the organization's rigid hierarchy, the outreach-oriented Abouel Fotouh engaged other political currents through his involvement in the Medical Syndicate. At times he battled the Brotherhood's Qutbists publicly, such as when he opposed the Brotherhood "party platform" that Morsi and others drafted in 2007, which prohibited women and Christians from running for president. As a result, Abouel Fotouh attracted a small but noteworthy following among the revolutionary-oriented segment of Brotherhood youths, such as those who participated in the 2011 uprising during its earliest days.[2]

Abouel Fotouh's disagreements with the Qutbists precipitated his ouster from the Guidance Office in 2009, but he remained a committed Muslim Brother nonetheless. He stayed on the organization's General Shura Committee and acted as one of the Brotherhood's most visible advocates to the international community. During the 2011 uprising, he penned a *Washington Post* op-ed emphasizing that "the Brotherhood has already decided not to field a candidate for president in any forthcoming elections."[3]

Less than three months after Mubarak's ouster, however, Abouel Fotouh chucked this promise and announced his presidential candidacy.[4] Coming on the heels of the March 2011 Brotherhood youth conference that criticized the Guidance Office for establishing the FJP, Abouel Fotouh's disobedience was yet another embarrassment for the organization and fed media rumors of deep splits within the organization. So the Brotherhood leadership moved swiftly to enforce discipline. It sidelined Abouel Fotouh immediately, formally expelled him from the organization in June 2011, and reportedly froze the memberships of four thousand Brotherhood youths who had joined his campaign.[5]

Yet the Brotherhood's dismissal of Abouel Fotouh and his supporters didn't put the issue to rest. As the presidential elections approached, Abouel Fotouh emerged as one of the most prominent candidates—as well as the candidate who was ideologically closest to the Brotherhood. The Guidance Office thus worried that many Muslim Brothers might ultimately vote for Abouel Fotouh, a Brotherhood outcast who had defied an institutional edict. Nothing would undermine the Brotherhood's hierarchical culture of obedience more profoundly. And even worse, *what if Abouel Fotouh actually won?* The ex-Brotherhood leader's transgression would be rewarded, and the Brotherhood's reputation as a strong, internally cohesive organization would be severely tarnished!

As a result, the Brotherhood decided that it couldn't sit out the presidential elections entirely. And while it had promised not to nominate a presidential candidate from within its own ranks, nothing prevented it from endorsing a candidate and then ordering its cadres to vote for that person.

But who would be a suitable candidate for the Brotherhood to endorse? This proved more challenging than the Brotherhood's leadership anticipated because it was dissatisfied with the emerging crop of candidates. The Brotherhood regarded the leading candidate, former foreign minister and Arab League secretary-general Amr Moussa, as a remnant of the Mubarak regime. It regarded Ahmed Shafik, Mubarak's last prime minster, as an even greater villain in this regard. On the other hand, it considered Hazem Abu Ismail, the lone Salafist candidate and a former Brotherhood parliamentary candidate, far too extreme, as well as too unpredictable. And the only other mainstream Islamist candidate other than Abouel Fotouh, scholar Selim al-Awa, was a total nonstarter, since al-Awa was affiliated with the Wasat Party—an organization that ex-Brotherhood activists had founded in defiance of the Guidance Office in 1996.[6]

So around February 2012, the Brotherhood went back to the drawing board, deliberating over candidates who might be persuaded to run. The Brotherhood first approached Islamist-oriented judge Hossam el-Gheriany, but he refused. "I'm a straight man," el-Gheriany told Guidance Office leader Mohamed Ali Bishr. "This period needs a political guy—a gray-area guy who can make compromises." Next the Brotherhood approached another Islamist-oriented judge, Mahmoud Mekki, but he similarly rejected the group's overtures.[7]

By late March, the Brotherhood still had no candidate to endorse in the presidential elections—and with the official nominations period fast-approaching, Abouel Fotouh was still the most credible Islamist candidate. Meanwhile, the SCAF was threatening the Brotherhood with a severe crackdown if it continued to challenge the junta's authority, while the Brotherhood's battles with non-Islamists over the Constituent Assembly left it increasingly isolated politically.

This is when the Brotherhood started seriously reconsidering its promise not to field a presidential candidate.

The deliberations began during the last two weeks of March 2012. At the lowest level of the organization, Muslim Brothers debated the prospect of a Brotherhood presidential candidate in their weekly *usar* meetings, which likely enabled the Brotherhood leadership to take an informal poll of the organization before making a decision.[8] Then on March 31, the Brotherhood's General Shura Committee held an intense meeting on the matter. Proponents of nominating a Brotherhood candidate argued that the organization faced an increasingly dangerous political environment and that winning executive power was necessary to protect the Brotherhood's gains. Opponents, however, worried that the Brotherhood would lose credibility if it broke its promise and additionally warned that a Brotherhood president would be vulnerable because the security services would never accept a civilian president.[9]

The ultimate General Shura Committee vote was extremely close: Fifty-six Brotherhood leaders voted to nominate a candidate, while fifty-two voted against.[10] The committee then selected the Brotherhood's nominee via secret ballot. Approximately 70 percent voted for Khairat al-Shater, the deputy supreme guide, on the first ballot.[11]

When the Brotherhood announced al-Shater as its presidential candidate during a press conference that day, journalists immediately questioned his eligibility. Convicted felons are barred from presidential elections for five years under Egyptian law, and although al-Shater's felony conviction under Mubarak was politicized, it was a felony conviction nonetheless. Supreme Guide Badie, however, emphasized that the organization had consulted with its lawyers, who saw no legal barriers to al-Shater's candidacy.[12] But, as an insurance policy, the Brotherhood quietly nominated a backup candidate: Mohamed Morsi, who had received approximately 60 percent of the General Shura Committee's votes during its March 31 meeting.[13] The plan was for Morsi to step aside as soon as the Supreme Presidential Elections Commission (SPEC) approved al-Shater's candidacy, and the Brotherhood initially kept Morsi's nomination a secret while it focused on al-Shater's campaign.[14]

In the immediate aftermath of the Brotherhood's announcement that it would nominate al-Shater, a few high-profile Brotherhood figures criticized the General Shura Committee for breaking its promise not to run a presidential candidate, and some resignations followed.[15] But for the most part, the Brotherhood's rank and file immediately fell behind al-Shater's candidacy, organizing ad hoc events in their governorates and posting al-Shater's campaign logo as their social media avatars.

Whether or not al-Shater would be Egypt's next president, the Brotherhood no longer feared that Abouel Fotouh would divide its base.

• • • • • • • •

While the Brotherhood's decision represented a substantial shift in tactics, its ideological output never changed. On the campaign trail, al-Shater identified himself unambiguously with the Brotherhood's longtime goal of implementing *sharī'ah* and establishing an Islamic state in Egypt. "Our faith commands us to build and organize our lives and our countries correctly, based on Islam and the guidelines that God Almighty brought to us," al-Shater declared during a campaign press conference.

Alluding to al-Banna's multistage program for achieving Islamist rule, al-Shater said that the parliamentary elections reflected Egyptians' embrace of Islamism. If elected president, al-Shater promised to continue this process, as the Brotherhood's Islamist vision would be "circulated on a greater scale with the aim of encouraging the entire Egyptian people to participate in executing the realization of its modern renaissance." And after his government mobilized Egyptians collectively behind this agenda, al-Shater envisioned a full societal push for enacting it: "In creating the renaissance, there is a role for government, a role for the people, the private sector, and for the family. These three wings—the government, the people, and the private sector—must all be integrated into one organization, whose first and foremost objective is to create this country's renaissance and to reach with it an honorable standard of living for all Egyptians, who have suffered acutely for a long time."

Al-Shater's presidency, in other words, would work to integrate all of society's sectors into one organization—namely, the Brotherhood—to advance the Brotherhood's Islamizing cause. Egypt was about to hold its first truly open presidential elections, and a leading candidate was offering a pathway to totalitarian rule.

But what kinds of policies would al-Shater actually implement if he won the presidency? What was an Islamist approach to education or housing or taxation? Like al-Banna many decades before him, al-Shater never gave specifics. "I'm not going to go into very much detail about this vision or our program," he said.[16]

Six days after the Brotherhood nominated al-Shater, another formidable figure threw his hat into the ring: Omar Suleiman, the former intelligence chief who served as Mubarak's vice president during the dictator's final days in office. While his opponents derided him as the SCAF's man and a counterrevolutionary figure, Suleiman quickly emerged as a serious contender for precisely these reasons. To the segment of Egyptians that feared further revolutionary tumult and distrusted the Brotherhood, Suleiman was the "stability" candidate.[17]

Suleiman's emergence rattled the Brotherhood considerably. After all, Suleiman was an architect of Mubarak's anti-Brotherhood repression, and he

now had a realistic shot at the presidency. And since the Brotherhood believed that Egyptians would never elect a figure from the previous regime
in fair and free elections, it viewed Suleiman's candidacy as a SCAF plot to
rig the next elections, destroy the revolution, and crush the Brotherhood.
"General Omar Suleiman will not win the presidential elections," al-Shater
said during a television interview. "And if he wins it will be through fraud, and
we will not allow this."[18]

Al-Shater repeated this warning on the campaign trail. "We strongly refuse
the idea of bringing back the prior political system in a different way, through
Omar Suleiman, and we see that this is insulting to the revolution," he said. "If
an attempt is made to steal the revolution or commit rigging, then, naturally,
we and others will go out to the streets because the situation won't have a
solution."[19] But the Brotherhood wasn't prepared to play wait-and-see. On
Friday, April 13, the Brotherhood organized street protests for the first time in
many months, busing Muslim Brothers to Tahrir Square and holding protests
in other governorates as well against Suleiman's candidacy.[20]

Meanwhile, the Brotherhood pushed back against Suleiman's candidacy
through the FJP-controlled Parliament, which drafted the Law of Political
Exclusion to bar former Mubarak regime officials from running for high office.
The law ultimately banned anyone who served in top offices during the final
decade of Mubarak's rule from elections for the next ten years. Beyond Suleiman, this proposed law would exclude former prime minister Ahmed Shafik,
who was spending much of his time campaigning among the rural clans and
tribes that had previously supported and participated in Mubarak's regime.[21]

Yet on April 14, the presidential election was upended once again, when
the SPEC disqualified ten candidates on various technicalities, including Suleiman and al-Shater. The SPEC ruled that Suleiman had failed to collect the
proper number of signatures on his nomination petitions and barred al-Shater
for his previous felony conviction. Both candidates appealed, but the SPEC
affirmed its decision three days later.[22]

Of course, the Brotherhood had expected legal challenges to al-Shater's
candidacy, which is why it nominated Morsi as a backup candidate. It therefore had its appeal ready to be filed as soon as the SPEC disqualified al-Shater.
Moreover, al-Shater wasn't the only candidate barred on the basis of a prior
conviction—the SPEC disqualified non-Islamist candidate Ayman Nour on
the same grounds—which is to say that the SPEC applied its standards for
disqualifying candidates quite evenly. But when the SPEC issued its final
decision, al-Shater declared that his exclusion was a conspiracy by former

Mubarak regime officials on the SPEC, and the Brotherhood immediately used the incident as yet another rallying cry against the SCAF.[23]

"The SCAF . . . isn't working seriously toward a transition of power but is seeking a power arrangement that it will manage from behind the scenes," al-Shater declared in a press conference on April 18, calling for new protests against the SCAF.[24] That Friday, Muslim Brothers once again mobilized toward Tahrir Square, where non-Islamist revolutionaries joined them for the biggest demonstrations in months, and the Brotherhood called for another million-man march for the next Friday, April 27, to "salvage the revolution."[25]

But four days prior to the April 27 marches, Field Marshal Tantawi signed the Law of Political Exclusion into effect, barring former Mubarak regime officials from running for higher office.[26] It was a major concession to the Brotherhood, which responded by announcing that it would demonstrate in the governorates but not in the more symbolic and centralized venue of Tahrir Square.[27]

The Brotherhood kept its promise. Only a few hundred protesters—and virtually no Muslim Brothers—participated in the Tahrir demonstrations that Friday. Once again, the Brotherhood had used its ability to mobilize, or not mobilize, to pressure the SCAF.[28]

• • • • • • • •

It is often said that Mohamed Morsi wasn't supposed to be the Brotherhood's presidential candidate, and, as a technical matter, this is true. Al-Shater was the Brotherhood's first choice, as well as the superior candidate in just about every respect. Whereas al-Shater was the organization's chief strategist, Morsi was a functionary. Whereas al-Shater partly built his charisma on the twelve years that he spent in prison under Mubarak, Morsi spent only a few months in jail. And whereas al-Shater was an accomplished businessman who spoke in full paragraphs, Morsi was a bumbling engineering professor who tended to drone on ad infinitum.

Yet from the moment that the Brotherhood decided to nominate a presidential candidate on March 31, it knew that the SPEC might disqualify al-Shater and that Morsi—the alternate—would likely be its man. And the Brotherhood was willing to stomach Morsi's shortcomings for one simple reason: By late March 2012, winning the presidency had become such a priority for the Brotherhood that the question of *who* should be president was of secondary importance. Indeed, Morsi's candidacy was the product of a strategic calculus that put power before proficiency.

At the same time, the Brotherhood's ultimate ambivalence regarding *which* man became president reflected the organization's fundamental belief in its internal uniformity. Recall that every Muslim Brother goes through the same lengthy *tarbiah* process and then swears an oath to follow orders in pursuit of the exact same Islamizing agenda. As a result, there is a tendency within the Brotherhood to view its leaders as interchangeable exponents of the same ideas. So from the typical Muslim Brother's perspective, even if al-Shater was preferable, a Morsi presidency would ultimately serve the same purpose because it would pursue identical goals.

This was the argument that the Brotherhood used as it switched gears from al-Shater's presidential campaign to Morsi's: The man didn't matter because both Morsi and al-Shater represented the same Brotherhood vision for Egypt.[29] And that vision had a proper name: the Renaissance Project, the vague policy platform that the Brotherhood distributed during the campaign, which called for the establishment of an economically prosperous state based on *shariah*.

For this reason, Morsi's presidential campaign was almost entirely devoid of egoism. On the campaign trail, Morsi rarely talked about himself, his life experiences, or his own specific vision for Egypt. The focal point of his campaign was that he was the Brotherhood's candidate and as president would implement the Brotherhood's Renaissance Project, whatever that meant.[30] Morsi's promise to be "president of all Egyptians" thus rang hollow, as did Supreme Guide Badie's declaration that Morsi was "relieved" of the oath he swore to the organization. At the end of the day, Morsi's campaign operation and platform were Brotherhood-branded products through and through.[31]

Morsi's standing among Salafists was the first casualty of this approach. The Salafists emerged as one of Egypt's most pivotal electoral blocs during the parliamentary elections, and, after the SPEC disqualified Salafist presidential candidate Hazem Abu Ismail in early April because of his mother's US citizenship, the Salafists were left to choose between two Islamist candidates: Abouel Fotouh and Morsi. But whereas Abouel Fotouh tried to widen his base by presenting himself as a more inclusive Islamist, Morsi presented himself as a more hardline one—which, in theory, should have appealed to the Salafists' fundamentalism.[32] And during the first week of his candidacy, Morsi actively courted the Nour Party in Alexandria, with much of the discussion focused on how *shariah* would be implemented.[33]

Yet the Salafists' long-running and often contentious competition with the Brotherhood made them skeptical of Morsi, given the lack of daylight between him and his organization. From their perspective, the Brotherhood put politics before doctrine and often embraced politically expedient *shari'ah* interpretations rather than the literalist ones that define Salafism.

Of course, the Salafists similarly viewed Abouel Fotouh—whose campaign team included prominent leftists—as too "moderate" and disagreed in particular with his call for a "civil state," as opposed to an Islamic one. But Abouel Fotouh reassured them by backtracking on his former calls for inclusiveness. For example, when asked during an interview on a Salafist satellite network whether non-Muslims should be permitted to run for president, Abouel Fotouh answered circumspectly. "It's the right of any faction, Islamist or non-Islamist, to nominate or not nominate [candidates]—it's up to them," he said. "But Egypt cannot have a president who does not have an Islamist orientation. The Egyptian people expressed this in the parliamentary elections and in other elections."[34] So on April 29, the Nour Party's leadership voted to back Abouel Fotouh over Morsi by a margin of 71 to 29 percent.[35] One week later, al-Gamaa al-Islamiya similarly backed Abouel Fotouh.[36]

The Morsi campaign's decision to elevate the candidate's Brotherhood affiliation over his own biography also fed a negative media narrative, which portrayed Morsi as a "spare tire"—a replacement for al-Shater, rather than a worthy candidate in his own right. It also contributed to his low polling numbers. An early May 2012 *Al-Ahram* poll pegged Morsi's support at just 7 percent—a distant fourth behind Amr Moussa (39 percent), Abouel Fotouh (24 percent), and Ahmed Shafik (17 percent).[37] After a May 10 televised debated between Moussa and Abouel Fotouh, which ultimately left both leading candidates looking less presidential, the polls shifted slightly. In a poll released just three days before the May 23 election, Moussa's support dropped to 31.7 percent, Abouel Fotouh fell to fourth place with 14.6 percent, and Shafik jumped to second place with 22.6 percent. Yet Morsi was still a distant third behind Moussa and Shafik, with 14.8 percent.[38]

The Brotherhood's deepening isolation from other political forces didn't help Morsi's standing either. In late April, the FJP pushed another measure to withdraw confidence from al-Ganzoury's government through Parliament, but the SCAF once again rejected this.[39] In response, on April 30, Speaker Saad al-Katatny froze Parliament, suspending all sessions for a week.[40] The move, however, instantly backfired: The Salafist and non-Islamist parliamentary blocs rejected al-Katatny's move and accused the Brotherhood of taking the entire Parliament into a fight with the SCAF without its permission. Al-Katatny ultimately backtracked.[41]

Table 7.1 *Al-Ahram* Polling, 2012 Presidential Elections (1,200 respondents)

	April 28–May 1	May 14–17
Amr Moussa	39.0	31.7
Abdel Moneim Abouel Fotouh	24.0	14.6
Ahmed Shafik	17.0	22.6
Mohamed Morsi	7.0	14.8
Hamdeen Sabahi	6.7	11.7
Other candidates / Undecided	6.3	4.6

As a result of these factors, many analysts believed that the Brotherhood was losing support and that Morsi would lose badly as a result. The *Wall Street Journal* reported that the Brotherhood's fortunes had "faded" due to "mounting public criticism" and "internal defections," while the *Washington Post* claimed that Morsi was "running an underdog campaign" and that the Brotherhood was contending with "a shift in public opinion as many Egyptians have soured on the venerable Islamist organization."[42] Yet these accounts underestimated the one advantage that Morsi possessed over every other candidate: the Muslim Brotherhood's unparalleled ground organization.

Indeed, among Egypt's various political forces and candidates, the Muslim Brotherhood was uniquely constructed to perform well electorally, even as its popularity declined. With thousands of five-to-ten-person *usar* scattered in virtually every district across the country, all of which marched at the orders of the Guidance Office, the Brotherhood was able to mobilize an unparalleled get-out-the-vote effort.

For the elections, however, the Brotherhood simplified its organization. Normally, the Guidance Office communicated its orders to the governorate leaders, and those commands would then be passed down through the multitiered chain of command until it reached the *usar* chiefs, who would then direct Brotherhood cadres on the ground. But during the elections, the Brotherhood adopted a "flat organization" in which orders were communicated from the governorate offices directly to a top official within each electoral district, which enabled swifter action.[43] Moreover, prior to the elections, individual cadres were given specific tasks, such as distributing brochures, handling the local media, or mobilizing specific numbers of residents to the polling places.[44]

So when the two-day voting period ended on May 24, the results shocked

Table 7.2 2012 Presidential Elections, Round 1 Results (Major Candidates)

Candidate	Total Votes	Percentage
Mohamed Morsi	5,553,097	25.30
Ahmed Shafik	5,210,978	23.74
Hamdeen Sabahi	4,739,983	21.60
Abdel Moneim Abouel Fotouh	3,936,264	17.93
Amr Moussa	2,407,837	10.97

many observers: Morsi came in first place with 5.5 million votes and 25.30 percent. Meanwhile, Shafik finished second with 5.2 million votes and 23.74 percent, essentially absorbing the "stability" vote that Omar Suleiman left behind
when he was disqualified a month earlier.[45] The fact that no candidate received an outright majority forced a June 16 runoff between Morsi and Shafik.

The first-round results indicated two interesting trends within Egypt's
electorate. First, given Morsi's utter lack of charisma and unambiguous at-
tachment to the Brotherhood, his vote totals could be interpreted as reflect-
ing the Brotherhood's hardcore support base—the types of voters who would
back the Brotherhood no matter the candidate. Second, non-Islamists won a
clear majority of the vote, since the two leading Islamist candidates—Morsi
and Abouel Fotouh, who finished in fourth place—received only 43 percent
combined. Egypt was thus far more divided between Islamists and non-
Islamist than the Islamists' overwhelming victory in the parliamentary elections suggested. The Islamists won because they were exceptionally well organized—not because they were extraordinarily popular.

• • • • • • • •

The second round of the 2012 presidential elections represented a tremendous opportunity for Mohamed Morsi. By running against Ahmed Shafik,
Mubarak's last prime minister, Morsi was able to broaden his base beyond the
Brotherhood's supporters by presenting himself as the candidate of Egypt's
revolution. So he changed his tone substantially during the second round.
Rather than emphasizing his Brotherhood credentials, Morsi now spoke
about himself and tied his personal story to the January 2011 uprising.

"Three of my children faced death during the revolution, including Abdullah," Morsi told TV host Mahmoud Saad during a May 26 interview. "I was in
Cairo, and Abdullah called me from Zaqaziq . . . on Wednesday, February 2.

There were about three hundred thugs around him. . . . He told me, 'Dad, they want to slaughter us, because security [forces] are surrounding us, and the thugs have knives. Save me, Dad, they will slaughter us.'" Morsi added that, during the uprising, pro-Mubarak thugs similarly beat two of his other sons, and he also discussed his own imprisonment on January 28, 2011. Morsi further emphasized core revolutionary demands, promising that Mubarak and his cronies would be convicted one way or another and that he would seek justice for the revolution's martyrs.

Morsi also appealed to Christians. "For our Christian brothers, I want to say that the nation of Egypt belongs to all," Morsi said, when asked to address Christian fears about the Brotherhood. "They are the sons of Egypt, just like Muslims, and in front of the law and the constitution they are like Muslims completely." Morsi then claimed that he would treat Christians as equals, unlike the previous regime, which he accused of being involved in the deadly January 2011 terrorist attack on an Alexandria church.[46]

Meanwhile, Morsi downplayed the Brotherhood's commitment to "implementing *shari'ah*," noting that *shari'ah* had been an important basis of the constitution since 1923. He similarly downplayed the Brotherhood's Renaissance Project. "We have proposed it to the people not as a final project but as a suggested project for the whole country's renaissance, not just for the FJP," he told TV host Yosri Fouda during a May 30 interview. The immediate priority, he said, would be addressing five basic problems that affect Egyptians' daily lives: security, sanitation, bread, fuel, and traffic. He further denied his allegiance to the supreme guide and promised that he'd regard the FJP "just like the other parties."

"As president," Morsi said, "Egyptians and Egypt will have my allegiance, after God of course. Everyone is equal."[47]

Shafik countered Morsi by presenting himself as the stability candidate, promising to "restore order" if elected.[48] Whereas Morsi highlighted his opposition to the Mubarak regime, Shafik emphasized his governmental experience under Mubarak, including his stints as air force chief of staff, minister of civil aviation, and, of course, prime minister. At one point he even referred to Mubarak as his role model.[49]

The two campaigns also pursued entirely different strategies. Whereas Morsi campaigned by appealing to Islamists and prorevolutionary non-Islamists, Shafik engaged the rural clans and tribes who had supported the Mubarak regime for decades and who could be counted on to mobilize their hundreds—and sometimes thousands—of family members during the elections. In this sense, the election was a contest between two very different organizational models: the Brotherhood's top-down chain of command, comprising obedient cadres who could mobilize supporters in practically every Egyptian neighborhood, and the Mubarakist model, which depended on the diffuse support of landed interests, particularly in the countryside. The problem with Shafik's model, however, was that the Arab Spring had revealed the weaknesses of these clans and tribes: Despite their local influence, they had been unable to stem the January 2011 uprising, and the Brotherhood and Salafists overwhelmed them during the winter 2011–12 parliamentary elections.

Shafik, however, faced an even more daunting challenge: the strong possibility that he might be eliminated from the election. After all, under the Law of Political Exclusion, which Tantawi signed into effect on April 23, former Mubarak regime officials were barred from elections for the next ten years. The SPEC, however, accepted Shafik's appeal of his disqualification under the new law, which permitted him to reenter the race pending ongoing legal challenges, which were due in mid-June.[50]

The Brotherhood viewed all of this as one big conspiracy—an attempt by remnants of the Mubarak regime within the state's institutions to steal the presidential election and restore Mubarak's regime under Shafik. From the Brotherhood's perspective, Shafik—or any Mubarakist—couldn't possibly win a fair and free election because Egyptians were overwhelmingly religious Muslims and therefore desired the implementation of *shari'ah*. Egyptians' broad support for the anti-Mubarak uprising and Islamists' overwhelming victory in the parliamentary elections proved this in the Brotherhood's eyes.

So to pressure the SCAF to enforce the Law of Political Exclusion against Shafik, the Brotherhood called mass protests demanding that he be put on trial, along with other previous Mubarak regime security officials.[51] Revolutionary groups, as well as three former presidential candidates who had lost during the first round, joined the demonstrations. On June 5, tens of thousands of Egyptians descended on Tahrir Square.[52]

The following day, the Brotherhood issued a firm warning in its daily Morsi campaign e-mail: "If Shafik is elected president, in this critical stage in Egypt's history, . . . we might return again to what we had prior to January 25, [2011], and we will rectify the matter quickly." The Brotherhood's message to the SCAF was clear: Let Shafik run and win, and we will launch another uprising.[53]

• • • • • • • •

On June 14, two days before the second round of the presidential election, the SCC suddenly declared that one-third of the FJP-controlled Parliament had been elected unconstitutionally. The court ruled that those parliamentary seats that had been elected through individual-candidacy voting (as opposed to party-list voting) should have been reserved for political independents and that "the makeup of the entire chamber is illegal and, consequently, it does not legally stand." At the same time, the court issued an additional ruling upholding Shafik's right to run in the presidential elections.[54]

The SCAF's rapid implementation of the court's decision was a tremendous blow to the Brotherhood. By dissolving Parliament, the SCAF effectively nullified the Brotherhood's primary political achievement since Mubarak's ouster and put the Brotherhood back at square one in its quest for power. Still, despite the politically tense environment in which the court issued its ruling, the decision had strong legal merit. After all, two consecutive Mubarak-era Parliaments were dissolved in 1987 and 1990 for similarly failing to include political independents sufficiently. And a judge had warned the Brotherhood and other political parties during the autumn 2011 negotiations over the parliamentary law that their insistence on allowing partisan candidates to run for all seats might render the elections unconstitutional.

From the Muslim Brothers' perspective, however, the court's decisions reflected yet another conspiracy against them. After all, during its late March confrontation with the SCAF regarding al-Ganzoury's government, the Brotherhood alleged that the government was using the threat of Parliament's dissolution to manipulate it—and now that warning had come true. So in response to the court's decision, the Brotherhood alleged a "coup" against "the democratic revolution" that might "hand over power to one of the most prominent symbols of the former era," meaning Shafik.[55]

Yet the Brotherhood refused to be distracted from Morsi's presidential campaign, since victory was now more urgent than ever. So rather than joining other political forces in street protests against the court's decision, the Brotherhood called on Egyptians to "prevent the return of the former regime" by voting for Morsi.[56] And in a separate statement, the supreme guide rejected calls for Morsi to drop out of the race to protest the court's decision, explaining that the Guidance Office and the FJP executive committee had voted to keep Morsi in the runoff.[57] The source of this announcement was noteworthy: Despite Morsi's second-round promises that he would not take orders from the Brotherhood's leadership, it was the Brotherhood leadership—and not his own campaign—that ultimately determined and declared his strategy during this critical moment.

The country was simmering when second-round voting began on June 16, but the Brotherhood kept its eye on the prize. To mobilize its cadres, the Brotherhood declared voting for Morsi a "political obligation." In certain districts, Brotherhood leaders encouraged their cadres by giving them targets for the number of voters that they had to bring to the polls.[58] Meanwhile, the Brotherhood dispatched two cadres apiece to all of Egypt's more than thirteen thousand polling stations and equipped them with laptops and proprietary software for tabulating the elections results in real time when the polls closed on June 17.[59]

At four o'clock the morning of June 18, the Brotherhood announced its estimated results in a press conference: Morsi was the winner, with 51.7 percent of the vote.[60] By declaring victory before the SPEC announced the official results, the Brotherhood hoped to control the narrative and, more important, preempt any attempt by the SCAF or others to deny Morsi the presidency.

• • • • • • • •

But what, exactly, did the Brotherhood think that Morsi had won? The election, after all, took place amid tremendous institutional uncertainty. There was no constitution, no Parliament, and thus no clear delineation of the next president's powers.[61] Even if the SPEC declared Morsi the winner, he still faced a power struggle with the SCAF to define his executive authority.[62]

The SCAF, however, wanted to get ahead of this game. On June 18—only hours after the Brotherhood declared Morsi's victory—it released an amended version of the March 2011 constitutional declaration that constrained the next president's powers considerably. Specifically, the amended declaration maintained that the "incumbent SCAF members are responsible for deciding on all issues related to the armed forces including appointing its leaders and extending the terms in office of the aforesaid leaders." The declaration further maintained that the president could only declare war with the SCAF's approval. Finally, the SCAF asserted total legislative authority until a new Parliament was elected. This implied that the SCAF had the authority to issue laws constraining the president's powers until a new constitution was written.[63]

For the most part, the amended declaration was a reiteration of the November 2011 el-Salmi Document—an attempt by the SCAF to insulate the military from a newly elected government. But whereas the Brotherhood had responded to the el-Salmi Document with a one-day demonstration followed by negotiations, the gloves were now off. The Brotherhood immediately declared the SCAF's latest declaration a "coup against democracy" and announced its participation in "all popular activities against the constitutional coup and the dissolution of Parliament" moving forward.[64] Two days later, the FJP declared an indefinite Tahrir Square sit-in until the SCAF restored the People's Assembly and canceled the amended constitutional declaration, "which reduced the powers of the presidency and created a justification for the survival of the SCAF."[65]

Most centrally, however, the Brotherhood's Tahrir Square sit-in sought to pressure the SCAF to recognize Morsi's presidential victory. The Brotherhood believed, based on its own tallying, that Morsi had won. And following the dissolution of the FJP-controlled Parliament and the SCAF's amended constitutional declaration that undercut the next president's power, the Brotherhood feared that the elections results would be forged in Shafik's favor.[66]

So the Brotherhood threw its full organizational weight behind the Tahrir Square sit-in. It commanded Muslim Brothers from all across Egypt to mobilize toward Cairo. The Brothers were organized within the square according to their *shu'abah*—the administrative unit that comprises six to twelve Brotherhood *usar*, totaling forty to ninety members each. To ensure that the Brotherhood maintained a constant and sizable presence in the square at all times, *shu'abah* members determined among themselves who would remain in the sit-in during the week and who would return to their jobs and families in their hometowns. But all cadres were required to attend the major demonstrations, such as on June 24 when the SPEC promised to announce the elections results.

To control the sit-in, the Brotherhood's Guidance Office appointed an official within the square to distribute orders to the *shu'abah* chiefs. These orders came in the form of handwritten memos, which were distributed to the chiefs multiple times a day in some instances and instructed cadres on prayer times, demonstration times, and other activities. This unified hundreds and sometimes thousands of cadres' actions within the square, and the structure further enabled the *shu'abah* chiefs to relay reports from Tahrir to the Guidance Office.

Looking ahead to the SPEC's announcement of the elections results on June 24, the Brotherhood envisioned two possible scenarios: Either the SPEC would declare Morsi the winner, or it would forge the elections in Shafik's favor. And if the latter scenario happened, the Brotherhood anticipated clashes with security forces and instructed its cadres to prepare for battle. "If Shafik wins, I will be a dead man," Fathi Ageez, who had come from the Nile Delta city of Mansoura, told me while setting up his Tahrir tent with his colleagues. "I will fight to the end," he said, explaining that his *usrah* leader had told him to do so a few days earlier. Other Muslim Brothers in the square said that they would merely defend the square and not engage in offensive violence. But either way, violence appeared inevitable.[67]

Of course, the Brotherhood's leaders denied any and all responsibility for escalating the crisis. Despite the Brotherhood's top-down mobilization of its cadres toward Tahrir Square and its chain of command within the square, Guidance Office officials repeatedly claimed that they would have no control over the situation if Shafik won. "The coming revolution may be less peaceful and more violent," Deputy Supreme Guide al-Shater told David Ignatius of the *Washington Post* a few days before the presidential runoff. "It may be difficult to control the streets. . . . Some parties, not the Muslim Brotherhood, may resort to further violence and extremism."[68] But in fact the Tahrir Square sit-in was a well-organized bargaining tactic—a way for the Brotherhood to make the SCAF fear a Morsi loss more than a Morsi win.

So while tensions mounted in Tahrir Square, the Brotherhood's leaders negotiated on two fronts. First, in the days leading up to the June 24 elections announcement, al-Shater and other Brotherhood leaders met with top SCAF figures, though no details of these meetings were ever released publicly.[69] Second, the Brotherhood engaged a wide variety of non-Brotherhood political figures and activists, working to win their support and thus present a unified front to the SCAF and the international community.

Morsi unveiled the outcome of his discussions with these other political forces during a June 22 press conference at the Fairmont Hotel in northern Cairo. With prominent revolutionary activists, writers, and non-Islamist figures standing behind him on stage, Morsi promised inclusive rule. Specifically, he promised not to appoint an FJP figure to the vice presidency. He added that there could be multiple vice presidents and said that he would consider appointing a woman, a Copt, and a youth figure to the position. He also promised to appoint a "broad coalition government" in which the majority would not be from the FJP and also promised to appoint a "nationalist, independent personality"—in other words, not a Muslim Brother—as prime minister. Finally, Morsi promised to uphold the independence of the judicial, legislative, and executive branches of government, insisting that he had no fight with the

SPEC's judges or the SCAF. "We await the results of the presidential election that the SPEC will announce, achieving the will of the people, as we all know it," Morsi said, as he concluded his remarks.[70]

• • • • • • • •

A dark mood hung over Tahrir Square on the afternoon of Sunday, June 24, 2012. The SPEC was supposed to announce the elections results at two o'clock in the afternoon, but the announcement was now over an hour late. According to a rumor that circulated rapidly through Cairo, the SCAF had already informed Shafik that he would be Egypt's next president, and businesses sent their workers home early in anticipation of severe violence.

Morsi's supporters in Tahrir Square expected to be at the front lines of that violence. The Brotherhood, of course, had instructed its cadres to be prepared to fight security forces in the event of a Shafik victory. Meanwhile, toward the southern end of the square, dozens of Salafists marched in lines of two carrying cloths meant to represent shrouds. "We are ready to die like the martyrs before us," one of them told me, referring to the approximately eight hundred people who died in the January 2011 uprising. "This is my coffin," said another, pointing to the cloth in his hands. "We win or we die."[71] The stultifying, hundred-degree heat, combined with the square's congestion, made the delayed announcement nearly unbearable.

When SPEC chair Farouk Sultan began his address at three thirty, he clarified nothing. For the next forty-five minutes, Sultan took Egyptians on a tortuous tour of the various bureaucratic decisions that the SPEC made during the course of determining the election's outcome, offering every statistic except the one that mattered. Finally, during the forty-sixth minute of his address, Sultan got to the point: Morsi had won the presidential election with 13,230,131 votes to Shafik's 12,347,380.

As soon as Sultan mentioned Morsi's name as Egypt's next president, Tahrir Square erupted in screams of "*Allāhu akbar!*"—"God is great!"—and many demonstrators threw themselves to the ground in prayer. Muslim Brothers had expected, and prepared for, the worst: a Shafik victory and immediate clashes. Instead they were celebrating a presidential victory and, with it, the promise of advancing their longtime goal of establishing an Islamic state in Egypt.

8 The Power Struggle Continues

After eight decades in Egypt's opposition, the Muslim Brotherhood had finally reached the seat of power. Brotherhood leader Mohamed Morsi would now be Egypt's first elected civilian president, and he was set to take his oath on June 30, 2012.

Yet despite his dramatic victory, Morsi's presidential powers were undefined. There was still no constitution and, following the June 14 SCC ruling, no People's Assembly either. The true power holder remained the SCAF, which declared total legislative authority, as well as control over all military-related affairs under its June 18 constitutional declaration. Meanwhile, Muslim Brothers were still camped out in Tahrir Square, rejecting the SCAF's declaration and vowing to stay until the FJP-controlled Parliament was restored. To be sure, Morsi's victory lowered the temperature considerably, and fears of a bloody confrontation between the Brotherhood and security forces subsided. But the power struggle between Egypt's strongest governmental institution and strongest political force still wasn't resolved.

Indeed, that power struggle was evident from the moment that Morsi's victory was announced on June 24. While Morsi struck a conciliatory tone during his acceptance speech, promising to be a president of "all Egyptians" and declaring his appreciation for the military, the police, and the judiciary, his surrogates went on the offensive.[1] That evening, his campaign spokesman Yasser Aly announced that Morsi would take his presidential oath before the People's Assembly and not before the SCC's general assembly, as the SCAF's June 18 declaration had mandated.[2] This was a sharp jab at the SCAF's declaration, as well as a blatant attempt to undo the SCC's dissolution of the lower house of Parliament. The tension intensified over the next few days, as Brotherhood figures echoed Morsi's implicit demand for restoring the People's Assembly and indicated that, as president, Morsi would have the authority to cancel the SCAF's decree.[3]

Ultimately, the Brotherhood negotiated an end to the standoff with the SCAF, and Morsi took his oath before the SCC's general assembly on June 30.[4] Yet despite this concession, Morsi made it quite clear that he did not consider the matter of the People's Assembly's dissolution settled. During an address at Cairo University that afternoon, he emphasized the dissolved parliamentary body's popular legitimacy. "The Egyptian people have imposed their will and exercised their inherent sovereignty, and for the first time in Egypt's modern history, the people have mastered their full powers," he said. "They have elected their representatives for the People's Assembly and the Shura Council in free and fair elections that reflected a true representation of all components of the Egyptian society."[5]

The strongest indication of the ongoing power struggle between the Brotherhood and the SCAF, however, came on Friday, June 29, one day before his inauguration, when Morsi swore the oath of office symbolically in Tahrir Square. The Brotherhood commanded its cadres to pack the square to ensure a massive crowd and hung banners on the main podium decrying the SCAF's constitutional declaration. When Morsi appeared on stage, the crowd went wild, and Morsi pushed away his bodyguards to wave to it. He then proceeded to the podium, where he chanted slogans in unison with the square: "Revolutionaries! Free men! We will complete the journey!"

"Oh great people!" Morsi declared in a fiery address.

> I've come before you because I completely believe that you are the source of authority and legitimacy that is above all. . . . No institution, body, or side is above this will! The nation is the source of all authorities. . . . And this is why I came here today. Everyone hears me now. All the people hear me—the ministries and the government, the army and the police, men and women of Egypt, at home and abroad. I say to them and with full force, "There is no authority above this authority! There is no authority above this authority!"

With that, Morsi walked out in front of his podium, screaming, "No authority is above this authority!" and waving his finger furiously. His bodyguards, already looking uneasy, scrambled to surround him as he continued screaming and gesticulating.

Suddenly, Morsi opened his sports coat. "I am not wearing a bulletproof vest," he declared. "Because I am confident, as I trust God and I trust you, and I fear only God. And I will always be fully accountable to you." Once again, the crowd went wild.[6]

As he wrapped up his address, Morsi noticed members from the US-designated terrorist organization al-Gamaa al-Islamiya in the audience, holding posters of their spiritual leader Omar Abdel Rahman. Better known as "the blind sheikh," Abdel Rahman was sentenced in 1996 to life imprisonment in the United States for plotting terrorist attacks on the United Nations (UN) headquarters, a federal office building, and major bridges and tunnels in New York City.[7] But al-Gamaa was also a Brotherhood political ally. So when Morsi saw the posters of Abdel Rahman during his Tahrir speech, he veered off script.

"Oh great Egyptian people," he said. "I will do my best to free all detainees, including the blind sheikh, Omar Abdel Rahman. This is their right onto me, and my duty towards them."[8]

· · · · · · · ·

The emergence of Mohamed Morsi as Egypt's first elected president should have greatly concerned Washington. While the American policy community was deeply divided over whether the Brotherhood would cooperate with the United States and abide by Egypt's international commitments, virtually every analyst who met Morsi came away with the same impression: This man hated the West deeply and unambiguously. Morsi volunteered 9/11 conspiracy theories unabashedly, dealt with American journalists brusquely, and routinely described the United States as a society in moral and physical decay.[9] And here he was, standing before many thousands of fundamentalists in Tahrir Square and making one concrete presidential promise: that he would demand that the United States release a convicted terrorist from prison.

The Obama administration, however, took the long view. For starters, the Egyptian military still held significant political power, particularly over the country's foreign relations and defense policy, and would thus remain Washington's key partner on strategic matters. The administration thus viewed the $1.3 billion in annual US military aid to Egypt as promoting continuity in the US–Egyptian relationship and ensuring that Egypt maintained its strategic coordination with Washington and its peace treaty with Israel.

But the administration also believed that it had to stay on the Brotherhood's good side. The Brotherhood was Egypt's dominant political force, and the administration anticipated that it would be a key political player within the Arab world's most populous state for many years to come. As many within the administration saw it, the Brotherhood's Islamist ideology resonated with Egypt's overwhelmingly religious and Muslim population, and Morsi's electoral victory reflected that. And now that Morsi had won the presidential election, the administration saw no alternative to working with the Brotherhood.[10]

So when Secretary of State Hillary Clinton was asked about Morsi's call for the United States to free Abdel Rahman, Clinton demurred. "I think it's very clear that he was given due process," she said. "He was tried and convicted for his participation in terrorist activities."[11]

A few days later, State Department spokeswoman Victoria Nuland similarly brushed questions about Morsi's remark aside. "President Morsi has just come into office," she said. "To my knowledge, neither he nor his people have contacted us on this case, but I think the Secretary was extremely clear in her interviews . . . about where we stand on it."[12]

In the Obama administration's view, Morsi's call for Abdel Rahman's release was purely rhetorical, and virtually nobody within the administration expected that it would be the last time that Morsi said something displeasing. Those US officials who worked on Egypt knew that the Brotherhood was anti-Semitic, anti-Christian, and hostile toward women's rights.

But in crafting its Egypt policy, the administration decided to choose its battles. If Washington made an international issue over every controversial Morsi remark, there was no telling how he and the Brotherhood might respond. So the administration decided that it would let his hostile rhetoric slide and focus instead on what Morsi, his government, and the Brotherhood actually *did*.[13] And to ensure that Morsi *did* the right things, the administration intensified its policy of "engagement," announcing on July 5 that Clinton would visit Egypt later that month to meet Morsi.[14]

Had Egypt been a consolidated democracy, this policy of "engagement" with Morsi and the Brotherhood might have made sense. But Egypt was in the throes of a power struggle between the SCAF and the Brotherhood. And it was also more polarized than ever: More than 48 percent of the country had just voted for Ahmed Shafik, Hosni Mubarak's last prime minister, while 57 percent had voted for non-Islamist candidates during the first round of the presidential election. Moreover, key Egyptian constituencies—including Coptic Christians and non-Islamists—were deeply fearful of the Brotherhood's theocratic project.

In its statements, the Obama administration signaled its recognition of this polarization. On the day that the presidential election results were announced, President Obama called both Morsi and Shafik—the call to the losing candidate being a very rare gesture, intended to encourage postelectoral conciliation. And during his congratulatory call to Morsi, Obama urged him to "take steps to advance national unity" and "respect the rights of all Egyptians, particularly women, minorities, Christians, et cetera."[15]

But just as the administration decided that it would judge Morsi by his actions rather than his words, Egypt's non-Islamists judged the Obama administration by the same standard. They ignored the many State Department press statements calling on Morsi to govern inclusively and tolerantly and instead focused on what the administration actually *did*. And from their perspective, the Obama administration's immediate, high-level outreach to Morsi didn't constitute acceptance of Egyptians' democratic choice. Rather, they viewed it as an endorsement of Morsi and the Brotherhood in a political struggle that was still unsettled.

The unsettled state of Egyptian politics was especially apparent during the second week of Morsi's presidency. On the evening of July 8, Morsi issued a presidential decree negating the SCAF's June 18 constitutional declaration and ordering the People's Assembly to return.[16] Did Morsi have the authority to issue such a decree? Nobody knew, because there was no constitution, no legislature, and no clarity about the extent of Morsi's presidential powers.

So in lieu of rules for resolving the dispute, a new political crisis emerged. The judiciary emphasized its June 14 ruling that the lower house of Parliament was elected unconstitutionally, and the SCAF warned Morsi to respect its constitutional declaration.[17] Meanwhile, Morsi played his hand quite poorly and apparently failed to prepare the Brotherhood for this showdown. While Brotherhood leaders expected him to call back Parliament, they had no idea that he would do it so soon after taking office.[18]

The Brotherhood responded to Morsi's decree slowly. Brotherhood leader Saad al-Katatny, the speaker of the dissolved People's Assembly, issued a statement on the night of Morsi's decree welcoming the move, but the Brotherhood's parliamentary delegation wasn't informed of any next steps.[19] The following day, the Brotherhood called for a mass demonstration on July 10 to "support the president of the Republic in his latest decisions."[20] But unlike during the Brotherhood protests in Tahrir Square during the week leading up to Morsi's victory, the Brotherhood did not tell its cadres to reoccupy the square and only commanded its youth activists in Cairo to participate. Brotherhood youths thus saw this demonstration call as half-hearted—a sign that their leaders weren't ready for the political battle into which Morsi had thrust them.[21]

So on the morning of July 10, al-Katatny convened a very brief session of Parliament. The members voted to refer the lower house's ability to convene to the Court of Cassation in Cairo and resolved not to assemble until the court rendered a decision. The People's Assembly then adjourned within minutes. Later that day, the SCC issued a ruling that affirmed its prior invalidation of the 2011–12 parliamentary elections.[22] Morsi announced the next day that he would respect the ruling, and, for the time being, Egypt's power struggle cooled down.[23]

Clinton landed in Egypt three days later, on July 14. The secretary intended to deliver a major address on Egyptian democracy in Alexandria, but, given the political crisis of the previous week, she ultimately thought better of it and focused on her meetings with Morsi and Defense Minister Tantawi instead. As a State Department official told the *New York Times*, Clinton's goal in Egypt was "to engage in . . . dialogue and to avoid the kind of confrontation that could potentially lead to the transition veering off track." Clinton would not address the SCAF's constitutional declaration or Morsi's attempt to reverse it and would leave these matters for Egyptian courts and politicians to decide.[24]

But even with this more modest agenda, Clinton's visit was a total disaster. No matter how hard she tried to appear nonpartisan, and no matter how broadly she tried to engage Egyptians beyond the Brotherhood, non-Islamists ultimately interpreted her meeting with Morsi as an embrace of the Brotherhood. Protests followed her everywhere. In Cairo, hundreds of anti-Morsi demonstrators gathered outside Clinton's hotel, accusing her of supporting the Muslim Brotherhood. In Alexandria, protesters taunted her with chants of "Monica, Monica" and threw tomatoes and shoes at her motorcade. At another point, during a meeting with civil society representatives and Christian leaders, participants accused the United States of pressuring the SCAF to ensure Morsi's victory during the presidential election, and one participant accused Clinton's aide Huma Abedin of being a "secret agent of the Muslim Brotherhood."[25] The experience left the American officials with a very low opinion of Egypt's non-Islamists and made the Brotherhood look reasonable by comparison.

Still, Clinton committed one major unforced error. During a press conference with the Egyptian foreign minister, Clinton was asked whether she was drawing a "moral equivalence" between Morsi, an elected president, and the SCAF, "which seems to have undemocratically overstayed its welcome in the political sphere." Clinton had intended to avoid addressing these polarizing questions but suddenly let her guard down. "This is first and foremost a question for the Egyptian people," Clinton replied. "But the United States supports the full transition to civilian rule with all that entails."[26]

Of course, to an American audience, Clinton's statement reflected two core democratic values: respecting electoral outcomes and supporting civilian rule. But coming amid Egypt's ongoing power struggle, her remark was interpreted as supporting Morsi and the Brotherhood against the military.

So the following day, only hours after meeting with Clinton, Tantawi offered a not-so-implicit response. "We believe in God, and the blood of Egyptians will not be shed for any reason, especially in light of attempts that are pushed from abroad, which are always trying to drive a wedge between the people and the armed forces," he said during an address to the Second Army. "We will not allow this." He added that the military would not allow "a certain group" to establish hegemony over Egypt—a clear threat to the Brotherhood.[27]

• • • • • • • •

Despite the ongoing power struggle with the SCAF, the Muslim Brotherhood's leaders were extremely optimistic about the path forward. In their view, Morsi's electoral victory had given him—and the organization's project more broadly—unparalleled political legitimacy. And while they knew that their confrontation with the military was far from over, the Brotherhood's leaders believed that Morsi's victory represented an unprecedented opportunity to finally fulfill the next step of Hassan al-Banna's historic program: Islamizing the Egyptian state.

"The Muslim Brothers have pointed to the same plan for eighty years," Brotherhood leader Saad al-Husseini told me a few days before Morsi took office. "And [we] have arrived at the stage whose name is 'reforming the government.' And we will continue reforming the society and building the family and the individual."[28] In this context, "reforming the government" meant "implementing *shari'ah*"—which is what the Brotherhood had promised to do throughout its eight-decade existence.

But now that the Brotherhood was in a position to implement *shari'ah*, what policies, exactly, did it have in mind? For example, what did a *shari'ah*-compliant housing policy look like, as opposed to what came before? How would a *shari'ah*-compliant tax policy differ from the tax policies of the Mubarak era? The Brotherhood had promised for decades that "Islam was the solution." But what, specifically, was that solution?

This wasn't a new dilemma for the Brotherhood. It had first wrestled with these questions a dozen years earlier when seventeen Muslim Brothers won seats in the 2000 People's Assembly elections. At that time, the Brotherhood was suddenly—and quite unexpectedly—the largest opposition group in a Parliament otherwise controlled by Mubarak's ruling party, and the Brotherhood's leadership decided that its parliamentarians needed policy guidance. It thus tasked Guidance Office leader Mohamed Habib, who managed the Brotherhood's political file, to oversee the drafting of a policy platform, which became known as the Renaissance Project.[29]

The Renaissance Project was the Brotherhood's program for building an Islamic state in Egypt, which Hassan al-Banna saw as a prerequisite for the "renaissance" of the Muslim world more broadly.[30] And the drafting of the Renaissance Project intensified considerably after the 2011 uprising. The project's work was divided between two teams of Muslim Brothers. One team, based in northern Cairo, worked under the direction of Deputy Supreme Guide Khairat al-Shater and focused on business and economic policy. A second team, based on the Cairo island of Manial under the direction of FJP leader Ahmed Soliman, devised plans for promoting the Brotherhood's agenda through the state institutions that it anticipated controlling.[31]

During the organization's rapid, post-Mubarak ascent to power, Brotherhood leaders routinely touted the Renaissance Project as a policy platform.[32] The Brotherhood claimed that over a thousand Egyptians participated in drafting the project and that it was based on consultations with political and business leaders in other developing countries.[33] But, in fact, the emperor had no clothes. Far from being a policy agenda, the Renaissance Project was a mix of aspirations and principles, without any real plan for achieving any of them.

For example, its economic objectives included "transitioning from a 1.8 percent to a 7 percent annual GDP growth rate," "doubling the per capita GDP rate to raise the capability of the citizen to meet his basic needs while achieving an adequate well-being for all classes," and "reducing the current rate of inflation, which exceeds 11 percent annually . . . to support the purchasing power of the local currency and reduce the cost of access to goods and services."[34] How, exactly, did the Brotherhood expect to realize these lofty goals? It never said.

At another point in the program, the Renaissance Project offered a series of "mechanisms" for achieving certain social "goals" and presented them in figure 8.1.[35]

But, once again, these mechanisms didn't represent a coherent policy.

Goals

- Reduce the inflation rate to less than half by 2016.

- Protect the dignity of the poor and marginalized.

- Include the poor in the process of economic development.

Mechanisms

- Increase the number of families benefiting from social security from 1.5 million to 3 million households.

- Allocate a portion of the proceeds from taxes to developing the slums.

- Strengthen governmental and civil oversight of markets.

- Cancel the debts of small farmers (one acre or less).

Figure 8.1 Renaissance Project Goals and Mechanisms

And, of course, the Renaissance Project never described how the mechanisms—all of which were quite expensive—would be funded.

Even at the theoretical level, the Renaissance Project was a sloppy patchwork of ideas. It emphasized certain capitalist ideas such as enacting antitrust policies, encouraging foreign trade, reducing Egypt's deficit, and cutting the red tape that inhibits the emergence of new businesses. Yet it also envisioned a large role for the state in managing the economy, including price controls for commodities, "strict oversight" of markets, "increasing support for farmers to confront the ongoing rise in the high cost of the agricultural process," and "reconsidering" the Mubarak-era privatization of state-owned enterprises. And, of course, it contained a critical Islamic component, such as encouraging the establishment of Islamic financial institutions, discouraging interest-based banking, and using *zakat* (religiously mandated charity) and *waqf* (Islamic endowments) to combat poverty.[36] The policy prescriptions were thus often contradictory. How, for example, could one simultaneously "expand the social security umbrella to include all Egyptians" and "reduce the internal and external public debt at a rate of 15 percent annually," especially without any concrete plan for attracting or raising revenue?[37]

Most surprising, however, the Renaissance Project offered little insight into how the Brotherhood would actually build an Islamic state in Egypt. Its section on implementing an "Islamic reference" was quite vague: It envisioned a "national, constitutional state," as opposed to a "military or police state," and otherwise offered bromides on "empowering women" and "realizing the principle of citizenship and equality."[38] At other points, the project refers to "*sharī'ah* principles" as the guideposts for economic and social policy questions. But, again, what did any of this mean in practice?

On the day after Morsi's inauguration, I posed this question to Brotherhood secretary-general Mahmoud Hussein: What would change once *sharī'ah* was implemented? Very little, he replied. "The principles of *sharī'ah* don't necessarily interfere with the details of everyday life," he said. "But rather [*sharī'ah*] gives a governing framework."

I thought he misunderstood me, so I tried to clarify. What would change in terms of policy if *sharī'ah* were implemented? How, for example, would education policy change?

"We are not saying that we want to change," he said. "We are talking about values, not matters of education, industry, farming, et cetera. Because we are talking about a framework. *Sharī'ah* does not interfere with the details."[39]

I was surprised by his vagueness. Like every top Brotherhood leader, Hussein had struggled for decades to "implement *sharī'ah*" and even spent years in prison for this cause. Yet now that his organization had won the presidency, he apparently had no concept of an Islamist policy and even suggested that nothing might change at all.

A week later, I posed the same question to Guidance Office leader Abdel Rahman al-Barr, an al-Azhar–educated sheikh who was nicknamed the "Brotherhood's mufti" due to his prolific legal opinion-writing. But, again, I got nothing. "What will change is that the entire society will realize that it is cooperating in the path of achieving the highest values," he said. He added that when *sharī'ah* was implemented, people would obey the laws not like "a flock of sheep" but because the educational system had spread Islamic morals, such that people viewed following the law as the right thing to do.

I pressed al-Barr for specifics. But like Hussein, he wouldn't provide any and instead presented a utopian vision. When *sharī'ah* is implemented, al-Barr explained, Islamic preachers will be "given the opportunity to reach the hearts of the people," so that they would learn how to behave morally. Drugs, sexual abuse, financial corruption, and other societal ills will thus disappear.[40] What kinds of *sharī'ah*-compliant policies could be implemented to bring Egypt closer to this model of perfection? Al-Barr, Hussein, and the many

Brotherhood figures that I interviewed during this period seemed to have no idea whatsoever. And, again, the Renaissance Project didn't say either.

Yet the Brotherhood's lack of a specific policy agenda was consistent with Hassan al-Banna's vision. Recall that al-Banna sought to resist Western political and cultural domination by implementing Islam as an "all-embracing concept" in Muslim lands from the ground up. The Muslim Brotherhood was al-Banna's organizational vehicle for achieving this. The five-to-eight-year *tarbīah* process is the Brotherhood's method for indoctrinating Muslim Brothers according to Al-Banna's teachings. And its nationwide chain of command renders Muslim Brothers foot soldiers for promoting Islam as an "all-embracing concept" within the society, until the organization and its ideology achieve sufficient support for establishing an Islamic state.

Neither al-Banna nor Brotherhood leaders many decades later seemed to know what specific policies an Islamic state would actually implement, other than banning certain vices. But according to the Brotherhood's political theory, establishing an Islamic state in Egypt had one unambiguous precondition: Muslim Brothers, or those who embraced the Brotherhood's ideology, had to occupy key governmental positions. Whatever these Islamists did in power was inherently Islamic because they were Islamists, according to this tautological way of thinking.

So while the Brotherhood didn't know what its leaders would actually *do* in power, it knew that its leaders needed to *be* in power. And the Brotherhood was very prepared for advising Morsi on his governmental appointments: By the time that Morsi won the presidential election, the organization had already selected potential ministers and deputy ministers for every cabinet post, and it later drafted a list of gubernatorial candidates for Morsi to appoint in certain governorates.[41]

At the same time, however, the Brotherhood knew that it couldn't fill the top governmental posts with its people immediately. After all, in the week before his victory was announced, Morsi promised that he would appoint a non-Muslim Brother as his prime minister and that his first government would not be majority FJP. Moreover, despite its rapid political ascent, the Brotherhood was still inclined toward caution. One Brotherhood leader said that the organization's transition from parliamentary party to governing party was like going from driving a car to driving an oil tanker: The Brotherhood had to make its turns very slowly, because if it drove an oil tanker like it drove a car, then the whole project would capsize and burn.

So the Brotherhood's Renaissance Plan governmental team devised a strategy for Morsi, highlighting the ministries that the Brotherhood should control, as well as the ministries that could be reserved for other political and societal forces. The Brotherhood was particularly interested in controlling service-oriented ministries, such as Education, Transportation, Health, and Housing, as well as those ministries that were relevant to the production sectors, such as Agriculture, Industry, and Energy.

Meanwhile, for Morsi's first cabinet appointments, the Brotherhood preferred to leave the Ministry of Tourism to a non-Islamist, since appointing an Islamist would spark fears of alcohol and bikini bans and thus drive away tourism. It similarly anticipated appointing an official from al-Azhar to the Ministry of Religious Endowments, which seemed to be an attempt to assuage, if not co-opt, Egypt's foremost religious institution. And given the ongoing power struggle with the SCAF, the Brotherhood knew that it would be many years before it could appoint a Muslim Brother to run the Ministry of Defense or the Ministry of Military Production and that the Ministry of the Interior was similarly off-limits for now.[42]

As a result of all these considerations, Morsi's first round of appointments included only a few Muslim Brothers. The first appointment came on July 24, when Morsi named Hesham Qandil as his prime minister. It was a surprising choice: Qandil had served as minister of irrigation in the Sharaf and al-Ganzoury governments. And at fifty years old, Qandil was relatively unknown, as well as the youngest person to serve as premier since Nasser in 1954. Qandil's key advantage, however, was that he was not a Brotherhood member but was widely believed to be a Brotherhood sympathizer.[43] This enabled Morsi to keep his promise that he would not appoint a Muslim Brother to the premiership, while at the same time reassuring his base.

The following week, Morsi unveiled his first cabinet. Muslim Brothers occupied only five of thirty-five ministerial positions, but the specific ministries to which they were appointed is worth noting. The five ministries—Education, Housing, Information, Manpower, and Youth—weren't the most powerful, but they represented mechanisms through which the Brotherhood could bolster its work Islamizing Egyptian society. In other words, by holding the Education, Youth, Manpower, and Information Ministries, the Brotherhood was now better positioned to spread its message among students, youths, labor unions, and the general public, respectively, while holding the Housing Ministry enabled the Brotherhood to bolster its support within the country's most impoverished sectors.

Meanwhile, Morsi retained seven ministers from the previous government, including those who held the most sensitive positions. The ministers of foreign affairs, finance, and military production remained the same, and of course Tantawi remained defense minister. And as expected, the minister of religious endowments was appointed from al-Azhar. Morsi filled the rest of the ministries with technocrats.[44]

Ultimately, Morsi's first round of appointments gave the Egyptian government a slight Islamist hue but was far more status quo than revolutionary. And most important, since the SCAF's field marshal was still the defense minister, the appointments did nothing to resolve the ongoing power struggle between the elected president and the military.[45]

· · · · · · · ·

While crime rose throughout the country in the year that followed Egypt's January 2011 uprising, the situation became especially perilous in the Sinai Peninsula, which had already been a hotbed of militant activity since the mid-2000s. Sinai was (and remains) the transit point for smuggled weapons and goods from northern Africa into Hamas-controlled Gaza, and the flow of weapons into Sinai and Gaza increased considerably following the February 2011 Libyan uprising and the Libyan state's subsequent breakdown. Moreover, as a result of underdevelopment and repressive governance, the peninsula was a tinderbox: Armed Bedouin tribes battled security forces in northern Sinai, and jihadi groups gained a foothold.[46]

During the 2000s, Sinai-based jihadis staged a number of deadly attacks on Egyptian resorts along the Red Sea, often targeting Israeli tourists vacationing there. But in the post-Mubarak period, the jihadis turned their guns on the pipeline that carried Egyptian natural gas to Israel and Jordan and attacked Israel as well. The jihadis' apparent goal was sparking an international crisis between Egypt and Israel that would embarrass the SCAF and generate domestic pressure within Egypt for canceling the 1979 peace treaty with Israel.

The jihadis' strategy very nearly succeeded. On August 18, 2011, twelve militants crossed from Sinai into Israel, killing eight Israelis and wounding thirty. Amid the chaos, Israeli forces chased some of the attackers back across the Egyptian border into Sinai and accidentally killed five Egyptian soldiers in the counterattack.[47] The death of the Egyptian soldiers sparked widespread outrage within Egypt, and, even after an official Israeli apology, protests continued outside the Israeli embassy in Giza for weeks. The crisis reached its climax on September 9, when protesters stormed the embassy and came within one locked door of the Israeli diplomats. Egyptian commandos ultimately rescued the Israelis, narrowly averting a severe international incident that might have destroyed Egyptian–Israeli relations.[48]

A year later, Sinai was just as unstable, and Morsi's presidency added new complications to an already risky situation. How would he and the Muslim Brotherhood respond if a similar cross-border attack occurred on his watch? The Brotherhood's behavior during the 2011 incidents was hardly reassuring. Two days after the August attacks, the Brotherhood released a statement that predictably ignored the attacks on Israel and instead called on the SCAF to respond to the accidental killing of the Egyptian soldiers by banishing the "Zionist" ambassador from Cairo and "reconsidering" the Camp David Accords.[49] It then led demonstrations against Israel throughout the country. And, following the September attack on the Israeli embassy, the Brotherhood released a statement blaming the SCAF for "not taking a decisive stand" against Israel, which "led to the explosion of nationalist feelings in the souls of Egyptians."[50]

The Brotherhood's policy toward Sinai also wasn't reassuring. As a long-term solution, the Renaissance Project envisioned developing the peninsula through major mining, agricultural, and technological projects but contained no insights on how any of this would be achieved.[51] The Brotherhood also believed that the jihadis were less likely to commit violence under a Brotherhood president. Indeed, when Secretary of State Clinton asked Morsi during their July 14 meeting how he planned to prevent extremist groups from further destabilizing Sinai, the newly elected president was puzzled. "Why would they do that?" he said, according to Clinton. "We have an Islamist government now."[52]

The absurdity of Morsi's position became clear three weeks later. On August 5, masked gunmen attacked an Egyptian military checkpoint in northern Sinai, killing sixteen soldiers during a Ramadan *iftār* meal. The assailants then crossed the Israeli border, where the Israeli air force ultimately killed them. It was the deadliest assault on the Egyptian military in many years and represented the first major test of Morsi's presidency.[53] While the Brotherhood issued a conspiracy-theory-laden statement alleging that Israeli intelligence orchestrated the attack "to abort the revolution," Morsi's initial response was measured.[54] He declared that there was "no room to appease this treachery, this aggression, and this criminality" and visited the northern Sinai city of El-Arish with Tantawi and other security officials the following day.[55]

Morsi and the Brotherhood, however, were hardly the only ones with severe misconceptions about the Sinai-based jihadis. Two days after the attack, Egyptian General Intelligence Service (EGIS) chief Gen. Murad Muwafi told a Turkish news agency that security forces had information on the attack before it occurred and also knew the radical Islamist group behind the attack but failed to anticipate the timing. "We never imagined that a Muslim would kill his Muslim brothers during an *iftār* on Ramadan," Muwafi said.[56]

The following day, on August 8, Morsi fired Muwafi and replaced him with Rafaat Shehata. Meanwhile, Morsi also fired the governor of North Sinai and the head of the Republican Guard, which is tasked with protecting the president, and instructed Tantawi to fire the head of military police, Gen. Hamdy Badeen.[57]

These were incredibly bold moves. As with his July 8 decree that called for restoring the dissolved People's Assembly, Morsi was once again testing the extent of his executive authority. But this time his orders were fully enforced. In the wake of the Sinai attacks, Morsi seemingly had the political capital to hold top security personnel accountable. And he used that political capital to try to gain control over a security apparatus that was historically hostile toward the Brotherhood.

In this way, his appointment of Shehata as intelligence chief was especially deft. While all previous EGIS directors had been appointed from the military, Shehata was the first intelligence chief to be promoted from within EGIS itself. Shehata's appointment thus appeared to be Morsi's strategy for putting some distance between EGIS and the SCAF and making EGIS answerable to him. Shehata also had a long history of dealing with the Brotherhood's Palestinian sister movement, Hamas. He previously headed EGIS's delegation to Gaza from 2005 to 2006 and played a pivotal role in brokering the prisoner swap between Israel and Hamas in October 2011, through which Hamas released captured Israeli soldier Gilad Shalit in exchange for 1,027 Palestinians.[58]

Four days later, Morsi made an even bolder move. On August 12, he decapitated the SCAF, firing Tantawi and chief of staff Gen. Sami Anan and appointing Gen. Abdel Fattah al-Sisi and Gen. Sedky Sobhy as their respective replacements. At the same time, Morsi issued a constitutional declaration that officially annulled the SCAF's June constitutional declaration, delegated full executive and legislative authority to himself, and empowered himself to appoint a new Constituent Assembly if the existing one was prevented from fulfilling its duties.[59] In the weeks that followed, an additional seventy generals were replaced.[60]

How did Morsi pull this off? How did he fire Tantawi and Anan and then appoint their replacements so seamlessly? How did he get the other generals to accept his assertion of executive and legislative powers? I unfortunately cannot say for sure. The planning and negotiating that likely preceded this move involved very few people, some of whom now sit in prison, and none of them have ever discussed the move in detail on the record.

There is, however, a generally accepted, and quite plausible, theory regarding this move. Recall that throughout the post-Mubarak period, Brotherhood leaders met frequently with SCAF officials. During those meetings, top Brotherhood leaders realized that lower-level generals were dissatisfied with the SCAF's management of the country and also resented the top generals, whom they viewed as barriers to their own promotions. Indeed, Tantawi had served as defense minister since 1991, Anan had been chief of staff since 2005, and younger generals believed that their turn to lead Egypt's armed forces had come. The Brotherhood's leaders, according to this theory, thus sensed an opportunity to make a deal with these younger Egyptian generals behind Tantawi's back.

Meanwhile, the Brotherhood's leaders believed that General al-Sisi, who was the director of military intelligence and one of the SCAF's youngest members at fifty-seven, was relatively sympathetic to their organization's ideology. By all accounts, al-Sisi was a religious man, and his wife was rumored to wear a full-face covering that is a sign of Islamic orthodoxy in Egypt, rather than the headscarf that is common among Egyptian Muslim women.[61] Moreover, former Brotherhood Guidance Office leader Abbas al-Sisi was reportedly one of the general's close ancestors.[62]

So, according to this theory, the Brotherhood's leaders reached an agreement with al-Sisi and his colleagues: Morsi would fire Tantawi and Anan, among many of the older military figures, and replace them with al-Sisi and a slew of younger generals. In exchange, the military would accept Morsi's cancellation of the SCAF's June constitutional declaration and cede full authority over Egypt's political sphere—executive and legislative authority—to Morsi. However, Morsi would respect the military's autonomy over its own affairs, including its budgets and perquisites. This meant that the military still had significant economic power, as well as power over Egypt's foreign and defense policy. But Morsi now held executive and legislative power when it came to managing Egypt's domestic affairs.

Again, there is simply no way to prove that this is how Morsi's decapitation of the SCAF transpired. But it is highly unlikely that Morsi could have fired top military leaders, named their replacements, canceled the SCAF's constitutional declaration, and—most important—achieved the Egyptian military's acceptance of these moves without a prearrangement with al-Sisi and his colleagues. So while Morsi's firing of Tantawi and Anan was widely described as a countercoup, it was likely the product of a coup within the military itself that Morsi deftly exploited.

9 Power, Not Policy

On August 13, Egypt awoke to a new political reality. For the first time since his election in June, President Morsi held executive and legislative authority under Egyptian law. Neither the military nor the judiciary had challenged his constitutional declaration's assertion of these powers, and he also held the legal authority to appoint a new Constituent Assembly if the present one failed.

To be sure, the military still held significant economic power, as well as autonomy over its own affairs, which meant power over Egypt's foreign and defense policy. But the new military leadership kept a remarkably low profile and largely withdrew from Egypt's political scene. Unlike Tantawi, new defense minister al-Sisi made few public appearances and saluted Morsi as Egypt's head of state. His wife mingled with the wives of Brotherhood leaders and Islamist ministers, as if she was just another official's wife.[1] Top generals also fell in line. In meetings with foreign visitors, the generals admitted the SCAF's failures in governing and said that the military would now follow Morsi's lead as Egypt's democratically elected leader.

Having moved beyond the power struggle that defined Morsi's first months in office, the Brotherhood believed that it finally had the opportunity to put its imprint on the Egyptian polity. And since the Brotherhood had no real policy vision apart from stacking the Egyptian government with Muslim Brothers or like-minded officials, that's precisely what Morsi did: He focused primarily on appointing Muslim Brothers and Brotherhood sympathizers to top governmental positions, while doing precious little in the way of governing.

Morsi's first major appointment came on August 12, the day that he fired SCAF leaders Tantawi and Anan, when he named Judge Mahmoud Mekki as his vice president. The appointment was similar to Morsi's selection of Hesham Qandil as prime minister. By choosing Mekki, Morsi technically kept his campaign promise not to appoint an FJP member to the vice presidency but nonetheless appointed someone who was widely considered sympathetic to the Brotherhood's political mission. Indeed, the Brotherhood had urged Mekki to run for president in early 2012 and only decided to nominate its own presidential candidate after he (and another pro-Islamist judge, Hossam el-Gheriany) declined. Mekki also had a long history of cooperating with the Brotherhood politically: He was a prominent figure in the 2005–6 "independent judiciary movement," which protested Mubarak's interference with the judiciary during the 2005 parliamentary elections, and the Brotherhood mobilized during that period to support Mekki and his colleagues.[2]

But Mekki's appointment was also a lost opportunity for Morsi to fulfill his campaign promise to govern inclusively. After all, in the days before his electoral victory was announced, Morsi suggested that he would appoint multiple vice presidents, possibly including a woman and a Christian, and the Brotherhood's Guidance Office had urged him to appoint as many as five vice presidents so that he could include a Salafist in the mix.[3] And since the vice presidency was a totally powerless position, Morsi could have appointed a non-Islamist—or even multiple non-Islamists—without in any way undercutting the Brotherhood's Islamizing project.

Two weeks later, Morsi once again missed an opportunity to fulfill his promise of inclusive rule when he unveiled his presidential team. Of its twenty-one members, at least fifteen were Islamists or members of Islamist parties. This included three Nour Party leaders, including its chair, Emad Abdel Ghafour; former presidential candidate and Islamist thinker Selim al-Awa; and Ahmed Omran, a leader of al-Gamaa al-Islamiya's political party.

Brotherhood affiliates constituted the plurality of Morsi's presidential team. This included Brotherhood businessman Husain al-Kazzaz, who was a prominent figure within al-Shater's Renaissance Project team; FJP vice-chair Essam el-Erian and second vice-chair Rafik Habib, who was also one of the presidential team's two Christian members; female Brotherhood politician Omaima Kamel; and two Guidance Office members—Essam el-Haddad, who served as the Guidance Office's point man on foreign relations and effectively became Morsi's national security adviser, and Mohi Hamed, who advised Morsi on workers' affairs.[4] Muslim Brothers similarly filled many of the presidential palace's other positions, such as foreign policy adviser (Khaled al-Qazzaz) and presidential spokesman (Yasser Aly).

Morsi once again demonstrated the narrowness of his emerging regime when he announced his gubernatorial appointments on September 5. Of

ten new governors, four were Muslim Brothers, including two former Guidance Office members, Kafr el-Sheikh governor Saad al-Husseini and Menou-
fiya governor Mohamed Ali Bishr. Another appointee, Osama Kamel, was
a prominent Brotherhood sympathizer who had affiliated with the Brotherhood during professional syndicate elections, and Morsi appointed Brotherhood leader Hassan al-Prince as the deputy governor of Alexandria.[5] For the
Brotherhood, these governorates represented starting points for implementing its Renaissance Project, and the day after their appointment, the Guidance Office reportedly met to draft a work plan for the new governors.[6]

Meanwhile, four of Morsi's remaining five gubernatorial appointees were
retired military or police generals, as were most of the seventeen other governors Morsi kept in office. This was consistent with the Mubarak-era pattern
of appointing retired security officials to governorships and signaled Morsi's
attempt to make peace with the security services rather than reform them.
More to the point, by stacking the governorships with retired security officials
and Muslim Brothers almost exclusively, Morsi demonstrated yet again that
he had no intention of honoring his campaign promise to rule inclusively.

To be sure, Morsi was completely within his rights as Egypt's elected
president to appoint whomever he wanted. He wasn't legally bound to keep
his campaign promise of ruling inclusively. And his appointment of Muslim
Brothers to top positions was hardly surprising: Leaders routinely appoint
members from their own parties to implement their policy visions.

But what was Morsi's policy vision? More than two months after taking
office, he still didn't appear to have one. All of Morsi's moves—the failed attempt to call back Parliament, the sacking of Tantawi and Anan, the constitutional declaration asserting total executive and legislative authority, and
the various rounds of appointments—were political in nature. Yet he offered
nothing in the way of an economic, health care, or education policy.

• • • • • • • •

In lieu of a policy vision, the Brotherhood had developed a hundred-day plan
prior to Morsi's inauguration that highlighted five main areas for immediate
improvement: public safety, traffic congestion, bread prices, public sanitation,
and fuel provision. A week after Morsi took office, the Brotherhood's General Shura Committee commanded its cadres nationwide to assist Morsi in
executing the hundred-day plan, apparently assuming that the same Brotherhood organizational infrastructure that helped Morsi win the presidency
could similarly help him implement public policy.[7] In turn, Brotherhood

cadres were suddenly picking up trash from the streets, organizing security patrols, and trying to solve traffic congestion by directing cars in the streets. Yet these efforts only reinforced the Brotherhood's utter unpreparedness for policymaking, since solving Egypt's urban traffic congestion, for example, required building new roads—not dispatching youths to stand in traffic circles. And many Egyptians found the fact that Muslim Brothers were behaving like police officers disconcerting: They had elected Morsi as their president but never asked for a Brotherhood takeover of their streets.

Meanwhile, from the presidential palace Morsi implemented a few policies to drive his hundred-day plan forward. He instituted stiff penalties for fuel smuggling and removed roadblocks that impeded traffic on certain thoroughfares. But when the hundred-day mark came, none of the five goals of Morsi's hundred-day plan had been achieved. Fuel shortages had worsened, bringing longer electricity blackouts and water cutoffs, and grew more severe shortly after the hundred-day mark passed, at which point Egypt had to suspend its natural gas exports. Traffic still congested major cities, especially when public transportation workers went on strike. And the long lines for bread continued.[8]

As a result, Egypt's economy was still in poor shape. From the start of the uprising in January 2011 until the start of Morsi's presidency in July 2012, Egypt's cash reserves had fallen from approximately $35 billion to $14.4 billion, and it was estimated that Egypt needed $9 billion to avoid economic calamity.[9] So Morsi spent much of his first hundred days trying to attract international donors and loans to boost Egypt's reserves, including two visits to Saudi Arabia, as well as visits to China and Europe.

But none of these trips yielded the requisite aid. Saudi Arabia had already deposited $1 billion in Egypt's Central Bank in May 2012, just prior to Morsi's election, and it appeared hesitant to send more. The Saudis distrusted the Brotherhood, given its explicit regional ambitions, and Morsi's outreach to Iran bolstered the Saudis' skepticism.[10]

Morsi's investment-focused trip to China was only slightly more successful. Arriving in Beijing with a delegation of Egyptian businessmen, Morsi discussed a variety of potential projects during his meeting with Chinese president Hu Jintao, including constructing a high-speed rail line between Cairo and Alexandria and building a fleet of fishing vessels. But Morsi's ultimate takeaway was small: China offered a grant of $71 million, payable over a three-year period.[11] To supplement these efforts, Morsi opened negotiations with the IMF in late August, seeking a $4.8 billion loan. But given the types of painful subsidy forms that the IMF requested as conditions, the negotiations stalled for months.[12]

Ultimately Morsi found two supporters: Qatar, which pledged $2 billion to Egypt during the emir's visit to Cairo in mid-August, and Turkey, which offered a $1 billion loan during Morsi's visit to Ankara in late September.[13] But Egypt's cash reserves only ticked upward slightly, from $14.4 billion in July to $15.4 billion in October, as Morsi's new spending offset Qatar and Turkey's generosity. During his first week in office, Morsi raised government salaries by 15 percent and increased social security payments, costing the Egyptian treasury an additional $414 million.[14] One hundred days after Morsi took office, Egypt remained at risk of economic calamity.

• • • • • • • •

Of course, the policy challenges that Morsi confronted during his early months in office were not his fault. He was not responsible for the country's economic troubles or its declining domestic security, both of which were the consequence of nearly two years of political uncertainty, as well as the incompetence of successive SCAF-appointed governments. But as Egypt's elected president, Morsi was now responsible for charting a way forward, and yet his government appeared aimless. By the hundred-day mark, few of his promises had been met. And to make matters worse, Morsi and the Brotherhood were in utter denial: The hundred-day plan, they claimed, was a success, and the revolution was moving forward.

Morsi chose to make this pronouncement during the annual October 6 holiday ceremonies, which commemorate Egypt's opening offensive during the 1973 Arab–Israeli War. In a rambling speech at Cairo Stadium that lasted nearly two hours, Morsi highlighted the hundred-day plan's five goals, claiming that his government had achieved 80 percent of his bread-provision goals, 40 percent of his public sanitation goals, 85 percent of his fuel goals, 70 percent of his security goals, and 60 percent of his goals regarding traffic improvement. These assertions, of course, were grounded in dubious metrics, and watchdog groups calculated a far lower success rate. But the Brotherhood-heavy crowd went crazy anyway, cheering through his entire address as if the event were a pep rally instead of an official ceremony.[15]

Beyond the total disconnect between Morsi's self-congratulatory declarations and reality, Morsi's speech was controversial for another reason. The president invited Tarek al-Zomor, an al-Gamaa al-Islamiya leader who spent three decades in prison for participating in President Anwar Sadat's assassination exactly thirty-one years earlier, to attend the October 6 ceremonies. For many Egyptians, al-Zomor's presence at an event commemorating the 1973 War—which Egyptians consider among Sadat's greatest achievements—was quite offensive, and the Sadat family later expressed its outrage.[16]

So after mostly steering clear of protest activity to give Morsi a chance during his first hundred days, leftist groups announced on his 101st day that they would organize demonstrations in multiple governorates on Friday, October 12. The protests carried a list of specific demands, including forming an inclusive Constituent Assembly, purging state institutions of corruption, bringing those responsible for killing revolutionaries to justice, raising the minimum wage, instituting a maximum wage, and developing policies for addressing "the deterioration of health, education, housing, and infrastructure services."[17] Two days before the protests were set to commence, a court acquitted twenty-four former Egyptian officials of orchestrating the February 2, 2011, Battle of the Camel attacks on Tahrir Square.[18] The activists highlighted the acquittals as additional evidence that little had changed under Morsi and intensified their protest calls.

The sudden emergence of anti-Morsi protests unnerved the Brotherhood. After eight-plus decades as Egypt's preeminent opposition movement, it had never been the target of antigovernment protests before. So in a brazen attempt to overwhelm the oppositionists' demonstrations, the FJP released a statement criticizing the Battle of the Camel verdict and commanded its cadres to join the October 12 demonstrations.[19]

It was a disastrous decision by the Brotherhood. As leftists chanted anti-Morsi slogans, Muslim Brothers charged into the square and tore down a podium. In response, many more leftist activists rushed to the square to support their comrades, and over a hundred people were injured in the ensuing clashes.

Embarrassed by these incidents, the Brotherhood's official Twitter account initially claimed that no Muslim Brothers were in Tahrir Square. But this was quickly discredited: Protesters located two buses that the Brotherhood used to transport its members to the square and promptly burned them.[20]

The Brotherhood's promise of pluralism never looked so dishonest. At the height of its power, it couldn't tolerate a relatively small Tahrir Square protest against Morsi.

• • • • • • •

In its many official statements on Egypt, the Obama administration repeatedly urged Morsi to govern inclusively. But two months after he took office, it was clear that he had no intention of doing so. His presidential team was overwhelmingly Islamist. His prime minister and vice president were widely viewed as Brotherhood sympathizers. And his first round of government appointments included a handful of Muslim Brothers but largely maintained the status quo: Former generals headed most of the governorates, and technocrats headed most of the ministries. Meanwhile, through his August 12 constitutional declaration, Morsi asserted total executive and legislative authority, thereby giving himself more legal power than Mubarak ever possessed.

At the same time, the Brotherhood used its political power to advance its intolerant ideology in other spheres. In early August, the Brotherhood-dominated Shura Council appointed Abdel-Nasser Salama as editor in chief of *Al-Ahram*, Egypt's largest state newspaper. Salama's selection shocked many within the journalism community because he had lost his column in 2010 for writing anti-Christian articles. The Shura Council's appointment of Gamal Abdel-Rahim to edit *Al-Gomhuria*, another major state newspaper, fell in the same category. Abdel-Rahim reportedly shut down a conference on religious freedoms in 2008 and called for the murder of a prominent Baha'i activist in 2009.[21]

Moreover, Morsi's early foreign policy moves were hardly reassuring. He refused to have any direct contact with Israeli officials, even as the situation on the Egyptian–Israeli border became tense following the August 5 Sinai attack.[22] And in late August, Morsi became the first Egyptian president in thirty-three years to visit Iran, which had broken off relations with Egypt after the 1979 peace treaty with Israel and later named a street in Tehran after Sadat's assassin.

The Obama administration, however, was hesitant to pressure Morsi because it feared his response. If the administration pushed Morsi on his foreign policy, the administration worried that the Brotherhood leader would rally his base around an even more hostile foreign policy. The administration similarly worried that pushing Morsi on his domestic policies would make the Brotherhood view Washington as its enemy. And there was one thing that practically everyone agreed on: Egypt was too important for Washington to make an enemy of its newly elected government.

The big mistake in the administration's thinking, however, was that the Brotherhood was even more afraid of Washington. After all, the Brotherhood's literature depicts the West as one of its sworn enemies, which works tirelessly to prevent Islamists from achieving power. The Brotherhood believed that the West supported Mubarak for exactly this reason and that Washington was therefore hell-bent on inhibiting its success now that it was in power. Yet the Obama administration didn't appreciate the depth of the Brotherhood's insecurities and was wary of testing the Brotherhood in any event. After a year and a half of tumult, it wanted to manage its Egypt policy cautiously. And in the administration's view, that meant winning Morsi's trust through "engagement" and trying to influence his foreign and domestic policies thereafter.

The administration focused on helping Morsi economically. The Brotherhood's Renaissance Project, after all, indicated a strong interest in economic development, and the Obama administration believed that it could demonstrate its goodwill—both to Morsi and the Egyptian people more broadly—by assisting these efforts. Unlike the oil-rich Gulf states, however, Washington couldn't simply send a few extra billion dollars. On Capitol Hill there was little interest in sending more money to anyone and especially to an Islamist government.

Instead the Obama administration encouraged investment in Egypt on two tracks. First, it strongly supported the Morsi government's pursuit of the $4.8 billion IMF loan. Second, in September, it assembled the largest-ever business delegation to Egypt, including over a hundred representatives of major American corporations.[23] "We hope that this delegation returns home with a very simple message: Egypt is open for business," Deputy Secretary of State Thomas Nides said on September 9 after the delegation met with Prime Minister Qandil.[24] It was an odd spectacle: Washington was trying to build relations with Morsi's government by boosting its economic image to the international business community—without compelling Morsi to do anything in return.

The effort rapidly exploded in the administration's face. On the evening of September 11, the delegation gathered in an upscale Cairo hotel ballroom for the concluding press conference of its trip, where it affirmed yet again that Egypt was "open for business." At that very moment, a mob of Salafists and youth protesters attacked the US embassy in downtown Cairo, rallying against an obscure Internet video that criticized the Prophet Muhammad.[25] The protesters scaled the embassy's walls, tore town the American flag, and raised a black jihadi flag in its place before Egyptian security forces finally controlled the situation.[26] Meanwhile, the Brotherhood's official Twitter account declared its support for the attack, tweeting that "Egyptians rise up to support Muhammad in front of the American Embassy."[27]

The incident coincided with the deadly terrorist attack on the US consulate in Benghazi, Libya, in which four Americans, including Ambassador

Chris Stevens, were murdered, and Washington expected Morsi to respond to the Egyptian situation immediately. After all, the administration had gone to great lengths to legitimize Morsi and drum up support for foreign investment in Egypt. But more to the point, denouncing an embassy attack within one's country is what a responsible leader does.

Instead, Morsi responded provocatively. The following day, his government called on the Obama administration to "take a firm position" against the producers of the film that portrayed the Prophet Muhammad negatively. Morsi's spokesman further announced that the president had instructed the Egyptian embassy in Washington "to take all possible legal procedures against those who are trying to damage relations and dialogue among countries and people" and alluded to the attack on the US embassy in Cairo only implicitly, stating, "Egypt is responsible for protecting private and public property, diplomatic missions and embassies of all states."[28] Meanwhile, the Muslim Brotherhood announced protests in all governorates against "the abuse of religious beliefs and defaming of the Messenger of Allah, peace be upon him."[29]

Morsi's behavior incensed the administration. When asked that evening about the situation in Egypt during an interview with Telemundo, Obama responded, "I don't think we would consider them an ally. But we don't consider them an enemy."[30] Then, during a twenty-minute phone call later that night, Obama sternly warned Morsi that US–Egyptian relations would be jeopardized if Egyptian authorities didn't take a firmer stand against the attack on the embassy.[31]

Obama's comments doubting Cairo's friendship greatly unnerved the Brotherhood, which scrambled to control the diplomatic fallout the following day. Morsi appeared on national television and said it was Egyptians' "religious duty to protect our guests and those who come to us from outside our nation," adding that those who attacked the US embassy "do not represent any of us." Morsi further expressed his condolences for Ambassador Stevens's murder in Libya and vowed to bring charges against those who attacked the embassy in Cairo.[32] Meanwhile, Deputy Supreme Guide al-Shater wrote a letter to the *New York Times* saying that the Brotherhood did "not hold the American government or its citizens responsible for acts of the few that abuse the laws protecting freedom of expression."[33]

These responses satisfied the administration. It believed that Obama's tough talk with Morsi, which White House officials later termed the "woodshed call," worked: The Brotherhood deescalated the crisis and thus demonstrated that it valued its relationship with Washington. Morsi's instincts might not be pro-American, the thinking went, but when his commitment to the broader US–Egyptian partnership was tested, Morsi passed.

Still, Morsi's slow response to the embassy attack quashed earlier deliberations within the administration about Obama meeting Morsi on the sidelines of the UN General Assembly in New York two weeks later. After all, Obama was in the middle of a reelection campaign, and his administration's response to the Benghazi attacks was quickly becoming a significant political controversy. Nonetheless, Morsi was treated like a VIP in New York. The Clinton Global Initiative hosted him for a talk, and former President Bill Clinton personally interviewed Morsi before an elite audience. Secretary of State Hillary Clinton also met with Morsi at the UN meeting, during which Morsi vowed to protect US diplomatic missions and keep the peace treaty with Israel. A State Department official described the meeting as "very warm and relaxed"—a sign that Washington had moved beyond its September 11 crisis with the Brotherhood.[34]

• • • • • • • •

The Islamic Resistance Movement, better known by its acronym Hamas, is the Palestinian Muslim Brotherhood. While Hamas is organizationally independent of the Egyptian Brotherhood and, for example, doesn't take its marching orders from the Brotherhood's supreme guide, it shares the Brotherhood's two most basic components: its hierarchical organization and its Islamizing mission.

Naturally, Hamas, which is a US-designated terrorist organization, viewed the Muslim Brotherhood's post-Mubarak rise as a strategic boon.[35] The Mubarak regime cooperated with Israel in enforcing a blockade on Hamas-controlled Gaza, and it backed Israel during the 2008–9 Gaza war. But now that a Muslim Brother governed Egypt, Hamas anticipated greater freedom of movement. And Morsi, who had been the Guidance Office leader responsible for communicating with Hamas, sent every signal that he intended to be Hamas's partner.[36] During his first month in office, Morsi met with top Hamas leaders at the presidential palace twice, reversing Egypt's decades-long policy of treating the Palestinian Authority as the sole official Palestinian representative.[37]

While Morsi's power struggle with the Egyptian military prevented him from lifting the Gaza blockade during his first months in office, his presidency nonetheless provided Hamas with unprecedented diplomatic cover. Hamas's leaders believed a Brotherhood president would never side with Israel against another Brotherhood movement. Morsi's victory thus granted Hamas greater freedom of action against Israel: From June through October 2012, 465 rockets and mortars were fired from Gaza, according to the Israel Security Agency. Israel occasionally returned fire or launched counterstrikes, but its concerns about how Egypt might respond were a major factor in deterring a large-scale Israeli response.[38]

But in November 2012, hostilities between Gaza and Israel intensified. On November 5, Israeli forces killed an unarmed man caught crawling along the Gaza–Israel border fence, whom Israeli soldiers believed was an attacker. Five days later, Palestinians fired an antitank missile at an Israeli military jeep near the border, wounding four soldiers, and six Palestinians were killed in the Israeli reprisals. Then, during the next forty-eight hours, Palestinian groups fired over one hundred rockets at Israel.[39]

By November 14, the gloves were off. Israel launched Operation Pillar of Defense, killing Hamas military commander Ahmed al-Jabari and launching a series of air strikes, while hundreds of rockets fell on Israel from Gaza. Predictably, Israel's offensive set off protests in Cairo, and Morsi immediately recalled Egypt's ambassador to Israel. It was a relatively small gesture, however, since Mubarak had done the same thing to calm domestic fury during the second Palestinian intifada in the early 2000s.[40] Meanwhile, as Washington and the UN scrambled to encourage a cease-fire, all eyes were on Egypt. Would Morsi fulfill Egypt's traditional role of handling cease-fire negotiations between Israel and Hamas? Or would Morsi use this crisis to downgrade relations with Israel, as he and the Brotherhood had long promised?

Predictably, the Brotherhood urged Morsi in the latter direction. When Israel announced its offensive, the Brotherhood called for "sever[ing] diplomatic and trade relations with this usurper entity," so that the Egyptian government can "begin to be a role model for Arabs and Muslims who keep relations with this entity." The Brotherhood then announced mass protests against Israel that Friday.[41]

Egypt's national security establishment, however, urged Morsi to respond cautiously. After all, even before Israel began its offensive, EGIS had been working for days to negotiate a cease-fire between Hamas and Israel, and it advised Morsi to let it continue this work.[42] Washington also intervened with Morsi. Obama called Morsi on November 14, immediately after Morsi withdrew Egypt's ambassador from Tel Aviv, and emphasized "Egypt's central role in preserving regional security."[43]

Ultimately, Morsi split the difference between these two competing pressures. On the one hand, he stood firmly with Hamas. During a fiery speech at a suburban Cairo mosque during Friday prayers, he warned Israel that it would "pay a high price for this assault."[44] He also dispatched Prime Minister Qandil to Gaza, which forced Israel to temporarily halt its fire. Palestinian groups used Qandil's visit as cover for shooting an additional fifty rockets at Israel.[45] Yet on the other hand, Morsi authorized EGIS to negotiate a cease-fire arrangement between Israel and Hamas. This enabled the Egyptian government to work toward a resolution without forcing Morsi to deal with Israel directly, which was an ideological red line for him and the Brotherhood.[46]

Meanwhile, as the fighting intensified over the next few days, Washington aggressively engaged Morsi to iron out the terms of a cease-fire. Of course, the administration had significant concerns about how a Brotherhood president might respond to a conflict between Israel and Hamas in Gaza, but Morsi assuaged the administration's fears and cooperated. During the eight-day conflict, Obama and Morsi spoke on the phone six times, sometimes multiple times a day, and senior administration aides later told the *New York Times* that Obama "felt they were making a connection" during these calls.[47]

Morsi played his cards extremely well. Ideologically, he conceded nothing. He never dealt with Israeli officials directly, he showcased his pro-Hamas sympathies in his public statements, and he permitted Hamas leader Khaled Meshal to declare victory from Cairo when the cease-fire went into effect on November 21.

At the same time, by authorizing EGIS to negotiate the cease-fire, Morsi got the credit for brokering it. At home, Egyptian military and security officials hailed "our president" for his deft handling of the crisis.[48] Meanwhile, Obama administration officials lavished Morsi with praise, telling the *New York Times* that he possessed an "engineer's precision" and touting his "pragmatic confidence."[49] From the administration's perspective, the Gaza crisis affirmed that, even despite his ideological inclinations, Morsi would preserve the 1979 peace treaty with Israel. Morsi might be an Islamist, the thinking went, but when push came to shove, he behaved like a leader, not an ideologue.

10 The Power Grab

On the evening of November 21, 2012, Mohamed Morsi was a highly respected world leader, widely praised for his pragmatism during the Gaza conflict. But within twenty-four hours, that perception radically changed.

On the afternoon of November 22, Morsi suddenly issued a new constitutional declaration granting himself virtually unchecked power. Of course, he had already asserted total executive and legislative authority through his August 12 declaration, which coincided with his firing of SCAF leaders Tantawi and Anan. But the new declaration removed the last legal check on his power by placing all of his presidential actions above judicial scrutiny.

Specifically the declaration mandated that all of Morsi's constitutional declarations were "final and binding and cannot be appealed by any way or to any entity" and ruled that all pending legal challenges to his previous declarations were "annulled." It further empowered Morsi to appoint a new prosecutor-general to a four-year term, thereby circumventing laws that protected the prosecutor from presidential interference. Finally, the declaration empowered Morsi to "take the necessary actions and measures to protect the country and the goals of the revolution"—a broad clause that effectively granted him the authority to do anything.

The declaration directly impinged on the judiciary's authority in two additional ways. First, it mandated that the judicial branch reopen investigations and prosecutions into cases of murder, attempted murder, and wounding of revolutionaries by "anyone who held a political or executive position under the former regime." Insofar as this was a presidential order to the judicial branch, it blatantly contradicted the principle of judicial independence. Second, Morsi's constitutional declaration asserted that "no judicial body" could dissolve the Shura Council, which was the Brotherhood-dominated upper house of Parliament, or the Constituent Assembly, which the Brotherhood-dominated People's Assembly had appointed before it was dissolved in June.[1]

Those who defended Morsi's declaration often focused on this final aspect of it. Morsi, they argued, was merely trying to prevent the judiciary from dissolving the Constituent Assembly, which was drafting Egypt's new constitution. After all, in October, the SCC started reviewing dozens of lawsuits against the assembly, which alleged that it had been selected unconstitutionally and did not sufficiently reflect the diversity of Egyptian society. And given that the judiciary had ruled to dissolve the first Constituent Assembly in April and the People's Assembly in June, Morsi had every reason to believe that the SCC would now dissolve the current Constituent Assembly as well.[2]

Yet this defense of Morsi's constitutional declaration, which the Brotherhood and its apologists offered repeatedly during the ensuing crisis, ignores some inconvenient facts. For starters, while the judiciary was an institutional barrier to Morsi and the Brotherhood in many instances, it was not an implacable enemy. The judiciary, after all, had supervised every post-Mubarak election, which the Brotherhood's candidates won overwhelmingly. The judiciary also administered Morsi's presidential oath. And contrary to the Brotherhood's depiction of the judiciary as a pro-Mubarak entity, the judiciary contained many individuals who were sympathetic to the Brotherhood, including the judges whom Morsi appointed as his vice president and justice minister. Moreover, in virtually every battle that Morsi fought with the judiciary during his five-month presidency, *he* had been the instigator: Morsi's July 8 decree reinstating Parliament directly contravened the SCC's ruling that the People's Assembly elections had been conducted unconstitutionally, and his previous attempt to fire the prosecutor-general in October similarly affronted judicial independence.

More to the point, however, Morsi's November 22 constitutional declaration didn't merely prevent the judiciary from dissolving the Constituent Assembly—it prevented the judges from overruling all of his edicts as well. It was, in other words, an assertion of absolute legal power, rendering Morsi a dictator and shattering his democratic legitimacy in the eyes of many Egyptians.

As a result, Morsi's constitutional declaration ignited immediate, massive, and often violent protests. Within hours, thousands of protesters descended on Tahrir Square, where they battled security forces, and demonstrators attacked Brotherhood offices in governorates across the country. Within the first two days, over a hundred protesters were injured.[3] The chaos evoked scenes from the January 2011 uprising, as police once again used brutal force to quell antigovernment protests, and protesters quickly shifted their attention from rejecting the constitutional declaration to demanding Morsi's ouster. As the anti-Morsi mobilization picked up steam, non-Islamist political figures rushed to support the anti-Morsi movement, and three prominent figures—former IAEA chief Mohamed ElBaradei, former foreign minister Amr Moussa, and prominent Nasserist politician Hamdeen Sabahi—declared the formation of the National Salvation Front (NSF), refusing to negotiate until Morsi withdrew his declaration.

Amid this exploding crisis, Morsi added fuel to the fire. At a rally outside the presidential palace on the day after he released his edict, Morsi told his supporters that his power grab was necessary to combat the revolution's enemies. "There are weevils eating away at Egypt's nation," he said. "It is my duty to move forward with the goals of the revolution and eliminate all of the obstacles which are linked to the past that we hate." Meanwhile, he belittled the opposition, which included many revolutionaries who had supported his presidential candidacy only a few months earlier. "Those who protest me are just a small few," he said, "and they are spiteful of the revolution."[4]

As Morsi chose confrontation over compromise, the crisis worsened considerably. On November 24, the Supreme Council of the Judiciary called Morsi's power grab "an unprecedented attack on judicial independence," and the Judges Club declared a nationwide strike.[5] Meanwhile, Morsi's political base narrowed: Three of his non-Islamist presidential advisers resigned in protest of his edict, as clashes continued throughout the country.[6]

Seeking to end the crisis, Morsi met with representatives from the Supreme Council of the Judiciary on Monday, November 26, and agreed to certain restrictions on his constitutional declaration but otherwise refused to amend its text. The following day, thousands of anti-Morsi protesters descended on Tahrir Square, calling for Morsi's fall. Clashes with security forces continued for days as the protesters declared an open sit-in, and downtown Cairo was a battle zone once again.[7]

· · · · · · · ·

In the wake of Morsi's constitutional declaration, the Brotherhood's leadership backed the president completely but appeared hesitant to escalate the crisis any further. It canceled its plans to demonstrate in support of Morsi on November 27 in northern Cairo, saying that it hoped to avoid bloody confrontations with the anti-Morsi protesters. The Guidance Office, it seems, had learned from the experience of October 12, when its call for protests led to violent clashes with leftist protesters in Tahrir Square—a huge embarrassment at the time.

But as a result of the sudden and massive anti-Morsi mobilization, the Brotherhood's youth cadres were growing restless. In their view, the Brotherhood's victory in every single post-Mubarak election indicated that *it* had majority support and that *it* represented the authentic will of the Egyptian people. By contrast, the cadres believed that Morsi's non-Islamist opponents represented a small minority—a minority that was now trying to remove Morsi via demonstrations because it could never beat him at the ballot box. So rather than standing pat, the cadres wanted the Brotherhood to launch an aggressive response—to call for a full mobilization that would overwhelm the anti-Morsi protests and prove to the world that Egyptians largely supported Morsi.

Indeed, the Brotherhood's youths were steeling for a fight and painting the crisis in life-and-death terms. "When [the] future of Egypt is in the balance, . . . we are more than willing to pay for it with our lives not votes," Brotherhood youth Gehad el-Haddad, the son of a Morsi adviser, wrote on Twitter. On Brotherhood Facebook groups, members called for "cleansing" the country of Morsi's critics, singling out prominent Christians and the NSF's leaders as foremost targets. Meanwhile, Khairat al-Shater's son accused Morsi's opponents of starting a "civil war" and ominously warned that "the Brotherhood has a surplus of manhood."[8]

Feeling pressure from below, the Guidance Office relented. It called for a "million-man march to support [electoral] legitimacy and *sharī'ah*," which would take place on Saturday, December 1.[9] With this formulation, the Brotherhood pushed Egypt's already severe polarization to the brink: Egyptians either stood with Morsi and with *sharī'ah*, or they were opponents of Islam. And it was a clear signal to the Brotherhood's cadres: They weren't just fighting for their president but for their religion.

Meanwhile, the Brotherhood took its fight to the Constituent Assembly, where its members suddenly announced that they would rush to complete a draft of the constitution within two days. On the evening of November 29, Morsi endorsed these efforts. During a televised interview, he announced that he would call a referendum on the constitution two weeks after the Constituent Assembly completed its work and would relinquish legislative authority to the Shura Council once the new constitution was ratified.[10]

The Constituent Assembly, however, was paralyzed. A few weeks earlier,

disagreements between its Islamist and non-Islamist members brought deliberations to a standstill. Many of the non-Islamist members withdrew on
November 18, accusing the assembly's Islamists of "writing a constitution for
an Islamist state rather than for a national-unity state."[11] That effectively left
the constitution-drafting process in the hands of two groups: the Brotherhood and the Salafists. And now that the Constituent Assembly was moving
full-steam ahead without its non-Islamist members, the end product was a
theocratic, nonpluralistic constitution.

The new constitution expanded the role of *shari'ah* significantly. While
the second article of the previous constitution declared that "Islam is the religion of the state" and "principles of Islamic *shari'ah* are the principal source
of legislation," the new constitution added an article (219) that defined the
"principles of Islamic *shari'ah*" as including "general evidence, foundational
rules, rules of jurisprudence, and credible sources accepted in Sunni doctrines and by the larger community." This effectively narrowed the range of
shari'ah interpretations to which legislators could refer. In addition, whereas
the previous constitution maintained that "the Egyptian people are part of
the Arab nation," the new draft constitution added that they were also part
of the "Islamic nation," thereby undermining the citizenship of non-Muslim
Egyptians.

The constitution also carved out a much greater role for the state in enforcing religious doctrines. Article 11 authorized the state to "safeguard ethics,
public morality, and public order and foster a high level of education and of
religious and patriotic values," while Article 44 prohibited the "insult or abuse
of all religious messengers and prophets." And Article 4 provided an official
role for al-Azhar, empowering the Sunni institution to give its opinion on all
matters pertaining to *shari'ah*.

The new constitution draft also limited the rights of religious minorities
significantly. While Article 3 permitted Christians and Jews to be governed
by their respective personal status laws, it was noticeably silent on the rights
of other groups, such as Baha'is and Shiites, who frequently suffer discrimination in Egypt. Article 43, which upheld the "freedom to practice religious
rites and to establish places of worship for the divine religions," similarly
ignored these groups, since "divine religions" referred only to Sunni Islam,
Christianity, and Judaism. And Article 33, which prohibits discrimination,
dropped the words "on the basis of sex, origin, religion and creed."[12]

Finally, the new constitution draft contained three new clauses that significantly undermined Christians' rights. Article 42 dropped previous con-

stitutional language prohibiting forced evacuations within Egypt. As Samuel Tadros of the Hudson Institute noted, this clause followed the forced evacuations of Coptic Christians in four instances since Mubarak's ouster. Article 132 removed the "protection of national unity" from the president's duties—a clause that had previously referred to the president's role in safeguarding Muslim–Christian unity. And Article 212 created the "Supreme Authority for Endowment Affairs," which was empowered to "regulate, supervise, and monitor public and private endowments." This placed church finances under the control of Egypt's Islamist government.[13]

Meanwhile, to win the military's cooperation in facilitating the draft constitution's passage, the Islamists satisfied two of the brass's key demands. First, the constitution granted the military autonomy over its own affairs. Article 195 maintained that the defense minister must be a member of the armed forces "appointed from among its officers." Article 197 established the National Defense Council to oversee the military's budgets and mandated that high-ranking military officials would fill at least eight of the council's fifteen seats, thereby preventing civilian oversight of military budgets under a new Parliament. And Article 198 established the military judiciary as "an independent judiciary," allowing civilians to be tried before military courts for "crimes that harm the armed forces."

Second, the new constitution granted the military substantial influence— and perhaps even veto power—over the conduct of war. Article 146 stated that the president cannot "declare war, or send the armed forces outside state territory, except after consultation with the National Defense Council and the approval of the House of Representatives with a majority of its members." The text also equalized the defense minister and the president during wartime: Article 146 called the president the "supreme commander of the armed forces," while Article 195 declared the defense minister the "commander-in-chief of the armed forces."[14] And to further ensure the military's cooperation in the rushed constitution-drafting process, the Constituent Assembly voted to approve these military-related articles before all others.

On December 1, Morsi announced that a constitutional referendum would be held two weeks later. Meanwhile, hundreds of thousands of Muslim Brothers and Salafists demonstrated near Cairo University to support the constitution.[15]

The following morning, the SCC was scheduled to rule on the constitutionality of the Constituent Assembly. Islamists gathered outside the courthouse in downtown Cairo, hoping to pressure the judges to approve the assembly and validate the upcoming referendum. But the Islamists overplayed their hand. The judges claimed that they felt physically threatened and suspended the court's activities indefinitely for the first time in Egypt's history.

While the Brotherhood accused the judges of manufacturing the controversy, noting that the crowd had not blocked the entryways into the courthouse, the judges' accusations against the Islamists carried the day in Egypt's private media.[16] And given that Morsi's edict blocked the judiciary from ruling on the Constituent Assembly, many Egyptians believed that the Brotherhood was now blocking the judiciary by force.

• • • • • • • •

Ever since Morsi issued his decree on November 22, his opponents had protested in Tahrir Square. On Tuesday, December 4, however, the protesters organized a "last warning" protest outside the presidential palace in northern Cairo. The scene was predictably violent: Security forces deployed batons and tear gas against approximately ten thousand activists, who successfully broke past the barriers and declared a sit-in until the president withdrew his decree. Amid the violence, Morsi was forced to leave the palace through the back door. That evening, after the fighting died down, the crowd swelled to nearly a hundred thousand, with protesters—an awkward coalition of revolutionaries, leftists, and Mubarakists—calling on Morsi to step aside.[17]

The massive demonstration outside the presidential palace unnerved the Brotherhood's leaders. From their perspective, the December 15 referendum on the new constitution draft represented the perfect exit to the current crisis. After all, the Brotherhood anticipated using its nationwide chain of command to mobilize for another victory at the polls, which would ensure the Islamist constitution's passage and implicitly affirm Morsi's popular legitimacy in the process. And the Brotherhood expected that once the referendum passed, the non-Islamists would have no choice but to move on, as they had done during every previous electoral loss.

But it was becoming clear that the opposition *wouldn't* move on, because Morsi's opponents viewed the referendum as the product of a power grab that they utterly rejected. Instead of turning toward the ballot box, the protesters stayed in the streets, demanding that Morsi withdraw his constitutional declaration, cancel the referendum, and even resign from office. The mounting calls for Morsi's ouster alarmed the Brotherhood in particular, especially since the security forces appeared either incapable of keeping Morsi safe within the presidential palace or unwilling to do so.

In theory, the Brotherhood's leaders could have taken this moment to reconsider Morsi's actions during the previous two weeks. They could have examined how his power grab looked to those Egyptians who were already quite wary of the Brotherhood's intentions and reassessed the new constitution that moved Egypt's legal system very far, and very rapidly, toward theocracy. They could have delayed their pursuit of an Islamist constitution draft for the time being, calming the crisis by reaching out to their adversaries and compromising.

But from the Brotherhood leaders' perspective, they didn't have to compromise. Morsi had won an election and had the "legitimacy" to take whatever steps were necessary to move the Brotherhood's Islamist agenda forward. They also saw no real threat from the military, since the new constitution had met the generals' core demands, or any real pushback from the international community, which was still satisfied with Morsi's handling of the Gaza conflict and wasn't saying much. To compromise with Morsi's opponents now thus meant conceding to opposition groups that spoke loudly but ultimately lost every single election. If anything, the Brotherhood believed, Morsi needed to show that he was strong—popularly supported and firmly in control.

So on the evening of December 4, as massive crowds chanted outside the presidential palace for Morsi's fall and the police stood to the side, the Guidance Office planned a response in consultation with Morsi.[18] From Morsi's perspective, the Interior Ministry had failed to protect the palace earlier that day, and, as a Brotherhood leader told the *New York Times*, Morsi thus "called on the Muslim Brotherhood to become a human shield and protect the presidency because he can't trust the state."[19]

The following morning, Guidance Office spokesman Mahmoud Ghozlan released a statement calling for demonstrations outside of the presidential palace "to protect the legitimacy," adding that the Brotherhood's turnout would show "that the Egyptian people are the ones who choose this legitimacy and elected it, and, God willing, they will be able to protect it, adopt their constitution, and protect their institutions."[20]

In midafternoon on December 5, a few thousand Morsi supporters stormed the area outside the presidential palace and attacked the anti-Morsi sit-in, where a few hundred anti-Morsi protesters camped out in tents.[21] Chanting Morsi's name and "God is great," the Islamists tore down the protesters' tents, chased the demonstrators away from the palace, and erected barriers to assert their control over the area.[22] More Morsi supporters then swarmed into the area, preparing to defend it from future opposition incursions.

News of the Brotherhood's attack on the protesters spread quickly. At approximately six thirty in the evening, new clashes erupted one block from the palace. The fighting continued through the night, growing deadly as it wore on. Opposition protesters threw Molotov cocktails, Morsi supporters threw rocks, and both sides carried guns.[23] By the time the fighting ended the next morning, hundreds had been injured, and ten people were killed, most of them Muslim Brothers.

Amid the chaos, Muslim Brothers captured anti-Morsi protesters, tied them up, and tortured them.[24] The Brotherhood's torture chambers appeared prearranged. As the *Egypt Independent* reported from the scene, the central torture chamber was located at the gate of the presidential palace and protected by iron barriers and CSF riot police. Inside the chamber, Muslim Brothers and plainclothes police officers tore off detainees' clothes, took their belongings, and beat them until they confessed to being paid thugs.[25]

As videos of bearded Islamists beating bloodied protesters spread on YouTube and social media, Egypt's crisis spiraled out of control. Three more of Morsi's non-Islamist presidential aides resigned in protest of the Brotherhood's violence, and Rafik Habib, the prominent pro-Brotherhood Christian, resigned from his post as vice-chair of the FJP.[26] The attacks bolstered criticisms of the Brotherhood within Egypt's private media, which aired the Brotherhood's violence on loop.

Twenty-four hours later, Morsi returned to the presidential palace and addressed the nation. But rather than calming the situation, he once again fanned the flames. Apparently using the Brotherhood's abusive interrogation of protesters from the previous day's clashes as evidence, Morsi claimed that "investigations" had revealed that the assailants were armed and paid by external actors. "Who gave them the money? Who offered them the weapons? Who stands to support them?" Morsi asked conspiratorially. "Previously we saw mysterious talk of a third party," he said, adding that this "third party" was also responsible for other deadly incidents between the government and protesters, such as the October 2011 massacre of Coptic protesters and the November 2011 Mohamed Mahmoud Street clashes that preceded the parliamentary elections.

Morsi further defended his power-grabbing decree and announced that it would remain in effect until the new constitution was approved via referendum, after which new parliamentary elections would take place. Finally, toward the end of his statement, he offered the opposition a nominal olive branch, inviting political party heads, revolutionary youths, church representatives, and "national symbols" to an exchange at the presidential palace two days later, on Saturday, December 8.[27]

However, the opposition, nominally represented by the NSF, refused to meet with Morsi. Earlier in the crisis, it conditioned any negotiation with Morsi on the withdrawal of his power-grabbing constitutional declaration, and it now demanded that he open the new constitution draft to revisions and postpone the referendum. But Morsi rejected all of these conditions. Moreover, since the exchange was to come only three days after the Brotherhood's assault on protesters, NSF leaders faced pressure from younger activists not to negotiate with a president whom they now called a "killer."[28]

On Saturday, December 8, a handful of mostly Islamist political figures and party leaders attended Morsi's meeting at the presidential palace.[29] Afterward, Morsi released a new constitutional declaration, which effectively canceled the clause from the November 22 declaration that empowered the president to "take the necessary actions and measures to protect the country and the goals of the revolution." But the new declaration otherwise doubled down on the original one: It still placed Morsi's edicts above judicial review and affirmed that the referendum on the new draft constitution would be held on December 15.[30] As a result, the protests continued outside the palace.

• • • • • • • •

As the crisis entered its third week, Egypt's military leadership started to stir. Of course, the generals had participated in the rushed Constituent Assembly sessions that produced the new constitution draft, and the military was one of the draft's primary beneficiaries. But the generals seemingly realized that Morsi's uncompromising behavior had catalyzed a severe backlash and that the country's political polarization was rapidly reaching the point of no return. Indeed, the situation on the ground had gotten so unstable that the military was now back on the streets: Its tanks were defending the palace of an increasingly unpopular president, and its soldiers were reinforcing the area with cement blocks.

On December 8, in an apparent attempt to encourage reconciliation between the Brotherhood and opposition forces, the military released its first statement since the crisis began. It warned of "disastrous consequences" if the standoff wasn't resolved through dialogue and said that failing to reach a consensus "is in the interest of neither side." It concluded by affirming the military's "responsibility in protecting the nation's higher interests" and state institutions.[31] A Brotherhood official welcomed the military's remarks as "balanced," and Morsi proceeded with his superficial exchange at the presidential palace that same day.

Three days later, however, as massive anti-Morsi protests continued, the military issued another statement. At an officers' club event on December 11, Defense Minister al-Sisi announced that he would host "a meeting for humanitarian communication." Morsi's office initially told the *New York Times* that he would attend, and Gen. Mohamed al-Assar confirmed Morsi's attendance during a television phone interview that evening. The NSF also accepted the invitation.[32]

But the following day, the meeting was mysteriously canceled. Morsi reportedly had changed his mind and worried that a dialogue hosted by al-Sisi would undermine his standing as Egypt's chief executive.[33] And while the military avoided assigning direct blame, it expressed its frustration with unnamed political forces—presumably the Brotherhood—that considered al-Sisi's invitation for dialogue "a kind of intervention by the military into political affairs."[34]

As a result, al-Sisi's "meeting for humanitarian communication" never happened. But it was a highly significant episode nonetheless. By calling for dialogue without Morsi's prior approval, al-Sisi signaled that the military was still a separate power from the presidency. And in the minds of many Egyptians, that meant that Morsi was no longer their only choice.

• • • • • • • •

Throughout the post-Mubarak era, the Obama administration defended its policy of friendly "engagement" with the Brotherhood on the grounds that the Brotherhood was a "nonviolent" and "democratic party" that "plays by the democratic rules of the game."[35] But Morsi was now behaving like a fascist. The Brotherhood leader had seized total power, rushed a theocratic constitution to a referendum, dispatched his followers to attack protesters outside the presidential palace, and then issued a second decree that affirmed his original power grab in most respects. Within Washington, almost every analyst who once touted the Brotherhood's supposed moderation now conceded that Morsi was an autocrat. The optimism that once surrounded the Brotherhood's rise to power, misplaced though it was, dissipated almost entirely.

Yet the Obama administration stood by Morsi. In its statements, the administration largely avoided criticizing him, even as his behavior worsened.

In the wake of Morsi's power grab, the State Department evenhandedly called "for all Egyptians to resolve their differences over these important issues peacefully and through democratic dialogue."[36] When the Constituent Assembly announced that it would rush to complete its Islamist constitution draft, Washington was similarly equivocal. "We reiterate the call that we've been making for many days now for a full and inclusive dialogue to address any differences," State Department spokeswoman Victoria Nuland said.[37] And although President Obama called Morsi following the Brotherhood's December 5 attack on anti-Morsi demonstrators, he was careful not to take sides. According to the White House, Obama "underscored that it is essential for Egyptian leaders across the political spectrum to put aside their differences and come together to agree on a path that will move Egypt forward."[38]

Meanwhile, throughout the crisis, the administration signaled repeatedly that it intended to cooperate with Morsi moving forward. At the very moment that Muslim Brothers attacked protesters outside the presidential palace, Morsi's top foreign policy adviser, Guidance Office leader Essam el-Haddad, was in Washington meeting with National Security Adviser Tom Donilon at the White House. President Obama "stopped by"—and proceeded to sit with el-Haddad for forty minutes.

Two days later, an NSC official explained the administration's thinking. "The president and Morsi have a good personal relationship," he told me. "They spoke on the phone six times during the Gaza crisis. And that might be the best leverage we have."

Needless to say, the notion that Obama and Morsi had a "good personal relationship" due to six phone calls was questionable. But the official's comment reflected the administration's basic analysis of the situation in Egypt. Whether or not Morsi was a democrat, he was still Egypt's elected leader. He was therefore likely to be in power for at least the remainder of his four-year term and possibly longer. And no matter how divisive Egypt's new constitution was, the administration fully expected the referendum to pass. So what was the upside of criticizing Morsi now, when the administration would then have to work with him and the Brotherhood for years to come? And why should the administration push back on the referendum, when most Egyptians would likely vote for it anyway?

From the administration's perspective, the referendum results validated its caution: The new constitution was approved by 64 percent of Egyptian voters. To be sure, that was a small majority relative to previous referenda—by comparison, 77 percent of voters had approved the March 2011 referendum—

and the turnout was a surprisingly low 33 percent.[39] Still, Egypt had once again moved from street protests to the ballot box. The anti-Morsi demonstrations petered out, a new constitution was in effect, parliamentary elections were on the horizon, and Morsi was still Egypt's president.

Indeed, the administration believed that Egypt would now move forward. Yet in the eyes of many Egyptians, the crisis that Morsi's power grab ignited wasn't settled.

11 In Power but Not in Control

*On December 25, 2012, the High Elections Commissions announced that the con-*stitutional referendum had passed, with 64 percent voting "yes." That number should have alarmed President Mohamed Morsi and the Muslim Brotherhood. They had expended every ounce of energy to mobilize in favor of the new Islamist constitution, and the result was the lowest "yes" vote of any referendum in contemporary Egyptian history. To make matters worse, turnout was only 33 percent, meaning that out of approximately fifty-two million registered Egyptian voters, only 21 percent actually approved the new constitution. The numbers in Cairo, ground zero of Egypt's revolution, should have been especially disquieting: 56.8 percent of Cairenes voted "no."

In other words, a critical mass of Egyptians—at least a significant minority—rejected the new rules of Egypt's new Brotherhood-dominated political system. And that created the obvious risk that these Egyptians wouldn't play by those rules and would instead pursue political change by other, extrainstitutional means.

Morsi and the Brotherhood, however, did not see it this way. Forget the final percentages and turnout rate, they argued. A win is a win, and for the fifth straight time since Mubarak's ouster, they had won, demonstrating yet again that they and their program reflected the authentic will of the Egyptian people.[1] And as they saw it, their opponents had once again spoken loudly but carried small sticks. The anti-Morsi NSF called Morsi a "dictator," boycotted the Constituent Assembly, and protested for weeks. And yet all of that oxygen added up to a paltry six million "no" votes—less than half of the votes that Mubarak's last prime minister, Ahmed Shafik, received during the presidential elections only six months earlier.

So the day after the referendum's passage was announced, Morsi declared victory. "This is a historic day," he said during a televised speech. "A free constitution has come to Egyptians—not by a king's endowment or a president's imposition or a dictate by colonists. Rather, it's a constitution chosen by the Egyptian people of their own free and conscious will." For a brief moment, Morsi sounded a conciliatory note, admitting that he "made some mistakes and missteps here and there" during the previous month's crisis. But his over-all message was that Egypt was now moving forward under the new consti-tution, "from the First Republic to the Second Republic." And as the next step in this transition process, Morsi announced that he was ceding legislative authority to the Shura Council, Egypt's upper parliamentary house.[2]

On the surface, that sounded like progress, since Morsi was effectively canceling his previous power grabs and devolving legislative authority to an elected legislative body. Nonetheless, it was a highly controversial move be-cause the Shura Council was now being granted far more power than it was ever elected to wield. After all, according to the constitution under which it was elected, the Shura Council's role was largely consultative. The Egyptian public thus had paid little attention to the 2012 Shura Council elections, and turnout rates were exceptionally low.[3] Moreover, given the Shura Council's limited authority, the non-Islamist parties focused their energies instead on the more pivotal People's Assembly elections and in some cases abstained from the Shura Council elections altogether. Islamists thus won nearly 79 per-cent of the Shura Council's seats, with the Brotherhood's FJP claiming a 58 percent majority. So in the eyes of Morsi's opponents, the Shura Council was yet another Brotherhood-dominated body with dubious popular legiti-macy that was now being granted tremendous authority.

To make matters worse, Morsi circumvented his own constitution to stack the Shura Council with appointees. The new constitution empowered the president to appoint only 10 percent of the Shura Council, or twenty seats—a sharp reduction from the Mubarak-era constitution, which empowered the president to appoint up to one-third of the Shura Council, or ninety seats. So two days before the constitutional referendum results were announced, Morsi acted under the expiring Mubarak-era constitution and appointed ninety new members.[4]

To some extent, Morsi tried to use his appointments to reconcile with certain non-Islamist constituencies that had protested his earlier power grab. To accomplish this, he asked the Coptic Orthodox, Evangelical, and Roman Catholic Churches to submit candidates, and he appointed ten Christians, only one of whom refused to take the oath of office.[5] He similarly asked the NSF for nominations. But given its rejection of the new constitution, the

NSF refused and accused Morsi of using his appointment power as "a kind of bribery."[6]

For the most part, however, Morsi distributed his Shura Council appointments to shore up his Islamist base. Thirty-one of his forty-one party-affiliated appointees hailed from Islamist parties, including thirteen FJP members, nine Wasat figures, and six Salafists, including two members affiliated with al-Gamaa al-Islamiya. Many of the nonpartisan appointees were similarly Islamists, including al-Azhar clerics, professional syndicate leaders, and legal scholars. Meanwhile, Morsi also rewarded those non-Islamist parties that had aligned with the Brotherhood, appointing six members from the Ghad al-Thawra Party, which had participated in the Brotherhood's electoral coalition during the 2011–12 parliamentary elections, and three members of the RDP, which had been part of the Brotherhood's People's Assembly coalition. And in another bid to co-opt Egypt's brass, Morsi appointed three military figures.[7]

To the opposition, the Shura Council thus looked like the same kind of rubber-stamp Parliament that Hosni Mubarak enjoyed during his three decades in power—except that it was now rubber-stamping the edicts of the increasingly polarizing Brotherhood president. The composition of the Shura Council leadership only bolstered those accusations. After all, the Shura Council speaker was Ahmed Fahmy, a Brotherhood figure from Sharkiya whose son was married to Morsi's daughter.[8] And the new Shura Council majority leader was Essam el-Erian—the former Guidance Office leader who previously served as one of Morsi's presidential advisers.

More to the point, these men—like Morsi and every other Muslim Brother—had taken an oath to follow the Brotherhood leadership's orders. This meant that the Guidance Office had outsized influence over two branches of the Egyptian government—the presidency and the legislature— whether or not it attempted to use it. Morsi's devolution of legislative authority to the Brotherhood-dominated Shura Council was thus viewed as perpetuating his November 22 power grab rather than resolving it.

• • • • • • • •

The Brotherhood's leaders insisted that all of Morsi's power plays were defensive. Morsi, they said, was battling a host of domestic adversaries and state institutions that were determined to see him fail. His electoral victory thus gave him the "legitimacy" to do whatever was needed to advance his agenda and protect his presidency, whether that meant overriding the judiciary's check on his power, ramming an Islamist constitution through to ratification despite a non-Islamists' walkout, or granting new powers to a Brotherhood-dominated legislature. The Brotherhood saw no need to compromise with opposition groups that it trounced repeatedly at the polls, and it viewed the backlash against Morsi as a conspiracy by a relatively small group of Egyptians that had to be quashed rather than accommodated.

To a large extent, the Brotherhood's paranoia was a product of its historical experience. The organization had only recently emerged from many decades of significant repression and believed that those who repressed the Brotherhood in the past would happily do so again. Brotherhood leaders therefore regarded media criticism, particularly from private networks that were owned by businessmen who were viewed as allies of the Mubarak regime, as mortally threatening—as virtual invitations for the military, judiciary, police, or whomever to intervene in Egyptian politics and send the Brothers back to their prison cells.

This was why Egypt was never likely to progress toward inclusive, let alone liberal, democracy under the Brotherhood's rule: The Brotherhood believed that its opponents were constantly plotting a coup and it couldn't tolerate criticism.

To be sure, some of the Brotherhood's loudest media critics *did* call for Morsi's toppling from the earliest days of his presidency. For example, following the Sinai attack that killed sixteen Egyptian soldiers on August 5, 2012, TV host and leading conspiracy theorist Tawfiq Okasha claimed that the Brotherhood and Morsi planned to kill him and threatened to kill them first. "You don't know what I have," Okasha warned the Brothers on air. "I have beasts and lions behind me. . . . If you don't control yourselves, I'll put it all to the torch."[9] Similarly, on August 11, the independently owned daily *Al-Dustor* ran a front-page editorial warning that Brotherhood rule would produce "the destruction of citizens' dignity" and calling for the "union of the army and the people" to remove Morsi from power.[10] In response to these incidents, the Egyptian government ordered Okasha's Al-Faraeen network off the air and seized the offending copies of *Al-Dustor*.[11] The prosecutor-general later charged Okasha with "insulting the presidency," and he was ultimately acquitted.[12]

Yet Morsi's media crackdown didn't stop at these blatantly violent and insurrectionary pronouncements. Rather, Muslim Brothers and their allies targeted Morsi's media critics quite broadly, accusing prominent journalists of "insulting the presidency" to intimidate opposition voices.[13] And although Egyptian law permits anyone to file a legal complaint on virtually any grounds, these "insulting the presidency" accusations gained traction after Morsi's November 22 power grab, as his newly appointed prosecutor-general appeared particularly inclined toward investigating and indicting journalists on this charge.

Many of the indictments were petty. In one instance, journalist Yousry al-Badry was accused of "circulating false news likely to disturb public peace and public security" when he claimed (incorrectly, of course) that Morsi would visit a military hospital where Mubarak was being treated.[14] In another case, leftist journalist Abdel Halim Qandil was charged with "provoking discord among the Egyptian people" and "provoking hatred against the president of the republic" for writing that Morsi's hundred-day promises had been lies and for printing offensive photos of the president.[15] In a third case, Morsi's presidential office filed a complaint against psychiatrist Manal Omar and TV host Mahmoud Saad, accusing them of "insulting the president" for discussing the psychological effects of jail on those in power, with reference to Morsi's prior imprisonment under Mubarak.[16]

The most infamous case, however, involved comedian Bassem Youssef, whose weekly satirical news show *Al-Bernameg* (meaning "*The Program*") achieved record-setting viewership during Morsi's presidency. During an episode shortly after Morsi's November 22 power grab, Youssef mocked Morsi by hugging a pink pillow that had a picture of Morsi's face printed on it. A Muslim Brotherhood lawyer sued to have Youssef's show pulled off the air for "sarcasm against the president," and the prosecutor-general opened a criminal investigation.[17]

During Morsi's first seven months in office, four times as many journalists were charged with "insulting the president" as during Mubarak's thirty-year reign.[18] The prosecutor also pushed cases against nine newspapers and two satellite television networks.[19] Meanwhile, the Brotherhood-dominated Shura Council stacked the state-run media with pro-Morsi supplicants who weeded out Morsi's critics.[20]

Yet none of these maneuvers staunched the media's criticism of Morsi—if anything, the attacks grew harsher over time. And while revolutionaries decried Morsi as a "new Mubarak" for his attempts to silence the media, many Egyptians focused instead on Morsi's *failure* to end the criticism. In their eyes, Morsi's regime wasn't just autocratic but utterly incapable in its authoritarianism. Rather than seeing Morsi as a "new Mubarak," they saw a weak and nasty man who made Mubarak look competent by comparison.

• • • • • • • •

On the same day that he ceded legislative authority to the Shura Council, Morsi announced an imminent governmental shake-up. Ten days later, on January 5, he appointed ten new ministers, three of whom were Muslim Brothers, thus expanding the Brotherhood's cabinet presence from five to eight ministerial portfolios. Of course, that wasn't even a quarter of the entire cabinet. But since most of the other ministers were ideologically undefined technocrats, the Brotherhood was the cabinet's dominant ideological stream, and oppositionists thus accused Morsi of "Brotherhoodizing" the government. Given the emerging consensus within Egypt that Morsi was both autocratic and inept, the "Brotherhoodization" allegation was a damning one: It suggested that Morsi was working for the exclusive benefit of his secret organization and otherwise governing Egypt into the ground.

The Guidance Office's reported involvement in Morsi's ministerial appointments bolstered this Brotherhoodization accusation. According to the Egyptian daily *El-Watan*, the Brotherhood's executive body prevented Morsi from appointing Guidance Office member Hossam Abu Bakr as the minister of transportation, and Morsi instead appointed Ain Shams University engineering professor Hatem Abdel-Latif, a lower-ranking Muslim Brother. The Guidance Office similarly pressed Morsi to appoint former Guidance Office member Mohamed Ali Bishr as the minister of local development. This was an especially critical appointment, since it gave a senior Muslim Brother tremendous power over municipal elections, which were slated for the following year. Finally, Morsi appointed Bassem Ouda, a Muslim Brother who oversaw the energy portfolio on al-Shater's Renaissance Project team, as his minister of supply and interior trade.[21]

Beyond these Muslim Brothers, Morsi added to his government's Islamist bent by appointing Alexandria University economics professor El-Morsi Hegazy as his finance minister. Hegazy's academic work focused on Islamic finance, and FJP economics chairman Abdullah Shehata had urged Morsi to select him.[22] Hegazy's appointment thus indicated that Morsi's government would work to expand the adoption of financial tools that avoid interest. While this wasn't controversial—many Egyptians already used Islamic banks and supported the expansion of *sharī'ah*-compliant finance tools—the timing was nonetheless surprising. After all, Egypt was in dire economic straits and actively negotiating a $4.8 billion loan from the IMF. Yet rather than appointing an experienced economic policymaker from within the Finance Ministry, Morsi selected an Islamic finance professor without any governmental experience.[23]

When it came to the Interior Ministry, however, Morsi opted for institutional continuity. He thus replaced Interior Minister Ahmed Gamal el-Din, whom the Brotherhood accused of failing to adequately secure the presidential palace during the late 2012 protests, with police general Mohamed Ibrahim, who had been responsible for securing a visit by Morsi to Asyut a few months earlier.[24] By promoting a new minister from within the ministry itself, Morsi seemingly sought to assuage Egypt's notoriously abusive police that he would not undertake security sector reform any time soon.

It is again worth emphasizing that, as Egypt's elected president, Morsi had the legal right to appoint whomever he wished to his cabinet. Elections, as the saying goes, have consequences, and there was nothing strange or surprising about a Brotherhood president appointing Islamists to high governmental positions. And since Morsi's cabinet was still largely technocratic, many Muslim Brothers believed that he was acting too conservatively and should have appointed more Muslim Brothers to take full advantage of his electoral mandate.

For many Egyptians, however, the problem wasn't the Brotherhood's Islamism or Morsi's noninclusive governing style. The problem was that Morsi and the Brotherhood were failing in power. Despite the economic prosperity that the Brotherhood's Renaissance Project promised, Egypt's economy was tanking. Egypt's cash reserves dropped from $15.5 billion when Morsi took office to a perilously low $13.6 billion in January 2013—and even that figure was largely thanks to $3 billion in loans and grants from Turkey and Qatar, most of which the Morsi government spent within a month. As a result, the Egyptian pound had weakened against the US dollar by approximately 9.7 percent since Morsi took office, and food prices rose 2.5 percent during January 2013 alone.[25]

The currency crisis put tremendous strain on the Egyptian government's ability to subsidize food and fuel for a mostly impoverished population, and by mid-February the funds allocated for diesel subsidies had completely run out.[26] This was, in other words, a major problem that required serious policy solutions, and fast. But with its popularity declining ever since Morsi's November 22 power grab, the Brotherhood-led government was in no position to cut fuel or food subsidies, since this would deepen the popular despair and risk a new round of anti-Morsi protests.

So the government pursued an Islamist solution instead. In mid-January, Finance Minister Hegazy unveiled a draft law to create sovereign Islamic bonds, known as *sukuk*, for financing the government's budget deficit and anticipated that the Islamic Development Bank would buy $6 billion of them.[27] It was an unrealistic plan that reflected the finance minister's utter inexperience, and the *sukuk* law languished in the Shura Council for months. Meanwhile, the Egyptian government's negotiations with the IMF stalled.

Then on January 14, a train collision in Giza killed nineteen police conscripts and injured 117 more.[28] It was the second major train accident in the previous two months, and rather than blaming the government or the transportation minister, who was a Muslim Brother, the Brotherhood quickly resorted to conspiracy theories. Brotherhood leader and Shura Council member Gamal Heshmat claimed that "hidden hands" had caused the incident.[29] Even more outrageously, Muslim Brothers alleged on social media that the accident was a Christian conspiracy to subvert Morsi's presidency.[30]

These mounting political, economic, and policy frustrations—and the Brotherhood's apparent incapacity to address them—exploded on January 25, 2013, when revolutionaries marked the second anniversary of the 2011 uprising with a day of violent rage. Tens of thousands of protesters descended on Tahrir Square, where they chanted "down with the supreme guide" and hanged an effigy labeled "the execution of Mohamed Morsi." Demonstrators threw rocks at the police, and battles between police and demonstrators raged outside the Interior Ministry, presidential palace, and state media headquarters. Meanwhile, masked assailants stormed the Brotherhood's media headquarters in the Cairo neighborhood of Manial, and Brotherhood offices were ransacked and burned in the Suez Canal city of Ismailia, as well as in two Nile Delta cities.[31] In at least a few of these instances, the police enabled the anti-Brotherhood assaults by standing to the side.

The most violent protests, however, happened in Suez, where six people were killed and hundreds injured. By the evening, the police withdrew, forcing the military to deploy.[32] It was an extremely significant development: Morsi's government had just lost control of a major city, and the military was back on the streets.

The following morning, in the northern Suez Canal city of Port Said, a judge sentenced twenty-one people to death for their roles in the February 2012 soccer stadium riot. The verdict ignited immediate, violent protests across the country and particularly within Port Said itself. At least thirty-seven people were killed in the ensuing clashes, and military tanks deployed in the streets of both Port Said and Ismailia to the south, as Morsi's government lost control of two more Suez Canal cities.[33] The following day, as the chaos continued, Morsi declared a state of emergency in all three Suez Canal cities that were now under military control, including a thirty-day curfew that would last from nine in the evening to six in the morning.[34]

Within the three Suez Canal cities, however, the military did little to re-store order. Soldiers protected official buildings but showed no interest in confronting protesters directly, since this meant putting themselves at risk for an unpopular president.[35] Indeed, when Port Said protesters defied Morsi's curfew by pouring into the streets at nine o'clock, soldiers playfully kicked soccer balls with them rather than enforce the curfew.[36]

While Egyptian oppositionists laughed at Port Said's defiance of Morsi, Defense Minister al-Sisi did not find the situation so amusing. In a speech to the military academy, he warned that "the continuation of conflict [between] different political forces and their differences regarding the administration of the country's affairs could lead to a collapse of the state, and threatens the fu-ture of coming generations."[37] The speech was another signal that the military envisioned a political role for itself—particularly if the crisis that began with Morsi's November power grab continued to spiral out of control.

The following day, the NSF and the Salafist Nour Party offered a proposal to resolve the crisis. It called on Morsi to form a unity government, estab-lish a committee to amend controversial constitutional articles, dismiss his prosecutor-general, investigate the recent violence, and agree to nonpartisan-ship in all state institutions.[38] The fact that the Nour Party—which had played a pivotal role in writing and ratifying the constitution—was siding with the non-Islamist NSF over the Brotherhood signaled that Morsi's base was nar-rowing rapidly. But once again, Morsi rejected this offer outright and offered no alternative proposal.[39]

• • • • • • • •

Morsi and the Brotherhood refused to negotiate for one simple reason: They didn't take the opposition seriously. As they saw it, the non-Islamist parties that made up the NSF had little appeal in a religious Muslim country like Egypt—which is why the Brotherhood had routed those parties in every sin-gle post-Mubarak election. "The Egyptian people don't like them," Brother-hood leader and Kafr el-Sheikh governor Saad al-Husseini told me during a February 2013 interview. "The Egyptian people have morals. . . . [Non-Islamists] have a culture [that] is not here. And that's not our mistake—that's their fault."[40]

So rather than negotiating with the NSF, the Brotherhood chose a different strategy for resolving the political crisis: It would focus its energies on winning the upcoming parliamentary elections, which were expected by April, and thus affirm its popular legitimacy. And the Brotherhood was quite confident that it would prevail. Its leaders projected capturing 55 percent of the legislature, after which the FJP would appoint the next cabinet.[41]

The Brotherhood thus pivoted sharply toward elections mode. It coordinated with Islamic satellite stations and asked local imams to tout the Brotherhood's program once campaign season began. It also developed a multipronged media strategy: It would create FJP social media pages for each electoral district, build a national campaign website, and appeal to the international community by placing op-eds written by top Brotherhood candidates in major American newspapers.[42] And to broaden its appeal, the Brotherhood planned to run more youth and female candidates than during the previous election and promised that most of its former parliamentarians wouldn't run this time around.[43]

Meanwhile, it used its extensive social services networks as campaign instruments. It ran a bread distribution project for impoverished Cairo neighborhoods, operated a medical caravan in Asyut that served thousands, and set up a temporary clinic in Fayoum, where doctors wrote prescriptions for patients on pads with the FJP logo and then filled those prescriptions for free.[44]

There was, however, one major stumbling block to the Brotherhood's all-consuming electoral push: The SCC had to approve the new elections law, which the Brotherhood-dominated Shura Council was empowered to draft. And that proved much harder than either Morsi or the Brotherhood anticipated.

The Shura Council passed its first version of the new parliamentary elections law on January 19. The new law effectively maintained the format of the 2011–12 elections, mandating that two-thirds of the seats would be elected via party-list voting and one-third would be elected through individual (first-past-the-post) voting.

But the law carried a few noteworthy changes that clearly benefited the Islamists and the Brotherhood in particular. It enabled parliamentarians to switch their party affiliations after the elections, which non-Islamists feared might encourage parliamentarians to join the FJP in the majority once the new Parliament was seated. It also removed prior restrictions on distributing religious campaign propaganda and campaigning in places of worship. And it placed a very high electoral threshold for parties to enter Parliament: Parties had to receive at least one-third of the votes within a district, and the remaining seats would go to the parties that received the greatest number of votes—which would likely pad the FJP's parliamentary bloc.[45]

So on February 18, the SCC ruled that the elections law violated the new constitution in several respects. Specifically, the SCC said that parliamentarians could not switch their parties after taking office because this would violate the rights of voters. It also cautioned the Shura Council to ensure that the new law's districting enabled "equitable representation of the population" and mandated that when an electoral list contained both party-affiliated candidates and independents, the candidates' specific affiliations should be listed.[46] The Shura Council quickly addressed some of these concerns in its next draft, which it passed four days later on February 22.[47]

Yet the Shura Council did not address all of the court's concerns. Specifically, it did not substantially change the electoral districts, and this meant that the SCC could ultimately invalidate the law by claiming that the Shura Council did not satisfy its requirement of "equitable representation of the population." Indeed, the preliminary districting entailed larger districts that advantaged better-organized parties—in other words, the Islamists. And in some cases, Islamist-heavy neighborhoods were established as separate districts.[48] Moreover, the Shura Council refused to resubmit its new law to the SCC for prior review, arguing that it was not required to do so—and this also left the law vulnerable to future legal challenges.[49]

The Brotherhood's hastiness was not surprising. With economic and security challenges mounting and its popularity declining, it *needed* the parliamentary elections to start immediately. With another electoral victory in hand, the Brotherhood believed it would have the political capital to enact painful subsidy reforms, "reform and restructure" the Interior Ministry, conclude negotiations with the IMF, and—perhaps most important—prove to Egyptians and the world that its media critics did not reflect the will of the Egyptian people.[50]

So one day before the Shura Council finished its revisions of the elections law, Morsi announced that the House of Representatives elections would begin on April 27 and take place in four phases. This plan would effectively keep Egypt focused on elections—and not street protests, he hoped—through June, with the new Parliament finally sitting for its first session on July 6, 2013.[51] But on March 6, Egypt's administrative court canceled Morsi's decision and referred the law back to the SCC for review.[52]

While Morsi unsuccessfully appealed the administrative court's decision, the Shura Council went back to the drawing board, amending certain aspects of the elections law while also drafting a political participation law. The Shura Council finally passed those laws on April 10 and then referred them to the SCC. But the SCC didn't issue its decision for over a month, effectively thwarting the Brotherhood's electoral strategy for escaping the political crisis.[53]

And so the crisis wore on.

• • • • • • • •

Washington's friendly "engagement" with the Brotherhood was based on a simple premise: By cooperating with the Brotherhood, the United States could influence it to govern democratically and soften its anti-Western inclinations. But by January 2013, this policy approach had failed. After all, Morsi's domestic behavior was increasingly autocratic. Moreover, the Brotherhood still promoted anti-Western vitriol. For example, in his statement on January 24, 2013, marking the Prophet Muhammad's birthday, Supreme Guide Mohamed Badie declared Islam's superiority over the West. "Western civilization failed in offering people justice, security, safety, and peace," he wrote. "It offered materialistic benefits to the world . . . but it lacks soul and mercy. . . . The cheapest thing in the world became blood and [people's] souls."[54]

Meanwhile, Morsi continued calling for the United States to release the spiritual leader of al-Gamaa al-Islamiya, the "blind sheikh" Omar Abdel Rahman, and told CNN's Wolf Blitzer that he would raise this matter with President Obama if the two leaders met.[55] At the same time, even as Morsi rejected Washington's repeated calls for his presidential office to establish a direct channel to the Israeli government, he expanded his outreach to Iran, with Iranian president Mahmoud Ahmadinejad visiting Cairo in February. It was the first visit by an Iranian leader to Egypt since the 1979 Iranian Revolution.

The Obama administration brushed off these incidents as either empty rhetoric or symbolic gestures. Morsi might raise the blind sheikh issue or meet with Ahmadinejad, the administration's argument went, but he was cooperating with Washington on strategic matters and, at the very least, hadn't broken the Egyptian–Israeli peace treaty.

Yet the administration found it increasingly difficult to dismiss Morsi's anti-Semitic outbursts. In January 2013, the Washington-based Middle East Media Research Institute unearthed a 2010 video in which Morsi—then a relatively unknown Brotherhood leader—referred to Israelis as "bloodsuckers" and "descendants of apes and pigs" and urged Egyptians to "nurse our children and our grandchildren on hatred" for Jews and Israelis.[56] The discovery ignited a firestorm within the American media, forcing the White House to issue a rare criticism of Morsi. "We believe that President Morsi should make clear that he respects people of all faiths and that this type of rhetoric is unacceptable in a democratic Egypt," White House spokesman Jay Carney said.[57]

The White House was eager to use the episode to demonstrate that its engagement with the Brotherhood was paying off—that cooperating with Morsi made him responsive to Washington's occasional criticisms. So the administration breathed a sigh of relief the following day when Morsi's presidential office issued a statement proclaiming Morsi's "commitment to upholding religious freedom and promoting inter-religious tolerance" and rejecting "derogatory statements regarding any religious or ethnic group."[58] Indeed, an NSC official forwarded me Morsi's statement almost immediately, apparently believing that it reflected the Obama administration's positive influence over Morsi.

There was, however, one problem: That conciliatory statement was issued in English for a Western audience; Morsi's presidential office issued a very different statement in Arabic for domestic consumption. Morsi's spokesman Yasser Aly explained that Morsi's anti-Semitic statements came in the context of "Israeli aggression on Gaza" and emphasized the difference "between the Jewish religion and the criticism of the racist practices of the Israelis against the Palestinians."[59] And that same day, during a meeting in Cairo with seven US senators, Morsi launched into a diatribe against Israel and insinuated that the controversy over his 2010 remarks was due to Jewish control over the American media. "I think we all know that the media in the United States has made a big deal of this and we know the media of the United States is controlled by certain forces and they don't view me favorably," Morsi reportedly said.[60]

Still, the Obama administration showed no signs of rethinking its friendly engagement with the Brotherhood and Morsi. As the administration saw it, turning its back on the Brotherhood meant abandoning Egypt's leading party. The Brotherhood would likely govern Egypt for many years to come, the administration reasoned, and it therefore made sense to build goodwill with it by helping it, rather than squeezing it.

So the White House weighed a few options for bolstering Morsi, such as inviting him to Washington. It also tried to assist Morsi in creating an interagency process, much like the NSC structure, so that Morsi could enhance his management of Egypt's foreign policy. (Unsurprisingly, the Egyptian military wasn't particularly enthusiastic because such a structure would institutionalize the presidency's authority over it. After a few meetings with Morsi government officials in Cairo and Washington, the project ultimately went nowhere.)[61] And despite rising calls on Capitol Hill for the administration to withhold economic aid from Egypt on account of Morsi's autocratic rule and hateful statements, Secretary of State John Kerry delivered $190 million when he visited Morsi during his first overseas trip in early March.[62]

Indeed, the Obama administration bet long on Morsi and the Brotherhood. It simply didn't see any realistic alternatives.

• • • • • • • •

The Obama administration's assessment of Egypt's political field wasn't entirely wrong: No other political organization could match the Brotherhood's nationwide mobilization. The non-Islamist parties remained badly underdeveloped. They lacked coherent policy platforms in many cases, and—with the exception of the Wafd—had little name recognition in the rural areas where most Egyptians live.

Meanwhile, the Salafist Nour Party, which finished second to the Brotherhood's FJP in the 2011–12 parliamentary elections, split in January 2013 when Nour Party chairman and Morsi presidential adviser Emad Abdel Ghafour broke away and established the Watan Party. Although the Nour Party remained the stronger of the two parties, the Salafists' unity in the 2011–12 parliamentary elections was vital to their success. The Nour Party's division thus meant a fragmented Salafist vote in any subsequent election. By contrast, the Brotherhood was structured for cohesion—and could therefore rely on its deeply committed base to get out the vote in the next parliamentary election as no other party could.

Despite the Brotherhood's political power and mobilizing prowess, however, Morsi's control of the country was deteriorating. By late February, violent protests against his rule were occurring regularly, and the police increasingly refused to suppress the demonstrations on behalf of his unpopular government. The police mutiny peaked on March 7, when thousands of police went on strike across the country, shutting down stations, holding their commanders hostage, and refusing to guard Morsi's motorcade.[63]

While the Brotherhood attributed the police mutiny to a conspiracy within the state, many Egyptians blamed Morsi and the Brotherhood. In their view, it reflected the Brotherhood's ineptitude in managing state institutions. And the Brotherhood's response to the mutiny only bolstered that impression. The FJP-dominated Shura Council proposed legislation allowing the state to hire private security firms to assume policing duties—a sign that the Brotherhood had completely given up hope of managing the state institutions. On the same wavelength, FJP parliamentarian Saber Abouel Fotouh recommended forming "popular committees" to safeguard citizens and state institutions, which the opposition decried as a Brotherhood attempt to empower its cadres to police the country. Meanwhile, al-Gamaa al-Islamiya deployed its members to assume police duties in the Upper Egyptian city of Asyut—a frightening signal of state breakdown under Islamist rule.[64]

Then, on March 22, violent clashes erupted between opposition protesters and Muslim Brothers outside the Brotherhood's headquarters in the Cairo suburb of Moqattam. At least forty were injured, and the media largely blamed the Brotherhood for the violence, as networks repeatedly played footage of a Brotherhood cadre slapping a female activist.[65] In the immediate aftermath, Morsi's prosecutor-general summoned a wide range of prominent opposition leaders for interrogations, accusing them of incitement.[66] Predictably, no Brotherhood leaders were similarly interrogated—despite the fact that Muslim Brothers reportedly captured opposition protesters, held them in a nearby mosque, and beat them during the clashes.[67]

In response to the uproar, the Brotherhood once again tried to intimidate its media critics. The day after the Moqattam clashes, Muslim Brothers joined an Islamist sit-in outside the Egyptian Media Production Cities, a complex that contains the studios and offices of many of the country's most prominent satellite news networks, and besieged it.[68] The Islamists assaulted TV guests when they arrived at the complex for on-air interviews and prevented the stations' employees from getting to work.[69] A week later, Morsi's prosecutor summoned comedian Bassem Youssef on new charges of insulting the presidency, after Youssef mocked a ceremonial hat that Morsi wore while accepting an honorary degree at a Pakistani university.[70] Of course, none of these moves silenced the Brotherhood's opponents or critics—which made Morsi look even more ineffective.

The Brotherhood's failure, however, wasn't just a matter of perception. Egypt's cash reserves remained dangerously low, and although they increased by nearly $1 billion to $14.42 by the end of April 2013, that was largely thanks to a $2 billion deposit from Libya.[71] As a result of the ongoing cash crunch, the government raised the price of state-subsidized cooking gas for the first time in two decades, increasing prices on gas cylinders by 60 percent for domestic use and doubling the prices for businesses.[72] Meanwhile, rising inflation catalyzed a significant energy crisis, and the Electricity Ministry announced that power would be cut twice a day during the summer, for four hours at a time. This meant depriving Egyptians of air conditioning during the hottest months—which, in 2013, coincided with the fasting period of Ramadan.[73]

Due to these mounting challenges, many Egyptians were desperate for an alternative to the Brotherhood. And most dangerously, the ballot box provided no realistic respite. After all, the Brotherhood-dominated Shura Council was still wrangling with the judiciary over the parliamentary elections law, and, even if a law was passed, the opposition parties were too weak and disorganized to win. But more to the point, the fact that the Brotherhood's failed governance had come via the ballot box meant that a growing number of Egyptians didn't see elections as the sole source of political legitimacy.

This shift in popular attitudes would send Egypt's revolution flying off its rails.

12 The Rebellion

*The earliest calls for Morsi's ouster began within the first two months of his pres-*idency and largely came from the most radical segments of the Egyptian media, such as the satellite station Al-Faraeen and the daily newspaper *Al-Dustor*, both of which are privately owned. Morsi's November 22 power grab, however, moved these calls from the periphery into the mainstream, with protests increasingly calling for Morsi's overthrow as the crisis wore on.

By the early months of 2013, the hostility toward the Brotherhood transformed into a new embrace of the Egyptian military—including among many revolutionary activists, who called for the military to remove the Brotherhood from power, govern temporarily, and oversee a new political transition. "There will be bloody action in the street, and the army will come," an Alexandria-based leader of the ESDP, told me in late February 2013. "I don't want this, but the people will be happy."[1] Non-Islamist opposition leaders echoed these sentiments. "If Egypt is on the brink of default, if law and order is absent, [the army has] a national duty to intervene," Mohamed ElBaradei told the BBC.[2]

To be sure, the revolutionaries' embrace of the military was a stark reversal, since they were chanting for the SCAF's fall only eight months earlier. Yet contrary to their portrayal as "liberals" in the Western media, many of these activists believed in the principle of "continuous revolution"—and they viewed the military as a tool for promoting political change whenever they hit a wall, whether that wall was a dictator such as Mubarak or an elected president such as Morsi. And from their perspective, Morsi had sacrificed his electoral legitimacy when he seized total power in November and then dispatched Muslim Brothers to beat protesters outside the presidential palace.

Then in mid-March, an Ibn Khaldun Center poll found that 82 percent of Egyptians wanted the military to return to power.[3] Given the difficulties associated with polling in Egypt, it is impossible to say whether this figure was accurate—and it should be noted that another poll, conducted by Baseera and published in the state-run newspaper *Al-Gomhuria* in early April, found that only 3 percent of Egyptians wanted "the defense minister or another military man" as their president.[4] But the mere fact that these polls were published reflected that it was suddenly acceptable to speak of the military as a realistic alternative to Morsi and the Brotherhood.

The military's internal deliberations during this period are unknown and perhaps unknowable. But the generals' outward signals suggested that they intended to cooperate with Morsi and the Brotherhood, despite the rising anger. In mid-March, the military announced that it would accept cadets from Brotherhood families into military academies, reversing a prior ban and signaling its acceptance of Islamists as "part of the national fabric."[5]

Meanwhile, the generals said repeatedly that they had no interest in governing again. The generals likely knew that toppling Morsi would put them in direct conflict with the Brotherhood and its allies—Islamists who could mobilize effectively, and possibly violently, against a coup. Moreover, the military likely worried about the international community's response. US law calls for suspending aid to countries in which the military topples an elected government. A coup would thus jeopardize a vital source of military aid. And every communication between US officials and the Egyptian military on the matter was quite clear: *Whatever you do*, the American officials told the generals, *do not launch a coup.*

But perhaps the most important factor in the military's hesitance was its own reading of recent history. Unlike the revolutionaries, the generals had not forgotten the bitterness of the period of SCAF rule and weren't eager to repeat it. In private conversations, military officials said that they were trained to fight wars and protect borders—not to govern or make policy. Yet they always closed these discussions with the following line: "But we won't let the country fall to chaos." What, exactly, did that mean? The generals refused to elaborate.[6]

Perhaps the generals weren't really sure what they meant. During meetings with US officials, top generals expressed their frustration with Morsi and the Brotherhood. But the generals also blamed the opposition parties for the ongoing crisis and accused them of being stubborn.[7] So, for the time being, the brass stayed put, apparently hoping that Morsi would find a way to reconcile with the opposition and end the deepening political crisis.

Morsi understood that his durability depended more than ever on the generals. He therefore worked assiduously to stay in their good graces. When the *Guardian* published a leaked government report on April 10 that detailed the military's abuses during the 2011 uprising, Morsi scrambled to quash it.[8] The following day, Morsi met with the SCAF to clear the air. After the meeting, Morsi tried to project unity by appearing alongside top generals, with al-Sisi to his right. "I will not ever allow slanders in any way, shape or form or . . . any means to attack any member of the armed forces," Morsi said. He further praised the military for "its great role in protecting the security and safety of this nation." Finally, Morsi vowed not to pursue development projects in areas where the military operates and announced the promotion of senior military officers.

These gestures seemingly pleased al-Sisi, who said that he found Morsi to be "understanding" of the military's concerns.[9] The implicit deal that Morsi had struck with the military when he fired top SCAF leaders in August 2012 still stood: Morsi respected the military's autonomy over its own affairs and economic interests, and in exchange the military respected his political authority—even though many Egyptians no longer did.

• • • • • • • •

By late April 2013, the popular mood within Egypt had shifted sharply and broadly against the Brotherhood. As the country's economic frustrations intensified and power outages became more frequent, ordinary Egyptians cursed at Muslim Brothers in the streets. The private media networks, many of which were targets of Morsi's media crackdown, fed this anger and increasingly portrayed the organization as a secretive fifth column that had commandeered Egypt's revolution for its own parochial interests.

The country was boiling and collapsing at the same time—and most dangerously, there was no resolution to the crisis in sight. The military showed little interest in confronting Morsi so long as its perquisites were protected. The opposition parties were too weak to meaningfully challenge the Brotherhood in elections. And the Brotherhood refused to negotiate with its opponents. Worst of all, Morsi lacked a coherent policy agenda and thus inspired no confidence that he could put the country on a better path.

Indeed, Egypt's crisis was reaching the point of explosion—yet nobody knew what that explosion would ultimately look like or how the political crisis might end.

On April 28, a group of revolutionary activists proposed a way forward for the anti-Morsi opposition. Calling their campaign Tamarod, meaning "Rebellion," the activists announced a petition drive to withdraw confidence from Morsi and demand early presidential elections. "Electing a president isn't a Catholic marriage," Tamarod spokesman Mohamed Abdel Aziz declared, arguing that Morsi had sacrificed his electoral legitimacy by killing protesters and seizing total power through his November 22 constitutional declaration. Abdel Aziz added that Tamarod hoped to collect fifteen million petition signatures against Morsi—more than the number of votes that Morsi received during the second round of the presidential elections only a year earlier. It further called for a "million-man march" on June 30, 2013, the one-year anniversary of Morsi's inauguration, with the hope of ending his presidency by July 1.[10]

The idea behind Tamarod wasn't new. For example, in early March, citizens in at least four governorates had petitioned the military to take control of the country, and according to one activist 13,500 people signed the petitions.[11] But while these earlier efforts received little media attention and quickly fizzled, Tamarod was an instant phenomenon. Its first press conference was broadcast on virtually every privately owned satellite network and covered in almost every major Egyptian newspaper.

Indeed, the amount of attention that Tamarod received was rather surprising, since Tamarod's five founding members were little-known youth activists who claimed to be affiliated with Kefaya, the virtually defunct opposition movement from the mid-2000s.[12] So while Tamarod presented itself as a grassroots effort to oust Morsi by early elections or a mass demonstration, its most critical support came from elites—particularly those in the media organizations that Morsi's prosecutor and the Brotherhood routinely threatened. And thanks to this attention, Tamarod hit the ground running, with activists lining up across the country to distribute its petition.

The Brotherhood, however, didn't view Tamarod as particularly significant. It regarded Egypt's non-Islamist opposition parties and movements as media contrivances with little presence on the ground, with Tamarod only being the latest example. Its primary concern was the state institutions, which it claimed were packed with Mubarak regime holdovers who were undermining Morsi's presidency. And Brotherhood leaders increasingly worried that Morsi was losing his battle with the *ancien régime* by appointing Muslim Brothers to high-ranking positions too gradually.[13]

So to bolster his Brotherhood base, Morsi issued another cabinet reshuffle on May 7. Four of the nine new ministers were Muslim Brothers, bringing the Brotherhood's total representation to twelve of thirty-five ministerial positions. The Brotherhood still held only a small fraction of all cabinet seats, but since four of the remaining five appointees were Islamists, the cabinet's ideological bent tilted further toward the Brotherhood.

The new appointments were also significant because Morsi broke with his previous pattern of appointing Muslim Brothers to service- and production-oriented ministries. He tapped FJP leader Amr Darrag to head the Ministry of International Cooperation and Planning and named FJP spokesman Yehia Hamed minister of investment. These two men, along with FJP economics chairman Abdullah Shehata, were charged with overseeing Egypt's negotiations with the IMF—a portfolio that grew more urgent by the day.[14]

Egypt's economy, after all, was in total free fall. Inflation skyrocketed, with the Egyptian pound depreciating from 6.06 pounds to the dollar at the time of Morsi's inauguration to 7 pounds to the dollar by mid-May 2013, and the black market exchange rates soared to approximately 8.25 pounds to the dollar.[15] Egypt was also more dependent than ever on Qatar, with a $3 billion low-interest Qatari loan boosting Egypt's reserves to $16.04 billion by the end of May.[16] At the same time, Egypt's energy prices skyrocketed, and electricity shortages grew more frequent as summer approached, with blackouts of seven hours reported in some governorates.[17]

The rising anger on the street was a boon for Tamarod's anti-Morsi petition drive. By mid-May, Tamarod's petition collectors were visible throughout the country, and the campaign claimed to have collected over two million signatures within its first ten days of work.[18] And Morsi's appointment of more Muslim Brothers to address the country's ongoing slide bolstered the opposition's argument that he was more concerned with Brotherhoodizing the government than fixing problems.

Meanwhile, the Brotherhood made matters worse by picking new fights at virtually every turn. On May 14, the Brotherhood-dominated Shura Council announced that it was reopening amendments on "judicial reform." This violated an earlier promise that Morsi had made to the Supreme Council of the Judiciary that the judges' input would guide any changes to the judiciary law.[19]

Morsi's government also started threatening revolutionary activists. On May 10, Cairo Airport police detained April 6 Youth movement founder Ahmed Maher for allegedly organizing protests outside the interior minister's house. The timing of the arrest was suspicious, however. The protests had taken place two months earlier, and at the time of his arrest Maher was returning from Washington, where he had criticized the Brotherhood during a public conference.[20]

At the same time, the Morsi government continued its assault on media critics. On May 19, Morsi's prosecutor referred the editor and managing editor of *El-Watan* to criminal trials for defamation and for "publishing false news that aims to disturb the public peace and stir panic" after the newspaper published Islamist militants' alleged assassination targets.[21] The prosecutor opened another investigation into three Tamarod founders and prominent TV hosts Amr Adib and Mohamed Sherdy, accusing them of "inciting and mobilizing people to overthrow an elected government, inciting hatred against the regime, and promoting a group suspected of violating the law." In response to the investigation, Sherdy and Adib defiantly signed Tamarod petitions on air.[22]

By the end of May, Tamarod claimed that it had collected over seven million signatures.[23] Whether or not this figure was accurate—and it is reasonable to doubt it—Tamarod was by that point a household name. And as a result of the Brotherhood's failed and increasingly autocratic governance, many Egyptians were now looking toward the June 30 Tamarod protests as a pivotal showdown against the Brotherhood regime.

• • • • • • • •

As the crisis wore on, new signs emerged of the military's discontent with Morsi. For example, when Morsi's reshuffled cabinet posed for a photo on May 7, Defense Minister al-Sisi was conspicuously absent. Still, al-Sisi continued to reject popular calls for the military to topple Morsi and urged Morsi and the opposition to negotiate a resolution. "No one is going to remove anyone," al-Sisi told an audience of troops and public figures on May 12, saying that the military was not a "solution" to political problems and that the country should decide its future through the ballot box.[24]

Four days later, however, new tensions emerged between Morsi and the military. On May 16, seven security officers were kidnapped in Sinai, and Morsi responded by saying that efforts to release the officers should seek to "preserve the lives of everyone, whether the kidnapped or the kidnappers."[25] Morsi's statement sparked significant outrage within the military, since it equated the kidnapped officers with their captors. The soldiers' outrage escalated when rumors circulated that top Muslim Brothers were negotiating with the tribes to secure the officers' release in exchange for releasing inmates from one of Egypt's highest-security prisons.[26]

The crisis worsened a few days later, when a video surfaced in which the captives begged Morsi to release Sinai's political detainees in exchange for their release. The images made Morsi look weak, and his attempt to project strength by declaring that there was "no room for dialogue with the criminals" and that "all options were on the table" fell flat.[27] When the kidnapped officers were finally freed on May 22, the military released a message thanking "the efforts of military intelligence with the help of the tribal chieftains and honorable people of Sinai"—noticeably excluding Morsi from receiving credit.[28]

Meanwhile, another controversy was brewing upstream along the Nile, where Ethiopia began constructing a new dam that Cairo feared would reduce Egypt's Nile water supply downstream. To present Egypt's concerns, Morsi flew to Addis Ababa on May 25 and received assurances from the Ethiopian prime minister that Egypt's water supply would not be affected.

Later that week, Ethiopia diverted one of the Nile's tributaries as part of the construction plan, and Morsi's spokesman said that the move wouldn't affect the amount of Nile water reaching Egypt. Still, Cairo remained concerned about the new dam's impact and awaited a report from the Tripartite Nile Basin Committee—a review board comprising Egyptian, Ethiopian, and Sudanese experts—before determining its next steps.[29] After reviewing the June 2 report with a small group of technical advisers, Morsi invited political party leaders to discuss it in a meeting at the presidential palace the following day.[30]

Unbeknownst to the party leaders, however, the meeting was broadcast on live television. It turned out to be a total circus. With Morsi listening attentively, the politicians offered a series of outlandish recommendations for forcing Ethiopia to abandon its dam project, such as leaking false "intelligence information" to Ethiopian newspapers that an Egyptian attack was imminent and supporting ethnic liberation movements within Ethiopia against the government. The meeting also became a forum for wild conspiracy theories about supposed American and Israeli involvement in the dam project. When one party leader urged his colleagues not to leak the meeting's proceedings to the media, Morsi finally revealed that they were on live television, and the attendees erupted in a nervous laughter.[31]

Then on June 10, Morsi addressed the nation. Speaking before hundreds of cheering supporters, Morsi announced that "all options are open" against Ethiopia's dam project, implying that military action was possible. Morsi seemingly hoped that this tough talk would counteract Tamarod's rising influence and rally the public around his leadership.[32] But his threats against Ethiopia angered the generals, who had no interest in a confrontation with Ethiopia.

Suddenly, the generals changed their tune and sent signals that they were considering alternatives to Morsi. With the military's permission, Egyptian newspapers started printing flattering photos of al-Sisi, depicting the defense minister running in shorts or smiling optimistically—and thus striking a sharp contrast to the potbellied, scowling Morsi. And in meetings with US officials, al-Sisi no longer promised that the military wouldn't intervene politically, and he ranted against Morsi for refusing to reconcile with the opposition.[33]

It is worth emphasizing, however, that these signals appear obvious mostly in hindsight. At the time, nobody knew exactly what the military might do if and when the anti-Morsi fervor boiled over, which is why Tamarod continued working to build momentum against Morsi and the Brotherhood. By mid-June, Tamarod claimed that it had collected more than thirteen million signatures and that it was on pace to exceed its goal of fifteen million petitions calling for early presidential elections.[34] Whether or not those figures were accurate—and, again, one should take them with a hefty grain of salt—there is no questioning Tamarod's impact on Egypt's political scene. Even in the Brotherhood's rural strongholds, Tamarod petition collectors were so ubiquitous that in mid-May the Brotherhood and its Islamist allies started an anti-Tamarod petition campaign that called for Morsi to complete his four-year term.[35]

Of course, the ongoing deterioration of conditions under Morsi fueled Tamarod's rise. The police mutiny that began in the spring of 2013 worsened, and by June the police's apparent unwillingness to enforce the law led many Egyptians to take matters into their own hands. An illicit arms trade exploded nationwide, and the proliferation of smuggled and smaller homemade weapons indicated that the state was coming apart at the seams. And in certain parts of the country, the state practically didn't exist, as armed gangs took control of major thoroughfares in Upper Egypt and Sinai.[36]

Meanwhile, Egypt's economy continued to plummet. Food prices rose further, creating longer lines at government-run bakeries. The decline of the Egyptian pound and weak cash reserves strained the country's energy resources, and the resulting electricity outages grew longer and more frequent as summer approached. At the same time, Egypt's fuel crisis worsened, with hours-long gasoline lines extending for miles in certain parts of the country and often blocking major thoroughfares. The outages hindered factory production and farming irrigation, costing the economy an estimated $14 billion.[37]

Morsi's government offered no policy solutions to these challenges. And

as conditions worsened, the Tamarod campaign downplayed its own petition's call for early presidential elections and instead focused on strategies
for convincing the military to remove Morsi immediately. The centerpiece of
these efforts was the June 30 protests, which Tamarod's backers hoped would
compel the military to intervene against Morsi, as it had against Mubarak in
February 2011.

But the activists worried that even a massive anti-Morsi demonstration
wouldn't be sufficient to catalyze a coup. After all, al-Sisi was a Morsi appointee, and in all of its public statements the military indicated that it had
no interest in governing again. So to force the military's hand, revolutionary activists planned to escalate their protests even after the June 30 demonstrations. According to one plan, activists would surround the presidential
palace and governorate offices in every province and lay siege until the military intervened. Another plan suggested reinforcing this siege by parking
cars at the protest grounds, forcing the military and police to either remove
Morsi or use significant force to upend the protesters' positions. And in the
Nile Delta, anti-Morsi unionists planned to shut down their factories after
June 30, thereby threatening severe economic devastation for as long as Morsi
remained in office.

Indeed, Tamarod's supporters were desperate to end Morsi's rule and saw
the June 30 protests as their pivotal showdown with Morsi and the Brotherhood. "We will leave our homes [on June 30] and not go back unless the regime steps down, or we will die," Abdel Fattah Sabry, the chief Tamarod organizer in the Nile Delta city of Al-Mahalla al-Kobra, told me during an early
June interview.[38]

• • • • • • • •

Even as calls for Morsi's ouster reached a fever pitch by mid-June, the Brotherhood still didn't take Tamarod seriously. In interviews, Muslim Brothers continued to portray Tamarod as the work of a tiny but vocal minority—non-
Islamists who had little support in a Muslim-majority country like Egypt. So
rather than viewing Tamarod as a sign that Morsi's presidency was off the
rails, Muslim Brothers argued that Tamarod's emergence indicated that Morsi
was doing the right things—that he was making the kinds of policies that
would inevitably outrage the Brotherhood's weak, non-Islamist adversaries.
"Hassan al-Banna told us this would happen seventy years ago," Mahmoud
Rashad, an FJP media official, told me at the time. "So I am not worried but
confident that we are on the right track."[39]

Despite this self-assuredness, the Brotherhood was in a combative mood. It was tired of the calls for Morsi's ouster and wanted to prove the opposition's weakness once and for all. Starting in early June, it planned to mobilize its cadres earlier and more emphatically than Tamarod, organizing a "series of million-man marches to protect legitimacy" during the week leading up to June 30, including a mass demonstration to support Morsi on June 28. The Brotherhood also indicated that it was willing to use violence to defend Morsi's presidency, as it had done during the December 2012 demonstrations outside the presidential palace. "What the organization or the Muslim Brotherhood [leaders] sees is right, we will obey," former FJP spokesman Ahmed Sobea told me.[40]

Meanwhile, as the June 30 protests approached, Morsi worked to solidify his Islamist base by appealing to the Salafists. While the Salafists generally preferred the Muslim Brotherhood to its non-Islamist opponents—Salafists largely supported Morsi during the June 2012 runoff against Ahmed Shafik— there were signs of rising discontent. Nour Party leaders believed that the Brotherhood had appointed too few Salafists to top positions and had warned for many months that Morsi's fights with the judiciary and exclusivist governing style were pushing Egypt toward the brink of a violent breakdown.[41]

In terms of policy substance, however, the Salafists particularly objected to Morsi's rapprochement with Iran. Salafists typically regard Shiites as apostates and warned that improved Iranian–Egyptian relations would open the doors to Shiite proselytization in Egypt. The Nour Party also warned that engaging Iran alienated longtime Gulf allies such as the United Arab Emirates and Saudi Arabia and thus drove away foreign investment.[42]

Moreover, given Tehran's support for Syrian dictator Bashar al-Assad's brutal crackdown on the Syrian uprising, in which over a hundred thousand people had been killed by that point, Morsi's outreach to Iran was increasingly controversial even among non-Salafist Islamists. The pressure on Morsi to reverse his Iran policy intensified after May 31, when the Qatar-based Sheikh Yusuf al-Qaradawi, one of the most prominent Sunni Islamist voices and a major ideological influence on the Brotherhood, lambasted Iranian support for al-Assad and urged Sunnis to take up arms in support of the Syrian opposition. "Iran is pushing forward arms and men [to back the Syrian regime], so why do we stand idle?" Qaradawi declared. "How could 100 million Shiites [worldwide] defeat 1.7 billion [Sunnis]?"[43]

In a bid to appease these rising anti-Iranian sentiments and bolster its Islamist base, Morsi's administration suddenly embraced a hard-line Syrian policy. On June 13, Morsi foreign policy adviser Khaled al-Qazzaz announced that Egypt wouldn't take any action against Egyptian citizens who traveled to Syria to join the jihadis against the al-Assad regime. "The right of travel or freedom of travel is open for all Egyptians," al-Qazzaz told the Associated Press, adding that Egyptians who returned from the Syrian jihad weren't a threat to Egypt.[44]

Then on June 15, Morsi delivered a major address before tens of thousands of screaming supporters. Standing alongside radical Salafist clerics at a massive rally in Cairo Stadium, Morsi threw Egypt's total support behind the Syrian opposition. "The Egyptian people support the struggle of the Syrian people, materially and morally, and Egypt, its nation, leadership . . . and army, will not abandon the Syrian people until it achieves its rights and dignity," Morsi declared. He further criticized Iran implicitly, calling on its proxy Hezbollah to leave Syria and accusing states in the region of feeding "a campaign of extermination and planned ethnic cleansing" in Syria.[45]

It was an incredibly dangerous speech on many levels. By explicitly saying that Egypt's "army will not abandon the Syrian people," Morsi suggested that Egypt might get involved militarily in Syria—a commitment that Morsi was in no position to make, given the military's autonomy over its own affairs. Moreover, although Morsi didn't explicitly call for jihad in Syria or embrace the Salafists' anti-Shiism, other speakers did, including prominent Salafist Sheikh Mohamed Hassan, who called for preventing Shiites from entering Egypt and declared participation in the Syrian jihad "incumbent on all Arab peoples."[46] Morsi's involvement in the Syria rally was thus viewed as the Egyptian state's endorsement of the Syrian jihad and an open invitation for Egyptians to join it.[47] And given the significant security threat that Egypt already faced from Sinai-based jihadis, Morsi's implicit embrace of the Syrian jihad gave the Egyptian military another reason to see Morsi's presidency as destabilizing.

The next day, Morsi threw his Islamist base another bone. He announced the appointment of seventeen new governors, including seven from the Brotherhood, five from the military, and one from the police. With these appointments, Brotherhood-affiliated governors outnumbered those from the security services for the first time, by a margin of eleven to nine—a tally that pleased the Brotherhood's rank and file but outraged the opposition, which once again accused Morsi of "Brotherhoodizing" the government.[48] As a result, violent protests erupted in those governorates where Muslim Brothers presided and continued for days. Rioters burned the FJP's headquarters in

Tanta, laid siege to the governor's home in Kafr el-Sheikh, and stormed the governors' offices in Dakhaliya and Ismailia.[49]

Morsi's most controversial gubernatorial appointment, however, came in Luxor: He appointed Adel al-Khayat, a founding member of al-Gamaa al-Islamiya. The organization was reviled in Luxor because its militants had killed sixty-two people—including fifty-eight tourists—in a November 1997 attack at the Temple of Hatshepsut. Moreover, al-Gamaa had declared its intention to ban alcohol and nightclubs—moves that would be especially damaging in a governorate that relied so heavily on tourism revenue.[50]

Al-Khayat's appointment thus sparked instant outrage. Tourism Minister Hesham Zaazou resigned almost immediately, explaining that putting an al-Gamaa member in charge of Luxor would have a disastrous impact on tourism. Meanwhile, local Luxor citizens—many of them connected to the tourism industry—mobilized to prevent al-Khayat from entering the governor's office.[51] The standoff ended a week later, when al-Khayat resigned from office.[52]

By that point, however, the Brotherhood and its allies were growing restless. Seemingly everything that Morsi did led to a new wave of violent protests, and now demonstrators were preventing Morsi's gubernatorial appointees from entering their offices. The Brotherhood's youth cadres were particularly eager to mobilize in support of Morsi and said that they were willing to die to protect his presidency.[53]

On Friday, June 21, hundreds of pro-Morsi protesters gathered outside Rabaa al-Adawiya mosque in northern Cairo, chanting Islamist slogans. From the podium, al-Gamaa al-Islamiya leader Assem Abdel-Maged declared that the following week's protests would be the "spark for an Islamic revolution," while pro-Brotherhood preacher Safwat Hegazy threatened to defend Morsi's presidency violently, saying that "whoever sprays [Morsi] with water, we will spray with blood." The demonstration also featured a martial arts performance by Islamist youths, as well as banners depicting Morsi's media critics in nooses—violent threats that sought to intimidate the opposition.[54]

• • • • • • • •

Egypt's rapidly deteriorating political environment greatly unnerved Washington. After months of trying to "moderate" Morsi's behavior through friendly "engagement," US officials now recognized privately that this policy had failed miserably. Morsi's exclusivist governing style had alienated a large segment of Egyptian society, and Washington's largely uncritical interactions with him fed the perception that the United States supported the Brother-hood. Still, the Obama administration viewed the June 30 Tamarod protests as a recipe for further instability, since Morsi's toppling would destroy Egypt's electoral institutions and risked severe civil strife.

In an apparent attempt to walk the opposition back from the brink, US ambassador Anne Patterson addressed the Cairo-based Ibn Khaldun Center on June 18. After explaining that Washington dealt with Morsi and the Muslim Brotherhood because they had won elections, Patterson turned to the up-coming June 30 Tamarod protests. "Some say that street action will produce better results than elections," she said. "To be honest, my government and I are deeply skeptical." Patterson added that "more violence on the streets" would encumber Egypt's economic progress and urged the opposition to organize politically. "Join or start a political party that reflects your values and aspirations," she said. "You will have to roll up your sleeves and work hard. Progress will be slow and you often will feel frustrated. But there is no other way."[55]

Of course, Patterson's point was that democratic institutions provided a more peaceful mechanism for resolving political disputes than uprisings. But in the context of Egypt's severe political polarization, Patterson was effec-tively blaming the opposition for Egypt's instability and touting Morsi's dem-ocratic credentials simply because he had won an election. As a result, Pat-terson's statement backfired, and Egypt's private media cited it as evidence of US support for the Brotherhood.

Two days later, Patterson visited Brotherhood Deputy Supreme Guide Khairat al-Shater.[56] The meeting was supposed to be private, but news of it leaked almost instantly, further feeding the perception of close US–Brother-hood ties. Yet Patterson's meeting with al-Shater wasn't chummy at all: The ambassador urged al-Shater to take Tamarod seriously and argued that Morsi needed to make substantial political concessions to calm the atmosphere, such as replacing the prime minister.

Al-Shater refused. The political parties backing Tamarod don't count for anything and have no support in the street, he said. From the Brotherhood's perspective, the only forces that mattered were the Brotherhood, the mili-tary, and the Mubarak regime's former supporters—and al-Shater alleged that the Mubarakists had plotted with corrupt members of the security services to topple Morsi from the moment that he was elected. So, as al-Shater saw it, there was nothing that Morsi could offer that would appease those particular forces.

Al-Shater further lambasted Egyptian Christians. He accused the new Coptic pope of being an "agent" against the Brotherhood and darkly vowed that the Copts would "pay a price" for supporting Tamarod. He also discussed the situation in the Sinai, claiming that the Brotherhood's relations with certain groups had kept violence on the peninsula to a minimum and threatening that all hell would break loose if Morsi were toppled.

Ultimately, al-Shater threw the ball back into Washington's court. "You have been big supporters of this transition in Egypt," he told Patterson. "And you need to make it clear that you'll stand by us. That will make a big difference."[57]

Washington, however, knew that it had little control over the situation. Neither the Brotherhood nor the opposition was heeding its calls for reconciliation, and that portended disaster.

• • • • • • • •

By late June, Egypt's political polarization had become so severe that both the Muslim Brotherhood and the opposition expected significant violence on June 30, and talk of a civil war was prevalent.[58] Political violence was already occurring daily: Muslim Brothers and their opponents clashed, Salafist political headquarters were torched, and all sides spoke of the June 30 protests in life-and-death terms.[59] This was precisely the scenario that the military likely feared most because severe violence would jeopardize its economic interests and undermine its credibility as the ultimate guarantor of security under the Egyptian constitution.

On June 23, Defense Minister al-Sisi demanded negotiations before the situation spun out of control. "There is a state of division in society," al-Sisi warned on the military's Facebook page. "Prolonging it poses a danger to the Egyptian state. There must be consensus among all. . . . We will not remain silent as the country slips into a conflict that is hard to control."

It was al-Sisi's most direct political statement yet—another indication that the military might intervene if the political forces didn't resolve their differences soon. Yet after meeting with al-Sisi, Morsi downplayed the statement's implications. His presidential office released a statement saying that the military was playing a "patriotic role" by trying to defuse "the rising tension between the different political factions."[60]

Rather than acting to defuse the tensions, however, the Brotherhood ramped up its mobilization. Partnering with radical Salafists such as al-Gamaa al-Islamiya and Brotherhood offshoot movements such as the Wasat Party, the Brotherhood announced a week of demonstrations to support Morsi, starting with a rally in Asyut on June 25 and rallies in five other cities the following day.[61] These activities were intended to counter Tamarod's claim that it represented the Egyptian people broadly and bolster Morsi ahead of a major address to the nation on June 26.[62]

As Morsi made quite clear in his address that evening, the Brotherhood and its allies were in no mood for compromise. With his government ministers—including al-Sisi—sitting in the front rows and hundreds of supporters howling throughout the rest of the auditorium, Morsi unleashed a rambling and mostly defiant two-and-a-half-hour speech. While the president admitted some mistakes during his year in office, he largely blamed Egypt's problems on conspiracies and claimed that the remnants of the Mubarak regime were actively working to sabotage his presidency.

"There are those who crave the ability to turn back the clock and revert to the state of corruption, oppression, monopolization and injustice," Morsi declared, accusing the "beneficiaries of the old regime" of "sparing no effort to sabotage the democratic experiment" through "violence, defamation, incitement, and corrupt financing."

Morsi then proceeded to name his enemies. "I issue a stern warning to Ahmed Bahgat and Mohamed al-Amin," he said, referring to the owners of two major satellite news networks. "They owe debts and taxes, but instead of paying them they stir up trouble on their TV channels. No one should think that they can escape justice!" Morsi followed this explicit threat with a more veiled threat against the country's historically powerful rural clans. "Studies have shown that only thirty-two families [control] the Egyptian economy," he said, blaming them for inequality.

Morsi also attacked the judiciary. "The involvement of some judges in politics has confused both the judiciary and the political circles," he said. "Judges appearing as politicians is considered by Egyptian judicial norms to violate the esteem of the judiciary." Once again, Morsi named an enemy, singling out the judge responsible for a case against former presidential candidate Ahmed Shafik as an "illegitimate judge" and announcing that twenty-one other judges would be investigated for "election fraud."

Meanwhile, in explaining how he would resolve the political crisis, Morsi proposed a series of purges. He promised to "order ministers and governors to immediately fire the troublemakers responsible for what citizens have been suffering, within one week." He also commanded governors to "appoint youth assistants, not older than forty years old, starting four weeks from now," which likely meant that Brotherhood cadres would be appointed to key positions throughout the country. And to address the energy crisis, he announced that the Brotherhood-dominated Ministry of Supply would take control of gas stations that refused to cooperate with the government.

At certain points in his address, Morsi offered to negotiate with the opposition. He suggested appointing an independent committee to propose amendments to the constitution. Morsi also offered to form a "high committee for national reconciliation" that would include "representatives from all factions of society, from the parties, al-Azhar, the church, youth, and NGOs."[63] The opposition, however, rejected these entreaties out of hand. From its perspective, Morsi's previous calls for dialogue were farcical, and it saw little upside to negotiating with a president who, at one point in his speech, referred to them as "criminals."

But more to the point, the opposition didn't believe that it had to negotiate with Morsi. It sensed that the political tide had turned against him decisively and that this latest speech was likely the final nail in his political coffin. After all, Morsi had just threatened influential media entrepreneurs by name, attacked the judiciary, blasted the country's most powerful families, and promised to fire en masse government workers whom his ministers deemed "troublemakers." Morsi, in other words, had just given infinitely more people a reason to see his ouster as vital to their own self-preservation!

Far from calming tensions, Morsi's speech exacerbated them. Protesters immediately took to the streets in multiple governorates following the speech, and demonstrators began a Tahrir Square sit-in that evening as a precursor to the June 30 protests.[64] Meanwhile, the following day, the NSF issued a statement saying that the address "reinforced Egyptians' belief about Morsi's inability to fill the position of president" and called for early presidential elections to prevent further deterioration.[65]

The Brotherhood, however, still didn't believe that Morsi's presidency was in danger. It continued to see the June 30 Tamarod protests as a media contrivance and told its cadres that Morsi was fully in control of the situation. And to demonstrate its own mobilizing strength, the Brotherhood held two mass protests on Friday, June 28: one at al-Nahda Square in Giza and a second at Rabaa al-Adawiya Square. These two locations were chosen to prevent Morsi's supporters from clashing with opposition protesters in Tahrir Square and in front of the presidential palace. Rabaa al-Adawiya is also, notably, adjacent to a Defense Ministry compound.[66]

June 28, however, was another severely violent day in Egypt. In Alexan-

dria, armed confrontations erupted between the Brotherhood and oppositionists. Dozens were injured, the Brotherhood's headquarters were set
ablaze, and an American student was stabbed to death. In Port Said, an explosion at a demonstration killed an Egyptian journalist and wounded twelve
others. Meanwhile, nine members of the Shura Council resigned to protest
Morsi's presidency.[67]

The country was on fire, and Morsi's government was beginning to crum-
ble. Yet the Brotherhood was still convinced that the president would sur-
vive. After all, Brotherhood leaders reasoned, who would topple him? The
Brotherhood believed that the military had Morsi's back, and al-Sisi's fluid
communication with Morsi seemingly fed the president's confidence. The
two met on the afternoon of June 29, and later that day Morsi stressed his faith
in the military in an interview with the *Guardian*.[68]

However, the military and police sent the opposition a very different set
of signals.

On the evening of June 29, two of Tamarod's five founders, Mouhib Doss
and Walid al-Masry, met a retired military officer at a café in downtown Cairo.
The retired officer told them that the military would take care of security the
following day and instructed the activists on protest routes, emphasizing that
the Tamarod protests shouldn't approach the Brotherhood's demonstration
site at Rabaa al-Adawiya Square. It was a tense meeting, and, given the extreme sensitivity regarding the military's stance toward the June 30 protests,
the retired officer did not share his name. But the Tamarod activists came
away from the discussion believing that the military would protect them.[69]

Meanwhile, in the days leading up to the June 30 protests, the Interior Ministry signaled its support for the anti-Morsi movement. The Police Officers
Club announced on June 20 that it would "secure peacefully demonstrating
citizens and not secure any partisan facilities"—meaning that it would protect those protesting against Morsi but not protect the Brotherhood's prop-
erties from attacks.[70] Then on June 28, the Interior Ministry put "Police of
the People" posters on its personnel carrier vehicles and reportedly updated
police uniform badges to prevent "elements" from posing as police officers
and "driving a wedge between the police and the people."[71] The message was
clear: Those who turned out on June 30 didn't have to worry about tear gas or
birdshot because the police stood with "the people"—in other words, those
protesting Morsi.

Still, during their last meeting before the Tamarod protests hit on June 30,
al-Sisi urged Morsi to defuse the situation. As the *New York Times* later re-

ported, al-Sisi pressed Morsi on a package of concessions, including the appointment of a new cabinet. Morsi refused, however, saying that he needed to consult with his Islamist coalition.[72]

• • • • • • • •

The June 30 protests were probably the largest protests in Egyptian history. All across the country, millions of Egyptians from all walks of life spilled into the streets, seemingly exceeding the number of protesters who participated in the largest demonstrations of the 2011 uprising. From Tahrir Square in downtown Cairo all the way to the Giza neighborhood of Dokki more than a mile westward, as well as in front of the presidential palace in northern Cairo, participants reported such crowded conditions that they could barely press forward. And beyond Cairo the outpouring was similarly overwhelming, as anti-Morsi demonstrators packed the central squares in virtually every governorate throughout the country.

Egyptian media outlets would later claim that fourteen million, seventeen million, or thirty-three million protesters turned out on that day—exaggerated figures, in all likelihood. But no matter how many Egyptians actually participated in the June 30 protests, the ultimate impact of those protests was undeniable. As anti-Brotherhood protesters clogged virtually every major thoroughfare and the security forces refused to suppress them, Morsi had no capacity to restore order. Indeed, by the evening of June 30 and arguably before that, he was a president in name only—he held the title but in fact controlled nothing.

The result was chaos. Clashes between Morsi's supporters and opponents broke out in multiple cities, killing at least seven people and injuring hundreds. In the Cairo suburb of Moqattam, police stood to the side as protesters attacked the Brotherhood's main headquarters and set it ablaze.

Indeed, the state participated very directly in the uprising. Uniformed police officers joined the anti-Morsi protesters in some locations, and army helicopters dropped Egyptian flags on the demonstrations from above.[73] Egypt's political crisis was now a full-blown insurrection—and all eyes turned toward Morsi and the Brotherhood, since only they had the ability to initiate a political solution, such as calling for new elections.

Morsi, however, made no such offers. While he recognized that the June 30 protests had been large, he still believed that Tamarod was a media creation and told his advisers that most protesters had gone home that evening. According to his analysis, the protests stemmed from popular frustrations regarding the country's deteriorating conditions, particularly the long fuel lines and worsening electricity outages. So rather than offering any political concessions, he organized a series of meetings with his ministers and advisers, believing that improved conditions would satisfy the protesters.[74]

The Brotherhood was similarly delusional and fed its members a completely alternative reality. At its main protest site in Rabaa al-Adawiya Square, the Brotherhood celebrated the one-year anniversary of Morsi's presidency with cake and fireworks and claimed that it had gathered four million people to support the president.[75] Only a few hundred thousand people had protested Morsi's presidency, the Brotherhood's leaders insisted, and the images of mass protests had been photoshopped.

The Brotherhood thus assured its members that Morsi's presidency was safe—that the army was on its side and that the organization had made preparations to secure the presidential palace.[76] The Brotherhood equipped hundreds of its cadres with helmets, shields, and sticks, and they marched in formation around the Brotherhood's protest site chanting pro-Morsi slogans. It was an astoundingly foolish move: The appearance of "Brotherhood militias," as the media branded them, stoked new fears of severe civil strife between Muslim Brothers and anti-Morsi protesters and indicated that the current crisis might still get worse.

So the following afternoon, the military issued a statement that gave "the political forces a 48 hour ultimatum as a last chance to carry the burdens of this historic situation that the nation is going through." The military's statement warned that if "the people's demands aren't set within the time frame," it would "declare a road map and procedures for overseeing it, with the cooperation of all sides and national directions, including the youth who started this glorious revolution, without excluding anyone."[77]

The statement was a clear warning to Morsi and the Brotherhood that the military would intervene if it failed to resolve the political crisis. Of course, this is precisely what the opposition wanted—and for the next forty-eight hours the masses returned to the squares in anticipation of a coup.

Shortly after the military's ultimatum, US officials met with two of Morsi's Brotherhood advisers, Essam el-Haddad and Khaled al-Qazzaz, and urged them to offer an electoral solution to the crisis, such as a referendum on Morsi's presidency. The advisers, however, refused, arguing that such a move had no constitutional basis. They further insisted that the June 30 protests had been meager and that the media images of large crowds had been photoshopped.

The US officials disputed that, noting that the protests had been quite large and that the military was poised to intervene if Morsi didn't act quickly. But Morsi's advisers still refused and alleged that the military had been plotting to topple Morsi from the moment he took office. Morsi's advisers then placed the onus on the United States, arguing that the military wouldn't intervene if Washington told it not to.

"You really shouldn't count on that," one of the US officials replied, adding that Washington had repeatedly told the military not to launch a coup but that the military would likely do it anyway.

When the meeting ended, al-Qazzaz walked the Americans out and told them that he expected to be killed.[78]

· · · · · · · ·

Indeed, within Morsi's inner circle, there was the growing sense that a military coup was imminent. Yet Morsi exuded an eerie calm around his advisers. Whether or not he believed that the military would intervene—and different advisers have told me different things—Morsi appeared resigned to his fate and didn't believe that there was much he could do either way.[79]

As the crisis continued without any presidential action, the situation in the streets deteriorated further. On July 2, eighteen people were reportedly killed in clashes near the Brotherhood's protest site in Giza, and dozens were injured in clashes between Morsi's opponents and supporters in Alexandria. Meanwhile, Morsi's political circle narrowed, with six ministers and two government spokesmen resigning. That afternoon, al-Sisi met with Prime Minister Hesham Qandil and Morsi, and, as the *New York Times* later reported, Morsi accepted the package of concessions that al-Sisi had recommended on the day before the protests began, including the appointment of a new cabinet. But later that evening, al-Sisi told Morsi that the opposition had refused those concessions.[80]

Late on July 2, the military signaled that it was poised to intervene. It took control of the state-run newspaper *Al-Ahram* and printed a transition plan on its front page that promised to remove Morsi if he failed to satisfy the protesters' demands.[81]

Around midnight, a visibly shaken Morsi addressed the nation. In another rambling speech, in which he emphasized his electoral legitimacy by using the word "legitimacy" fifty-seven times, the president refused to resign or call early elections. "I cannot permit, allow, or say anything to violate legitimacy or take steps or actions that would shake legitimacy," he said, adding that he was ready to protect his electoral legitimacy with his own blood. Still, for the first time, Morsi offered some concessions: He promised to form a coalition government and create a committee to review constitutional articles. He also suggested that he would fire his prosecutor-general.[82]

Had Morsi made these concessions a week earlier, he might have survived. But by the evening of July 2, the mass protesters and key state institutions had converged around the same point of consensus: Morsi had to go. The only question was *how* he would exit—whether he would strike a deal and accept early elections or whether the military would ultimately intervene.

The military seemingly preferred the former. On the morning of July 3, Defense Minister al-Sisi sent three emissaries to Morsi—Prime Minister Qandil, Shura Council speaker Ahmed Fahmy, and former presidential adviser Selim al-Awa—to urge the president to accept a referendum on his presidency within the next few weeks. According to Fahmy's account of these discussions, Fahmy counteroffered with Morsi's subsequent approval: The president would appoint al-Sisi as his prime minister, hold parliamentary elections, allow Parliament to form a new cabinet, and then agree to either early presidential elections or a referendum on his presidency.

But al-Sisi refused. "This is the only option, the masses demand this," he reportedly said, referring to his demand for a referendum on Morsi's presidency in the next few weeks. "I cannot wait any longer."[83]

Later that day, an Arab foreign minister called Morsi on behalf of Washington and asked whether he would accept the appointment of a new cabinet that would assume all legislative power and also replace the governors that he had appointed. According to the *New York Times*, Morsi responded by suggesting that he'd rather die than accept what he considered a de facto coup.[84]

Shortly after the military's forty-eight-hour ultimatum expired at four o'clock on the afternoon of July 3, security forces surrounded the Brotherhood's protest at Rabaa al-Adawiya Square. Later that evening, al-Sisi addressed the nation. Flanked by a broad range of Egyptian figures—including the Coptic pope, the sheikh of al-Azhar, youth activists, non-Islamist politicians, and a representative from the Salafist Nour Party—he announced that Morsi was toppled, the controversial December 2012 constitution had been suspended, and the chief justice of the SCC would serve as interim president.

As millions of Egyptians rejoiced throughout the country, the Brotherhood rapidly transitioned from ruling party to repressed opposition movement. Within minutes of al-Sisi's declaration, the Brotherhood's satellite television stations were taken off the air, two high-ranking Brotherhood leaders were arrested, and warrants were issued for three hundred more.[85]

While Morsi and his advisers knew that his toppling was likely after the military issued its forty-eight-hour ultimatum, every Brotherhood leader and cadre that I've interviewed since Morsi's ouster has told me the same thing: The Brotherhood never expected a coup. Until the very last minute, Brotherhood leaders told their members at their protest sites that the military would stand by Morsi and that the president would prevail.

The Brotherhood was thus entirely unprepared for the brutal period to come.

Conclusion
Broken Brothers

*When Defense Minister Abdel Fatah al-Sisi responded to mass protests by top-*pling Mohamed Morsi on July 3, 2013, he won the admiration of many millions of Egyptians. But he also thrust himself into a life-and-death struggle with the Brotherhood. From the Brotherhood's standpoint, al-Sisi was the face of the coup that ousted its elected president, and the Brotherhood vowed to fight him and his fellow "putschists" until Morsi was restored to power. Al-Sisi and his colleagues thus viewed the Brotherhood's destruction as essential to their own survival, and they were quite willing to use severe violence to prevent the Brotherhood from seeking retribution.

Indeed, despite American and European efforts to promote reconciliation, there was no chance at fostering compromise between the Brotherhood and Egypt's new military-backed regime after Morsi's ouster. After all, the military was not prepared to permit the restoration of a president that it just removed from power. And the Brotherhood refused to participate in any post-Morsi process because doing so meant legitimating the coup.

To some extent, the Brotherhood's demand that Morsi be reinstated was a matter of principle: Morsi had been elected, and it wouldn't accept his undemocratic deposal. But it also reflected the Brotherhood's particular organizational realities. Accepting the coup would have stoked significant discord within the Brotherhood's ranks and undermined its internal unity during the most dangerous moment in its history. Then on July 8, security forces killed fifty-one Morsi supporters and wounded at least four hundred more outside the Republican Guard headquarters in northern Cairo, where Morsi was rumored to be held.[1] From that point forward, the Brotherhood viewed any negotiation with the new military-backed regime as a betrayal of its martyrs.

So rather than negotiating, the Brotherhood prepared for a prolonged confrontation with the regime. It gathered its members in Rabaa al-Adawiya

Square and al-Nahda Square and vowed to occupy those areas indefinitely. It also organized a series of mass protests throughout the country, where it blocked major thoroughfares, confronted security forces, and clashed with ordinary citizens. These activities were designed to send a very clear message: Egypt would not know stability until the coup was reversed.

Despite the military's obvious advantages in arms and capacity, the Brotherhood sincerely expected to prevail. It believed that only a small group of generals had plotted the coup and that at least a few military officials opposed Morsi's ouster. "They're already talking to us—not just low level, but high level," Gehad el-Haddad, a spokesman for the organization, told me a few days after Morsi's ouster. "They're telling us that Morsi is all right. . . . They are briefing us on what's going on."

The Brotherhood thus believed that prolonged protests would bring the regime to its knees, paving the way for Morsi's return.[2] And it tried to appeal to these supposed allies within the military by distinguishing the "putschists" from the broader military institution. Accordingly, in one of its first statements following the coup, the Brotherhood attributed Morsi's toppling to "some members of the military council" but emphasized, "We fully trust in our great army that redeems us and we redeem it, and which loves us and which we love, and which could not have participated in this conspiracy."[3]

Moreover, the Brotherhood believed that it possessed the manpower to continue resisting the new regime indefinitely. Its hundreds of thousands of deeply committed members could keep the Brotherhood's protest sites occupied. And the Brotherhood believed that its members' willingness to die for the cause would make it difficult for the military to disperse the protests. "If they want to disperse the sit-in, they'll have to kill 100,000 protesters," el-Haddad, the Brotherhood's spokesman, told journalist Maged Atef. "And they can't do it [because] we're willing to offer one hundred thousand martyrs."[4]

Once again, the Brotherhood badly miscalculated. It profoundly overestimated its own capabilities and catastrophically underestimated the new regime's eagerness to crush it.

Like the Brotherhood, the new military-backed regime saw the post-Morsi period as an existential struggle—one that it was similarly determined to win. According to its narrative, the Brotherhood wasn't a patriotic organization but a fifth column that sought to take control of Egypt for its own power promotion. The Egyptian military had answered the public's call by removing the Brotherhood from power, saving Egypt from becoming a failed state like Syria, and narrowly averting a civil war. Yet rather than accepting Morsi's ouster, the Brotherhood had chosen to continue its struggle against a country that already rejected it. The regime thus had no choice but to take the battle to the Brotherhood because the fate of Egypt was at stake.

The regime viewed the Brotherhood's protest sites at Rabaa al-Adawiya and al-Nahda Squares as ground zero of this war. These sites were effectively no-go zones for the Egyptian police, and they became sanctuaries where wanted Brotherhood leaders held meetings and addressed the international media. Moreover, Morsi supporters reportedly detained, abused, and tortured alleged "infiltrators" within these sites, while pro-Morsi snipers shot at local residents from within al-Nahda Square.[5] And the Egyptian media, which now referred to the Brotherhood as a terrorist organization, claimed (incorrectly) that protestors at these sites were heavily armed, leading many Egyptians to view these sites as major national security threats.

When it became clear that a negotiated resolution with the Brotherhood was impossible, the military-backed government signaled that it would disperse the protests by force. On July 24, al-Sisi asked Egyptians to hold mass demonstrations to "authorize" him to confront "terrorism," which Egyptians understood as a mandate for confronting the Brotherhood.[6] Two days later, hundreds of thousands of Egyptians joined promilitary protests.[7] Then on July 31, during its second meeting, the new cabinet announced that it had "delegated the minister of interior . . . to take all necessary measures to disperse protests or sit-ins at Rabaa Al-Adawiya and Al-Nahda [Squares]."[8]

It was widely understood that clearing these two protest sites would be very bloody. So to reduce the scale of bloodshed, some ministers advocated encircling the protests to prevent goods and protesters from entering, while permitting protesters to leave. This would have been a far more gradual approach to ending the protests but also promised far fewer casualties. The interior minister refused, however, arguing a siege strategy would give the Brotherhood the advantage of deciding when to initiate hostiles with the security forces that would surround the sites, forcing the police to be reactive rather than kinetic. Ultimately, the cabinet deferred to the security professionals and authorized the dispersal of the pro-Morsi protesters whenever the police were ready.[9]

On August 14, 2013, Egyptian security forces converged on both Rabaa al-Adawiya and al-Nahda Squares, killing hundreds of Morsi supporters in the deadliest massacres in contemporary Egyptian history.[10] By the end of the day, the Brotherhood's two protest sites—and its entire strategy for reversing the coup—lay in ruins.

In the months that followed, the regime effectively decapitated the Brotherhood. By the end of 2013, most of the Brotherhood's Guidance Office was in prison, and its other top leaders were either in exile or hiding. The regime similarly arrested many of the Brotherhood's General Shura Committee and provincial leaders, thereby shutting down the top two tiers of the Brotherhood's chain of command and disrupting its ability to make and execute decisions.

· · · · · · · ·

As the Guidance Office lost control over the organization's chain of command, internal disagreements suddenly exploded to the fore. One set of Brothers, generally older leaders and members living in exile or hiding within Egypt, took a long-term view of the organization's predicament. While they strongly rejected the coup, they urged Brotherhood cadres in Egypt to protest it nonviolently, arguing the Brotherhood's violence would play into the regime's hands. They also understood that the organization was unlikely to return to power in the near term and thus urged a more gradualist approach.

"The situation appears very serious," London-based Brotherhood leader Gomaa Amin wrote in July 2014. "The Islamic nation has faced a gradual, systematic, organized extermination campaign for many decades, and it continues to this day. . . . Because of this, Muslims are in need of consciousness, capability, cleverness, wisdom, and precision in planning to confront all of this."[11] Amin, who served as one of the Brotherhood's chief ideologists until his death in January 2015, thus advocated a return to societal outreach to raise "consciousness," which meant that the Brotherhood would effectively defer its power ambitions. To some extent, this conservative approach reflected the older leaders' personal experiences: They had worked for decades under very repressive conditions and—with the brief exception of the 2011–13 period—tended to view the Brotherhood's Islamizing mission as a long-term project.

Another, mostly younger set of Muslim Brothers, however, favored a more aggressive approach. They blamed the "old guard" leadership for the Brotherhood's predicament, arguing that Morsi and his colleagues had been too trusting of the military and should have moved more aggressively against the Brotherhood's domestic adversaries. So rather than deferring their power ambitions, these younger Muslim Brothers advocated revolutionary tactics to destabilize the "coup regime" as soon as possible and took matters into their own hands. They formed a variety of low-profile insurgent organizations, such as the Molotov Movement and Revolutionary Punishment, which targeted security personnel, infrastructure, and roads.[12]

While Egypt's security forces successfully shuttered many of these pro-- Morsi insurgent groups, this younger Brotherhood faction gained the upper hand within the organization by early 2015. When the Brotherhood held new elections, it replaced 65 percent of its leadership, and 90 percent of the new leaders hailed from the younger generation. The Brotherhood's public mes- saging reflected this shift toward more overt confrontation with the regime: It called for "jihad" and "martyrdom" in fighting the regime in a January 2015 statement and then demanded a "revolution that cuts the heads from the rotten bodies" after a court sentenced Morsi to death in May. Meanwhile, as more Muslim Brothers escaped to exile, Brotherhood leaders in Istanbul established a special division for Muslim Brothers abroad, which sought to resist the post-Morsi regime at the international level. "There will not be a political solution before the demands of the revolutionaries on the ground are met," Ahmed Abdel Rahman, who oversees the organization's activities for exiled Muslim Brothers, said during an interview with Al Jazeera. "We will continue our revolution until victory."[13]

The old guard attempted to rein in the Brotherhood's younger faction. It warned in a series of statements that embracing violence so explicitly would backfire. But the younger Muslim Brothers rejected these entreaties, took control of the Brotherhood's media outlets, and reportedly ousted these old guard leaders from the organization in May 2015.[14] While the extent of the new leadership's support among the Brotherhood's rank and file within Egypt is unknowable, the very public nature of this rift between the old guard and younger leaders suggests that the Brotherhood's culture of obedience is as broken as its chain of command.

Can the Brotherhood reemerge? History suggests that it would be foolish to predict otherwise. After all, the Brotherhood's ideology—like all ideolo- gies, perhaps—cannot be repressed out of existence and has in fact prospered under previous crackdowns. The Brotherhood's interpretation of Islam as an "all-embracing concept" meant to govern every aspect of life resonates with even non-Brotherhood Islamists. Moreover, Brotherhood movements beyond Egypt will continue to promote its vision for Islamizing the world from the grass roots up—from the individual to the family to the society to the state, until a "global Islamic state" can be established.

But the Brotherhood isn't simply an ideology. It is a hierarchical vanguard whose recruitment procedures and internal structures are designed to empower that ideology. And the Egyptian government's crackdown has dealt the Brotherhood's organization a very significant blow, which is why the Brotherhood hasn't executed a clear or successful strategy within Egypt in the years since Morsi's ouster.

Of course, the Brotherhood's organization can be rebuilt. But the longer the current crackdown persists, the harder this will be. As Brotherhood leader Khairat al-Shater noted in his April 2011 address on the Renaissance Project, it took the Brotherhood over a decade to rebuild itself after Nasser practically obliterated the organization during the 1950s and 1960s: "This matter took ten or even fifteen years, not just a few days, because as I said from the beginning, if the incarcerated [Muslim Brothers] had served just two years and then [been] released, it would have been easy; they would have exerted a little effort and organized what had existed before. However the matter took a much, much longer time."[15]

So how long will the post-Morsi crackdown on the Brotherhood last? It is extremely difficult to say. In March 2014, Defense Minister al-Sisi resigned from the military, announced his presidential candidacy, and won the barely contested elections two months later with nearly 97 percent of the vote. At the time, he was widely viewed as a hero for "saving" Egypt from the Brotherhood's misrule. Many, and perhaps most, Egyptians were also exhausted after nearly three years of political tumult and were thus willing to accept autocracy so long as al-Sisi could improve security and the economy.

Beyond his support among Egyptians, al-Sisi enjoyed two other benefits during his first year in office. First, Saudi Arabia, the United Arab Emirates (UAE), and Kuwait kept Egypt afloat economically by sending approximately $20 billion in aid during the two years following Morsi's ouster. These three Gulf monarchies feared that the Brotherhood's rise would inspire Brotherhood affiliates within their own kingdoms to escalate their antiregime activities. The Brotherhood fed these fears during its brief period in power by picking fights with the UAE in particular, and there is some indication that these Gulf states promised significant aid to encourage Egypt's military to oust Morsi prior to the June 2013 protests.[16] Either way, the Gulf's generosity rescued Egypt's economy, which was teetering at the time of Morsi's ouster, and gave al-Sisi a significant cushion for enacting fuel-subsidy reforms, updating the country's electricity grid, and undertaking new infrastructure projects.

Second, amid a collapsing regional order, al-Sisi's Egypt looked stable by comparison. By mid-2014, Libya was fractured among rival militant groups, the Syrian government controlled only a fraction of its territory, the Iraqi government was losing control of Sunni areas, the Iranian-backed Houthis were surging again in Yemen, and Syrian refugee flows into southern Turkey and Jordan squeezed both countries' resources. Then on June 10, only days after al-Sisi's inauguration, the Islamic State of Iraq and Syria (ISIS) captured Mosul, declared an Islamic state, and proceeded to occupy a vast swath of territory across Iraq and Syria. Before long, jihadists in Libya and the Sinai declared their allegiances to ISIS.

This regional context forced a hesitant Washington to engage al-Sisi as a strategic partner. After all, in October 2013, following a series of deadly crackdowns on pro-Morsi protests, the Obama administration announced that it would withhold "big ticket" weapon systems from Egypt "pending credible progress toward an inclusive, democratically elected civilian government through free and fair elections," and it deferred the Egyptian government's request for a "strategic dialogue" for over a year. But the rise of ISIS, as well as the Obama administration's desire to reassure Sunni Arab allies as it pursued a nuclear deal with Iran, impelled the administration to refocus its Egypt policy on security rather than human rights concerns. To this end, Obama met with al-Sisi on the sidelines of the 2014 UN General Assembly meeting and announced a resumption of weapon shipments in March 2015. Nearly four months later, Secretary of State John Kerry flew to Cairo to open a "strategic dialogue."

The chaotic regional context also bolstered al-Sisi at home. Even as the country's economy sputtered and new domestic crises emerged, many and perhaps most Egyptians viewed al-Sisi's repressive state as far preferable to the state breakdown that had occurred in Syria, Libya, and elsewhere. And in this environment, the Brotherhood became an especially useful enemy for the al-Sisi government. The Brotherhood's escalating calls for revolutionary violence fed the regime's narrative that it was a terrorist organization that sought to destabilize Egypt and thus bolstered al-Sisi's hand against it. And to some extent, the onslaught against the Brotherhood served as the glue that held the regime's constituent power centers together. The military, judiciary, police, private media, rural tribal interests, and the business community all viewed the Brotherhood's hypothetical reemergence as a significant threat to their respective interests and thus backed al-Sisi even as policy challenges otherwise mounted.

Throughout this period, the Brotherhood remained visible internationally. From its primary base in Istanbul, it broadcast its message through sympathetic satellite networks and lobbied Western capitals against al-Sisi—albeit with very little success. But by the end of 2015, it had faded almost entirely from view within Egypt. With tens of thousands of its leaders in prison, perhaps hundreds more in exile, and over one thousand Muslim Brothers killed since the coup, most of the Brotherhood's remaining cadres seemingly lay low. Indeed, during a visit to Cairo in November 2015, a high-ranking Egyptian security official told me that the Brotherhood had been neutralized on the ground, and many ordinary Egyptians seconded that assessment. Two and a half years after Morsi's ouster, the overall consensus was that Cairo's war against the Brotherhood had ended in victory.

As a result, the Brotherhood no longer represents a political challenge for al-Sisi's regime. But the regime faces a slew of daunting policy challenges, none of which have easy answers. Security forces are still battling ISIS-linked insurgents in the Sinai and the Western Desert with little success. Terrorism has driven away tourism, and the drop in global oil prices has forced the once-generous Gulf states to reduce their commitment to Cairo. As a result, the economy is sputtering: Commodity prices have risen due to subsidy reforms and inflation, and the fall in cash reserves means that Egypt is once again living on the economic edge. Meanwhile, there are constant whispers of rifts within the regime—none of which can be confirmed, but all of which suggest that there are still more chapters of Egypt's Arab Spring story to be written.

Except that these next chapters, like the ones that preceded it, won't be so springlike. During the past five years, Egyptians have learned the hard way that regime change doesn't necessarily yield improvement and may leave the country worse off. And for the time being, this is the Muslim Brotherhood's legacy in Egypt: It left the country worse off. It rushed to power without a coherent policy agenda. It picked fights with virtually every political institution and made enemies of almost every political force. And it responded to virtually every crisis by either demanding or grabbing more power, deepening Egypt's political polarization and bringing the country to the brink of severe civil strife.

Of course, the Brotherhood's leaders don't see it this way. They believe that Morsi's ouster was largely the product of a conspiracy within the Egyptian state and have vowed to use future moments of regime change to seek vengeance. In other words, if the Brotherhood gets a second chance, it is prepared to repeat many of the same mistakes.

APPENDIX
Interviews

Interviews with the Muslim Brotherhood

Name	Title	Date(s) Interviewed
Mohamed Morsi	Guidance Office member (2000–11), FJP chair (2011–12), Egyptian president (2012–13)	Aug. 3, 2010
Mehdi Akef	Former supreme guide	Jan. 24, 2011; June 9, 2013
Mahmoud Ezzat	Deputy supreme guide	Mar. 14, 2011
Khairat al-Shater	Deputy supreme guide	Mar. 13, 2011
Mahmoud Hussein	Secretary-general	July 1, 2012
Mahmoud Ghozlan	Spokesman	July 15, 2012
Gehad el-Haddad	Spokesman (2013)	July 9, 2013
Mohamed Habib	Former deputy supreme guide	Mar. 8, 2011; June 8, 2013
Abdel Moneim Abouel Fotouh	Guidance Office member (1987–2009), presidential candidate (2012)	Mar. 2, 2011
Abdel Rahman al-Barr	Guidance Office member	July 7, 2012
Mohamed Ali Bishr	Guidance Office member, governor of Menoufiya (2012–13), minister of local development (2013)	Oct. 14, 2014
Essam el-Erian	Guidance Office member (2009–11), FJP vice-chair (2012–13), Brotherhood/FJP parliamentarian (1987–1990, 2012), Morsi presidential adviser (2012), Shura Council member (2013)	Mar. 14, 2011
Mustafa Ghoneimy	Guidance Office member	July 4, 2012
Mohi Hamed	Guidance Office member, Morsi presidential adviser (2012–13)	Dec. 3, 2011

Name	Title	Date(s) Interviewed
Saad Esmat al-Husseini	Guidance Office member (2008–11), FJP executive committee member (2011–12), parliamentarian (2012), governor of Kafr el-Sheikh (2012–13)	Mar. 2, 2011; Dec. 10, 2011; June 28, 2012; Feb. 27, 2013
Saad al-Katatny	Guidance Office member, Brotherhood parliamentary bloc chair (2005–10), FJP parliamentarian (2012), parliamentary speaker (2012), FJP chair (2013)	Mar. 29, 2011
Abbas Abdel Aziz	Brotherhood/FJP parliamentarian (2005–2010, 2011), Shura Council presidential appointee (2013)	Feb. 28, 2013
Saber Abouel Fotouh	Brotherhood/FJP parliamentarian (2005–2010, 2012), Brotherhood labor leader in Alexandria	Dec. 11, 2011; Feb. 25, 2013
Magdy Ashour	Brotherhood parliamentarian (2005–10), independent parliamentarian (2010–11)	Mar. 7, 2011
Mohamed al-Beltagy	Brotherhood/FJP parliamentarian (2005–10, 2012)	Mar. 26, 2011; Mar. 2, 2013
Ali Fath al-Bab	Brotherhood parliamentarian (1995–2010), Shura Council majority leader (2012)	Dec. 4, 2011
Khaled el-Deeb	Brotherhood parliamentarian (2012)	June 30, 2012
Ahmed Fahmy	Brotherhood parliamentarian (2005–10), speaker of Shura Council (2012–13)	July 16, 2012
Azza al-Garf	FJP parliamentarian (2012), Muslim Brotherhood Sisters leader in October 6 City	June 26, 2012
Helmy al-Gazzar	FJP parliamentarian (2012), Brotherhood leader in Giza medical syndicate	Dec. 10, 2011; July 14, 2012

Name	Title	Date(s) Interviewed
Huda Ghania	FJP parliamentarian (2012), Muslim Brotherhood Sisters leader	July 9, 2012
Gamal Hanafi	Brotherhood parliamentarian (2005–10)	Jan. 13, 2011
Gamal Heshmat	Brotherhood/FJP parliamentarian (2000–3, 2012)	July 3, 2012; Mar. 23, 2014
Farid Ismail	Brotherhood/FJP parliamentarian (2005–10, 2012)	July 9, 2012
Essam Mukhtar	Brotherhood parliamentarian (2005–10), FJP parliamentary candidate (2011)	Dec. 4, 2011
Salah Naaman	FJP parliamentarian 2012	June 21, 2012
Sobhi Saleh	Brotherhood/FJP parliamentarian (2005–10, 2012), member of constitution-amending committee (2011)	Mar. 29, 2011; Dec. 11, 2011
Al-Mohamadi al-Sayyid Ahmed	Brotherhood/FJP parliamentarian (2005–10, 2012)	Dec. 11, 2011
Osama Suleiman	FJP parliamentarian (2012), Brotherhood Shura Committee	July 3, 2012
Mohamed Touson	FJP Shura Council member (2012–13), Mohamed Morsi's lawyer	Mar. 29, 2014
Osama Yassin	Brotherhood field coordinator during 2011 uprising, FJP parliamentarian (2012), minister of youth (2012–13)	Mar. 2, 2013
Sameh el-Essawy	FJP spokesman	June 24, 2012
Amr Farag	Rassd journalist, Brotherhood cadre	Oct. 8, 2014
Reda Ghanem	FJP communications chairman in Al-Gharbiya	June 10, 2013
Khaled Hamza	Editor in chief, IkhwanWeb	Jan. 10, 2011
Abdullah al-Mehi	TV anchor on Rabaa TV, Brotherhood cadre	Mar. 23, 2014
Mahmoud Rashad	FJP media chief in Tanta	June 10, 2013

Name	Title	Date(s) Interviewed
Ahmed Sobea	FJP spokesman (2011–12), Aqsa TV (Hamas) Cairo bureau chief (2013)	June 20, 2012; June 6, 2013
Mohamed Abdel Qadoos	Brotherhood Journalists Syndicate leader, Kefaya member	Mar. 31, 2011
Ali Abdelfattah	Brotherhood leader in Alexandria	Mar. 22, 2011
Ashraf Abdel Ghaffar	Brotherhood leader in Istanbul	Oct. 8, 2014
Hoda Abdel Moneim	Brotherhood Sisters leader in Nasr City, Mohamed Morsi's lawyer	Oct. 14, 2014
Badr Mohamed Badr	Brotherhood leader in Giza, journalist	Nov. 9, 2013
Murad Mohamed Aly	Member of Renaissance Project team, Morsi presidential campaign official, Brotherhood businessman	July 5, 2012
Ashraf Serry	Member of Renaissance Project team, Brotherhood businessman	June 27, 2012
Ahmed Soliman	Member of Renaissance Project team, FJP leader	July 12, 2012
Moaz Malek	Brotherhood businessman, Morsi presidential campaign volunteer	July 2, 2012
Muharram Oqba	Brotherhood/FJP leader in Kafr el-Sheikh	Feb. 27, 2013
Mohamed Sudan	FJP Foreign Affairs Committee, Alexandria	Dec. 11, 2011
Mohamed Abdel Rahim	Brotherhood cadre at Rabaa al-Adawiya	July 2, 2013
Ahmed Abdel Salam	Brotherhood cadre	June 24, 2012
Mohamed Abdel Wahed	Brotherhood cadre in Fayyoum	Nov. 29, 2011
Sayyid Aboul Nega	Brotherhood cadre	June 21, 2012
Said Ali	Brotherhood cadre at Rabaa al-Adawiya	July 2, 2013
Hesham Afifi	Brotherhood cadre	June 22, 2012

Name	Title	Date(s) Interviewed
Fathi Ageez	Brotherhood cadre from Mansoura	June 21, 2012
Ahmed Ali	Brotherhood cadre	June 30, 2012
Ammar al-Beltagy	Brotherhood cadre, son of Brotherhood leader Mohamed al-Beltagy	Mar. 9, 2011; June 22, 2012; July 9, 2012
Mohamed Desouki	Brotherhood cadre from Damanhour	June 24, 2012
Mohamed Fathi	Brotherhood cadre	July 18, 2012
Mohamed Fouad	Brotherhood cadre in Heliopolis	Nov. 28, 2011
Mohamed Gouda	Brotherhood cadre from Alexandria	June 30, 2012
Mamdouh Hammouda	Brotherhood cadre at Rabaa al-Adawiya	July 2, 2013
Mahmoud Helal	Brotherhood cadre in Fayoum	Nov. 29, 2011
Imad Ibrahim	Brotherhood cadre in Sayyida Zeinab	Nov. 28, 2011
Mohamed Mansour	Brotherhood cadre in Manial	Nov. 28, 2011
Imad Mohamed	Brotherhood cadre at Rabaa al-Adawiya	July 2, 2013
Hussein Morsi	Brotherhood cadre in El-Adwa, Mohamed Morsi's brother	Nov. 14, 2013
Ahmed Okail	Brotherhood cadre	July 12, 2012
Anas al-Qassas	Brotherhood cadre	Mar. 9, 2011
Ammar Sadik	Brotherhood cadre	Mar. 21, 2011
Hesham Sadik	Brotherhood cadre from Mansoura	June 29, 2012
Ahmed Selim	Brotherhood cadre at Rabaa al-Adawiya	July 2, 2013
Ahmed Shams el-Din	Brotherhood cadre in Heliopolis	Nov. 28, 2011
Salah al-Sharbiny	Brotherhood cadre	June 29, 2012

Name	Title	Date(s) Interviewed
Ihab Sultan	Brotherhood cadre	June 29, 2012
Jehan Darwish	FJP elections worker in Manial	Nov. 28, 2011
Ahmed Abdel Fattah	Former Brotherhood blogger	June 26, 2010
Abdel Moneim al-Mahmoud	Former Brotherhood blogger	June 30, 2010
Abdel Galil al-Sharnouby	Former Brotherhood media team member	June 3, 2013; Oct. 12, 2014
Kamel el-Helbawy	Former Brotherhood leader	Feb. 24, 2013; Nov. 8, 2013
Ibrahim el-Houdaiby	Former Brotherhood youth	Mar. 1, 2011
Mohamed Abbas	Revolutionary activist, former Brotherhood youth	Feb. 28, 2011; June 22, 2012
Moaz Abdel Karim	Revolutionary activist, former Brotherhood youth	Mar. 10, 2011
Mohamed al-Qassas	Revolutionary activist, former Brotherhood youth	Mar. 21, 2011; July 15, 2014; July 17, 2014; Oct. 9, 2014; Oct. 11, 2014
Islam Lotfy	Revolutionary activist, former Brotherhood youth	Mar. 2, 2011
Mosab Ragab	Revolutionary activist, former Brotherhood youth	Mar. 7, 2011
Abouleila Madi	Wasat Party Chairman	Jan. 26, 2011

Other Relevant Interviews

Name	Title	Date(s) Interviewed
Mustafa Abdel-Aziz	Conservatives Party chair	July 4, 2010
Esraa Abdel Fattah	Revolutionary activist, founder of April 6 Youth movement	Mar. 6, 2011
Emad Abdel Ghafour	Nour Party chairman (2011–12), Watan Party chairman (2013–present), Morsi presidential adviser (2012–13)	Dec. 7, 2011; Nov. 12, 2013; Mar. 27, 2014; Oct. 11, 2014
Hassan Abdel-Gowad	Wafd board member	July 24, 2010
Nasser Abdel Hamid	Revolutionary activist, Coalition of Revolutionary Youth leader	Mar. 15, 2011
Said Abdel-Khaliq	Wafd board member, editor of Al-Wafd (1998–ca. 2000, 2009–10)	July 17, 2010
Assem Abdel-Maged	Al-Gamaa al-Islamiya leader	July 7, 2012
Mounir Fakhry Abdelnour	Wafd secretary-general (2006–11), former MP (2000–5), minister of tourism (2011–12), minister of industry, trade, and investment (2013–15)	Aug. 10, 2010
Nasser Amin	Human rights lawyer	Oct. 12, 2014
Said Ashmawy	Former judge, State Security Court	Jan. 7, 2011
Ahmed Ashour	Ghad Party (Moussa Mustafa Moussa's faction) board member	July 27, 2010
Sheikh Mahmoud Azab	Al-Azhar official	July 11, 2012
Hatem Azzam	Wasat Party leader	June 5, 2013
El-Sayyid el-Badawy	Wafd chairman (2010–present)	Mar. 1, 2013
Ziad Bahaa-Eldin	ESDP leader, parliamentarian (2012), deputy prime minister (2013–14)	July 6, 2012

Name	Title	Date(s) Interviewed
Nader Bakkar	Nour Party spokesman	Oct. 14, 2014
Hazem el-Beblawi	Prime minister (2013–14)	Oct. 12, 2014
Essam Derbala	Al-Gamaa al-Islamiya leader	June 21, 2012
Bilal Diab	Revolutionary youth activist	Mar. 20, 2011
Mouhib Doss	Tamarod founder	Oct. 9, 2014
Hany Enan	Kefaya financier	Mar. 1, 2011
Amr Ezz	Revolutionary youth activist, Coalition of Revolutionary Youth leader, April 6 Youth	Mar. 8, 2011
Abdel Rahman Faris	Revolutionary youth activist, Coalition of Revolutionary Youth leader, Egypt Current Party founder	Mar. 9, 2011; Dec. 5, 2011
Bassem Fathi	Revolutionary youth activist	Mar. 10, 2011
Samir Fayyad	Tagammu vice-chair	Aug. 3, 2010
Mohamed Fouad	Parliamentary candidate (2011), parliamentarian (2015)	Feb. 24, 2013
Shadi el-Ghazali Harb	Revolutionary youth activist, Coalition of Revolutionary Youth leader, El-Gabha Party	Mar. 8, 2011; June 22, 2012
Mohamed Haikal	Tamarod founder	June 5, 2013
Amr Hamzawy	Free Egypt Party leader, parliamentarian (2012)	Dec. 5, 2011
Nadia Henry	Presidential appointee to Shura Council (2013)	Jan. 28, 2015
Mahmoud Ibrahem	Former NDP youth	July 31, 2010
Nageh Ibrahim	Former al-Gamaa al-Islamiya leader	Feb. 25, 2013
George Ishak	Kefaya leader	Mar. 5, 2011

Name	Title	Date(s) Interviewed
Gameela Ismail	Former Ghad Party (Ayman Nour's faction) secretary-general (2006–8)	July 22, 2010
Bassem Kamel	Revolutionary activist, ESDP parliamentarian (2012)	June 24, 2012
Ahmed al-Kattan	Nour Party leader in Al-Mahalla al-Kobra	June 10, 2013
Judge Mahmoud el-Khodeiry	FJP-aligned independent parliamentarian (2012)	June 25, 2012
Tarek el-Kholy	Revolutionary youth activist, Coalition of Revolutionary Youth leader, April 6 Youth	Mar. 13, 2011
Rami Lekah	Reform and Development / Our Egypt parliamentarian (2012)	June 23, 2012
Ahmed Maher	Revolutionary activist, founder of April 6 Youth	Mar. 9, 2011
Gamal Metwally	Nour Party parliamentarian (2012)	July 17, 2012; Nov. 14, 2013
Hossam Moones	Revolutionary activist, Karama Party	Mar. 15, 2011
Sally Moore	Revolutionary youth activist, Coalition of Revolutionary Youth leader	Mar. 13, 2011
Amr Moussa	Foreign minister (1991–2001), Arab League secretary-general (2001–11), presidential candidate (2012)	July 12, 2012
Dalia Moussa	Revolutionary activist	Mar. 3, 2011
Moussa Mustafa Moussa	Ghad Party (Moussa Mustafa Moussa faction) chairman	June 27, 2010
Gen. Abbas Mukhaymer	FJP parliamentarian (2012)	July 4, 2012
Ibrahim Nasser el-Din	Ghad Party (Moussa Mustafa Moussa faction) board member	July 17, 2010
Wael Nawara	Ghad Party (Ayman Nour faction) secretary-general	Mar. 29, 2011
Amina al-Niqash	Tagammu Party vice-chair	Jan. 10, 2011

Name	Title	Date(s) Interviewed
Farida al-Niqash	Tagammu Party board member, editor in chief of Al-Ahaly	Aug. 11, 2010
Mohamed Nour	Nour Party spokesman (2011–12), Watan Party spokesman (2013)	Dec. 1, 2011; Feb. 24, 2013
Hamdeen Sabahi	Karama Party chairman, presidential candidate (2012 and 2014)	Mar. 1, 2013; Apr. 2, 2014
Mohamed Anwar Esmat Sadat	Reform and Development Party leader, parliamentarian (2005–10, 2012)	Oct. 14, 2014
Mahmoud Salem	Revolutionary activist, blogger	Jun. 28, 2010
Ahmed Samih	Revolutionary youth activist, Andalus Institute for Tolerance and Anti-Violence Studies	Feb. 10, 2011
Magdy Selim	Nour Party leader in Kafr el-Sheikh	Feb. 27, 2013
Riad al-Shaqfeh	Syrian Muslim Brotherhood leader (2010–14)	July 4, 2013; Mar. 23, 2014; Oct. 8, 2014
Mustafa Shawqi	Revolutionary activist, Justice and Freedom Movement	Mar. 5, 2011
Essam Shiha	Wafd board member	Jan. 17, 2011; Jan. 23, 2011
Amr el-Shobaky	Independent parliamentarian (2012)	July 10, 2012
Camilia Shokry	Wafd board member	Aug. 1, 2011
Yasin Tag el-Din	Wafd vice-chair	July 19, 2010
Khaled Telema	Revolutionary activist, Tagammu	Mar. 17, 2011
Ashraf Thabet	Nour Party leader, parliamentarian (2012)	June 27, 2012; Feb. 25, 2013
Awatif Wali	Wafd leader	July 18, 2010
Bassam al-Zarqa	Nour Party leader	Mar. 27, 2014
Aboud al-Zomor	Al-Gamaa al-Islamiya leader	Dec. 4, 2011

NOTES

Introduction: Rapid Rise, Faster Fall

1. Eric Trager, "The Muslim Brotherhood Won an Election, but Is It Really Democratic?" *New Republic*, June 26, 2012, http://www.newrepublic.com/article/104412/eric-trager-muslim-brotherhood-won-election-it-really-democratic.

2. Amr Bargisi et al., "Khairat al-Shater on 'The Nahda Project' (Complete Translation)," *Current Trends in Islamic Ideology*, April 10, 2012, http://www.hudson.org/research/9820-khairat-al-shater-on-the-nahda-project-complete-translation. In quoting from this source, I have adjusted some of the editors' grammar and translation choices to fit my own styling.

3. Eric Trager, "Witnessing a Coup in Egypt," *Wall Street Journal*, July 3, 2013, http://www.wsj.com/articles/SB10001424127887324853704578589911687210152.

4. Hazem Kandil, *Inside the Brotherhood* (Cambridge: Polity Press, 2015), 48.

5. The exact number of Muslim Brothers in Egypt prior to Morsi's ouster is unknown. During a 2010 interview, Morsi told me that the number was 750,000, though former deputy supreme guide Mohamed Habib told me in a 2013 interview that the number was closer to 250,000. The generally accepted number is roughly 500,000, and that is the number that I have normally used as a baseline. But there are some indications that the Brotherhood inflated this number to exaggerate its strength.

6. Alison Pargeter, *The Muslim Brotherhood: From Opposition to Power* (London: Saqi Books, 2013), 17–18.

7. Carrie Rosefsky Wickham, *The Muslim Brotherhood: Evolution of an Islamist Movement* (Princeton, NJ: Princeton University Press, 2013), 2.

8. As Kandil writes in *Inside the Brotherhood*, "the effectiveness of the Brotherhood's cultivation process was such that it has never suffered a major dissent in its 85 years of existence. There were numerous individual resignations, but not a single notable split. When high-profile members left, they blamed administrative corruption, organizational autocracy, or differences in priorities and strategies. None of them . . . questioned the ideological premises of Islamism" (147).

9.   Ibid., 47.
10.   For an examination of the revolutionary activists, I recommend Thanassis Cambanis's *Once upon a Revolution: An Egyptian Story* (New York: Simon & Schuster, 2015) and Wendell Steavenson's *Circling the Square: Stories from the Egyptian Revolution* (New York: Ecco, 2015). For an outstanding critique of the revolutionaries' ideas, I recommend Samuel Tadros's *Reflections on the Revolution in Egypt* (Stanford, CA: Hoover Institution Press, 2014).
11.   Steavenson echoes this point in *Circling the Square*: "Hindsight eats stories. It might seem inevitable now that Mubarak would fall; inevitable, that two and a half years later the army would take back control. But at the time there was nothing sure about it at all" (6).
12.   Interview with a former member of the Brotherhood's media team, October 2014.

1. Late to the Revolution
1.   Interview with Mohamed al-Qassas, March 21, 2011; interview with Amar Sadik, March 21, 2011. Unless otherwise noted, all interviews were conducted by the author.
2.   International Monetary Fund, *World Economic Outlook, April 2012: Growth Resuming, Dangers Remain* (Washington: International Monetary Fund, 2012), http://www.imf.org/external/pubs/ft/weo/2012/01/pdf/text.pdf, 196; "Egypt: The Arithmetic of Revolution," *GallupWorld*, http://www.gallup.com/poll/157043/egypt-arithmetic-revolution.aspx.
3.   Abbas P. Grammy, "The Economics of Revolution in Egypt," *Premier Thoughts: The CSUB Business Blog*, February 14, 2011, https://www.csub.edu/kej/_files/revolutionEgypt.pdf.
4.   "Egypt 2012," *African Economic Outlook* (2012), http://www.africaneconomicoutlook.org/fileadmin/uploads/aeo/PDF/Egypt%20Full%20PDF%20Country%20Note_01.pdf, 8
5.   Joel Beinin, "Egyptian Workers after June 30," *MERIP*, August 23 2013, http://www.merip.org/mero/mero082313.
6.   "Official Results: 16 Opposition, 424 NDP, 65 'Independents,'" *Ahram Online*, December 6, 2010, http://english.ahram.org.eg/NewsContent/1/5/1321/Egypt/Egypt-Elections-/Official-results—opposition,—NDP,—independents.aspx.
7.   Eric Trager, "The Cairo Files: Pre-Revolutionary Egypt?" *Commentary Magazine*, July 30, 2008, http://www.commentarymagazine.com/2008/07/30/the-cairo-files-pre-revolutionary-egypt/.
8.   Interview with Mohamed al-Qassas, March 21, 2011.
9.   Interview with Mohamed al-Qassas, July 15, 2014.
10.   Fatemah Farag, "The Students, Again and Again," *Al-Ahram Weekly*, no. 605, September 26–October 2, 2002; interview with Mohamed al-Qassas, July 15, 2014.
11.   Amira Howeidy, "Solidarity in Search of a Vision," *Al-Ahram Weekly*, no. 581, April 11–17, 2002.

12.   Ashraf Khalil, *Liberation Square: Inside the Egyptian Revolution and Rebirth of a Nation* (New York: St. Martin's, 2011), 39–40.

13.   Paul Schemm, "Egypt Struggles to Control Anti-War Protests," *MERIP*, March 31, 2003, http://www.merip.org/mero/mero033103.

14.   Amira Howeidy, "A Day at 'Hyde Park,'" *Al-Ahram Weekly*, no. 631, March 27–April 2, 2003; Khalil, *Liberation Square*, 40.

15.   Interview with Hany Enan, March 1, 2011; interview with George Ishak, March 5, 2011; Popular Campaign for Change, "Statement to the Egyptian People" (in Arabic [AR]), September 9, 2004, http://www.alarabnews.com/alshaab/2004/24-09-2004/n5.htm.

16.   Gamal Essam el-Din, "Space to Say 'No' to the President," *Al-Ahram Weekly*, no. 721, December 16–22, 2004; Amira Howeidy, "Arrests at the Fair," *Al-Ahram Weekly*, no. 728, February 3–9, 2005; Amira Howeidy, "Enough Is Not Enough," *Al-Ahram Weekly*, no. 731, February 24–March 2, 2005.

17.   Nadia Oweidat et al., *The Kefaya Movement: A Case Study of a Grassroots Reform Initiative* (Santa Monica, CA: Rand Corp., 2008) 28–35; Shaden Shehab, "That's Enough," *Al-Ahram Weekly*, no. 775, December 29–January 4, 2005; interview with Hany Enan, March 1, 2011; interview with Ahmed Salah, March 13, 2011.

18.   Interview with Islam Lotfy, March 2, 2011; interview with Mustafa Shawqi, March 5, 2011.

19.   Khalil, *Liberation Square*, 51.

20.   Samantha M. Shapiro, "Revolution, Facebook-Style," *New York Times Magazine*, January 22, 2009, http://www.nytimes.com/2009/01/25/magazine/25bloggers-t.html?pagewanted=all&_r=1.

21.   Interview with Mohamed al-Qassas, July 15, 2014.

22.   Interview with Esraa Abdel Fattah, March 6, 2011; interview with Ahmed Maher, March 9, 2011; interview with Nasser Abdel Hamid, March 15, 2011; Heba Saleh, "ElBaradei Returns to Cairo Amid Poll Speculation," *Financial Times*, February 20, 2010, http://www.ft.com/intl/cms/s/0/884308la-1dbe-11df-9e98-00144feab49a.html#axzz41fbDBfQP.

23.   Gamal Essam el-Din, "Statement for Change," *Al-Ahram Weekly*, no. 988, March 4–10, 2010.

24.   WhatsApp discussion with Mohamed al-Qassas, July 17, 2014.

25.   Wael Ghonim, *Revolution 2.0: The Power of the People Is Greater than the People in Power; A Memoir* (Boston: Houghton Mifflin Harcourt, 2012), 58–61, 73–81.

26.   Jack Shenker, "Mohamed ElBaradei Joins Egyptian Sit-In over Police Death Case," *Guardian*, June 25, 2010, http://www.theguardian.com/world/2010/jun/25/egypt-police-death-protest.

27.   WhatsApp discussion with Mohamed al-Qassas, July 17, 2014.

28.   "Egypt Church Blast Death Toll Rises to 23," Reuters, January 4, 2011, http://www.reuters.com/article/2011/01/04/us-egypt-church-idUSTRE7010M020110104.

29.   Mahmoud Mosalem, "Mubarak Mocks Oppositions Proposed Shadow Parliament," *Egypt Independent,* December 19, 2010, http://www.egyptindependent.com/news/mubarak-mocks-oppositions-proposed-shadow-parliament.

30.   Eric Trager, "After Tunisia, Is Egypt Next?" *Atlantic,* January 17, 2011, http://www.theatlantic.com/international/archive/2011/01/after-tunisia-is-egypt-next/69656/.

31.   Ahmed Zaki Osman, "Egypt's Police: From Liberators to Oppressors," *Egypt Independent,* January 24, 2011, http://www.egyptindependent.com/news/egypts-police-liberators-oppressors.

32.   Interview with Moaz Abdel Karim, March 10, 2011; interview with Tarek el-Kholy, March 13, 2011.

33.   Interview with Islam Lotfy, March 2, 2011; interview with Moaz Abdel Karim, March 10, 2011; interview with Mohamed al-Qassas, March 21, 2011.

34.   Alaa al-Din Arafat, *The Mubarak Leadership and Future of Democracy in Egypt* (New York: Palgrave Macmillan, 2009), 174; Amira Howeidy, "Back to Square One," *Al-Ahram Weekly,* no. 801, June 29–July 5, 2006.

35.   Samer Shehata and Joshua Stacher, "Boxing In the Brothers," *MERIP,* no. 8, August 2007, http://www.merip.org/mero/mero080807; Sophia Ibrahim, "Judgment Day," *Al-Ahram Weekly,* no. 893, April 17–23, 2008.

36.   Gamal Essam el-Din, "Brothers Fight On," *Al-Ahram Weekly,* no. 841, April 19–25, 2007; Gamal Essam el-Din, "Fait Accompli?" *Al-Ahram Weekly,* no. 888, March 13–19, 2008; "Egypt Muslim Brotherhood Says More than 1,000 Arrested," BBC News, November 21, 2010, http://www.bbc.co.uk/news/world-middle-east-11807640.

37.   Interview with Mohamed Abbas, February 28, 2011.

38.   The Muslim Brotherhood, "Statement from the Muslim Brotherhood regarding the Uprising of the Tunisian People and the Escape of President Ben Ali" (AR), *Egypt Window,* January 15, 2011, http://www.egyptwindow.net/news_Details.aspx?News_ID=10887.

39.   The Muslim Brotherhood, "Statement from the Brotherhood regarding the Uprising of Tunisia and the Demands of the Egyptian People," January 19, 2011, https://www.facebook.com/note.php?note_id=184162464940672.

40.   There is some disagreement about when, exactly, these threatening calls from the regime came. In interviews, Brotherhood leader Essam el-Erian indicated that they were received on January 20, and Saad al-Katatny indicated that they came on either January 20 or 21. In an interview with Al Jazeera, however, Brotherhood leader Osama Yassin indicated that the threatening calls arrived on January 19. Either way, it is clear that State Security did, in fact, threaten the Brotherhood directly and that this impacted the Brotherhood's approach prior to the January 25 protests, as this section is arguing.

41.   Interview with Mohamed al-Beltagy, March 26, 2011; interview with Sobhi Saleh, March 29, 2011.

42.   Michael Slackman, "Technology Helps Spread Discontent of Workers," *New*

York Times, April 7, 2008, A6; "Muslim Brotherhood Joins Strike Campaign," *International Herald Tribune*, April 30, 2008, 6.

43. Ahmed Abdel Fatah, "Statement of the Muslim Brothers regarding the April 6 Strikes," *Yalally* (blog), April 2, 2009, http://yalally.blogspot.com/2009/04 /6.html; "Egypt's Muslim Brotherhood Official Defends Stand on 6 April Strike," *BBC Monitoring Middle East*, April 9, 2009, retrieved from LexisNexis on May 11, 2012.

44. Interview with Mohamed al-Qassas, March 21, 2011; interview with Mohamed al-Qassas, October 9, 2014.

45. Fawzi Awis, *Defectors from the Brotherhood: A Look into the Organization's Rule* (AR) (Cairo: Sama House for Publication and Distribution, 2013), 194, 201–2.

46. Interview with Ali Abdelfattah, March 22, 2011; interview with Saad al-Katatny, March 29, 2011.

47. Mohamed Badie, "Statement from the Muslim Brotherhood on the Issue of the State of Popular Tension and Security Corruption in Egypt" (AR), *IkhwanWiki*, January 23, 2011, http://www.ikhwanwiki.com/index.php?title= بيان_من_الإخوان_المسلمين_بشأن_حالة_الاحتقان_الشعبي_والاستبداد_الأمني_في_مصر.

48. Interview with Wael Nawara, March 29, 2011.

49. Interview with Mohamed al-Qassas, March 21, 2011.

50. Interview with Osama Yassin, March 2, 2013.

51. "Witness to the Revolution: Dr. Osama Yassin, Part 2" (AR), Al Jazeera, November 13, 2011, https://www.youtube.com/watch?v=ha7EW_ZVbdA ; interview with Anas al-Qassas, March 9, 2011.

52. "Word of Engineer Saad al-Husseini to the Youths regarding Participation in January 25" (AR), YouTube, January 24, 2011, https://www.youtube.com /watch?v=oVelD9cRrTc.

53. Interview with Dalia Moussa, March 3, 2011; interview with Shadi el-Ghazali Harb, March 8, 2011; interview with Abdel Rahman Faris, March 9, 2011; interview with Ahmed Maher, March 9, 2011; interview with Sally Moore, March 13, 2011; interview with Tarek el-Kholy, March 13, 2011; interview with Nasser Abdel Hamid, March 15, 2011; interview with Hossam Moones, March 15, 2011; interview with Mohamed al-Qassas, March 21, 2011.

54. Interview with Ahmed Maher, March 9, 2011; interview with Sally Moore, March 13, 2011; interview with Hamdeen Sabahi, March 14, 2011; interview with Nasser Abdel Hamid, March 15, 2011; interview with Hossam Moones, March 15, 2011; interview with Bilal Diab, March 20, 2011.

55. Interview with Ahmed Maher, March 9, 2011; interview with Nasser Abdel Hamid, March 15, 2011; interview with Hossam Moones, March 15, 2011; interview with Khaled Telema, March 17, 2011;

56. Interview with Ahmed Maher, March 9, 2011; interview with Bassem Fathi, March 10, 2011.

57. Interview with Amr Ezz, March 8, 2011; interview with Ahmed Maher,

March 9, 2011; interview with Tarek el-Kholy, March 13, 2011; interview with Hossam Moones, March 15, 2011; interview with Bilal Diab, March 20, 2011.

58. "The Beginning of the January Revolution from in Front of the High Court," YouTube, March 31, 2012, https://www.youtube.com/watch?v=NXIIuwk4T _8; Mustafa Riad, "Eve of 'Friday of Decisiveness': Activists Exchange a Photo of Al-Beltagy in the Demonstrations of January 25" (AR), *Masress*, August 30, 2013, http://www.masress.com/fjp/82234.

59. Eric Trager, "Scenes from Egypt's Would-Be Revolution," *Atlantic*, January 25, 2011, http://www.theatlantic.com/international/archive/2011 /01/scenes-from-egypts-would-be-revolution/70191/; Kareem and Mona el-Naggar, "Violent Clashes Mark Protests against Mubarak's Rule," *New York Times*, January 25, 2011, http://www.nytimes.com/2011/01/26/world /middleeast/26egypt.html?pagewanted=all.

60. Interview with Mohamed al-Qassas, October 9, 2014.

61. "Witness to the Revolution: Dr. Osama Yassin, Part 2"; interview with Mohamed al-Qassas, October 9, 2014. The three youths were Islam Lotfy, Hany Mahmoud, and Ahmed Nazily.

62. Interview with Mohamed al-Qassas, October 9, 2014. This is not a word-for-word quotation.

63. Ibid.

64. The Muslim Brotherhood, "Statement from the Muslim Brotherhood regarding the Events of January 25 and Their Aftermath," *Ikhwan-Wiki*, January 26, 2011, http://www.ikhwanwiki.com/index.php?title= بيان_من_الإخوان_المسلمين_حول_أحداث_يوم_25_يناير_2011م_وتداعياتها.

65. Interview with Mohamed al-Beltagy, March 26, 2011; "Witness to the Revolution: Dr. Osama Yassin, Part 2."

66. Interview with Mohamed al-Beltagy, March 26, 2011; interview with Sobhi Saleh, March 29, 2011.

67. Interview with Saad al-Husseini, March 2, 2011; interview with Anas al-Qassas, March 9, 2011; interview with Amr al-Beltagy, March 9, 2011; interview with Mohamed Abdel Qadoos, March 31, 2011.

68. "Egypt Arrests Muslim Brotherhood Leaders," Reuters, January 27, 2011, http://www.realclearworld.com/news/reuters/international/2011/Jan/27 /egypt_arrests_muslim_brotherhood_leaders.html; interview with Mohamed al-Beltagy, March 26, 2011; interview with Sobhi Saleh, March 29, 2011; "Witness to the Revolution: Dr. Osama Yassin, Part 2."

69. Maggie Michael, "Egypt Sets Jan. 28 for Ousted Morsi's 3rd Trial," Associated Press, January 2, 2014, http://news.yahoo.com/egypt-sets-jan-28-ousted -morsi-39-3rd-110409016.html.

70. Essam el-Erian, "Diary of the Revolution," *IkhwanWiki*, http://www.ikhwan wiki.com/index.php?title=%D8%AF._%D8%B9%D8%B5%D8%A7%D9%85 _%D8%A7%D9%84%D8%B9%D8%B1%D9%8A%D8%A7%D9%86_%D9%8A %D9%83%D8%AA%D8%A8:_%D9%8A%D9%88%D9%85%D9%8A%D8 %A7%D8%AA_%D8%A7%D9%84%D8%AB%D9%88%D8%B1%D8%A9.

71. "President Mubarak Address," C-Span, January 28, 2011, http://www.c-span
.org/video/?297759-1/president-mubarak-address.

72. David D. Kirkpatrick, "Mubarak Orders Crackdown, with Revolt Sweeping
Egypt," *New York Times*, January 28, 2011, http://www.nytimes.com/2011/01
/29/world/middleeast/29unrest.html?pagewanted=all; Eric Trager, "Excess
Point," *New Republic*, January 30, 2011, https://newrepublic.com/article
/82453/egypt-riots-mubarak-public-opinion.

73. Interview with Mahmoud Ghozlan, July 15, 2012.

74. "Witness to the Revolution: Dr. Osama Yassin, Part 4" (AR), YouTube,
November 28, 2011, https://www.youtube.com/watch?v=308w4VgjVX8.

75. "Witness to the Revolution: Dr. Osama Yass [*sic*], Part 5" (AR), YouTube,
December 4, 2011, https://www.youtube.com/watch?v=T-TDls2trto.

76. Shady Talaat, "The Revolution . . . January 29 until February 1 2011," *Ahl al-
Qur' ān*, June 16, 2011, http://www.ahl-alQuran.com/arabic/show_article
.php?main_id=8279.

77. "Witness to the Revolution: Dr. Osama Yassin, Part 3" (AR), YouTube,
November 21, 2011, https://www.youtube.com/watch?v=FYC91OAnpl4;
"Witness to the Revolution: Dr. Osama Yassin, Part 4"; interview with Osama
Yassin, March 2, 2013. Morsi referenced his responsibility for the Brother-
hood's activities in Tahrir Square during a November 2012 interview with
Time. See Richard Stengel et al., "An Interview with Egyptian President
Mohamed Morsi: 'We're Learning How to Be Free,'" *Time*, November 28,
2012, http://world.time.com/2012/11/28/an-interview-with-egypts-president
-mohamed-morsi-were-learning-how-to-be-free/.

78. "Witness to the Revolution: Dr. Osama Yassin, Part 4"; "Witness to the Revolution: Dr. Osama Yass [*sic*], Part 5"; interview with Osama Yassin, March 2,
2013.

79. "Witness to the Revolution: Dr. Osama Yassin, Part 3."

80. Interview with Abdel Galil al-Sharnouby, June 3, 2013.

81. Gehad al-Ansary, "Former Muslim Brother: The Brotherhood Met with Omar
Suleiman before the Battle of the Camel" (AR), *Rassd*, April 14, 2013): http://
rassd.com/1-59134.htm.

82. Ibid.; Anthony Shadid, "Obama Urges Faster Shift of Power in Egypt," *New
York Times*, February 1, 2011, http://www.nytimes.com/2011/02/02/world
/middleeast/02egypt.html?pagewanted=all.

83. Interview with Mohamed al-Qassas, October 9, 2014.

84. "Hosni Mubarak's Speech: Full Text," *Guardian*, February 1, 2011, http://
www.theguardian.com/world/2011/feb/02/president-hosni-mubarak-egypt
-speech.

85. Khalil, *Liberation Square*, 217; "Live Blog Feb 2: Egypt Protests," Al Jazeera,
February 2, 2011, http://blogs.aljazeera.com/blog/middle-east/live-blog-feb
-2-egypt-protests.

86. Khalil, *Liberation Square*, 219–26.

87. Interview with Mohamed al-Qassas, October 9, 2014.

88. "Witness to the Revolution: Dr. Osama Yass [*sic*], Part 5."

89. Khalil, *Liberation Square*, 227–31; "Witness to the Revolution: Osama Yas [*sic*], Part 6," YouTube, December 11, 2011, https://www.youtube.com/watch?v=ZnFXW4aERb4.

90. Khalil, *Liberation Square*, 232–34.

91. Will Englund and Debbi Wilgoren, "Protesters Fill Tahrir Square for 'Day of Departure' Rally: Journalists Targeted," *Washington Post*, February 4, 2011, http://www.washingtonpost.com/wp-dyn/content/article/2011/02/03/AR2011020302747.html.

92. Khalil, *Liberation Square*, 230.

93. "Witness to the Revolution: Osama Yassin, Part 7" (AR), YouTube, December 18, 2011, https://www.youtube.com/watch?v=Z4GzvSojz8Q.

94. Interview with Mohamed al-Beltagy, March 26, 2011; "Witness to the Revolution: Osama Yassin, Part 7."

95. Griff Witte et al., "In Egypt, Muslim Brotherhood Reverses Course, Agrees to Talks on Transition," *Washington Post*, February 6, 2011, http://www.washingtonpost.com/wp-dyn/content/article/2011/02/05/AR2011020501707.html.

96. Dan Murphy, "Egypt Protests: Muslim Brotherhood's Concessions Prompt Anger," *Christian Science Monitor*, February 7, 2011, http://www.csmonitor.com/World/Middle-East/2011/0207/Egypt-protests-Muslim-Brotherhood-s-concessions-prompt-anger. The Brotherhood's apparent willingness to let Mubarak remain president is also reflected in its February 6 statement, which makes a number of demands but none pertaining to Mubarak. See "Statement from the Muslim Brotherhood Regarding the Dialogue Session That Was Held Today between the Political, National and Youth Forces and the Vice President of the Republic" (AR), *IkhwanWiki*, February 6, 2011, http://www.ikhwanwiki.com/index.php?title=بيان_من_الإخوان_المسلمين_حول_جلسة_الحوار_التى_تمت_اليوم_بين_القوى_السياسية_والوطنية_والشبابية_ونائب_رئيس_الجمهورية.

97. Muslim Brotherhood, "Press Statement from the Muslim Brotherhood on the Fourteenth Day of the Blessed Popular Revolution," *IkhwanWiki*, February 7, 2011, http://www.ikhwanwiki.com/index.php?title=بيان_صحفى_من_الإخوان_المسلمين_فى_اليوم_الرابع_عشر_من_الثورة_الشعبية_المباركة.

98. Trager, "After Tunisia, Is Egypt Next?"

99. Muslim Brotherhood, "Statement from the Muslim Brotherhood regarding the Events of Thursday, February 3, 2011," *IkhwanWiki*, February 3, 2011, http://www.ikhwanwiki.com/index.php?title=بيان_من_الإخوان_المسلمين_حول_أحداث_يوم_الخميس_الثالث_من_فبراير_2011م.

100. Muslim Brotherhood, "Statement from the Muslim Brotherhood regarding the Events of the Great Friday 2/4/11" (AR), *IkhwanWiki*, February 5, 2011, http://www.ikhwanwiki.com/index.php?title=بيان_من_الإخوان_المسلمين_حول_أحداث_الجمعة_العظيمة_4/2/2011م.

101. "Witness to the Revolution: Osama Yassin, Part 7."

102. Abdel Moneim Abou el-Fotouh, "Democracy Supporters Should Not

Fear the Muslim Brotherhood," *Washington Post*, February 9, 2011, http://www.washingtonpost.com/wp-dyn/content/article/2011/02/09 /AR2011020905222.html.

103. "CNN: Muslim Brotherhood, VP Suleiman to Meet," YouTube, February 6, 2011, https://www.youtube.com/watch?v=YSdBfYT8lDU.

104. Essam el-Errian, "What the Muslim Brothers Want," *New York Times*, February 9, 2011, http://www.nytimes.com/2011/02/10/opinion/10erian.html?_r=1 &ref=opinion.

105. Frank Newport, "Americans Sympathetic to Egyptian Protesters," *Gallup Politics*, February 7, 2011, http://www.gallup.com/poll/145979/americans -sympathetic-egyptian-protesters.aspx.

106. "Live Blog Feb 10: Egypt Protests," Al Jazeera, February 10, 2011, http://blogs .aljazeera.com/blog/middle-east/live-blog-feb-10-egypt-protests.

107. "Hosni Mubarak's Speech to the Egyptian People: 'I Will Not . . . Accept to Hear Foreign Dictations,'" *Washington Post*, February 10, 2011, http://www .washingtonpost.com/wp-dyn/content/article/2011/02/10/AR2011021005290 _pf.html.

108. Interview with Ahmed Samih, February 10, 2011.

109. "Live Blog Feb 11: Egypt Protests," Al Jazeera, February 11, 2011, http://blogs .aljazeera.com/blog/middle-east/live-blog-feb-11-egypt-protests.

110. "Statement from the Muslim Brotherhood regarding the Fall of Mubarak and His Regime," *IkhwanWiki*, February 11, 2011, http://www.ikhwanwiki.com /index.php?title=بيان_من_الإخوان_المسلمين_بمناسبة_سقوط_مبارك_ونظامه.

111. David D. Kirkpatrick, "Wired and Shrewd, Young Egyptians Guide Revolt," *New York Times*, February 9, 2011, http://www.nytimes.com/2011/02/10 /world/middleeast/10youth.html?pagewanted=all.

2. An Islamist Vanguard

1. Jeremy M. Sharp, "Egypt: Background and U.S. Relations," Congressional Research Service, June 5, 2014, http://fas.org/sgp/crs/mideast/RL33003.pdf, 14–17.

2. "International Security Threats," C-SPAN, February 10, 2011, http://www .c-span.org/video/?297949-1/international-security-threats.

3. "Obama Administration Corrects Clapper's Claim That Muslim Brotherhood Is 'Secular,'" Fox News, February 10, 2011, http://www.foxnews.com/politics /2011/02/10/administration-corrects-dni-clapper-claim-muslim-brotherhood -secular.html.

4. George W. Bush, "Text: Address to the Nation," *Washington Post*, September 20, 2001, http://www.washingtonpost.com/wp-srv/nation/specials /attacked/transcripts/bushaddress_092001.html.

5. Richard P. Mitchell, *The Society of Muslim Brothers* (Oxford: Oxford University Press, 1993), 30–32, 55–58, 61–67, 71.

6. Said K. Aburish, *Nasser: The Last Arab; A Biography* (New York: Thomas Dunne Books, 2004), 45–47, 51, 53–55.

7. Mitchell, *Society of Muslim Brothers*, 141.

8. Seyyid Qutb, *Milestones* (Damascus: Dar al-Ilm, n.d.), 10–11, 39, 55, 57, 72, 79–80.

9. Thomas H. Kean and Lee H. Hamilton, *The 9/11 Commission Report* (New York: W.W. Norton, 2004) 51, 72, 362.

10. Barbara H. E. Zollner, *The Muslim Brotherhood: Hasan al-Hudaybi and Ideology* (London: Routledge, 2009), 3, 65–70.

11. Hassan al-Hudaybi, "Preachers Not Judges," *IkhwanWiki*, http://www.ikhwan wiki.com/index.php?title=قضاة_لا_دعاة.

12. Zollner, *Muslim Brotherhood*, 84–85, 92–93.

13. Robert S. Leiken and Steven Brooke, "The Moderate Muslim Brotherhood," *Foreign Affairs* 86, no. 2 (March–April 2007): 108, 113.

14. Marc Lynch, "Assessing the MB 'Firewall,'" *Abu Aardvark*, May 13, 2008, http://abuaardvark.typepad.com/abuaardvark/2008/05/assessing-the-m .html.

15. Marc Lynch, "No Brothers in Doha," *Abu Aardvark*, February 23, 2008, http://abuaardvark.typepad.com/abuaardvark/2008/02/no-brothers-in.html.

16. Scott Shane, "As Islamist Group Rises, Its Intentions Are Unclear," *New York Times*, February 3, 2011, http://www.nytimes.com/2011/02/04/world /middleeast/04brotherhood.html?pagewanted=all.

17. Bruce Riedel, "Don't Fear Egypt's Muslim Brotherhood," *Daily Beast*, January 27, 2011, http://www.thedailybeast.com/articles/2011/01/27/muslim -brotherhood-could-win-in-egypt-protests-and-why-obama-shouldnt-worry .html.

18. Leiken and Brooke, "The Moderate Muslim Brotherhood," 116.

19. Nathan Brown, "The Muslim Brotherhood," Carnegie Endowment for International Peace, April 13, 2011, http://carnegieendowment.org/files/0413 _testimony_brown.pdf, 6.

20. Bertus Hendriks, "Egypt's Elections, Mubarak's Bind," *MERIP*, no. 129 (January 1985): 17–18.

21. Erika Post, "Egypt's Elections," *MERIP*, no. 147 (July–August 1987): 17.

22. Mona el-Ghobashy, "The Metamorphosis of the Egyptian Muslim Brothers," *International Journal of Middle East Studies* 37, no. 3 (August 2005): 384; Eberhard Kienle, "More Than a Response to Islamism: The Political Deliberalization of Egypt in the 1990s," *Middle East Journal* 52, no. 2 (Spring 1998): 228.

23. Samer Shehata and Joshua Stacher, "The Brotherhood Goes to Parliament," *MERIP*, no. 240 (Fall 2006): http://www.merip.org/mer/mer240 /brotherhood-goes-parliament.

24. Carrie Rosefsky Wickham, "The Muslim Brotherhood after Mubarak: What the Brotherhood Is and How It Will Shape the Future," *Foreign Affairs*, February 3, 2011, https://www.foreignaffairs.com/articles/egypt/2011-02-03 /muslim-brotherhood-after-mubarak.

25. El-Ghobashy, "Metamorphosis of the Egyptian Muslim Brothers," 390.

26. Shadi Hamid, "The Rise of the Islamists: How Islamists Will Change Politics, and Vice Versa," *Foreign Affairs*, May/June 2011, https://www.foreignaffairs .com/articles/north-africa/2011-04-03/rise-islamists.

27. Marc Lynch, "MB and Democracy, Again," *Abu Aardvark*, March 11, 2008, http://abuaardvark.typepad.com/abuaardvark/2008/03/mb-and-democrac .html.

28. Marc Lynch, "Did We Get the Muslim Brotherhood Wrong?" *Foreign Policy*, April 10, 2013, http://foreignpolicy.com/2013/04/10/did-we-get-the-muslim -brotherhood-wrong/.

29. Samuel Tadros, *Motherland Lost: The Egyptian and Coptic Quest for Modernity* (Stanford, CA: Hoover Institution Press, 2013), 137–42; P. J. Vatikiotis, *The History of Modern Egypt: From Muhammad Ali to Mubarak*, 4th ed. (Baltimore: Johns Hopkins University Press, 1991), 38–39.

30. Sayyid Jamal al-Din al-Afghani, "Teaching and Learning," in *Modernist Islam, 1840–1940: A Sourcebook*, ed. Charles Kurzman (Oxford: Oxford University Press, 2002), 104–6.

31. Muhammad 'Abduh, *The Theology of Unity*, trans. Ishaq Musa'ad and Kenneth Cragg (London: George Allen & Unwin, 1966), 115.

32. Hasan al-Banna, *Five Tracts of Hasan al-Banna (1906–1949): A Selection from the Majmu'at Rasa'il al-Imam al-Shahid Hasan al-Banna*, trans. Charles Wendell (Berkeley: University of California Press, 1978) 3.

33. Zhyntativ, "Hasan al-Banna and His Political Thought of Islamic Brotherhood," *IkhwanWeb*, May 13, 2008, http://www.ikhwanweb.com/article.php ?id=17065.

34. Hasan al-Banna, "Between Yesterday and Today,"in *Five Tracts of Hasan al-Banna*, 14, 16.

35. Hassan al-Banna, "Message to the Fifth Conference" (AR), *IkhwanWiki*, January 4, 2003, http://www.ikhwanwiki.com/index.php?title=رسالة_المؤتمر_الخامس.

36. Hasan al-Banna, "Our Mission," in *Five Tracts of Hasan al-Banna*, 46.

37. Mustafa Mashhour, "Jihad Is the Way" (AR), *IkhwanWiki*, http://www .ikhwanwiki.com/index.php?title=الجهاد_هو_السبيل.

38. Hassan al-Banna, "The Governing System" (AR), *IkhwanWiki*, http://www .ikhwanwiki.com/index.php?title=نظام_الحكم....رسائل_البنا.

39. Hassan al-Banna, "The Economic System" (AR), *IkhwanWiki*, http://www .ikhwanwiki.com/index.php?title=النظـام_الاقتصـادي.

40. Hasan al-Banna, "To What Do We Summon Mankind?" in *Five Tracts of Hasan al-Banna*, 89–91.

41. Al-Banna, "Our Mission," 61.

42. Al-Banna, "Between Yesterday and Today," 31.

43. Hassan al-Banna, "Message on Teaching," *IkhwanWiki*, August 12, 2006, https://docs.google.com/viewer?url=http://www.ikhwanwiki.com/images/1 /1c/رسالة_التعاليم.pdf&chrome=true, 5–6.

44. Al-Banna, "To What Do We Summon Mankind?" 71.

45. Interview with Magdy Amr, January 17, 2011.

46.   Interview with Khaled Hamza, January 10, 2011; interview with Magdy Amr, January 17, 2011; interview with Ibrahim Houdaiby, Marcy 1, 2011.

47.   Interview with Mosab Ragab, March 7, 2011.

48.   Interview with Abdel Moneim al-Mahmoud, June 30, 2010; interview with Khaled Hamza, January 10, 2011; interview with Islam Lotfy, March 2, 2011; interview with Amr al-Beltagy, March 9, 2011; interview with Moaz Abdel Karim, March 10, 2011.

49.   Interview with Islam Lotfy, March 2, 2011; interview with Mosab Ragab, March 7, 2011; interview with Amr al-Beltagy, March 9, 2011.

50.   Interview with Islam Lotfy, March 2, 2011; interview with Mosab Ragab, March 7, 2011; interview with Amr al-Beltagy, March 9, 2011.

51.   Interview with Islam Lotfy, March 2, 2011; interview with Mosab Ragab, March 7, 2011.

52.   Interview with Khaled Hamza, January 10, 2011; interview with Islam Lotfy, March 2, 2011.

53.   Interview with Khaled Hamza, January 10, 2011.

54.   Interview with Mosab Ragab, March 7, 2011; interview with Magdy Ashour, March 7, 2011; interview with Mohamed Habib, March 8, 2011.

55.   Interview with Khaled Hamza, January 10, 2011; interview with Islam Lotfy, March 2, 2011.

56.   Adham Mahmoud and Mohamed Hamid, "The Ten Pillars of the Oath to the Muslim Brotherhood" (AR), *Masress*, May 9, 2012, http://www.masress.com /almesryoon/117222. The *bay'a* has changed at different points throughout the Brotherhood's history. See Ella Landau-Tasseron, "Leadership and Allegiance in the Society of the Muslim Brothers," Hudson Institute, Research Monographs on the Muslim World, 2.5, December 2010, http://www.hudson.org /content/researchattachments/attachment/1153/20110110_baya2010_layout4 .pdf.

57.   "'Al-Masry al-Youm' Opens the File of the Oath in the 'Muslim Brotherhood' (Special File)" (AR), *Al-Masry al-Youm*, May 7, 2012, http://www.almasry alyoum.com/news/details/177248.

58.   "The Muslim Brotherhood," *IkhwanWiki*, http://www.ikhwanwiki.com /index.php?title=%D8%AC%D9%85%D8%A7%D8%B9%D8%A9_%D8%A7 %D9%84%D8%A5%D8%AE%D9%88%D8%A7%D9%86_%D8%A7%D9%84 %D9%85%D8%B3%D9%84%D9%85%D9%8A%D9%86#.D8.A7.D9.84.D9 .85.D9.86.D8.B7.D9.82.D8.A9; Mitchell, *Society of Muslim Brothers*, 164.

59.   Interview with Magdy Amr, January 17, 2011; interview with Mohamed Abbas, February 28, 2011; interview with Ibrahim Houdaiby, March 1, 2011; interview with Islam Lotfy, March 2, 2011; interview with Mosab Ragab, March 7, 2011; interview with Anas al-Qassas, March 9, 2011.

60.   Abdel Moneim al-Mahmoud, "List of the Internal Populace of the Muslim Brothers" (AR), *IkhwanWiki*, http://www.ikhwanwiki.com/images/4/40 /لائحة_الشعبة_الداخلية_للاخوان_المسلمين.pdf; interview with Mosab Ragab, March 7, 2011.

61. Al-Mahmoud, "List of the Internal Populace of the Muslim Brothers."

62. Interview with Khaled Hamza, January 10, 2011.

63. Ibid.

64. "The General Organization of the Muslim Brotherhood (1994)," *IkhwanWiki*,
     https://ar.wikisource.org/wiki/29%1994_عام28%_المسلمين_للإخوان_العام_النظام.

65. Mitchell, *Society of Muslim Brothers*, 164; "The Muslim Brotherhood," *Ikhwan-
     Wiki*, http://www.ikhwanwiki.com/index.php?title=المسلمين_الإخوان_جماعة#.D8
     .A7.D9.84.D9.85.D9.86.D8.B7.D9.82.D8.A9; interview with Khaled Hamza,
     January 10, 2011.

3. Postrevolutionary Posturing

1.   "Constitutional Statement for the Egyptian Supreme Council of the Armed
     Forces" (AR), State Information Service, February 13, 2011, http://www
     .sis.gov.eg/Ar/Templates/Articles/tmpArticles.aspx?ArtID=44103#
     .VtcNkDZOKlJ.

2.   Eric Trager, "Is Egypt's Military Turning against the Revolution?" *Atlantic*,
     March 1, 2011, http://www.theatlantic.com/international/archive/2011/03/is
     -egypts-military-turning-against-the-revolution/71859/.

3.   Steven A. Cook, *Ruling but Not Governing: The Military and Political Devel-
     opment in Egypt, Algeria, and Turkey* (Baltimore: Johns Hopkins University
     Press, 2007), 76–77.

4.   Alex Blumberg, "Why Egypt's Military Cares about Home Appliances,"
     NPR, February 4, 2011, http://www.npr.org/sections/money/2011/02/10
     /133501837/why-egypts-military-cares-about-home-appliances; David D.
     Kirkpatrick, "Egyptians Say Military Discourages an Open Economy," *New
     York Times*, February 17, 2011, http://www.nytimes.com/2011/02/18/world
     /middleeast/18military.html?pagewanted=all&_r=0; Joseph Hammond and
     James Wan, "Egypt's Military Economy: Money Is Power, Power Is Money,"
     Daily News Egypt, April 14, 2014, http://www.dailynewsegypt.com/2014/04
     /14/egypts-military-economy-money-power-power-money/.

5.   "Egypt Army in Emergency Law Pledge," Al Jazeera, February 11, 2011,
     http://www.aljazeera.com/news/middleeast/2011/02/201121161511674298
     .html.

6.   "The Generation Changing the World," *Time*, February 28, 2011, http://
     content.time.com/time/covers/0,16641,20110228,00.html.

7.   "Security Men in Solidarity with the Demonstrators and '6 April' Demands
     the Immediate Release of All Detainees: The Army Clears Tahrir Square and
     Calls for an End to Protests" (AR), *Al-Emarat al-Youm*, February 15, 2011,
     http://www.emaratalyoum.com/politics/news/2011-02-15-1.356420.

8.   "Referendum on Amendments to the Constitution of Egypt This Month"
     (AR), Al Jazeera, March 1, 2011, http://www.aljazeera.net/news/arabic/2011
     /استفتاء-تعديلات-دستور-مصر-هذا-الشهر/3/1.

9.   Khulud Khairi, "Field Marshal Tantawi Meets with the Committee to Amend
     the Constitution" (AR), *Masress*, February 15, 2011, http://www.masress.com

/alwakei/7170; "Million-Man March in Tahrir Square to Pay Tribute to the Martyrs of the Revolution and Emphasize Its Demands" (AR), *Al-Arabiya*, February 18, 2011, http://www.alarabiya.net/articles/2011/02/18/138153 .html.

10. Jack Shenker, "Egyptian Army Hijacking Revolution, Activists Fear," *Guardian*, February 15, 2011, http://www.theguardian.com/world/2011/feb/15 /egyptian-army-hijacking-revolution-fear.

11. Mohamed Gamal Arafa, "Al-Bayoumi: Our Youths Protected the Revolution from the Thugs" (AR), *Al-Wafd*, February 17, 2011, http://alwafd.org تحقيقات-وحوارات/17068/البيومي-شبابنا-حمى-الثورة-من-البلطجية/.

12. Nathan J. Brown and Michele Dunne, "Egypt's Controversial Constitutional Amendments," Carnegie Endowment for International Peace, March 23, 2007, http://carnegieendowment.org/files/egypt_constitution _webcommentary01.pdf.

13. Mohamed Habib, *The Muslim Brotherhood: Between the Rise to Power and Eating the Legitimacy* (AR) (Cairo: Sama for Publishing and Distribution, 2013), 33; interview with Saad al-Katatny, March 29, 2011; "Khairat al-Shater with Mona al-Shazli on the Program 'Ten in the Evening'" (AR), YouTube, March 8, 2011, https://www.youtube.com/watch?v=Lm-R6j9bIa8; "Headline: Dr. Mohamed Al-Beltagy; Freedom and Justice Party 3/3" (AR), YouTube, February 23, 2011 https://www.youtube.com/watch?v=zm_jQH -MxuE.

14. Brotherhood leader Sobhi Saleh, who was later appointed to the constitution-amending commission, explained this reasoning during an interview: "Why didn't we start directly with a constitution? I will tell you simply: . . . The constitutional assembly comes either by appointment or election. We don't want it to come through appointment because the one that appoints is the army." See "Mr. Sobhi Saleh Explains Why We'll Vote Yes for the Constitutional Amendments," YouTube, March 12, 2011, https://www.youtube.com/watch?v =L9orhB1LwwE.

15. "Press Statement from the Muslim Brotherhood regarding the Constitutional Declaration That Was Published on 13 February 2011," *Ikhwan-Wiki*, February 13, 2011, http://www.ikhwanwiki.com/index.php?title= بيان_صحفى_من_الإخوان_المسلمين_حول_الإعلان_الدستورى_الصادر_اليوم_الأحد_13_فبراير_2011م.

16. "Press Statement: The Supreme Guide and His Deputies and the Press Spokesmen Express the Opinion of the Society Only" (AR), *Egypt Window*, February 14, 2011, http://www.egyptwindow.net/ar_print.aspx?print_ID= 11213.

17. Arafa, "Al-Bayoumi: Our Youths Protected the Revolution from the Thugs" (AR).

18. Shaaban Abdel Sittar et al., "Million-Man March for Victory in Tahrir: And Al-Qaradawi Leads the Worshipers after an Absence of 30 Years" (AR), *Al-Sharq Al-Awsat*, February 19, 2011, http://archive.aawsat.com/details.asp ?section=4&issueno=11771&article=608944#.VtcONjZOKlK; "Statement

from the Muslim Brotherhod regarding the Events of February 25, 2011," *IkhwanWiki*, February 26, 2011, http://www.ikhwanwiki.com/index.php?title =بيان_من_الإخوان_المسلمين_بخصوص_أحداث_الجمعة_25_فبراير_2011م.

19. Ahmed Sobea, "The Decision to Release al-Shater and Malek from Tora's Grounds" (AR), *IkhwanWiki*, March 2, 2011, http://www.ikhwanwiki.com /index.php?title=قرار_الإفراج_عن_الشاطر_ومالك_يصل_مزرعة_طرة.

20. Interview with Khairat al-Shater, March 13, 2011; Mohamed Shaaban, "For the First Time: The Secret File of the Family of Khairat al-Shater" (AR), *Al-Mogaz*, February 27, 2013, http://www.elmogaz.com/node/67632; "Khairat al-Shater" (AR), *IkhwanWiki*, http://www.ikhwanwiki.com/index.php?title= خيرت_الشاطر.

21. Amira Howeidy, "Meet the Brotherhood's Enforcer: Khairat el-Shater," *Ahram Online*, March 29, 2012, http://english.ahram.org.eg/NewsContent/1/64 /37993/Egypt/Politics-/Meet-the-Brotherhood's-enforcer-Khairat-ElShater .aspx.

22. David D. Kirkpatrick, "Keeper of Islamic Flame Rises as Egypt's New Decisive Voice," *New York Times*, March 12, 2012, http://www.nytimes.com/2012/03 /12/world/middleeast/muslim-brotherhood-leader-rises-as-egypts-decisive -voice.html?pagewanted=all.

23. Interview with Abdel Moneim al-Mahmoud, June 30, 2010; interview with Mohamed al-Beltagy, March 26, 2011.

24. Alaa al-Din Arafat, *The Mubarak Leadership and the Future of Democracy in Egypt* (New York: Palgrave Macmillan, 2009), 174; Amira Howeidy, "Back to Square One," *Al-Ahram Weekly On-line*, no. 801, June 29–July 5, 2006; Amira Howeidy, "The Same Old War of Attrition," *Al-Ahram Weekly On-line*, no. 810, August 31–September 6, 2006. (Many *Al-Ahram Weekly On-line* articles have not been archived on the Internet, so URLs for them are unavailable.)

25. Sophia Ibrahim, "Judgment Day," *Al-Ahram Weekly On-line*, no. 893, April 17–23, 2008; Samer Shehata and Joshua Stacher, "Boxing In the Brothers," *MERIP*, August 8, 2007, http://www.merip.org/mero/mero080807; Robert Springborg, "The Hounds That Did Not Bark: Solving the Mystery of Business without Voice in Egypt," in *Business Politics in the Middle East*, ed. Steffen Hertog et al. (London: C. Hurst, 2013), 255.

26. Kirkpatrick, "Keeper of Islamic Flame Rises."

27. "First Meeting with Khairat al-Shater after His Leaving Imprisonment" (AR), YouTube, March 8, 2011, https://www.youtube.com/watch?v=UyYFi7Ln9tw.

28. Steve Hendrix and William Wan, "Egyptian Prime Minister Ahmed Shafiq Resigns Ahead of Protests," *Washington Post*, March 3, 2011, http://www .washingtonpost.com/wp-dyn/content/article/2011/03/03/AR2011030301569 .html.

29. "Speech of Primes Minister Essam Sharaf from Tahrir Square," YouTube, March 4, 2011, https://www.youtube.com/watch?v=nuknV-IlM7U.

30. "Egypt PM Addresses Tahrir Rally," Al Jazeera, March 5, 2011, http://www .aljazeera.com/news/middleeast/2011/03/20113483827365222.html.

31. Interview with Abdel Rahman Faris, March 9, 2011.

32. Mohsen Samika et al., "The Army Disperses 'Tahrir' Sit-In after a Battle with Bullets and Swords in the Square" (AR), *Al-Masry al-Youm*, March 10, 2011, http://today.almasryalyoum.com/article2.aspx?ArticleID=290076&IssueID =2070; David D. Kirkpatrick, "Egypt's Women Find Power Still Hinges on Men," *New York Times*, January 9, 2012, http://www.nytimes.com/2012/01 /10/world/middleeast/egyptian-women-confront-restrictions-of-patriarchy .html.

33. Nathan J. Brown and Michele Dunne, "Egypt's Draft Constitutional Amendments Answer Some Questions and Raise Others," Carnegie Endowment for International Peace, March 1, 2011, http://carnegieendowment.org/2011/03 /01/egypt-s-draft-constitutional-amendments-answer-some-questions-and -raise-others#.

34. "Statement from the 'Salafist Call' Regarding the Referendum on the Constitutional Amendments," *Ana Salafy*, March 7, 2011, http://www.anasalafy.com /play.php?catsmktba=24581.

35. Eric Trager, "In a Divided Egypt, the Military and Islamists Play for Political Advantage," *Atlantic*, March 18, 2011, http://www.theatlantic.com /international/archive/2011/03/in-a-divided-egypt-the-military-and-islamists -play-for-political-advantage/72715/.

36. "The Complete Text of the Constitutional Amendments on Which There Will Be a Referendum in Egypt" (AR), *Al-Arabiya*, March 8, 2011, http://www .alarabiya.net/articles/2011/03/08/140716_1.html.

37. "Conference of the Society of the Muslim Brothers regarding the Constitutional Amendments 1" (AR), YouTube, March 12, 2011, https://www.youtube .com/watch?v=NDaRJvTGMaI.

38. "Statement of the Coalition of Revolutionary Youth regarding the Referendum on the Constitutional Amendments" (AR), Facebook, March 14,2011, https:// www.facebook.com/notes/الثورة-شباب-ائتلاف-بيان/يناير-25-شباب- /حول-الاستفتاء-على-التعديلات-الدستورية/132701383468689.

39. "The Muslim Brotherhood Tops the List of Supporters of the Constitutional Amendments" (AR), *Al-Ahram*, March 14, 2011, http://gate.ahram.org.eg /NewsContentPrint/13/70/49163.aspx.

40. "Moussa: I Will Participate in the Referendum on Constitutional Amendments, but I Won't Vote in Their Favor" (AR), *Al-Masry al-Youm*, March 16, 2011, http://www.almasryalyoum.com/news/details/119372.

41. "Majority of Egyptians against Constitutional Amendments, Says Poll," *Egypt Independent*, March 11, 2011, http://www.egyptindependent.com//news /majority-egyptians-against-constitutional-amendments-says-poll.

42. Shaimaa Al-Qarnshawi, "Cairo Voters Said 'No' the Most: And Those Agreeing to the Amendments Won in Every Governorate" (AR), *Al-Masry al-Youm*, March 21, 2011, http://www.almasryalyoum.com/news/details/120474.

43. Hesham al-Awadi, *In Pursuit of Legitimacy: The Muslim Brothers and Mubarak, 1982–2000* (London: Tauris Academic Studies, 2004), 82–84.

44. Interview with Saad al-Husseini, March 2, 2011.

45. Interview with Mohamed Morsi, August 2, 2010; Salah al-Din Hassan, "El-Erian: The Muslim Brotherhood Doesn't Need Legitimacy, and the Experiences of Partisan Brothers Were Failures" (AR), *Islam Online*, January 17, 2011, https://groups.google.com/forum/#!topic/salaheldinhassan /KpY6XNdYfPM.

46. Interview with Abdel Moneim Abouel Fotouh, March 2, 2011; Salah al-Din Hassan, "Abouel Fotouh: I Reject the Establishment of a Party for the Muslim Brothers in Egypt" (AR), *IslamOnline*, March 17, 2011, http://salaheldinhassan .blogspot.com/2011/03/blog-post.html.

47. Mohamed Badie, "Press Statement regarding the Freedom and Justice Party and the Presidential and Parliamentary Elections" (AR), *Egypt Window*, March 15, 2011, http://www.egyptwindow.net/news_Details.aspx?News_ID= 11581.

48. Interview with Islam Lotfy, March 2, 2011; interview with Moaz Abdel Karim, March 10, 2011; interview with Amr al-Beltagy, March 9, 2011.

49. Abdel Galil al-Sharnouby, "Dr. Morsi: The Guidance Office Didn't Agree to the Youths' Conference on Saturday" (AR), *IkhwanWiki*, March 25, 2011, http://www.ikhwanwiki.com/index.php?title=على_يوافق_لم_الإرشاد_مكتب_:مرسي.د _مؤتمر_الشباب_يوم_السبت.

50. "Recommendations of the Brotherhood Youth Conference" (AR), Facebook, March 26, 2011, https://www.facebook.com/notes/توصيات/رصد-شبكة /مؤتمر-شباب-الاخوان/-199071970127804.

51. Hassan Mahmoud, "Dr. Abuzeid Tells the Full Details of the Youth Conference in Dokki" (AR), *Dakahlia Ikhwan*, March 27, 2011, http://dakahliaikhwan .com/viewarticle.php?id=7796; Eric Trager, "Western Media Is Fixated on the Wrong Arrest in Egypt," *New Republic*, September 23, 2013, https:// newrepublic.com/article/114820/gehad-el-hadded-arrest-egypt-what-media -doesnt-understand.

52. Interview with Anas al-Qassas, March 9, 2011.

53. Nathan J. Brown and Kristen Stilt, "A Haphazard Constitutional Compromise," Carnegie Endowment for International Peace, April 11, 2011, http:// carnegieendowment.org/2011/04/11/haphazard-constitutional-compromise#; Dalia Othman, "'Al-Masry al-Youm' Publishes the Text of the 'Constitutional Declaration': And Presidential Elections before the End of the Current Year" (AR), *Al-Masry al-Youm*, March 30, 2011, http://www.almasryalyoum.com /news/details/122361; "Text of the 71 Constitution and 2007 Amendments" (AR), State Information Service, September 30, 2009, http://www.sis.gov.eg /Ar/Templates/Articles/tmpArticles.aspx?CatID=73#.VBSAS0tRSpQ.

54. Brown and Stilt, "Haphazard Constitutional Compromise."

55. "Mr. Sobhi Saleh Explains."

56. Eric Trager, "Struggling to Restart Egypt's Stalled Revolution," *Atlantic*, April 2, 2011, http://www.theatlantic.com/international/archive/2011/04 /struggling-to-restart-egypts-stalled-revolution/73362/.

57. Neil MacFarquhar, "Protesters Scold Egypt's Military Council," *New York Times*, April 1, 2011, http://www.nytimes.com/2011/04/02/world/middleeast/02egypt.html?_r=1&.

58. "Mubarak's Former Chief of Staff Arrested," Al Jazeera, April 7, 2011, http://www.aljazeera.com/news/middleeast/2011/04/20114720540306784.html.

59. AFP, "Egyptian Protesters Call for Mubarak Trial," *Emirates 24/7*, April 8, 2011, http://www.emirates247.com/news/world/egyptian-protesters-call-for-mubarak-trial-2011-04-08-1.378569.

60. Ivan Watson and Mohamed Fadel Fahmy, "Protesters Gather in Tahrir Square to Pressure Egyptian Military," CNN, April 8, 2011, http://www.cnn.com/2011/WORLD/meast/04/08/egypt.protest/.

61. Yosri al-Badry and Ahmed Shalabi, "Al-Sherif' in Jail after His Capture for 15 Days Pending Investigation, and 'Mubarak' and His Two Sons Receive Investigation Announcement in Sharm el-Sheikh" (AR), *Al-Masry al-Youm*, April 12, 2011, http://today.almasryalyoum.com/article2.aspx?ArticleID=293394; Patrick J. McDonnell and Jeffrey Fleishman, "Mubarak's Arrest a Watershed Moment for Egypt," *Los Angeles Times*, April 13, 2011, http://articles.latimes.com/2011/apr/13/world/la-fg-egypt-mubarak-20110414.

62. "First Meeting with Khairat al-Shater."

63. "Khairat al-Shater with Mona al-Shazli."

64. "Engineer Khairat al-Shater Deputy Supreme Guide: Meeting of Al-Aqsa Channel 2" (AR), *IkhwanTube*, March 11, 2011, http://www.ikhwantube.com/video/1659133/.

65. Bargisi "Khairat al-Shater on 'The Nahda Project' (Complete Translation)," *Current Trends in Islamist Ideology* (April 10, 2012), http://www.hudson.org/research/9820-khairat-al-shater-on-the-nahda-project-complete-translation. Quotations have been lightly edited for style.

4. Preparing for Power

1. Interview with Abdel Moneim al-Mahmoud, June 30, 2010.

2. Interview with Islam Lotfy, March 2, 2011.

3. "Dr. Mohamed Morsi" (AR), *IkhwanWiki*, http://www.ikhwanwiki.com/index.php?title=محمد_مرسي#.D8.A7.D9.84.D8.B9.D9.85.D9.84_.D8.A7.D9.84.D8.B3.D9.8A.D8.A7.D8.B3.D9.8A.

4. Mohamed Habib, *The Muslim Brotherhood: Between the Rise to Power and Eating the Legitimacy* (AR) (Cairo: Sama for Publishing and Distribution, 2003), 17–18.

5. Tarek Masoud, "Mohamed Morsi Will Have His Hands Full Uniting a Deeply Divided Egypt," *Daily Beast*, June 25, 2012, http://www.thedailybeast.com/articles/2012/06/25/mohamed-morsi-will-have-his-hands-full-uniting-a-deeply-divided-egypt.html.

6. Interview with Abouleila Madi, January 26, 2011; interview with Mohamed Habib, March 8, 2011; interview with Essam el-Erian, March 14, 2011; interview with Mohamed al-Beltagy, March 26, 2011; interview with Sobhi Saleh,

March 29, 2011; Eric Trager, "Meet the Islamist Political Fixer Who Could Be Egypt's Next President," *New Republic*, April 27, 2012, https://newrepublic .com/article/102988/egypt-muslim-brotherhood-election-mohamed-morsi.

7. David D. Kirkpatrick, "In Egypt Race, Battle Is Joined on Islam's Role," *New York Times*, April 23, 2012, http://www.nytimes.com/2012/04/24/world /middleeast/in-egypt-morsi-escalates-battle-over-islams-role.html?_r=1& pagewanted=all.

8. Trager, "Meet the Islamist Political Fixer."

9. Ibrahim El-Houdaiby, "The Muslim Brotherhood's Trial of Pluralism," *Ahram Online*, April 23, 2011, http://english.ahram.org.eg/NewsContentPrint/4/0 /10662/Opinion/0/The-Muslim-Brotherhoods-trial-of-pluralism.aspx.

10. Interview with Mohamed Morsi, August 3, 2010.

11. Mahmoud Hussein, "The Final Statement Issued by the Shura Council of the Muslim Brotherhood in Its Second Meetings during the Fourth Session of Years 2010–14" (AR), April 30, 2011.

12. "Dr. Mohamed Morsi, Member of the Guidance Office and Chairman of the Freedom and Justice Party in a Complete and Important Discussion" (AR), YouTube, May 11, 2011, https://www.youtube.com/watch?v=FdM9Gf3crTM &list=UUk8lzqE3cS2kZrC3THDDaXgMay%2011th%202011.

13. Mustafa Shahin, "A New Headquarter for the Freedom and Justice Party Opens in the Walidiya Area in Assiut" (AR), *IkhwanOnline*, May 4, 2013 (no longer available online); Salah al-Masan and Abdullah Salah, "Medical Caravan of 'Freedom and Justice' in Al-Hakarub Area in Aswan" (AR), *Al-Youm al-Sabaa'*, July 29, 2011, http://www.youm7.com/story/2011/7/29/_قافلة_طبية #464308/الحرية_والعدالة_فى_منطقة_الحكروب_بأسوان.VtcuXTZOKlI.

14. Diaa Mustafa, "Agreement on Establishing the Freedom and Justice Party after the Sixty Days without a Complaint Ends" (AR), *Masress*, June 6, 2011, http:// www.masress.com/misrelgdida/63319.

15. Ahmed Abu al-Qassem, "Opening of the Freedom and Justice Headquarters in al-Dakhaliya in the Presence of Morsi and el-Erian" (AR), *Al-Nahhar Egypt*, July 4, 2011, http://www.alnaharegypt.com/t~38551.

16. "Dr. Mohamed Morsi, Member of the Guidance Office."

17. Islam Tawfiq, "Dr. Morsi Meets a German Federation Parliamentary Delegation" (AR), *IkhwanWiki*, July 12, 2011, http://www.ikhwanwiki.com/index .php?title=د._مرسي_يلتقي_وفدًا_من_البرلمان_الاتحادي_الألماني.

18. Osama Abdel Salam, "Dr. Morsi: My Chairmanship of the Freedom and Justice Party Is a Transitional Phase" (AR), *IkhwanWiki*, April 30, 2011, http://www.ikhwanwiki.com/index.php?title=د._مرسي:_رئاستي_لحزب_الحرية%22_والعدالة%22_مرحلة_انتقالية.

19. Maye Kassem, *In the Guise of Democracy: Governance in Contemporary Egypt* (Reading, UK: Ithaca Press, 1999), 186–87.

20. Alaa al-Din Arafat, *The Mubarak Leadership and Future of Democracy in Egypt* (New York: Palgrave Macmillan, 2009), 15.

21. Interview with Ibrahim Nasser el-Din, July 17, 2010; interview with Said Ab-

dul Khaliq, July 17, 2010; interview with Awatif Wali, July 18, 2010; interview with Yasin Tag el-Din, July 19, 2010; interview with Gameela Ismail, July 22, 2010; interview with Hassan Abdel Gowad, July 24, 2010; interview with Ahmed Ashour, July 27, 2010; interview with Mahmoud Ibrahem, July 31, 2010; interview with Camilia Shokry, August 1, 2010; interview with Mounir Fakhry Abdelnour, August 10, 2010; interview with Amina Niqash, January 10, 2011.

22. Interview with Samir Fayyad, August 3, 2010.

23. Interview with Moussa Mustafa Moussa, June 27, 2010; interview with Mustafa Abdel-Aziz, July 4, 2010; interview with Farida Niqash, August 11, 2010.

24. Interview with Mahmoud Salem, June 28, 2010; interview with Said Ashmawy, January 7, 2011; interview with Essam Shiha, January 23, 2011; Lisa Blaydes, *Elections and Distributive Politics in Mubarak's Egypt* (Cambridge: Cambridge University Press, 2011), 10; Mona el-Ghobashy, "The Dynamics of Egypt's Elections," *MERIP*, September 29, 2010, http://www.merip.org/mero/mero092910.

25. "Toward an Electoral Alliance: For Egypt Includes 12 Parties, Most Notably Freedom and Justice, al-Wafd, and al-Tagammu" (AR), *Egypt Window*, June 15, 2011, http://www.egyptwindow.net/news_Details.aspx?News_ID=12942.

26. "Document of the Democratic Alliance for Egypt," Facebook, June 21, 2011, https://www.facebook.com/notes/الدكتور-محمد-سعد-الكتاتني/وثيقة-التحالف-الديمقراطي-من-أجل-مصر/226793187340266-.

27. Tarek Osman, *Egypt on the Brink: From Nasser to Mubarak* (New Haven: Yale University Press, 2010), 26, 31–32; Hany Raslan and Rada Mohamed Helal, *The New Wafd Party* (AR) (Cairo: Al-Ahram Center for Political and Strategic Studies, 2010), 11; Joel Gordon, "The False Hopes of 1950: The Wafd's Last Hurrah and the Demise of Egypt's Old Order," *International Journal of Middle East Studies* 21, no. 2 (May 1989): 197–98.

28. Bertus Hendriks, "Egypt's Elections, Mubarak's Bind," *MERIP*, no. 129 (January 1985): 11.

29. Eric Trager, "Egypt's New Political Alliance Could Boost the Islamists," Washington Institute for Near East Policy, PolicyWatch no. 1822, June 24, 2011, http://www.washingtoninstitute.org/policy-analysis/view/egypts-new-political-alliance-could-boost-the-islamists.

30. "Eng. Khairat al-Shater with Mahmoud Saad in 'The Square'" (AR), YouTube, June 13, 2011, https://www.youtube.com/watch?v=kuz9IoII6T8&index=4&list=WL.

31. "Statement from the Muslim Brotherhood: Regarding the Assassination of Sheikh Osama bin Laden" (AR), *Egypt Window*, May 2, 2011, http://www.egyptwindow.net/news_Details.aspx?News_ID=12352.

32. Mohamed Badie, "Palestine in a New Era" (AR), *Egypt Window*, May 5, 2011, http://www.egyptwindow.net/news_Details.aspx?News_ID=12405.

33. Mohamed Badie, "In Memory of the Catastrophe the Arab Peoples Siege the

Zionist Entity" (AR), *Dakhaliya Ikhwan*, May 19, 2011, http://dakahliaikhwan
.com/viewarticle.php?id=8393.

34. Mark Landler, "Obama Seeks Reset in Arab World," *New York Times*, May 11,
2011, http://www.nytimes.com/2011/05/12/us/politics/12prexy.html
?pagewanted=all&_r=0. Thanks to my friend Samuel Tadros for pointing me
to this piece.

35. Barack Obama, "Remarks by the President on the Middle East," White House,
May 19, 2011, https://www.whitehouse.gov/the-press-office/2011/05/19
/remarks-president-middle-east-and-north-africa.

36. "Clinton: U.S. 'Would Welcome' Dialogue with Muslim Brotherhood," CNN,
July 1, 2011, http://www.cnn.com/2011/WORLD/meast/06/30/egypt.muslim
.brotherhood.us/.

37. "The Words of Dr. Mohamed Morsi in Dakhaliya 1-3" (AR), YouTube, July 6,
2011, https://www.youtube.com/watch?v=YGr29o9AtzY.

38. "Katatni Criticizes US Policies in Middle East in Meeting with American
Officials," *IkhwanWeb*, October 5, 2011, http://ikhwanweb.com/article.php?id
=29075.

39. "The French Ambassador in the Hospitality of the Freedom and Justice Party"
(AR), *Egypt Window*, June 30, 2011, http://www.egyptwindow.net/news
_Details.aspx?News_ID=13145.

40. "Freedom and Justice Welcomes a Representative from the French Senate"
(AR), e-mailed press release, October 20, 2011.

41. David D. Kirkpatrick, "Crime Wave in Egypt Has People Afraid, Even the
Police," *New York Times*, May 12, 2011, http://www.nytimes.com/2011/05/13
/world/middleeast/13egypt.html?pagewanted=all.

42. "Demands of the Second Egyptian Anger Revolution" (AR), Facebook,
May 15, 2011, https://www.facebook.com/notes/مطالب-ثورة-الغضب-المصرية-الثانية
/ثورة-الغضب-المصرية-الثانية/-131227183618632.

43. "Statement from the Muslim Brotherhood on Nonparticipation in the Activities of Friday, May 27, 2011" (AR), *Dakhalia Ikhwan*, May 27, 2011, http://
www.dakahliaikhwan.com/viewarticle.php?id=8477.

44. Salma Shukrallah, "Tahrir Protest Swells by Midday," *Ahram Online*, May 27,
2011, http://english.ahram.org.eg/NewsContent/1/64/13075/Egypt/Politics
-/Tahrir-protest-swells-by-midday.aspx.

45. Sarah Lynch, "The Aftermath of Another Clash at Egypt's Tahrir Square,"
Christian Science Monitor, June 29, 2011, http://www.csmonitor.com/World
/Middle-East/2011/0629/The-aftermath-of-another-clash-at-Egypt-s-Tahrir
-Square.

46. Robert Mackey, "Protesters Return to Cairo's Tahrir Square," *New York Times*,
June 29, 2011, http://thelede.blogs.nytimes.com/2011/06/29/protesters
-return-to-cairos-tahrir-square/.

47. "The Muslim Brotherhood's Position regarding the Activities of Friday,
7/8/2011" (AR), *IkhwanWiki*, July 6, 2011, http://www.ikhwanwiki.com
/index.php?title=موقف_الإخوان_المسلمين_من_فعالية_الجمعة_8/7/2011م.

48. Salma Shukrallah, "Hundreds of Thousands Revitalise Egypt's Revolution
     on Determination Friday," *Ahram Online*, July 8, 2011, http://english.ahram
     .org.eg/NewsContent/1/64/15899/Egypt/Politics-/Hundreds-of-thousands
     -revitalise-Egypts-revolution.aspx; "Live Updates: A Blow by Blow Ac-
     count of Egypt's 'Friday of Determination,'" *Ahram Online*, July 8, 2011,
     http://english.ahram.org.eg/~/NewsContentP/1/15863/Egypt/Friday-of
     -Determination-a-blow-by-blow-account-of-.aspx.

49. Anthony Shadid, "Islamists Flood Square in Cairo in Show of Strength,"
     New York Times, July 29, 2011, http://www.nytimes.com/2011/07/30/world
     /middleeast/30egypt.html?pagewanted=all.

50. Kristen Chick, "Egyptian Army Empties Tahrir Square," *Christian Science
     Monitor*, August 1, 2011, http://www.csmonitor.com/World/Middle-East
     /2011/0801/Egyptian-Army-empties-Tahrir-Square.

5. The Road to Parliament

1.   Interview with Magdy Amr, January 17, 2011; interview with Salah Naaman,
     June 21, 2012.

2.   See, for example, "Aspects of the Muslim Brotherhood Camp of a Known
     Populace 2" (AR), YouTube, July 9, 2011, https://www.youtube.com/watch?v
     =zR4pIjguFQU.

3.   Interview with Magdy Amr, January 17, 2011.

4.   "Dr. Mahmoud Ezzat and the Muslim Brotherhood's Matrouh Camp
     2011" (AR), YouTube, July 28, 2011, https://www.youtube.com/watch?v=
     V0ImkXgFL6I.

5.   "Engineer Khairat al-Shater in the Matrouh Camp of the Muslim Brother-
     hood" (AR), YouTube, July 28, 2011, https://www.youtube.com/watch?v=
     sNVz_h4fzY0.

6.   Mokhtar Awad, "The Salafi Dawa of Alexandria: The Politics of a Religious
     Movement," *Current Trends in Islamist Ideology*, August 14, 2014, http://www
     .hudson.org/research/10463-the-salafi-dawa-of-alexandria-the-politics-of-a
     -religious-movement-.

7.   Ibid.

8.   Eric Trager, "Egypt's Looming Competitive Theocracy," *Current Trends in
     Islamist Ideology*, December 27, 2012, http://www.hudson.org/research/9791
     -egypt-s-looming-competitive-theocracy.

9.   Souad Mekhennet and Nicholas Kulish, "With Muslim Brotherhood Set to
     Join Egypt Protests, Religion's Role May Grow," *New York Times*, January 27,
     2011, http://www.nytimes.com/2011/01/28/world/middleeast/28alexandria
     .html?module=Search&mabReward=relbias%3Ar.

10. Interview with Emad Abdel Ghafour, October 11, 2014.

11. Ibid.

12. "The Salafist Nour Party Withdraws from the Democratic Alliance Because
     of Secularist Parties" (AR), *Masress*, September 4, 2011, http://www.masress
     .com/kelmetna/31522.

13. Sami Aboudi, "Egypt Changes Election System in Favour of Party Lists," Reuters, September 24, 2011, http://af.reuters.com/article/topNews/idAFJOE 78N09Q20110924?pageNumber=1&virtualBrandChannel=&sp=true.

14. "Muslim Brotherhood-led Bloc Threatens Egypt Vote Boycott," Al-Arabiya, September 29, 2011, http://english.alarabiya.net/articles/2011/09/29/169271 .html.

15. Interview with Nasser Amin, October 12, 2014.

16. Adel Al-Dargali, "Mustafa Al-Tawil: 'The Brotherhood' Cheated 'the Wafd' in the Year 1984 . . . and Reneged on Any Agreement" (AR), Al-Masry al-Youm, October 9, 2011, http://www.almasryalyoum.com/news/details/116726.

17. Eric Trager, "Policywatch 1868: Tensions Grow between Egypt's Military Leaders and the Muslim Brotherhood," Washington Institute for Near East Policy, November 8, 2011, http://www.washingtoninstitute.org/policy -analysis/view/tensions-grow-between-egypts-military-leaders-and-the -muslim-brotherhood.

18. Farida Ali, "Statement from Badrawy and Morsi: The Democratic Alliance Continues, and We Will Pursue a Document of Basic Principles" (AR), Sidi el-Balad, October 2, 2011, http://www.el-balad.com/3889.aspx; "The Wafd Decides to Conduct Elections via an 'Independent List' from the Democratic Alliance" (AR), Al-Fagr, October 6, 2011, http://www.elfagr.org/64804#.

19. "Egypt: Sharp Differences among the Factions of the 'Democratic Alliance' after the Brotherhood Demands to Achieve a Third of the Parliament" (AR), Al-Mokhtsar, October 3, 2011, http://www.almokhtsar.com/node/15959

20. Hany al-Waziri, "'Freedom and Justice': The Democratic Alliance Has Prepared 70% of Its Lists for the Elections" (AR), Al-Masry al-Youm, October 14, 2011, http://m.almasryalyoum.com/news/details/118026.

21. Mostafa Ali, "Finally, Egypt's Parties Set to Begin the Battle for Post-Mubarak Parliament," Ahram Online, October 25, 2011, http://english.ahram.org.eg /News/25030.aspx. There is reason to believe that the FJP actually ran for a much higher percentage of the seats, and some estimates have suggested that FJP candidates ultimately ran for 90 percent of all seats. However, because the full lists of candidates are not available, this number has been difficult to verify.

22. Interview with Essam Mukhtar, December 4, 2011; interview with Mohamed Sudan, December 11, 2011; interview with al-Muhammadi al-Sayyid, December 11, 2011; interview with Saber Abouel Fotouh, December 11, 2011; interview with Azza al-Garf, June 26, 2012; interview with Osama Suleiman, July 3, 2012.

23. "The Text of the Document of Ali El-Salmi for Supra-Constitutional Principles" (AR), Facebook, November 8, 2011, https://www.facebook.com/notes /164653623629773/وائل-حشاد-المحامى/نص-وثيقة-السلمي-للمبادئ-فوق-الدستورية.

24. "'Prevent Sedition': The Brotherhood Demands el-Salmi's Fall" (AR), Egypt Window, November 2, 2011, http://www.egyptwindow.net/news_Details .aspx?News_ID=15243.

25. Mohamed Hassan Shaaban, "The Political Forces in Egypt Line Up to Confront the 'el-Salmi Document'" (AR), *Al-Sharq al-Awsat*, November 3, 2011, http://archive.aawsat.com/details.asp?section=4&article=648051&issueno=12028#.VtdW2TZOJFI.

26. "Al-Jamaa Al-Islamiya to Egypt's Army: Withdraw the Constitutional Amendments Plans or Else," *Ahram Online*, November 4, 2011, http://english.ahram.org.eg/NewsContent/1/64/25945/Egypt/Politics-/AlJamaa-AlIslamiya-to-Egypts-army-Withdraw-the-con.aspx.

27. Zeinab El Gundy, "Egypt Deputy PM and Political Forces Look for Common Ground over 'Supra-Constitutional Principles,'" *Ahram Online*, November 15, 2011, http://english.ahram.org.eg/NewsContent/1/64/26606/Egypt/Politics-/Egypt-Deputy-PM-and-political-forces-look-for-comm.aspx.

28. Marwa Awad, "Thousands Protest in Egypt's Tahrir against Army Rule," Reuters, November 18, 2011, http://www.reuters.com/article/us-egypt-protest-army-idUSTRE7AH0WX20111118; Sherif Tarek, "Egypt's Islamists Dominate Tahrir Square's Dense Friday Protest," *Ahram Online*, November 18, 2011, http://english.ahram.org.eg/NewsContent/1/64/26902/Egypt/Politics-/Islamists-dominate-Egypts-Tahrir-Squares-dense-Fri.aspx.

29. David D. Kirkpatrick and Liam Stack, "Violent Protests in Egypt Put Thousands against Police," *New York Times*, November 19, 2011, http://www.nytimes.com/2011/11/20/world/middleeast/violence-erupts-in-cairo-as-egypts-military-cedes-political-ground.html.

30. Mohamed Faris, "Rights Activists Condemn the Dispersal of the Tahrir Sit-In with Force: And Call for the Dismissal of 'Sharaf' and 'Issawy'" (AR), *Al-Masry al-Youm*, November 19, 2011, http://www.almasryalyoum.com/news/details/126958; Amira Wahba, "Central Security Forces Disperse 'Tahrir' Sit-In with Force and Capture a Number of the Demonstrators" (AR), *Al-Ahram*, November 19, 2011, http://gate.ahram.org.eg/News/138814.aspx.

31. Hossam Zayed, "The Number of Deaths from the Events in Tahrir Rises to 38 after the Death of Those Injured at Kasr Al-Eini Today" (AR), *Al-Ahram*, November 24, 2011, http://gate.ahram.org.eg/News/141141.aspx.

32. "Statement by State Department Spokesperson Victoria Nuland at the Press Briefing," Embassy of the United States, Cairo, Egypt, November 21, 2011, http://egypt.usembassy.gov/tr112211.html.

33. Ahmed Said, "Cancellation of 63 Flights at Cairo Airport Due to the Events in Tahrir" (AR), *Al-Youm al-Sabaa*, November 21, 2011, http://www.youm7.com/story/2011/11/21/إلغاء_63_رحلة_طيران_بمطار_القاهرة_بسبب_أحداث_التحرير/537272#.VFTO-r5RQrd.

34. David D. Kirkpatrick, "Egypt Cabinet Offers to Resign as Protests Rage," *New York Times*, November 21, 2011, http://www.nytimes.com/2011/11/22/world/middleeast/facing-calls-to-give-up-power-egypts-military-battles-crowds.html.

35. Adel al-Daragali, "'The Wafd' Requests the Postponement of the Elections for Two Weeks At Least: And Elect a President within 60 Days" (AR), *Al-Masry*

al-Youm, November 22, 2011, http://www.almasryalyoum.com/news/details /127959.

36. Interview with Riad Haddad, November 27, 2011; Mohamed Al-Gali, "Political Sources: 'The Military' Is Studying Charging ElBaradei with Forming a Salvation Government" (AR), *Al-Youm al-Sabaa*, November 22, 2011, http:// www.youm7.com/story/2011/11/22/مصادر_سياسية_العسكرى_يدرس_تكليف_البرادعى #537690/بتشكيل_حكومة_إنقاذ.VFUWGb5RQrd.

37. "Al-Beltagy to 'Military': We Can Gather Millions against Any Force" (AR), *Al-Youm al-Sabaa*, November 20, 2011, http://youm7.com/news/newsprint ?newid=536249.

38. "Dr. Morsi after Annan Meeting: Military Pledges to Hand Over Power End of June," *IkhwanWeb*, November 22, 2011, http://www.ikhwanweb.com/article .php?id=29237.

39. "Statement from Field Marshal Tantawi" (AR), YouTube, November 22, 2011, http://www.youtube.com/watch?v=hDssEDm0i6Q.

40. David D. Kirkpatrick, "Deal to Hasten Transition in Egypt Is Jeered at Protests," *New York Times*, November 22, 2011, http://www.nytimes.com/2011/11 /23/world/middleeast/egypts-cabinet-offers-to-quit-as-activists-urge-wider -protests.html?pagewanted=all.

41. Interview with Imad Ibrahim, November 28, 2011.

42. This contention is drawn from my personal observations and interviews in Egypt during the 2011–12 parliamentary elections.

43. Ibid. When I asked people who they voted for and why in various neighborhoods in multiple cities, a frequent response was "Islamists" because—and I'm paraphrasing here—"we want to be ruled by our religion."

44. Interview with Amr Hamzawy, December 5, 2011; interview with Abdel Rahman Faris, December 5, 2011.

45. Sherif Tarek, "Al-Nour and Brotherhood: Arch Foes in Elections Runoff," *Ahram Online*, December 4, 2011, http://english.ahram.org.eg/NewsContent /33/100/28502/Elections-/News/AlNour-and-Brotherhood-Arch-foes-in -elections-runo.aspx.

46. Hesham Sallam, ed., *Egypt's Parliamentary Elections: A Critical Guide to a Changing Political Arena* (Washington: Tadween Publishing, 2013) 153.

6. Powerless Parliamentarians

1. Interview with Abdel Galil al-Sharnouby, October 12, 2014.

2. Interview with Saad al-Katatny, March 29, 2011; Gamal Essam Eddin, "'Information' of the People: Saad al-Katatny Is a Graduate of the College of Sciences of Asyut University and Has No Background in Constitutional Law" (AR), *Al-Ahram*, January 16, 2012, http://gate.ahram.org.eg/News/161126.aspx; "Mohamed Saad al-Katatny" (AR), *IkhwanWiki* http://www.ikhwanwiki.com /index.php?title=محمد_سعد_الكتاتني.

3. TV interview with Saad al-Katatny (AR), YouTube, May 8, 2009, https:// www.youtube.com/watch?v=YfMx2FqpeGo.

4. Gamal Essam el-Din, "Changing Brotherhood Faces," *Al-Ahram Weekly On-line*, no. 984, February 4–10, 2010.

5. Khaled Salam, "Katatny–Hoyer Meeting, Step in the Right Direction," *IkhwanWeb*, April 16, 2007, http://www.ikhwanweb.com/article.php?id=600.

6. Gihan Shahine, "Smoke and Mirrors," *Al-Ahram Weekly On-line*, no. 842, April 26–May 2, 2007; "Katatni Praises Obama's Speech, Urges for Real Change in US Policies," *IkhwanWeb*, June 4, 2009, http://www.ikhwanweb.com/article.php?id=20359.

7. Liam Stack, "Egypt's Child Protection Law Sparks Controversy," *Christian Science Monitor*, July 24, 2008, http://www.csmonitor.com/World/Middle-East/2008/0724/p05s01-wome.html.

8. Gamal Essam el-Din, "Stand Off Escalates," *Al-Ahram Weekly On-line*, no. 860, August 30 –September 5, 2007.

9. Gamal Essam el-Din, "Before the Vote," *Al-Ahram Weekly On-line*, no. 836, March 15–21, 2007; Gamal Essam el-Din, "Pick and Mix," *Al-Ahram Weekly On-line*, no. 882, January 31–February 6, 2008.

10. "The Supreme Guide Entrusts a Brotherhood Delegation with Congratulating Meshal and Haniyeh" (AR), *Amal al-Ummah*, January 24, 2009, http://www.amlalommah.net/new/index.php?mod=article&id=3400.

11. Nancy Metwally, "Chairman of the Revolution Parliament" (AR), *Al-Ahram*, January 23, 2012, http://gate.ahram.org.eg/Malafat/161/1047/الكتاتني.aspx.

12. Interview with Saad al-Katatny, March 29, 2011.

13. Amr Abdel Rahman, "The Brotherhood Shura Decides: Taha Wahdan Instead of al-Husseini" (AR), *Masress*, January 14, 2012, http://www.masress.com/misrelgdida/82625.

14. Interview with Mahmoud Hussein, July 1, 2012; interview with Gamal Heshmat, July 3, 2012; interview with Osama Suleiman, July 3, 2012; interview with Mustafa Ghoneimy, July 4, 2012; interview with Helmy al-Gazzar, July 14, 2012; interview with Mahmoud Ghozlan, July 15, 2012; interview with Ahmed Fahmy, July 16, 2012.

15. Interview with Helmy al-Gazzar, July 14, 2012.

16. Ahmed Eleiba, "Government Must Be Approved by New Parliament, Says FJP Leader," *Ahram Online*, December 4, 2011, http://english.ahram.org.eg/NewsContent/33/100/28484/Elections-/News/Government-must-be-approved-by-new-parliament,-say.aspx.

17. "Press Statement from the Freedom and Justice Party" (AR), January 16, 2012.

18. Gamal Essam el-Din, "Brothers Seek Parliamentary Alliance," *Al-Ahram Weekly On-line*, no. 1081, January 19–25, 2012; Hussein Mahmoud, "Dr. Morsi: New Parliament Formation Will Be All-Inclusive," *IkhwanWeb*, January 16, 2012, http://www.ikhwanweb.com/article.php?id=29560.

19. Interview with Ziad Bahaa-Eldin, July 6, 2012; interview with Mohamed Anwar Esmat Sadat, October 14, 2014.

20. "President of the Egyptian Wafd Party: We Won't Enter Parliamentary Coali-

tions" (AR), *Al-Arabiya*, January 19, 2012, http://www.alarabiya.net/articles /2012/01/19/189153.html.

21. Ahmed al-Sukri, "Nominations of Freedom and Justice to the 19 People's [Assembly] Committees" (AR), *Al-Wafd*, January 23, 2012, http://www.alwafd .org/19-الشعب-الشعب-للجان-والعدالة-الحرية-ترشيحات-152291/السياسي20%الشارع-13/وتقارير-أخبار.

22. Abu Al-Abbas Mohamed and Sameh Lashin, "Crisis in the Committee Elections: The Wafd Withdraws—and Social Democrats and Free Egyptians Threaten" (AR), *Al-Ahram*, January 25, 2012, http://www.ahram.org.eg /archive/Revolution-Parliament/News/126963.aspx.

23. The complete list of the Brotherhood's General Shura Committee isn't public, but a partial list is available at http://www.ikhwanwiki.com/index.php?title= الانتشار_ومرحلة_الشورى_مجلس.

24. Eric Trager et al., "Who's Who in Egypt's Muslim Brotherhood," Washington Institute for Near East Policy, September 2012, http://www.washington institute.org/policy-analysis/view/whos-who-in-the-muslim-brotherhood; interview with Saber Abouel Fotouh, December 11, 2011.

25. Amr al-Nadi, "The Muslim Brothers Win the Chairmanship of Most Parliamentary Committees —and 3 Members from the Wafd Violate the Decision to Boycott" (AR), *Al-Masry al-Youm*, January 31, 2012, http://m.almasryalyoum .com/news/details/148238.

26. Interview with Abbas Mukhaymer, July 4, 2012.

27. Nour Ali et al., "Al-Katatny in His Words" (AR), *Al-Youm al-Sabaa*, January 23, 2012, http://www1.youm7.com/story/2012/1/23/_مصر_كلمته_فى_الكتاتنى #585036/والديمقراط_الحرية_أجل_من_ها_أبناء_قدمت.VGrDZ4dRT4g.

28. Gamal Essam el-Din, "Difficult Debut," *Al-Ahram Weekly On-line*, no. 1082, January 26–February 1, 2012.

29. "Comment of Dr. Amr Hamzawy in the Second Session of the Parliament" (AR), YouTube, January 24, 2012, https://www.youtube.com/watch?v= GMzquzhxhMA&list=UU42WdA_gO2tV1MorxgobTfA.

30. "Comment of Dr. Essam el-Erian during the Second Session of Parliament" (AR), YouTube, January 24, 2012, https://www.youtube.com/watch?v= _Ggh49ijLVg&list=UU42WdA_gO2tV1MorxgobTfA.

31. "Video: Letter of Field Marshal Tantawi to the Members of the People's Assembly by the Tongue of Al-Katatny" (AR), *Dunya al-Watan*, January 24, 2012, http://www.alwatanvoice.com/arabic/news/2012/01/24/240923.html.

32. H. A. Hellyer, "Egypt: The Politics of Remembering Death," Brookings Institution, October 8, 2013, http://www.brookings.edu/research/opinions/2013 /10/08-egypt-deaths-hellyerh.

33. Yasmine El Rashidi, "Massacre in Cairo," *New York Review of Books*, October 16, 2011, http://www.nybooks.com/daily/2011/10/16/massacre-cairo/; Eric Trager, "Crossed," *Tablet*, October 12, 2011, http://www.tabletmag.com /jewish-news-and-politics/80586/crossed.

34. "Egypt Clashes Continue into Third Day as Army Cracks Down," *Guardian*,

December 18, 2011, http://www.theguardian.com/world/2011/dec/18/egypt
-violence-day-three.

35. Associated Press, "US Senator Kerry Meets with Egypt's Brotherhood," *Real
Clear Politics*, December 10, 2011, http://www.realclearpolitics.com/news/ap
/politics/2011/Dec/10/us_senator_kerry_meets_with_egypt_s_brotherhood
.html.

36. Mahmoud Fayyad, "The Brotherhood: A Referendum on Camp David
Is Inevitable" (AR), *Al-Wafd*, August 23, 2011, http://www.alwafd.org
/أخبار-وتقارير/13-الشارع%20السياسي/86126-الإخوان-لابد-من-استفتاء-شعبي-علي-كامب-ديفيد.

37. Interview with Saad al-Husseini, December 10, 2011.

38. "Chairman of the Freedom and Justice Party Meets the American Deputy
Secretary of State" (AR), Freedom and Justice Party press release, January 11,
2012.

39. "Interview with Lamis el Hadidi, CBC TV," US Department of State, January 11, 2012, http://www.state.gov/s/d/former/burns/remarks/2012/180455
.htm.

40. "Press Statement" (AR), e-mail from Muslim Brotherhood, January 18, 2012.

41. "Document from the Secret Video Recording of Morsi's Meeting with the
Supreme Guide and the Members of the Society after His Presidential Inauguration" (AR), YouTube, July 22, 2012, https://www.youtube.com/watch
?v=P3FWdGTffoI. This video, which became public after the July 2013 coup
and was likely released by Egypt's domestic intelligence services, appears to
be mislabeled online. The issues that Morsi discusses in the video suggest that
it was filmed before his presidency, right after US deputy secretary of state
William Burns's January 2012 visit to Egypt.

42. "Draft Law for Azhar Reform Draws Ire of Egypt's Younger Islamic Scholars,"
Islam Today, January 9, 2012, http://en.islamtoday.net/artshow-234-4316
.htm.

43. Ahmed al-Buhairi, "'SCAF' Agrees on the Law of 'Al-Azhar's Independence';
'Al-Shater': Flagrant Aggression against the People's Assembly" (AR), *Al-
Masry al-Youm*, January 28, 2012, http://today.almasryalyoum.com/article2
.aspx?ArticleID=326327.

44. Wafa Bakry et al., "'SCAF' Decides on Presidential Elections Law without
Presenting It to Parliament" (AR), *Al-Masry al-Youm*, January 31, 2012,
http://today.almasryalyoum.com/article2.aspx?ArticleID=326687.

45. Mohamed Ismail, "The Brotherhood: We Ask 'SCAF' and the Interior Ministry to Fulfill Its Responsiblities in Protecting the Parliament from Groups
That Adopt the Theory of Destroying the State and Military" (AR), *Al-Youm
al-Sabaa*, February 1, 2012, http://www.youm7.com/story/2012/2/1/الإخوان_
نطالب_العسكرى_والداخلية_بتحمل_مسئولياتهما_فى_حماية/592058#.VtHFKzZOLlI.

46. David D. Kirkpatrick, "Egyptian Soccer Riot Kills More Than 70," *New
York Times*, February 1, 2012, http://www.nytimes.com/2012/02/02/world
/middleeast/scores-killed-in-egyptian-soccer-mayhem.html; Mohamed Fadel
Fahmy, "Eyewitnesses: Police Stood Idle in Egypt Football Massacre," CNN,

February 2, 2012, http://www.cnn.com/2012/02/02/world/africa/egypt
-soccer-deaths-color/.

47. Khaled Dawoud, "Mohamed Mahmoud II," *Al-Ahram Weekly On-line*, February 9–15, 2012.

48. "People's Assembly Agrees on Indicting the Interior Minister for Negligence" (AR), *Masress*, February 2, 2012, http://www.masress.com/saiedonline/9137.

49. "Tantawi Vows [to Pursue] Those Involved in the Port Said Incidents" (AR), Al Jazeera, February 2, 2012, http://www.aljazeera.net/news/arabic/2012/2
/2/طنطاوي-يتوعد-المتورطين-بأحداث-بورسعيد.

50. Mohamed Abdel Qadir and Mohamed Gharib, "'National Security' Demands the Cleansing of the Police and 'Interior Ministry'" (AR), *Al-Masry al-Youm*, February 5, 2012, http://today.almasryalyoum.com/article2.aspx?ArticleID=327270.

51. Emad Fouad, "'Defense' Committee Recommends the Sacking of the General Prosecutor—and Requests Authorization to Investigate the 'Intelligence, Military Police, and Central Security'" (AR), *Al-Masry al-Youm*, February 6, 2012, http://today.almasryalyoum.com/article2.aspx?ArticleID=327398.

52. Mohamed Badie, "Statement from the Supreme Guide to the Umma" (AR), *Masress*, February 4, 2012, http://www.masress.com/misrelgdida/83760.

53. "Dr. Mohamed al-Beltagy Speaks on the Political Outlook and the Future Role of the Military Council" (AR), YouTube, February 4, 2012, https://www.youtube.com/watch?v=9Q7FXQaZKcs.

54. "Ghozlan: Bringing Forward Presidential Elections Acceptable," *IkhwanWeb*, February 5, 2012, http://www.ikhwanweb.com/article.php?id=29637.

55. Associated Press, "Egypt's Muslim Brotherhood Wants Government Sacked," *USA Today*, February 9, 2012, http://usatoday30.usatoday.com/news/world/story/2012-02-09/egypt-muslim-brotherhood/53027196/1; Mohamed Haggag, "Khairat al-Shater: I Won't Form the Coming Coalition Government" (AR), *Al-Youm al-Saba'*, February 10, 2012, http://www.youm7.com/story/2012/2/10/#598865/خيرت_الشاطر_لن_أشكل_الحكومة_الائتلافية_القادمة.VtHGVDZOJFJ.

56. "The Brotherhood Begins Consultations on the Formation of the Coalition Government" (AR), *Masress*, February 10, 2012, http://www.masress.com/altaghieer/57600; Mohamed Gharib and Hany al-Waziri, "Meeting at the Guidance Office to Convince 'Shater' to Head 'Coalition Government'" (AR), *Al-Masry al-Youm*, February 11, 2012, http://m.almasryalyoum.com/news/details/151062; Kamel Kamel, "'Bakkar': We Haven't Had Communications with the 'Brotherhood' Regarding Forming a Coalition Government" (AR), *Al-Youm al-Saba'*, February 15, 2012, http://www.youm7.com/story/2012/2/15/#603374/بكار_لم_نتلق_اتصالات_من_الإخوان_حول_تشكيل_الحكومة_الائتلافي.VtHGeDZOJFJ.

57. Walaa Naamah et al., "'The Brotherhood' Retreats from the Idea of a Coalition Government" (AR), *Al-Wafd*, February 14, 2012, http://alwafd.org/أخبار-وتقارير/13-الشارع20%السياسي/162936-الإخوان-يتراجعون-عن-فكرة-الحكومة-الائتلافية.

58. Hany Ezzat, "Intensive Consultations for the Muslim Brotherhood to Resolve the Issue of the Coalition Government" (AR), *Al-Ahram*, February 26, 2012, http://www.ahram.org.eg/Archive/821/2012/2/26/60/133728.aspx.

59. Matt Bradley and Charles Levinson, "In Standoff, Egypt Blocks Americans from Leaving," *Wall Street Journal*, January 27, 2012, http://www.wsj.com /articles/SB10001424052970204573704577184751313941924.

60. "The Muslim Brotherhood Calls for Islamist Aversion to Stop the Baathist Aggression and Demand That the Honorable Reject Forbidden (American) Money" (AR) *Egypt Window*, August 17, 2011, http://www.egyptwindow.net /news_Details.aspx?News_ID=13791.

61. "Opinion of the Brotherhood: Regarding Civil Disobedience and the Formation of the Government and Dialogue for the Sake of Egypt" (AR), *Egypt Window*, February 15, 2012, http://www.egyptwindow.net/ar_print.aspx ?print_ID=17123.

62. "FJP Receives Assistant U.S. Secretary of State for Democracy and Human Rights, Discuss NGO," *IkhwanWeb*, January 27, 2012, http://www.fjponline .com/article.php?id=379.

63. Matt Bradley, "U.S., Egypt Look to Settle Nerves over Aid, Trial," *Wall Street Journal*, February 21, 2012, http://www.wsj.com/articles/SB1000142 4052970204131004577235000880596674.

64. "Senators Issue Statement on Decision to Dismiss Travel Restrictions on American Employees of NGOs in Egypt," press release from Sen. John McCain's office, March 1, 2012, http://www.mccain.senate.gov/public/index.cfm /press-releases?ID=cf34de54-d3b5-651d-c3ee-505c71941ff2.

65. "Press Statement" (AR), Muslim Brotherhood, March 3, 2012, https://drive .google.com/viewerng/viewer?a=v&pid=forums&srcid=MTcwNDczNzYlNj UxMDE0OTczODgBMTA0NDA5NjI1OTQxOTQ3NDA0NTMBbnE0NDN 6WUlQN0VKATAuMQEBdjI.

66. Hamza Hendawi, "Egypt Parliament to Consider Cutting Off US Aid," Associated Press, March 11, 2012, http://news.yahoo.com/egypt-parliament -consider-cutting-off-us-aid-151250364.html.

67. Gamal Essam el-Din, "Letting Off Steam," *Al-Ahram Weekly On-line*, no. 1089, March 15–21, 2012.

68. "Daily Press Briefing," US Department of State, March 12, 2012, http://www .state.gov/r/pa/prs/dpb/2012/03/185626.htm#EGYPT.

69. "Press Briefing by Press Secretary Jay Carney, 4/5/12," White House, April 5, 2012, https://www.whitehouse.gov/the-press-office/2012/04/05/press -briefing-press-secretary-jay-carney-4512; "Daily Press Briefing," US Department of State, April 5, 2012, http://www.state.gov/r/pa/prs/dpb/2012/04 /187486.htm#EGYPT.

70. Tamim Elyan, "Egyptian Liberal Party to Boycott Upper House Vote" Reuters, January 9, 2012, http://www.reuters.com/article/us-egypt-election-boycott -idUSTRE8081WF20120109; "The Participation Rate in the Shura Council Elections is 15%" (AR), *Akhbarak*, February 1, 2012, http://www.akhbarak

.net/articles/6754426-انتخابات-في-المشاركة-نسبة-المصدر-من-المقال; "'High Elections Committee': 12.2% Participation Rate in the Second Round of 'Shura'" (AR), *Al-Masry al-Youm*, February 17, 2012, http://www.almasryalyoum.com/news /details/152416.

71. "Al-Beltagy: We Are Preparing a Constitution with Full National Consensus" (AR), YouTube, March 3, 2012, https://www.youtube.com/watch?v= xgG9rLjx6uQ.

72. Gamal Essam el-Din, "The Struggle for Consensus," *Al-Ahram Weekly On-line*, no. 1088, March 8–14, 2012.

73. Gamal Essam el-Din, "Dubious Addition," *Al-Ahram Weekly On-line*, no. 1091, March 29–April 4, 2012; Gamal Essam el-Din, "Constitution by Numbers," *Al-Ahram Weekly On-line*, no. 1090, March 22–28, 2012; Bel Trew and Sarah Mourad, "Coalition to Create 'Alternative Constituent Assembly," *Ahram On-line*, March 27, 2012, http://english.ahram.org.eg/NewsContent/1/64/37832 /Egypt/Politics-/Coalition-to-create-alternative-constituent-assemb.aspx.

74. Gamal Essam el-Din, "Dubious Addition."

75. "Al-Azhar Withdraws from Constituent Assembly," *Ahram Online*, March 29, 2012, http://english.ahram.org.eg/NewsContentPrint/1/0/38022/Egypt/0 /AlAzhar-withdraws-from-constituent-assembly-.aspx.

76. Heba Fahmy, "Church Withdraws from Constituent Assembly, SCAF Asked to Step In," *Daily News Egypt*, April 2, 2012, http://www.dailynewsegypt .com/2012/04/02/church-withdraws-from-constituent-assembly-scaf-asked -to-step-in/; Gamal Essam el-Din, "A 'Stillborn' Assembly," *Al-Ahram Weekly On-line*, no. 1092, April 5–11, 2012.

77. Gamal Essam el-Din, "Tied Up in Knots," *Al-Ahram Weekly On-line*, no. 1093, April 12–18, 2012, ; "Egypt's Supreme Administrative Court Suspends Embattled Constituent Assembly," *Ahram Online*, April 10, 2012, http://english .ahram.org.eg/NewsContent/1/64/38936/Egypt/Politics-/Egypts-Supreme -Administrative-Court-suspends-embat.aspx; "The Judges: Establishment of the 'Constituent Assembly' Is Void" (AR), *Al-Masry al-Youm*, April 11, 2012, http://today.almasryalyoum.com/article2.aspx?ArticleID=334659.

78. "Constitutional Affairs Presents the Amendment to the Presidential Law" (AR), YouTube, February 27, 2012, https://www.youtube.com/watch?v= DkKtiELm4iY&list=UU42WdA_gO2tV1MorxgobTfA.

79. Mohamed Hamdy, "Egypt's Foreign Cash Reserves Up to US$ 15.4 Bln," *Amwal Al Ghad*, November 5, 2012, http://amwalalghad.com/en/business/banks /10996-egypts-foreign-cash-reserves-up-to-us-154-bln.html.

80. "New Fuel Crisis Cripples Egypt's Traffic," *Ahram Online*, March 21, 2012, http://english.ahram.org.eg/NewsContent/3/12/37386/Business/Economy /New-fuel-crisis-cripples-Egypts-traffic.aspx; "Egypt Falters on Fuel Payments, Suppliers Say," Reuters, June 1, 2012, http://www.reuters.com/article /egypt-fuel-idUSL5E8GPAE120120601; "PA to Propose Binding Solutions to Bread Crisis," *Daily News Egypt*, February 12, 2012, http://www.dailynews egypt.com/2012/02/12/pa-to-propose-binding-solutions-to-bread-crisis/.

81. "Al-Katatny: The Government Creates the Crises for Us—and This Isn't Logical" (AR), YouTube, March 20, 2012, https://www.youtube.com/watch ?v=e0FZ2gkpHEc#action=share.
82. Interview with Helmy al-Gazzar, July 14, 2012.
83. "Statement on the Meeting of the Executive Office of the Freedom and Justice Party on 3/1/2012" (AR), FJP Facebook page, March 2, 2012, https://www .facebook.com/SayedKady/posts/402830239733356.
84. Ihsan al-Sayyid, "'Freedom and Justice': The Formation of a Government Supported by the Majority Must Be Accelerated" (AR), *Al-Youm al-Saba'*, March 9, 2012, http://www.youm7.com/story/2012/3/9/-الحرية-والعدالة—لابد-من #621730/بالأغلب-مدعومة-حكومة-لتشكيل-الإسراع.VtHK0zZOLlI; Gamal Essam el-Din, "Egypt MPs Move Closer to Vote of No Confidence in Ganzouri's Govt," *Ahram Online*, March 11, 2012, http://english.ahram.org.eg/NewsContent/1/64 /36522/Egypt/Politics-/Egypt-MPs-move-closer-to-vote-of-no-confidence -in-.aspx.
85. Reuters, "Egypt Parliament to Challenge el-Ganzouri Govt: Brotherhood's FJP," *Ahram Online*, March 9, 2012, http://english.ahram.org.eg/News Content/1/64/36351/Egypt/Politics-/Egypt-parliament-to-challenge -ElGanzouri-govt-Brot.aspx.
86. Interview with Emad Abdel Ghafour, October 11, 2014.
87. Interview with Ahmed Sobea, June 20, 2012; Zeinab el-Gundy, "MPs Inch Closer to Vote of No-Confidence in el-Ganzouri Government," *Ahram Online* (March 29, 2012): http://english.ahram.org.eg/NewsContent/1/64/38042 /Egypt/Politics-/MPs-inch-closer-to-vote-of-noconfidence-in-ElGanzo.aspx.
88. "'The Brotherhood': SCAF's Keeping of the Ganzoury Government Is an Attempt "to Make Parliament Fail" (AR), *RT*, March 18, 2012, https://arabic .rt.com/news/581047-_محاولة_الجنزوري_حكومة_على_العسكري_المجلس_ابقاء_الاخوان /. البرلمان_افشال_/.
89. "Statement of the Muslim Brotherhood on Obstacles to the Handover of Power to the Representatives of the People from among the Civilians" (AR), Facebook, March 25, 2012, https://www.facebook.com/notes /412560075436258/المسلمين-الاخوان-جمـــاعة-بيان/علي-الرحيم-عبد. /.
90. MENA, "In Sunday Statement, SCAF Hits Back at Brotherhood Criticisms," *Ahram Online*, March 25, 2012, http://english.ahram.org.eg/NewsContent/1 /0/37691/Egypt/0/In-Sunday-statement,-SCAF-hits-back-at-Brotherhood .aspx.
91. Sarah Mourad, "Brotherhood Crushed in 1954: Could History Repeat Itself in 2012?" *Ahram Online*, April 5, 2012, http://english.ahram.org.eg/News Content/1/64/38409/Egypt/Politics-/Brotherhood-crushed-in—Could -history-repeat-itsel.aspx.

7. The Road to Ittahidiya Palace

1. Abdel Moneim Abouel Fotouh, *Witness to the History of the Islamist Movement in Egypt, 1970–1984* (AR) (Cairo: Dar al-Shorouk, 2010), 67–70, 91–94.

2.   Eric Trager, "The American Media Gets an Egyptian Presidential Candidate All Wrong," *New Republic*, May 3, 2012, http://www.newrepublic.com/article /world/103072/egypt-elections-islamist-muslim-brotherhood-president.

3.   Abdel Moneim Abou el-Fotouh, "Democracy Supporters Should Not Fear the Muslim Brotherhood," *Washington Post*, February 9, 2011, http://www.washingtonpost.com/wp-dyn/content/article/2011/02/09 /AR2011020905222.html.

4.   Mohamed Abduh Hassanein, "Brotherhood Leader Abdel Moneim Abouel Fotouh: I Think It's Good to Nominate Myself for the Presidency Independent of the Society" (AR), *Al-Sharq al-Awsat*, April 6, 2011, http://archive.aawsat .com/details.asp?section=4&article=615967&issueno=11817#.VtH0ADZOJFI.

5.   "The Muslim Brotherhood Expels Abouel Fotouh from Its Membership" (AR), *Al-Hiwar*, June 19, 2011, http://www.alhiwar.net/ShowNews.php?Tnd =19123#.VIN4VIdRT4g; Hany al-Waziri and Ghada al-Sharif, "4000 Brother-hood Youths Join the Campaign to Support 'Abouel Fotouh'—and the Society Freezes Their Membership" (AR), *Al-Masry al-Youm*, June 23, 2011, http:// today.almasryalyoum.com/article2.aspx?ArticleID=301407.

6.   Zeinab El Gundy, "Muslim Brotherhood on a Quest for a Presidential Candidate," *Ahram Online*, March 8, 2012, http://english.ahram.org.eg/News ContentPrint/1/0/36222/Egypt/0/Muslim-Brotherhood-on-a-quest-for-a -presidential-c.aspx.

7.   Interview with Mohamed Ali Bishr, October 14, 2014.

8.   Interview with Ammar al-Beltagy, July 9, 2012. One interviewee, Muslim Brotherhood parliamentarian Salah Naaman (June 21, 2012), disputed this. However, given that a full ten days elapsed between the first reports that the Brotherhood was considering nominating a presidential candidate and the General Shura Committee's ultimate decision, it seems likely that this was discussed in the *usar* meetings that occurred during that period and that these discussions would have enabled the Brotherhood to take an informal poll of its membership.

9.   Interview with Gamal Heshmat, March 23, 2014.

10. Mustafa Suleiman and Ahmed Othman, "Political Controversy Causes the Brotherhood to Nominate al-Shater for the Presidency of Egypt" (AR), *Al-Arabiya*, March 31, 2012, http://www.alarabiya.net/articles/2012/03/31 /204463.html.

11. Interview with Mohamed Ali Bishr, October 14, 2014.

12. "The Muslim Brotherhood Announces Nomination of al-Shater for Presi-dent 2" (AR), YouTube, April 1, 2012, https://www.youtube.com/watch?v= 9VEyBRFS8P4.

13. Interview with Mohamed Ali Bishr, October 14, 2014.

14. "Statement from the Muslim Brotherhood and Freedom and Justice Party" (AR), *Ikhwan al-Beheira*, April 8, 2012, http://www.elbehira.net/elbehira/nd _shnws.php?shart=19107.

15. Hany al-Waziri, "Leaders in the 'Brotherhood': We're Trapped by the Nom-

ination of 'al-Shater'" (AR), *Al-Masry al-Youm* (April 4, 2012): http://today
.almasryalyoum.com/article2.aspx?ArticleID=333856.

16. "Press Conference for the Campaign of Khairat al-Shater" (AR), YouTube,
April 9, 2012, https://www.youtube.com/watch?v=qft1Cez2O4Y.

17. Mohsen Samika, "'Moussa': Omar Suleiman Is the Candidate of the Military
Council to Face al-Shater" (AR), *Al-Masry al-Youm*, April 3, 2012, http://m
.almasryalyoum.com/news/details/169872; Kristen Chick, "Omar Suleiman,
Mubarak's No. 2, Enters Egypt's Presidential Race," *Christian Science Monitor*,
April 6, 2012, http://www.csmonitor.com/World/Middle-East/2012/0406
/Omar-Suleiman-Mubarak-s-no.-2-enters-Egypt-s-presidential-race.

18. Bahi Hassan, "Khairat al-Shater: Omar Suleiman Won't Win Except through
Fraud, and We Won't Allow This" (AR), *Al-Masry al-Youm*, April 9, 2012,
http://m.almasryalyoum.com/news/details/171077.

19. "People Book—Al-Shater: Nomination of 'Omar Suleiman' Humiliates and
Burns the Revolution" (AR), YouTube, April 9, 2012, https://www.youtube
.com/watch?v=FK_WCnn8qnw.

20. "The Brotherhood Returns to Tahrir Square against Omar Suleiman" (AR),
Al-Sharq al-Awsat, April 14, 2012, http://archive.aawsat.com/details.asp
?section=4&article=672645&issueno=12191#.VtHlmTZOJFI.

21. Mostafa Suleiman, "Egypt's Parliament Moves to Ban Ex-Spy Chief, Ex-PM
from Running for President," *Al-Arabiya News*, April 10, 2012, https://english
.alarabiya.net/articles/2012/04/10/206712.html.

22. Sherif Tarek, "Eliminated Presidential Contenders to Appeal Disqualification Decision," *Ahram Online*, April 15, 2012, http://english.ahram.org.eg
/NewsContent/36/122/39326/Presidential-elections-/Presidential-elections
-news/Eliminated-presidential-contenders-to-appeal-disqu.aspx; Associated
Press, "Egypt Panel Definitively Bars 3 Presidential Hopefuls," *USA Today*,
April 17, 2012, http://usatoday30.usatoday.com/news/world/story/2012-04
-17/egypt-presidential-race-ban/54364670/1.

23. "Statement from the Muslim Brotherhood and the Freedom and Justice
Party," April 17, 2012; "Statement from the Muslim Brotherhood and the
Freedom and Justice Party," April 18, 2012; "Eng. Khairat al-Shater and the
Conspiracy to Remove Him from the Presidential Elections," YouTube,
April 18, 2012, https://www.youtube.com/watch?v=eMt84ZXrreo.

24. "Al-Shater: SCAF Isn't Serious about Withdrawing from Power" (AR), You-
Tube, April 18, 2012, https://www.youtube.com/watch?v=p3WphHUPOrI.

25. Aya Batrawy, "Tens of Thousands Protest Military's Rule in Egypt," Associated Press, April 20, 2012, http://news.yahoo.com/tens-thousands-protest
-militarys-rule-egypt-123923499.html; Saleh Shalabi, "The Brotherhood to
Participate in Million-Man March April 27" (AR), *Masress*, April 23, 2012,
http://www.masress.com/almesryoon/114938.

26. "Egypt Army Backs Law on Presidential Bid Ban: Report," Reuters, April 23,
2012, http://af.reuters.com/article/egyptNews/idAFL5E8FNCL020120423.

27. Muslim Brotherhood, "Press Statement regarding Friday of Salvaging the Revolution 27 April 2012" (AR), April 25, 2012.

28. Edmund Blair and Tamim Elyan, "Egyptians Protest amid Fears over Mubarak Old Guard," Reuters, April 27, 2012, http://www.reuters.com/article/us -egypt-protest-idUSBRE83Q0PD20120427; "'Tahrir' without Brothers: Salafists Occupy the Square" (AR), Al-Masry al-Youm, April 27, 2012, http:// today.almasryalyoum.com/article2.aspx?ArticleID=336586.

29. Khairat al-Shater said, "We Will All Work for the Renaissance Project, Whoever the Next President Will Be." See "Morsi's Presidential Campaign Kicks Off," FJP Online, April 18, 2012, http://www.fjponline.com/article.php?id=628.

30. Mohamed al-Khatib, "Morsi: The Revolution Must Remain Lit, and We Will Never Allow the Return of a New Dictator" (AR), Masress, April 24, 2012, http://www.masress.com/egynews/168713.

31. "Dr. Mohamed Morsi: The President Must Be Leader of All Egyptians," FJP Online, April 22, 2012, http://www.fjponline.com/article.php?id=637; Hany al-Waziri and Mohamed Aboul Dahab, "Badie Excuses Morsi from the Oath— and the Candidate 'Heard and Obeyed'" (AR), Al-Masry al-Youm, May 3, 2012, http://today.almasryalyoum.com/article2.aspx?ArticleID=337190.

32. Thanassis Cambanis, "Race for Egypt: Inside the 3-Way Fight for the Presidency," Atlantic, May 11, 2012, http://www.theatlantic.com/international /archive/2012/05/race-for-egypt-inside-the-3-way-fight-for-the-presidency /257062/; Marwa Essam el-Din, "Paper and Pencils: Is the Brotherhood Presidential Candidate Mohamed Morsi on Borrowed Time?" Al-Ahram, April 22, 2012, http://shabab.ahram.org.eg/UI/Front/Inner.aspx?NewsContentID= 3127.

33. Hamdy Dabash et al., "Morsi Presents His Program to al-Dawa al-Salafiyya and Requests Its Support for the Presidency" and "Bourhamy: Our Decision after 'the Final List'" (AR), Al-Masry al-Youm, April 25, 2012), http://today .almasryalyoum.com/article2.aspx?ArticleID=336219.

34. Mohamed Fathy, "In Details: Why Did the Salafists Support Abouel Fotouh Despite His Refusing the Idea of 'the Islamist Candidate'?!" (AR), Al-Ahram, April 29, 2012, http://shabab.ahram.org.eg/News/3215.aspx; "Dr. Abdel Moneim Abouel Fotouh on Al-Hafiz Channel 02-05-2012" (AR), YouTube, February 5, 2012, https://www.youtube.com/watch?v=hgWJRuVOyDc&list =UUQpLme0GRI0L8MRC_d2aSrA&index=9&feature=plcp&fb_source= message.

35. "Conference of Nour Party and al-Dawa al-Salafiyya regarding Supporting Abouel Fotouh" (AR), YouTube, April 29, 2012, https://www.youtube.com /watch?v=qH5OFBf62bM.

36. Ramy Nawwar and Kamel Kamel, "Al-Gamaa al-Islamiya Announces Its Support for Abouel Fotouh in the Presidential Elections" (AR), Al-Youm al-Sabaa, May 6, 2012, http://www.youm7.com/story/2012/5/6/_الجماعة_الإسلامية #671338/تعلن_دعمها_لأبو_الفتوح_فى_انتخابات_الرئاسة.VtH4xjZOJFJ.

37.   "Moussa Continues to Lead *Al-Ahram* Opinion Polls for the Presidential Elections of Egypt" (AR), *Al-Ahram*, May 7, 2012, http://arabi.ahram.org.eg /NewsQ/6516.aspx.

38.   "Moussa, Shafiq Lead Egypt Presidential Race: Opinion Polls," *Ahram Online*, May 20, 2012, http://english.ahram.org.eg/NewsContent/36/122/42121 /Presidential-elections-/Presidential-elections-news/Moussa,-Shafiq-lead -Egypt-presidential-race-Opinio.aspx.

39.   "Press Statement by People's Assembly Speaker about Dr. Ganzouri's Recent Remarks," *FJP Online*, April 27, 2012, http://www.fjponline.com/article.php ?id=653&ref=search.php.

40.   "Parliament Suspends Sessions for One Week to Protest Ganzouri Government," *FJP Online*, April 30, 2012, http://www.fjponline.com/article.php?id= 661&ref=search.php.

41.   Gamal Essam el-Din, "Parliament Freeze, Reshuffle Rumours Aggravate Ongoing Political Crisis," *Ahram Online*, April 30, 2012, http://english.ahram.org .eg/NewsContent/1/64/40536/Egypt/Politics-/Parliament-freeze,-reshuffle -rumours-aggravate-ong.aspx; interview with Bassem Kamel, June 24, 2012; interview with Emad Abdel Ghafour, October 11, 2014.

42.   Matt Bradley, "Islamists' Fortunes Fade before Egypt Vote," *Wall Street Journal*, April 26, 2012, http://www.wsj.com/news/articles/SB100014240527 02303990604577367654212903644?KEYWORDS=muslim+brotherhood& mg=reno64-wsj; Ernesto Londoño, "Muslim Brotherhood Presidential Candidate an Underdog in Egypt," *Washington Post*, May 16, 2012, https://www .washingtonpost.com/world/middle_east/muslim-brotherhood-presidential -candidate-an-underdog-in-egypt/2012/05/16/gIQAP3yVUU_story.html.

43.   Interview with Ahmed Okail, July 12, 2012.

44.   Ibid.; interview with Mohamed Fathi, July 18, 2012.

45.   "Relive Vote Count in 1st Round of Egypt Presidential Race: How Morsi and Shafiq Moved On," *Ahram Online*, May 25, 2012, http://english.ahram.org.eg /News/42755.aspx.

46.   "Dr. Mohamd Morsi President of Egypt God Willing on Al-Nahar Channel" (AR), YouTube, May 27, 2012, https://www.youtube.com/watch?v= DGWjAogF4QI&list=UUk8lzqE3cS2kZrC3THDDaXg.

47.   "Discussion of Dr. Mohamed Morsi with Yosri Fouda: Complete" (AR), YouTube, December 18, 2012, https://www.youtube.com/watch?v= KGFpcwP2I1M.

48.   Kristen Chick, "Egypt Presidential Candidate: Ahmed Shafiq, Former Mubarak Man," *Christian Science Monitor*, June 1, 2012, http://www .csmonitor.com/World/Middle-East/2012/0601/Egypt-presidential -candidate-Ahmed-Shafiq-former-Mubarak-man.

49.   Patrick Martin, "Ahmed Shafik: Military Man Tied to Egypt's Old Regime Vows to Restore Order," *Globe and Mail*, May 31, 2012, http://www.theglobe andmail.com/news/world/ahmed-shafik-military-man-tied-to-egypts-old -regime-vows-to-restore-order/article4223730/.

50. "Election Bar on Egypt Ex-PM Reversed," Al Jazeera, April 25, 2012, http://
www.aljazeera.com/news/middleeast/2012/04/2012425213117151622.html.

51. Mohamed Ismail, "'The Brotherhood' Participates in Million-Man March
Tomorrow and Demands Trying Shafik and Wagdy" (AR), *Al-Youm al-Saba'*,
June 4, 2012, http://www.youm7.com/story/2012/6/4/-الإخوان-تشارك-فى-مليونية
غدٍ-وتطالب-بمحاكمة-شفيق-ووجدى/696229#.VtH5SzZOJFJ.

52. Maggie Michael, "Egypt Rulers Demand Constitution Panel in 48 Hours,"
Associated Press, June 5, 2012, http://bigstory.ap.org/article/egypt-rulers
-demand-constitution-panel-48-hours.

53. Mohamed Okasha, "3 Letters: Before You Elect the Brotherhood" (AR),
Ikhwan el-Beheira, June 6, 2012, http://www.elbehira.net/elbehira/nd_shnws
.php?shart=20462.

54. "Egypt Court Rules Entire Parliament Illegally Elected, Orders Body to
Dissolve after Unconstitutional Vote," CBS News, June 14, 2012, http://www
.cbsnews.com/news/egypt-court-rules-entire-parliament-illegally-elected
-orders-body-to-dissolve-after-unconstitutional-vote/.

55. "Statement from the Muslim Brotherhood Regarding the Unconstitutionality
of the Political Isolation Law" (AR), *Egypt Window*, June 14, 2012, http://
egyptwindow.net/news_Details.aspx?Kind=8&News_ID=20223.

56. Sami Beltagy, "'The Brotherhood Calls for Excluding Shafik from the Ballot
Boxes" (AR), *Masress*, June 14, 2012, http://www.masress.com/elwady/18311.

57. "Statement from the Supreme Guide of the Muslim Brotherhood" (AR),
Egypt Window, June 14, 2012, http://www.egyptwindow.net/news_Details
.aspx?News_ID=20224.

58. Interview with Mohamed Fathi, July 18, 2012.

59. Interview with Sameh Essawy, June 24, 2012.

60. Abdel-Rahman Hussein, "Mohamed Morsi Claims Victory for Muslim
Brotherhood in Egypt Election," *Guardian*, June 18, 2012, http://www
.theguardian.com/world/2012/jun/18/mohamed-morsi-muslim-brotherhood
-egypt.

61. Marc Lynch smartly compared Egypt's institutional uncertainty during this
period to "Calvinball," a game of constantly changing rules from the comic
strip *Calvin and Hobbes*. See Marc Lynch, "Calvinball in Cairo," *Foreign Policy*,
June 18, 2012, http://foreignpolicy.com/2012/06/18/calvinball-in-cairo/.

62. Eric Trager, "The Next Egyptian President: Likely Scenarios," Washington Institute for Near East Policy, PolicyWatch no. 1954, June 15, 2012, http://www
.washingtoninstitute.org/policy-analysis/view/the-next-egyptian-president
-likely-scenarios.

63. "English Text of SCAF Amended Egypt Constitutional Declaration," *Ahram
Online*, June 18, 2012, http://english.ahram.org.eg/NewsContent/1/64/45350
/Egypt/Politics-/English-text-of-SCAF-amended-Egypt-Constitutional
-.aspx.

64. "Statement from the Freedom and Justice Party regarding the Complemen-
tary Constitutional Declaration" (AR), June 18, 2012.

65. "Statement from the Executive Office of the Freedom and Justice Party regarding the Continuation of Activities to Complete the Revolution" (AR), June 20, 2012.

66. Interview with Mustafa Ghoneimy, July 4, 2012.

67. Eric Trager, "The Muslim Brotherhood Won an Election, but Is It Really Democratic?" *New Republic*, June 26, 2012, https://newrepublic.com/article /104412/eric-trager-muslim-brotherhood-won-election-it-really-democratic.

68. David Ignatius, "In Egypt, a Sense of Dread," *Washington Post*, June 14, 2012, https://www.washingtonpost.com/opinions/david-ignatius-in-egypt-a-sense -of-dread/2012/06/14/gJQAHVb2cV_story.html.

69. Mahmoud Muslim, "Wahid Abdel Magid: Anan Met al-Shater before the Announcement of Morsi as President and Details of the Meeting of the 'Missing Link' Meeting" (AR), *El-Watan*, September 18, 2012, http://www.elwatan news.com/news/details/50382.

70. "Press Conference for Candidate Mohamed Morsi and the Political Forces" (AR), YouTube, June 22, 2012, https://www.youtube.com/watch?v= Cnc8TDDy5Wk.

71. Trager, "Muslim Brotherhood Won an Election."

8. The Power Struggle Continues

1. "Speech of Dr. Mohamed Morsi, President of Arab Republic of Egypt" (AR), YouTube, June 24, 2012, https://www.youtube.com/watch?v=CRZ6VphJrXE.

2. "Morsi Will Take the Oath before the People's Assembly and Not before the Constitutional Court as the Constitutional Declaration States" (AR), *Al-Quds*, June 24, 2012, http://www.alquds.com/news/article/view/id/365827.

3. Mahmoud al-Suifi, "Abdel Maqsoud: Morsi Has the Right to Cancel the 'Decree'" (AR), *Al-Wafd*, June 27, 2012, http://alwafd.org/-13/أخبار-وتقارير السياسي20%الشارع/231293/عبد-المقصود-مرسى-من-حقه-إلغاء-المكمل; "Al-Husseini to 'Al-Ahram Portal': Morsi Won't Waive His Oath in Front of Parliament" (AR), *Al-Ahram*, June 24, 2012, http://gate.ahram.org.eg/NewsContent/24/109 ملفات/مرسى-رئيساً-لمصر/الحسينى-لـبوابة-الأهرام-مرسى-لن-يتنازل-عن-حلف-اليم/224109/.aspx.

4. Rana Khazbak and Mohamed Elmeshad, "Morsy Strikes a Power-Sharing Deal to Shore Up Presidency," *Egypt Independent*, July 1, 2012, http://www .egyptindependent.com/news/morsy-strikes-power-sharing-deal-shore -presidency. Negotiations between the Brotherhood and the SCAF continued throughout this period. As FJP parliamentarian Khaled el-Deeb told me during an interview on June 30, 2012, three FJP leaders—Saad al-Katatny, Essam el-Erian, and Osama Yassin—handled the discussions with the SCAF over whether Parliament would be reinstated.

5. Maha El-Kady, "Texts: Egypt's Political Transition," *Cairo Review of Global Affairs*, June 30, 2012, http://www.thecairoreview.com/texts/egypts-political -transition/.

6. "Speech of President Mohamed Morsi in Tahrir Square: Complete 2012-6-29" (AR), YouTube, June 29, 2012, https://www.youtube.com/watch?v=N

_DqkzqHTAM; "President Morsi: The People Are the Source of Authority and Legitimacy That Is above All" (AR), State Information Services, June 30, 2012, http://www.sis.gov.eg/Ar/Templates/Articles/tmpArticles.aspx?ArtID =59755#.VJ8EwClYCM.

7.   Joseph P. Fried, "Sheik Sentenced to Life in Prison in Bombing Plot," *New York Times*, January 18, 1996, http://www.nytimes.com/1996/01/18/nyregion /sheik-sentenced-to-life-in-prison-in-bombing-plot.html?pagewanted=all.

8.   "President Mohamed Morsi's Speech in Tahrir Square, Friday June 29, 2012," *IkhwanWeb*, June 30, 2012, http://www.ikhwanweb.com/article.php?id= 30153.

9.   Shadi Hamid, "Brother Number One," *Foreign Policy*, June 7, 2012, http:// foreignpolicy.com/2012/06/07/brother-number-one/.

10. This is based on my many conversations with US officials during this period, all of which were off-the-record discussions.

11. "Interview with Jill Dougherty of CNN," US Department of State, June 30, 2012, http://www.state.gov/secretary/20092013clinton/rm/2012/06/194337 .htm.

12. "Daily Press Briefing," US Department of State, July 2, 2012, http://www .state.gov/r/pa/prs/dpb/2012/07/194449.htm#EGYPT.

13. This is based on my many conversations with US officials during this period, all of which were off-the-record discussions.

14. "Daily Press Briefing," US Department of State, July 5, 2012, http://www.state .gov/r/pa/prs/dpb/2012/07/194614.htm.

15. "Daily Press Briefing," US Department of State, June 25, 2012, http://www .state.gov/r/pa/prs/dpb/2012/06/193995.htm#EGYPT. It is worth noting that the White House readout of President Obama's congratulatory call to Morsi contained none of this language about national unity. See "Readout of the President's Call with President-Elect Morsi of Egypt," White House, June 24, 2012, https://www.whitehouse.gov/the-press-office/2012/06/24 /readout-president-s-call-president-elect-morsi-egypt.

16. Ahmed Shalabi et al., "The President Cancels the Field Marshal's Decision" (AR), *Al-Masry al-Youm*, July 9, 2012, http://today.almasryalyoum.com /article2.aspx?ArticleID=345800.

17. Abdel-Rahman Hussein, "Egypt's Ruling Generals Warn Morsi to Respect the Constitution," *Guardian*, July 9, 2012, http://www.theguardian.com/world /2012/jul/09/egypt-generals-warn-morsi-constitution.

18. Interview with Farid Ismail, July 9, 2012.

19. Interview with Hoda Ghania, July 9 2012; interview with Farid Ismail, July 9, 2012; Eric Trager, "What's Going On in Egyptian Politics? Don't Ask Egyptians," *New Republic*, July 9, 2012, https://newrepublic.com/article/104792 /eric-trager-whats-going-egyptian-politics-dont-ask-egyptians; "Al-Katatny Welcomes the Restoration of the People's Assembly" (AR), *Masress*, July 8, 2012, http://www.masress.com/moheet/388433.

20. "The Muslim Brotherhood Participates in Million-Man March to Support the

President Tomorrow" (AR), *Egypt Window*, July 9, 2012, http://www.egypt window.net/news_Details.aspx?Kind=23&News_ID=20923.

21. Interview with Ammar al-Beltagy, July 9, 2012; Trager, "What's Going On in Egyptian Politics?"

22. Abdel-Rahman Hussein, "Decree to Restore Egypt's Parliament Cancelled," *Guardian*, July 10, 2012, http://www.theguardian.com/world/2012/jul/10 /egypt-parliament-reconvenes-five-minutes.

23. "The President Declares Respect for the 'Constitutional Court's' Ruling—and the Brotherhood Gathers for 'Million-Man March'" (AR), *Al-Masry al-Youm*, July 12, 2012, http://today.almasryalyoum.com/article2.aspx?ArticleID=346154.

24. David D. Kirkpatrick, "Clinton Visits Egypt, Carrying a Muted Pledge of Support," *New York Times*, July 14, 2012, http://www.nytimes.com/2012/07/15 /world/middleeast/clinton-arrives-in-egypt-for-meeting-with-new-president .html?pagewanted=all&_r=0.

25. Elise Labott, "Protests as Clinton Holds Meetings in Egypt," CNN, July 16, 2012, http://www.cnn.com/2012/07/15/world/africa/egypt-clinton/; Hillary Rodham Clinton, *Hard Choices* (New York: Simon & Schuster, 2014), 348.

26. "Remarks by Clinton, Egyptian Foreign Minister Amr in Cairo," US Department of State, July 15, 2012, http://iipdigital.usembassy.gov/st/english /texttrans/2012/07/201207159066.html#axzz3NDV2YSGy.

27. Mohamed Ahmed Tantawi, "Tantawi: We Won't Permit a Group to Control Egypt, and Foreign Fronts Are Pushing Us to Shed Blood" (AR), *Al-Youm al-Sabaa'*, July 15, 2012, http://www.youm7.com/story/2012/7/15/-لن—طنطاوى نسمح-بسيطرة-مجموعة-على-مصر-وجهات-أجنبية-تدفعنا-لإ/732175#.VKF4IClYCM; Hamdi Mubaraz, "*W. Times*: Hilary Asked Tantwi [sic] to Hand Over Power," *Al-Wafd*, July 15, 2012, http://alwafd.org/السلطة-بنقل-طنطاوى-طالبت-هيلارى-تايمز-و-240280/صحف.

28. Interview with Saad al-Husseini, June 28, 2012.

29. Interview with Ahmed Soliman, July 12, 2012.

30. For example, see al-Banna's letter, "12. Responsibility of the Keeper" (AR), http://www.ikhwanwiki.com/index.php?title=البنا_حسن_الشهيد_الإمام_رسائل.

31. Interview with Ashraf Serry, June 27, 2012; interview with Ahmed Soliman, July 12, 2012.

32. Marc Lynch, "Did We Get the Muslim Brotherhood Wrong?" *Foreign Policy*, April 10, 2013, http://foreignpolicy.com/2013/04/10/did-we-get-the-muslim -brotherhood-wrong/; "The Historic, Great Speech of President Morsi That Led to His Success" (AR), YouTube, November 6, 2012, https://www .youtube.com/watch?v=LkxE99y7TS4.

33. Interview with Ashraf Serry, June 27, 2012.

34. "Presidential Program for Dr. Mohamed Morsi" (AR), distributed by the Freedom and Justice Party, 29.

35. Ibid., 39.

36. Eric Trager, "Think Again: The Muslim Brotherhood," *Foreign Policy*, January 28, 2013, http://foreignpolicy.com/2013/01/28/think-again-the-muslim -brotherhood/; "Presidential Program for Dr. Mohamed Morsi," 14.

37. "Presidential Program for Dr. Mohamed Morsi," 11, 29.

38. Ibid., 8.

39. Interview with Mahmoud Hussein, July 1, 2012.

40. Interview with Abdel Rahman al-Barr, July 7, 2012.

41. Interview with Saad al-Husseini, June 28, 2012; "Governors Movement: Guidance Office Submits Candidates for Morsi and Source: Brotherhood Representatives in 8 Governorates" (AR), *Al-Masry al-Youm*, August 21, 2012, http://m.almasryalyoum.com/news/details/158401.

42. Interview with senior Renaissance Project official, July 2012.

43. "Profile: Egypt Prime Minister Hisham Qandil," BBC News, August 3, 2012, http://www.bbc.com/news/world-middle-east-18977436.

44. "Egypt's Newly Appointed Cabinet Ministers," American Chamber of Commerce in Egypt, August 2012, http://www.usegyptcouncil.org/wp-content/uploads/2012/08/AmCham-Egypt-Newly-Appointed-Cabinet-Ministers.pdf.

45. Abdel-Rahman Hussein, "Egypt Swears In First Post-Revolution Cabinet with Plenty of Old Guard," *Guardian*, August 2, 2012, http://www.theguardian.com/world/2012/aug/02/egypt-middleeast.

46. Ehud Yaari, "Sinai: A New Front," Washington Institute for Near East Policy, Policy Note no. 9, January 2012, http://www.washingtoninstitute.org/uploads/Documents/pubs/PoilicyNote09.pdf.

47. Maggie Michael and Ian Deitch, "Egypt to Withdraw Ambassador to Israel over Ambush," *Independent*, August 20, 2011, http://www.independent.co.uk/news/world/middle-east/egypt-to-withdraw-ambassador-to-israel-over-ambush-2341011.html.

48. Barak Ravid et al., "Israeli Diplomatic Staff and Families Evacuated after Egyptians Storm Embassy in Cairo," *Ha'aretz*, September 10, 2011, http://www.haaretz.com/israel-news/israeli-diplomatic-staff-and-families-evacuated-after-egyptians-storm-embassy-in-cairo-1.383588.

49. Samir al-Sayyid, "The Brotherhood Demands Establishing National Sovereignty over Sinai and Banishing the 'Zionist' Ambassador" (AR), *Al-Ahram*, August 20, 2011, http://gate.ahram.org.eg/NewsContentPrint/13/70/106937.aspx.

50. Muslim Brotherhood, "Statement from the Muslim Brotherhood regarding the Events of Friday 9-9-2011" (AR), e-mailed statement, September 9, 2011.

51. "Presidential Program for Dr. Mohamed Morsi," 43, 58–60.

52. Clinton, *Hard Choices*, 473.

53. Kareem Fahim and Mayy El Sheikh, "Gunmen Kill 15 and Steal Vehicle in Attack on Egypt Base," *New York Times*, August 5, 2012, http://www.nytimes.com/2012/08/06/world/middleeast/gunmen-storm-egyptian-base-killing-15-soldiers.html; Yaakov Katz, "The Sinai Attack: Blow by Blow," *Jerusalem Post*, August 6, 2012, http://www.jpost.com/Defense/The-Sinai-attack-Blow-by-blow.

54. Muslim Brotherhood, "Statement from the Muslim Brotherhood regarding the Sinful Aggression That Happened Yesterday on Our Soldiers in Rafah" (AR), e-mailed statement, August 6, 2012.

55.   Fahim and El Sheikh, "Gunmen Kill 15 and Steal Vehicle"; "Morsi and Tantawi Arrive in El-Arish to Inspect the Security Situation after 'Sinai Attacks,'" *Al-Masry al-Youm*, August 6, 2012, http://m.almasryalyoum.com/news/details /155278.

56.   "Intelligence Chief to 'Turkish Agency': We Had Information about the Sinai Attacks" (AR), *Al-Youm al-Saba'*, August 7, 2012, http://www.youm7.com /story/2012/8/7/#751766/رئيس-المخابرات-لوكالة-تركية—كانت-لدينا-معلومات-بهجوم-سيناء .VtITAzZOJFJ.

57.   "Egypt President First Intelligence Chief," Al Jazeera, August 9, 2012, http:// www.aljazeera.com/news/middleeast/2012/08/201288151651222389.html.

58.   Yusuf Ayoob and Mohamed Tantawi, "We Publish the First Picture of the Acting Egyptian Intelligence Chief" (AR), *Al-Youm al-Saba'*, August 8, 2012, http://www.youm7.com/story/2012/8/8/-ننشر-أول-صورة-للقائم-بأعمال-رئيس-المخابرات #752684/المصرية.VtITHzZOJFJ.

59.   "English Text of President Morsi's New Egypt Constitutional Declaration," *Ahram Online*, August 12, 2012, http://english.ahram.org.eg/News/50248 .aspx.

60.   "Newspaper: Sisi Moves 70 Generals to Retirement and a Member of the Military: The Changes Are 'Routine'" (AR), *Al-Masry al-Youm*, September 3, 2012, http://www.almasryalyoum.com/news/details/161115.

61.   Zeinab El Gundy, "Meet General el-Sisi, Egypt's Defence Minister," *Al-Ahram Online*, August 13, 2012, http://english.ahram.org.eg/NewsContent/1/0 /50305/Egypt/0/Meet-General-ElSisi,-Egypts-defence-minister.aspx. The rumor about al-Sisi's wife wearing a full-face covering was later discredited. She does, however, wear a *hijab*.

62.   Hany al-Waziri and Mohamed Tarek, "Son of 'Abbas Sisi,' Previous Member of Brotherhood Guidance Office, to *El-Watan*: The Defense Minister Is from [Our] Family—and Doesn't Belong to the Organization" (AR), *El-Watan*, August 20, 2012, http://www.elwatannews.com/news/details/39609.

9. Power, Not Policy

1.   Interview with Hoda Abdel Moneim, October 14, 2014.

2.   Ahmed Aboulenein, "Mahmoud Mekki: Activist Judge Turned Vice President," *Daily News Egypt*, August 13, 2012, http://www.dailynewsegypt.com /2012/08/13/vice-presidents-long-history-of-activism/.

3.   Interview with Mahmoud Hussein, July 1, 2012.

4.   Ahmed Aboulenein, "Morsy Appoints Islamist-Dominated Presidential Team," *Daily News Egypt*, August 27, 2012, http://www.dailynewsegypt.com /2012/08/27/morsy-appoints-islamist-dominated-presidential-team/; Hany al-Waziri, "'Mohi Hamed': The Third Man" (AR), *El-Watan*, December 12, 2012, http://www.elwatannews.com/news/details/94626.

5.   Nancy Messieh, "Who Are Egypt's New Governors?" Atlantic Council, September 5, 2012, http://www.atlanticcouncil.org/blogs/egyptsource/who-are -egypts-new-governors.

6.   Mahmoud Shaaban Bayoumi, "The 'Guidance' Office Puts a Work Plan for the
      'Brotherhood' Governors to Ensure Their Success" (AR), *Al-Masry al-Youm*,
      September 6, 2012, http://m.almasryalyoum.com/news/details/161910.

7.   Interview with Azza al-Garf, June 26, 2012; Ahmed Ragab, "The Brotherhood
      Shura Decides to Begin to Execute the 100-Day Program of the Presidency"
      (AR), *El-Balad*, July 7. 2012, http://www.el-balad.com/211385.

8.   Shaimaa Khalil, "Egypt: President Morsi's 100 Days in Power," BBC, Octo-
      ber 9, 2012, http://www.bbc.com/news/world-middle-east-19882135; Tom
      Perry, "Analysis: Egypt's Mursi Dogged by Own Promises in First 100 Days,"
      Reuters, October 5, 2012, http://www.reuters.com/article/us-egypt-mursi
      -idUSBRE8940FB20121005; Salma El Wardany, "Egypt Halts Gas Exports
      Amid Shortage, Plans Fuel-Subsidy Cut," Bloomberg, October 16, 2012,
      http://www.bloomberg.com/news/articles/2012-10-16/egypt-halts-gas
      -exports-amid-shortage-plans-fuel-subsidy-cut.

9.   Mohamed Hamdy and Sayed Badr, "Egypt's Foreign Cash Reserves Drop
      US$448 Mln at End of November," *Amwal al-Ghad*, December 6, 2012,
      http://www.amwalalghad.com/en/?tmpl=component&option=com_content
      &id=12014; David D. Kirkpatrick, "In Simply Meeting, Egyptian and Saudi
      Leaders Open New Era," *New York Times*, July 12, 2012, http://www.nytimes
      .com/2012/07/13/world/middleeast/in-simply-meeting-egyptian-and-saudi
      -leaders-open-new-era.html?_r=0.

10.   Joel Gulhane and Mariam Iskander, "Egyptian Foreign Affairs: One Year in
      Power," *Daily News Egypt*, June 29, 2013, http://www.dailynewsegypt.com
      /2013/06/29/egyptian-foreign-affairs-one-year-in-power/.

11.   "Following Morsi's Visit, Chinese Investors See Promising Opportunities in
      'Gate to Africa' Egypt," *IkhwanWeb*, August 30, 2012, http://www.ikhwanweb
      .com/article.php?id=30268.

12.   Ahmad Shokr, "Back to the Table, Egypt and the IMF," *Jadaliyya*, August 23,
      2012, http://www.jadaliyya.com/pages/index/7011/back-to-the-table-egypt
      -and-the-imf-.

13.   "Qatar Pledges $2bn for Egypt's Central Bank," Al Jazeera, August 12, 2012,
      http://www.aljazeera.com/news/middleeast/2012/08/201281261018425841
      .html; "Egypt Signs $1 Billion Turkish Loan Deal," Reuters, September 30,
      2012, http://www.reuters.com/article/us-egypt-turkey-loan-idUSBRE
      88T0G920120930.

14.   Islam Zayed, "Morsi Raises Government Salaries," *Daily News Egypt*,
      July 3, 2012, http://www.dailynewsegypt.com/2012/07/03/morsi-raises
      -government-salaries/.

15.   "President Mohamed Morsi's Speech at Cairo Stadium" (AR), YouTube, Oc-
      tober 6, 2012, https://www.youtube.com/watch?v=Vk_Ms5gsOFA; Hamza
      Hendawi and Sarah El Deeb, "Egypt's New President Gives Himself High
      Grades," Associated Press, October 7, 2012, http://bigstory.ap.org/article
      /egypts-new-president-gives-himself-high-grades.

16.   Ahmed Eleiba, "Those Missing and the Uninvited," *Masress*, October 11, 2012,

http://www.masress.com/en/ahramweekly/30884; "Sadat Family Angry over Tarek Al-Zomor's Attendance of War Ceremony," *Egypt Independent*, August 10, 2012, http://www.egyptindependent.com/news/sadat-family -angry-over-tarek-al-zomor-s-attendance-war-ceremony.

17. Rahab Abdel Lah, "24 Parties and Movement Publish a Map of Marches for the Demonstrations on October 12" (AR), *Al-Youm al-Saba'*, October 9, 2012, http://www.youm7.com/story/2012/10/9/ننشر_خريطة_مسيرات_24_حزبا_وحركة_في #810671/مظاهرات_جمعة_12_أكتوبر.VtJGxDZOJFI.

18. "Egypt's Court Acquits 24 in 'Camel Battle' Trial," Reuters, October 10, 2012, http://www.reuters.com/article/us-egypt-court-camel-idUSBRE8991 GK20121010.

19. "Statement from the Freedom and Justice Party regarding the Rulings of the Camel Battle" (AR), Facebook, October 11, 2012, https://www.facebook.com /lkhwanonline/posts/511574815537589.

20. "Rival Protesters Clash in Egypt's Capital," Al Jazeera, October 13, 2012, http://www.aljazeera.com/news/middleeast/2012/10/20121012133639 244689.html.

21. Zeinab El Gundy, "Egypt Shura Council Announces New Heads for 3 State Papers," *Ahram Online*, August 9, 2012, http://english.ahram.org .eg/NewsContent/1/64/49968/Egypt/Politics-/Egypt-Shura-Council -announces-new-heads-for—state.aspx; Eric Trager, "Egypt's New President Moves against Democracy," *Wall Street Journal*, August 15, 2012, http:// www.wsj.com/articles/SB10000872396390444772404577587611785521668 ?autologin=y.

22. The one exception to Morsi's refusal to communicate with Israeli officials came in October 2012, when Egypt's new ambassador to Israel presented his credentials to Israeli president Shimon Peres in Jerusalem in the form of a letter from Morsi to Peres. In the letter, Morsi referred to Peres as a "dear and great friend" and affirmed his commitment to the 1979 peace treaty. Morsi's presidential office later said that this wording reflected the Ministry of Foreign Affairs' protocol, and it was the only instance of official communication between the Egyptian presidency and the Israeli government during Morsi's presidency.

23. "U.S. Chamber to Lead Largest-Ever Business Delegation to Egypt," US Chamber of Commerce, September 3, 2012, https://www.uschamber.com /press-release/us-chamber-lead-largest-ever-business-delegation-egypt.

24. Islam Serour, "US Business Delegation Promises Support for Egyptian Econ- omy," *Daily News Egypt*, September 9, 2012, http://www.dailynewsegypt .com/2012/09/09/us-business-delegation-promisese-support-for-egyptian -economy/.

25. Ashraf Khalil, "US Ambassador's Death: First Blood to the Bigots on Both Sides," *National*, September 13, 2012, http://www.thenational.ae/news/world /us-ambassadors-death-first-blood-to-the-bigots-on-both-sides.

26. David Schenker and Eric Trager, "How to Send Egypt a Message," *New York*

Daily News, September 12, 2012, http://www.nydailynews.com/opinion/send
-egypt-message-article-1.1157828.

27. David D. Kirkpatrick et al., "Egypt, Hearing from Obama, Moves to Heal
the Rift from Protests," *New York Times*, September 13, 2012, http://www
.nytimes.com/2012/09/14/world/middleeast/egypt-hearing-from-obama
-moves-to-heal-rift-from-protests.html?pagewanted=all&_r=0.

28. "Morsi Calls for 'Legal' Action in US against Filmmakers," trans. Joelle el-
Khoury, *Al-Monitor*, September 13, 2012, http://www.al-monitor.com/pulse
/politics/2012/09/egypt-morsi-tells-ambassador-to-take-legal-action-against
-us-filmmaker.html##ixzz3OTekadzz .

29. Muslim Brotherhood, "Press Statement regarding Demonstrations, Friday
September 14, 2012," received via e-mail, September 12, 2012.

30. Aliyah Shahid, "Obama: Egypt Is Neither 'Ally' nor 'Enemy,'" MSNBC, September 12, 2012, http://www.msnbc.com/melissa-harris-perry/obama-egypt
-neither-ally-nor-enem.

31. Kirkpatrick et al., "Egypt, Hearing from Obama."

32. Ibid.

33. Khairat el-Shater, "'Our Condolences,' the Muslim Brotherhood Says," *New
York Times*, September 13, 2012, http://www.nytimes.com/2012/09/14
/opinion/our-condolences-the-muslim-brotherhood-says.html?smid=tw
-share.

34. Dana Hughes, "Mideast Unrest Tops Clinton Agenda at Start of UN Meeting,"
ABC News, September 25, 2012, http://abcnews.go.com/blogs/politics/2012
/09/mideast-unrest-tops-clinton-agenda-at-start-of-un-meeting/.

35. "Word of Ismail Haniyeh after Morsi's Victory" (AR), YouTube, June 27, 2012,
https://www.youtube.com/watch?v=V3bn-zV_yFo.

36. Interview with Saad al-Husseini, June 28, 2012.

37. Reuters, "Hamas Chief Meets Egypt's Morsi in Cairo, Hails 'New Era,'"
Ha'aretz, July 19, 2012, http://www.haaretz.com/middle-east-news/hamas
-chief-meets-egypt-s-morsi-in-cairo-hails-new-era-1.452281; "Egypt's President Meets Hamas Leader," Associated Press, July 27, 2012, http://bigstory.ap
.org/article/egypts-president-meets-hamas-leader.

38. Dan Murphy, "How Many Rockets Were Fired from Gaza at Israel This Year?"
Christian Science Monitor, November 15, 2012, http://www.csmonitor.com
/World/Security-Watch/Backchannels/2012/1115/How-many-rockets-were
-fired-from-Gaza-at-Israel-this-year.

39. Ibid.; Aron Heller and Ibrahim Barzak, "Israel, Gaza Militants Trade Fire in
Escalation," Associated Press, November 11, 2012, http://news.yahoo.com
/israel-gaza-militants-trade-fire-escalation-121805200.html.

40. Salma Shukrallah, "Hundreds March in Cairo to Demand an End to Diplomatic Ties with Israel," *Ahram Online*, November 14, 2012, http://english
.ahram.org.eg/NewsContent/1/64/58146/Egypt/Politics-/Hundreds-march
-in-Cairo-to-demand-an-end-to-diplom.aspx.

41. Conor Molloy, "Brotherhood Calls for Protests against Israeli Action," *Daily*

News Egypt, November 14, 2012, http://www.dailynewsegypt.com/2012/11
/14/brotherhood-calls-for-protests-against-israeli-action/; Eric Trager, "The
Gaza Invasion: Will It Destroy Israel's Relationship with Egypt?" *Atlantic*, November 15, 2012, http://www.theatlantic.com/international/archive/2012/11
/the-gaza-invasion-will-it-destroy-israels-relationship-with-egypt/265265/.

42. Trager, "Gaza Invasion."
43. Barak Ravid and Reuters, "Obama Calls Netanyahu, Morsi in Wake of Gaza Offensive," *Ha'aretz*, November 14, 2012, http://www.haaretz.com/israel-news
/obama-calls-netanyahu-morsi-in-wake-of-gaza-offensive.premium-1.477882.
44. Ashraf Khalil, "Morsi's Gaza Challenge: How New Can the New Egypt Afford
to Be?" *Time*, November 16, 2012, http://world.time.com/2012/11/16/morsys
-gaza-challenge-how-new-can-the-new-egypt-afford-to-be/; "#Egypt President #Morsi Statements About #Gaza Nov 16 2012," YouTube, November 16,
2012, https://www.youtube.com/watch?v=hhKg0bcde5w.
45. "Egypt PM's Visit to Gaza Fails to Cease Rockets," *Jerusalem Post*, November 16, 2011, http://www.jpost.com/Defense/Egypt-PMs-visit-to-Gaza-fails
-to-cease-rockets.
46. Interview with Mustafa Ghoneimy, July 4, 2012.
47. Peter Baker and David D. Kirkpatrick, "Egyptian President and Obama Forge
Link in Gaza Deal," *New York Times*, November 21, 2012, http://www.nytimes
.com/2012/11/22/world/middleeast/egypt-leader-and-obama-forge-link-in
-gaza-deal.html?pagewanted=all.
48. Interview with Egyptian intelligence official, November 21, 2012; interview
with Egyptian military official, November 21, 2012.
49. Baker and Kirkpatrick, "Egyptian President and Obama Forge Link."

10. The Power Grab

1. "Video: We Publish the Articles of the New Constitutional Declaration
of President Morsi" (AR), *Al-Youm al-Saba'*, November 22, 2012, http://
www.youm7.com/story/2012/11/22/-الجديد-الدستورى-الإعلان-مواد-ننشر-بالفيديو
#854577/للرئيس-مرسى.VLVw7cZRT4g; "English Text of Morsi's Constitutional
Declaration," *Ahram Online*, November 22, 2012, http://english.ahram.org.eg
/News/58947.aspx.
2. "Egypt's Constitutional Assembly Case Referred to Supreme Court," *Al-
Arabiya*, October 23, 2012, http://english.alarabiya.net/articles/2012/10/23
/245476.html; Abdel-Rahman Hussein, "Egyptian Court Decides Whether to
Dissolve Islamist-Dominated Assembly," *Guardian*, October 22, 2012, http://
www.theguardian.com/world/2012/oct/23/egypt-mohamed-morsi; "Egypt
Supreme Court to Decide on Constitutional Panel," BBC, October 23, 2012,
http://www.bbc.com/news/world-middle-east-20043721.
3. Kareem Fahim and David D. Kirkpatrick, "Clashes Break Out after Morsi
Seizes New Power in Egypt," *New York Times*, November 23, 2012, http://
www.nytimes.com/2012/11/24/world/middleeast/amid-protest-egypts
-leader-defends-his-new-powers.html?hp&pagewanted=all; Aya Batrawy

and Maggie Michael, "Clashes Erupt across Egypt over Morsi's New Powers," *Washington Times*, November 23, 2012, http://www.washingtontimes.com /news/2012/nov/23/presidents-backers-rivals-clash-egypt/?page=all.

4. Michael Birnbaum and Joby Warrick, "President's Decree of New Powers Divides Egypt," *Washington Post*, November 23, 2012, https://www.washington post.com/world/middle_east/morsis-decree-sparks-rival-rallies-in-egypt /2012/11/23/288a1436-3571-11e2-bfd5-e202b6d7b501_story.html; Soheila Hamed, "'El-Watan' Publishes the Full Text of Morsi's Speech from in Front of Ittahadiya" (AR), *El-Watan*, November 23, 2012, http://www.elwatannews .com/news/details/82539.

5. David D. Kirkpatrick, "Egyptian Judges Challenge Morsi over New Powers," *New York Times*, November 24, 2012, http://www.nytimes.com/2012/11/25 /world/middleeast/morsi-urged-to-retract-edict-to-bypass-judges-in-egypt .html?pagewanted=all.

6. David D. Kirkpatrick, "Pressure Grows on Egyptian Leader after Judicial Decree," *New York Times*, November 25, 2012, http://www.nytimes.com/2012/11 /26/world/middleeast/morsis-judicial-decree-draws-high-level-dissent.html ?pagewanted=all.

7. Abdel-Rahman Hussein, "Mohamed Morsi Indicates Judicial Decree Will Be Limited," *Guardian*, November 26, 2012, http://www.theguardian.com/world /2012/nov/26/mohamed-morsi-decree-sovereign-matters; Abdel-Rahman Hussein, "Egypt: Protesters Descend on Tahrir Square," *Guardian*, November 27, 2012, http://www.theguardian.com/world/2012/nov/27/egypt -protesters-descend-tahrir-square.

8. Eric Trager, "Shame on Anyone Who Ever Thought Mohammad Morsi Was a Moderate," *New Republic*, November 26, 2012, https://newrepublic.com /article/110447/shame-anyone-who-ever-thought-mohammad-morsi-was -moderate.

9. Mohamed Haggag, "'The Brotherhood: Feloul Are Frustrating the Achievements of the People" (AR), *Al-Youm al-Saba'*, November 28, 2012, http:// www.youm7.com/story/2012/11/28/الإخوان-الفلول-يجهضون-إنجازات-الشعب-ويعملون- #861088/على-هدم-المؤسسا.VtJUyzZOJFJ.

10. Ahmed Al-Bahnasawi, "Morsi to 'Egyptian Television': I Won't Retreat from the Constitutional Declaration—and There Is a Minority Trying to Drag the Country Backward" (AR), *El-Watan*, November 29, 2012, http://www .elwatannews.com/news/details/86954.

11. Gamal Essam el-Din, "The Constitution-Drafting Assembly Faces Fatal Threats," *Ahram Online*, November 19, 2012, http://english.ahram.org.eg /NewsContent/1/64/58539/Egypt/Politics-/The-constitutiondrafting -assembly-faces-fatal-thre.aspx.

12. Robert Satloff and Eric Trager, "Egypt's Theocratic Future: The Constitutional Crisis and U.S. Policy," Washington Institute for Near East Policy, December 3, 2012, http://www.washingtoninstitute.org/policy-analysis/view /egypts-theocratic-future-the-constitutional-crisis-and-u.s.-policy; Samuel

Tadros, "Egypt's Draft Constitution: Religious Freedom Undermined," *National Review*, December 5, 2012, http://www.hudson.org/research/9480 -egypt-s-draft-constitution-religious-freedom-undermined.

13. Tadros, "Egypt's Draft Constitution"; "Egypt's Draft Constitution Translated," trans. Nariman Youssef, *Egypt Independent*, December 2, 2012, http:// www.egyptindependent.com/news/egypt-s-draft-constitution-translated; "Constitution of the Arab Republic of Egypt 1971," State Information Service, http://www.sis.gov.eg/En/Templates/Articles/tmpArticles.aspx?CatID=208 #.VLwq2MZRT4g.

14. Satloff and Trager, "Egypt's Theocratic Future."

15. David D. Kirkpatrick, "Amid Egypt's Duel on Democracy, Morsi Calls for Vote," *New York Times*, December 1, 2012, http://www.nytimes.com/2012/12 /02/world/middleeast/in-egypt-a-clash-over-whos-a-threat-to-democracy .html?pagewanted=all&_r=0.

16. David D. Kirkpatrick, "Egyptian Court Postpones Ruling on Constitutional Assembly," *New York Times*, December 2, 2012, http://www.nytimes.com /2012/12/03/world/middleeast/egypt-morsi-constitution-vote.html?_r=0.

17. Stephanie McCrummen and Abigail Hauslohner, "Egyptians Take Anti- Morsi Protests to Presidential Palace," *Washington Post*, December 4, 2012, https://www.washingtonpost.com/world/middle_east/egyptians-take-anti -morsi-protests-to-presidential-palace/2012/12/04/b16a2cfa-3e40-11e2-bca3 -aadc9b7e29c5_story.html; Aya Batrawy and Hamza Hendawi, "Protest at Egypt President's Palace Turns Violent," *Washington Times*, December 4, 2012, http://www.washingtontimes.com/news/2012/dec/4/egypt-increases -security-ahead-opposition-march/?page=all.

18. Interview with Mustafa Ghoneimy, December 5 2012; interview with Mohi Hamed, December 5, 2012; interview with Mahmoud Hussein, December 5, 2012. The interviews with Ghoneimy and Hamed were conducted with the assistance of Washington Institute research assistants Katie Kiraly and Heba Dafashy.

19. David D. Kirkpatrick, "Morsi Turns to His Islamist Backers as Egypt's Crisis Grows," *New York Times*, December 7, 2012, http://mobile.nytimes.com /2012/12/08/world/middleeast/egypt-islamists-dialogue-secular-opponents -clashes.html.

20. "The Brotherhood Demonstrates in Front of Ittahidiya This Afternoon" (AR), *Masress*, December 5, 2012, http://www.masress.com/almesryoon/172552.

21. Haroon Siddique, "Mohamed Morsi's Supporters and Opponents Clash in Cairo," *Guardian*, December 5, 2012, http://www.theguardian.com/world /2012/dec/05/morsi-supporters-opponents-clash-cairo.

22. "Time of the Brotherhood's Attacks on the Protesters at Ittahidiya Palace 12/5/2012" (AR), YouTube, December 5, 2012, https://www.youtube.com /watch?v=vQ3k1YEOu_4; "Egypt during the Middle Ages (Video of the Reason for the Ittahidiya Palace Incidents)" (AR), YouTube, December 5, 2012, https://www.youtube.com/watch?v=dfGi89NFs4E.

23. Evan Hill, "'This Is Just the Beginning': A Bloody Night with Egypt's Protest-
     ers," *Atlantic*, December 7, 2012, http://www.theatlantic.com/international
     /archive/2012/12/this-is-just-the-beginning-a-bloody-night-with-egypts
     -protesters/266018/.

24. Robert Mackey, "Evidence of Torture by Egyptian Islamists," *New York Times*,
     December 11, 2012, http://thelede.blogs.nytimes.com/2012/12/11/evidence
     -of-torture-by-egyptian-islamists/; Nancy A. Youssef, "In Egypt's Battle
     over Morsi's Powers, No Criminal Charges and No Winners," *McClatchy DC*,
     December 7, 2012, http://www.mcclatchydc.com/news/nation-world/world
     /article24741412.html; Cambanis (2015) 212.

25. Mohamed el-Garhi, "*Al-Masry al-Youm* Goes inside the Brotherhood's
     Torture Chambers," *Egypt Independent*, December 7, 2012, http://www.egypt
     independent.com/news/al-masry-al-youm-goes-inside-brotherhood-s-torture
     -chambers.

26. Salma Shukrallah et al., "A Bloody Night at Egypt's Presidential Palace,"
     Ahram Online, December 6, 2012, http://english.ahram.org.eg/News/59852
     .aspx; David D. Kirkpatrick, "Morsi Defends Wide Authority as Turmoil Rises
     in Egypt," *New York Times*, December 6, 2012, http://www.nytimes.com
     /2012/12/07/world/middleeast/egypt-islamists-secular-opponents-clashes
     .html?pagewanted=all.

27. "Full Speech of President Mohamed Morsi after the Incidents of Ittahidiya"
     (AR), YouTube, December 6, 2012, https://www.youtube.com/watch?v=
     zPXfwjEHgMs.

28. Abdel-Rahman Hussein and Ian Black, "Egypt Opposition Rejects Morsi's
     Call for Talks amid Thousands-Strong Protests," *Guardian*, December 7,
     2012, http://www.theguardian.com/world/2012/dec/07/egypt-opposition
     -morsi-talks; "Tensions High after Thousands March in Cairo," Al Jazeera,
     December 8, 2012, http://www.aljazeera.com/news/middleeast/2012/12
     /201212714262703105.html ; Ahmed Ghoneim and Amr Hamed, "Revolu-
     tionaries: No Dialogue with a 'Killer' and the Fall of Martyrs Means 'End of
     the Regime's Legitimacy'" (AR), *El-Watan*, December 8, 2012, http://www
     .elwatannews.com/news/details/92078.

29. Ayat Al-Sukri et al., "Between Participating and Boycotting: Division among
     the Political Forces regarding the President's Dialogue" (AR), *Rassd*, Decem-
     ber 9, 2012, http://rassd.com/7-50826.htm.

30. "Text of the New Constitutional Declaration the President Morsi Issued"
     (AR), *Shorouk*, December 9, 2012, http://www.shorouknews.com/news
     /view.aspx?cdate=09122012&id=ac870987-0412-4dd8-ace9-a21b83213115.

31. Associated Press, "Egypt: Military Warns of 'Disastrous Consequences,'" CBS
     News, December 8, 2012, http://www.cbsnews.com/news/egypt-military
     -warns-of-disastrous-consequences/.

32. David D. Kirkpatrick and Kareem Fahim, "In Cairo, Effort to Broaden Sup-
     port for Charter," *New York Times*, December 11, 2012, http://www.nytimes
     .com/2012/12/12/world/middleeast/egypt-morsi-referendum-International

-Monetary-Fund-.html; Abdel Rahman Sayyid, "'Video: Al-Assar: Sisi's Dialogue Isn't Political, and Morsi Will Attend" (AR), *Al-Dostor*, December 11, 2012, http://www.dostor.org/111407.

33. Moahmed Ahmed Tantawi, "Egypt Passes the Most Dangerous 18 Hours; Al-Sisi Calls for Dialogue in the Evening, and Cancels It the Next Morning; Sources: Ittahidiya Palace Pressured to Postpone It after the Salvation Front Agreed; and the Armed Forces Issue a Vague Statement Increasing the Confusion" (AR), *Al-Youm al-Saba'*, December 12, 2012, http://www.youm7 .com/story/2012/12/12/-أخطر-18-ساعة-مرت-بها-مصر-السيسي-يدعو-للحوار-مساء-ويلغيه #874355/-ظهر.VtJXKjZOJFJ.

34. Fatiha al-Dakhakhani, "Military Source: Some Doubt the Intention of the Meeting and Expectations of Failure behind the Postponement" (AR), *Al-Masry al-Youm*, December 13, 2012, http://today.almasryalyoum.com /article2.aspx?ArticleID=363675.

35. Arshad Mohammed, "U.S. Shifts to Closer Contact with Egypt Islamists," Reuters, June 30, 2011, http://www.reuters.com/article/us-usa-egypt -brotherhood-idUSTRE75T0GD20110630; "Deputy Secretary Burns' Interview in Cairo with CBC TV," US Department of State, January 11, 2012, http://iipdigital.usembassy.gov/st/english/texttrans/2012/01/201201111710 42su0.9611323.html#axzz3PJaDxNjM.

36. Victoria Nuland, "The United States' Reaction to Egypt's November 22 Decisions," US Department of State, November 23, 2012, http://www.state.gov/r /pa/prs/ps/2012/11/200983.htm.

37. Victoria Nuland, "Daily Press Briefing," US Department of State, November 28, 2012, http://www.state.gov/r/pa/prs/dpb/2012/11/201168.htm #EGYPT.

38. "Readout of the President's Phone Call with Egyptian President Morsi," White House, December 6, 2012, https://www.whitehouse.gov/the-press -office/2012/12/06/readout-president-s-phone-call-egyptian-president -morsi.

39. Rayna Stamboliyska, "Egypt's Constitutional Referendum Results," *Jadaliyya*, December 25, 2012, http://www.jadaliyya.com/pages/index/9234/egypt's -constitutional-referendum-results.

11. In Power but Not in Control

1. The five votes were the March 2011 constitutional referendum, the 2011–12 People's Assembly elections, the 2012 Shura Council elections, the 2012 presidential election, and the December 2012 constitutional referendum. It's important to emphasize that this is how the Brotherhood counted their wins and that it's not entirely accurate to call the March 2011 referendum a Brotherhood win because they were one of many forces campaigning for it, including the Salafists, the military, and the Mubarak regime's previous support networks.

2. Al-Sayyid Khodeiry, "We Publish the Text of the President to the Nation regarding the Ratification of the Constitution" (AR), *Al-Youm al-Saba'*, De-

cember 26, 2012, http://www.youm7.com/story/2012/12/26/-خطاب-نص-ننشر
‏VMP.الرئيس-للأمة-مناسبة-إقرار-الدستور-تحملت-مسئولي/889112889112#.

3. "Carter Center Preliminary Statement on Egypt's Shura Council Election,"
    Carter Center, February 28, 2012, http://www.cartercenter.org/resources
    /pdfs/news/peace_publications/election_reports/egypt-022812-shoura
    -council-elections.pdf .

4. "Rights Lawyer Challenges Morsi's Appointment of 90 Shura Members," *Ah-
    ram Online*, December 24, 2012, http://english.ahram.org.eg/NewsContent/1
    /64/61228/Egypt/Politics-/Rights-lawyer-challenges-Morsis-appointment-of
    --Sh.aspx .

5. Interview with Nadia Henry, January 28, 2015.

6. Mary Wagdy, "Morsi Completes the Shura Council by Appointing 90 New
    Members among Them 'Islamists'" (AR), *Al-Sharq al-Awsat*, December 22,
    2012, http://archive.aawsat.com/details.asp?section=4&issueno=12443&
    article=709816#.VMhSI8ZRT4g.

7. "Great Partisan, Community Diversity in Appointed Shura Council Mem-
    bership by Presidential Edict," *IkhwanWeb*, December 24, 2012, http://www
    .ikhwanweb.com/article.php?id=30510.

8. Interview with Ahmed Fahmy, July 16, 2012.

9. Maggie Michael and Lee Keath, "With a Sneer, Egypt TV Host Challenges
    Islamists," Associated Press, August 24, 2012, http://bigstory.ap.org/article
    /sneer-egypt-tv-host-challenges-islamists.

10. Shadi Hamid, "Egypt's Uncomfortable Challenge: Balancing Security and
    Civil Liberties," *Atlantic*, August 20, 2012, http://www.theatlantic.com
    /international/archive/2012/08/egypts-uncomfortable-challenge-balancing
    -security-and-civil-liberties/261260/.

11. "Egypt Newspaper Censored over Insult to President," *USA Today*, August 11,
    2012, http://usatoday30.usatoday.com/news/world/story/2012-08-11/egypt
    -press/56980934/1.

12. "Egypt TV Host Acquitted of Charges of Incitement against President Morsi,"
    Ahram Online, January 8, 2013, http://english.ahram.org.eg/NewsContent/1
    /0/62036/Egypt/Egypt-TV-host-acquitted-of-charges-of-incitement-a.aspx.

13. "More 'Insulting President' Lawsuits under Morsi than Mubarak," *Ahram
    Online*, January 20, 2013, http://english.ahram.org.eg/NewsContent/1/64
    /62872/Egypt/Politics-/More-insulting-president-lawsuits-under-Morsi-than
    .aspx.

14. Dan Murphy, "For Egypt's Satirists, Morsi's Power Is No Joke," *Christian Sci-
    ence Monitor*, January 2, 2013, http://www.csmonitor.com/World/Security
    -Watch/Backchannels/2013/0102/For-Egypt-s-satirists-Morsi-s-power-is-no
    -joke.

15. "Investigation of the Egyptian Journalist Abdel Halim Qandil Accused of
    Insulting President Morsi" (AR), *Elaph*, January 2, 2013, http://elaph.com
    /Web/news/2013/1/783777.html.

16. "More 'Insulting President' Lawsuits."

17. Mayy El Sheikh, "Egypt: Prosecutor Opens Criminal Investigation against Comedian Accused of Insulting the President," *New York Times*, January 1, 2013, http://www.nytimes.com/2013/01/02/world/middleeast/comedian-accused-of-insulting-egyptian-president-to-be-investigated.html.

18. Hazem Youssef, "Complaint Accusing Abdel Halim Qandil of 'Insulting the President' Referred to Investigation" (AR), *Al-Masry al-Youm*, January 2, 2013, http://www.almasryalyoum.com/news/details/269347; "Mursi's Crackdown on Media Sets a New Record in Egypt's History," *Al-Arabiya*, January 20, 2013, http://english.alarabiya.net/articles/2013/01/20/261444.html.

19. "The Crime of Insulting the President, the Crime of a Tyrannical Regime" (AR), Arabic Network for Human Rights Information, January 20, 2013, http://www.anhri.net/wp-content/uploads/2013/01/22اهانة_الرئيس_نهائي.pdf.

20. Patrick Kingsley, "Egyptian Editor Says He Was Forced Out by Muslim Brotherhood," *Guardian*, February 18, 2013, http://www.theguardian.com/world/2013/feb/18/egyptian-editor-muslim-brotherhood-hani-shukrallah.

21. Hany al-Waziri, "Four Ministries of the 'Brotherhood' in Ministerial Amendments—and a Fifth Is Close to Them for Finance" (AR), *El-Watan*, January 5, 2013, http://www.elwatannews.com/news/details/108944.

22. Interview with high-ranking Muslim Brotherhood official, January 7, 2013.

23. Issandr El Amrani, "On Egypt's New Cabinet Lineup," *Arabist*, January 7, 2013, http://arabist.net/blog/2013/1/7/on-egypts-new-cabinet-lineup.html.

24. Yosri al-Badry, "'Mohamed Ibrahim' Man of the 'Prisons': Interior Minister" (AR), *Al-Masry al-Youm*, January 5, 2013, http://www.almasryalyoum.com/news/details/270361.

25. "UPDATE 2-Egypt Signals $2 Bln Qatar Loan Already Spent," Reuters, January 10, 2013, http://in.reuters.com/article/egypt-economy-qatar-idUSL5E9CA95P20130110; Alaa Shahine and Tarek El-Tablawy, "Egypt Inflation Climbs Most in Two Years as Pound Weakens," Bloomberg, February 10, 2013, http://www.bloomberg.com/news/articles/2013-02-10/egypt-s-inflation-rate-jumps-most-in-two-years-as-pound-weakens.

26. "Official: Funds Allocated to Diesel Subsidies Have Run Out," *Egypt Independent*, February 16, 2013, http://www.egyptindependent.com/news/official-funds-allocated-diesel-subsidies-have-run-out.

27. "Egypt Approves Law to Issue Sovereign Islamic Bonds," *Ahram Online*, January 16, 2013, http://english.ahram.org.eg/NewsContent/3/12/62636/Business/Economy/Egypt-approves-law-to-issue-sovereign-Islamic-bond.aspx.

28. Bradley Hope, "Egypt's Decaying Rail System Caused Train Crash: Transport Minister," *National*, January 16, 2013, http://www.thenational.ae/news/world/africa/egypts-decaying-rail-system-caused-train-crash-transport-minister.

29. Ahmed Fouad, "Gamal Heshmat to *Al-Shorouk*: Hidden Hands behind the Train Accident in Badrashin" (AR), *Al-Shorouk*, January 15, 2013, http://www.shorouknews.com/news/view.aspx?cdate=15012013&id=d916d9ec-dc89-4538-8a2c-6b5014f1b551.

30. Zeinobia, "And the Brotherhood Blames the Christians for #Badrashin Now!!" *Egyptian Chronicles*, January 16, 2013, http://egyptianchronicles.blogspot .com/2013/01/and-brotherhood-blames-christians-for.html?utm_source =feedburner&utm_medium=feed&utm_campaign=Feed%3A+Egyptian Chronicles+%28Egyptian+chronicles%29.

31. David D. Kirkpatrick, "Deadly Riots Erupt across Egypt on Anniversary of Revolution," *New York Times*, January 25, 2013, http://www.nytimes.com /2013/01/26/world/middleeast/tens-of-thousands-fill-tahrir-square-on -anniversary-of-egyptian-revolt.html?pagewanted=all; Jon Henley, "Clashes in Cairo as Egypt Marks Revolution Anniversary," *Guardian*, January 25, 2013, http://www.theguardian.com/world/2013/jan/25/egypt-uprising-violence -live#block-5102ad61b57993532c9aa4ac; "Angry Protests Leave 7 Dead on Egypt Anniversary," CBS News, January 25, 2013, http://www.cbsnews.com /news/angry-protests-leave-7-dead-on-egypt-anniversary/.

32. "Deadly Clashes as Egyptians Mark Uprising," Al Jazeera, January 26, 2013, http://www.aljazeera.com/news/middleeast/2013/01/201312571638570662 .html.

33. Nancy A. Youssef, "Port Said Soccer Riot Verdict Sparks Deadly Clashes in Egypt," McClatchy, January 26, 2013, http://www.mcclatchydc.com/news /nation-world/world/middle-east/article24743752.html .

34. Patrick Kingsley, "Mohamed Morsi Declares Emergency in Three Egyptian Cities," *Guardian*, January 27, 2013, http://www.theguardian.com/world /2013/jan/27/mohamed-morsi-emergency-provinces.

35. Nancy A. Youssef, "Another Day of Violence Leaves Egypt Wondering How This Will End," McClatchy, January 28, 2013, http://www.mcclatchydc .com/news/nation-world/world/article24743869.html; Abigail Hauslohner and Ingy Hassieb, "Egypt's Military Chief Says Clashes Threaten the State," *Washington Post*, January 29, 2013, https://www.washingtonpost.com/world /middle_east/egypts-military-chief-says-clashes-threaten-the-state/2013/01 /29/8a8ee7ae-6a1b-11e2-ada3-d86a4806d5ee_story.html.

36. Vivian Salama and Mike Giglio, "Egyptians Defy Curfew as Army Warns of 'Collapse,'" *Daily Beast*, January 29, 2013, http://www.thedailybeast.com /articles/2013/01/29/egyptians-defy-curfew-as-army-warns-of-collapse.html.

37. "Gen. Abdel Fattah al-Sisi during a Meeting with Students of the Military Academy," Facebook, January 29, 2013, https://www.facebook.com/decided .to.speak/posts/279271338867105.

38. "Salafist Nour Party, NSF Call for Unity Government," *Ahram Online*, January 30, 2013, http://english.ahram.org.eg/NewsContent/1/64/63689/Egypt /Politics-/Salafist-Nour-Party,-NSF-call-for-unity-government.aspx.

39. Kareem Fahim and Nicholas Kulish, "Opposition in Egypt Urges Unity Government," *New York Times*, January 30, 2013, http://www.nytimes.com/2013 /01/31/world/middleeast/egypt-protests.html.

40. Interview with Saad al-Husseini, February 27, 2013.

41. "FJP Predicts Winning 55% of Parliamentary Seats in Next Elections," *Egypt*

Independent, January 21, 2013, http://www.egyptindependent.com/news/fjp
-predicts-winning-55-parliamentary-seats-next-elections; "Katatny: If FJP
Takes Paliamentary Majority, Would Reassemble Cabinet," *Egypt Independent*, January 18, 2013, http://www.egyptindependent.com/news/katatny-if
-fjp-takes-parliament-majority-would-reassemble-cabinet.

42. Mahmoud Shaaban Bayoumi, "El-Watan Publicized the Plan of Freedom and
Justice to Support Its Candidates in the Parliamentary Elections" (AR), *El-
Watan*, January 6, 2013, http://www.elwatannews.com/news/details/109258;
Dina Ezzat, "Morsi and Brotherhood Embark on Pre-Elections PR Drive,"
Ahram Online, January 19, 2013, http://english.ahram.org.eg/NewsContent/1
/64/62789/Egypt/Politics-/Morsi-and-Brotherhood-embark-on-preelections
-PR-dr.aspx.

43. Yasser Ali, "Sources: 'Katatny' Meets with 'Shater' to Research Alliances and
the Party's Candidates during the Elections" (AR), *Al-Masry al-Youm*, February 11, 2013, http://www.almasryalyoum.com/news/details/284904; "FJP
Election List to Exclude Most Former MPs," *Egypt Independent*, February 13,
2013, http://www.egyptindependent.com/news/fjp-election-list-exclude
-most-former-mps?utm_source=dlvr.it&utm_medium=twitter.

44. Ahmed Hiza', "'Freedom and Justice' Begins Activating the Bread Plan in
Cairo Neighborhoods" (AR), *IkhwanOnline*, February 6, 2013 (no longer
available online); Mustafa Shahin, "9 Thousand Benefit from 20 Medical Car-
avans of the Brotherhood in Asyut" (AR), *IkhwanOnline*, February 9, 2013(no
longer available online); Nancy A. Youssef, "Amid Clashes of Egypt's Brotherhood, Opposition: The Quiet Struggle of Those in the Middle," McClatchy,
January 25, 2013, http://www.mcclatchydc.com/news/nation-world/world
/article24743734.html.

45. Nour Ali, "We Publish the Text of the Laws of Elections and Political Rights
before They Are Presented to the 'Supreme Constitutional Court'" (AR),
Al-Youm al-Saba', January 19, 2013, http://www.youm7.com/story/2013/1/19
/#914614/عرضهم-قبل-السياسية-الحقوق-مباشرة-و-الانتخابات-قانوني-نص-ننشر.VNI758ZRReQ;
Ayman el-Dessouki, "Egypt's New Elections Law: Too Controversial and
Too Biased," *Al-Arabiya*, January 23, 2013, http://english.alarabiya.net/views
/2013/01/23/262003.html.

46. Farouk el-Dessouki, "*Al-Masry al-Youm* Publishes 'Constitutional' Remarks
on Elections Law" (AR), *Al-Masry al-Youm*, February 18, 2013, http://www
.almasryalyoum.com/news/details/288618.

47. "Egypt's Opposition Wary of Election Plan, Islamists Satisfied," *Ahram Online*,
February 22, 2013, http://english.ahram.org.eg/News/65335.aspx.

48. Interview with Mohamed Fouad, February 24, 2013. Fouad noted that
whereas the 2011–12 parliamentary elections districting placed the Islamist-
dominated Giza neighborhood of Imbaba in the same electoral district as
Mohandessin and Dokki, the 2013 districting made Imbaba its own district.

49. Nathan Brown, "Is Egypt's New Parliamentary Election Law Constitutional?"
Arabist, February 22, 2013, http://arabist.net/blog/2013/2/22/is-egypts-new

-parliamentary-election-law-constitutional.html; "Shura Council: SCC Not Entitled to Review Election Law Amendments," *Egypt Independent*, February 28, 2013, http://www.egyptindependent.com/news/shura-council-scc -not-entitled-review-election-law-amendments.

50. Interview with Mohamed al-Beltagy, March 2, 2013; interview with FJP economics official, March 2, 2013.

51. "We Publish the Text of Morsi's Decisions in Calling for the House of Representatives Elections and Its Schedule and the Governorates of Its Four Stages" (AR), *Al-Ahram*, February 21, 2013, http://gate.ahram.org.eg/News/312051 .aspx.

52. "Parliamentary Elections in Egypt Stopped by a Decision from the Administrative Judges" (AR), BBC Arabic, March 6, 2013, http://www.bbc.com /arabic/middleeast/2013/03/130306_egypt_decree_morsi_elections; Ahmed Aboulenein, "Administrative Court Suspends Elections," *Daily News Egypt*, March 6, 2013, http://www.dailynewsegypt.com/2013/03/06/administrative -court-suspends-elections/.

53. Ahmed Aboulenein, "Shura Council Finalises Elections Law," *Daily News Egypt*, April 10, 2013, http://www.dailynewsegypt.com/2013/04/10/shura -council-finalises-elections-law/.

54. Mohamed Badie, "Muhammad, Peace Be upon Him and the Messenger of the Renaissance and the Maker of Civilization" (AR), Facebook, January 24, 2013, https://www.facebook.com/photo.php?fbid=437434682995251&set=a .392330860838967.87974.384587744946612&type=1&theater.

55. "Egyptian Pres. on the Release of Blind Egyptian Cleric: 'I Want Him to Be Free,'" CNN, January 7, 2013, http://cnnpressroom.blogs.cnn.com/2013/01 /07/egyptian-pres-on-the-release-of-blind-egyptian-cleric-i-want-him-to-be -free/.

56. David D. Kirkpatrick, "Morsi's Slurs against Jews Stir Concern," *New York Times*, January 14, 2013, http://www.nytimes.com/2013/01/15/world /middleeast/egypts-leader-morsi-made-anti-jewish-slurs.html?hp&_r=0& pagewanted=all.

57. Associated Press, "U.S. Condemns Comments from Egypt's Morsi," *USA Today*, January 16, 2013, http://www.usatoday.com/story/news/world/2013 /01/16/egypt-morsi-comments/1838445/.

58. Mohamed Farid, "Statement on the Egyptian Administration's Commitment to Upholding Religious Freedom and Promoting Inter-Religious Tolerance," CNN, January 21, 2013, http://ireport.cnn.com/docs/DOC-913705.

59. Ahmed Al-Bahnasawi, "Morsi: My Statements against America and Zionism Were Taken out of Context, and I Said Them Because of the Aggression on Gaza" (AR), *El-Watan*, January 16, 2013, http://www.elwatannews.com/news /details/114583.

60. Josh Rogin, "Exclusive: Morsy Implies Jews Control the American Media," *Foreign Policy*, January 23, 2013, http://foreignpolicy.com/2013/01/23 /exclusive-morsy-implies-jews-control-the-american-media/.

61.   Interview with senior US official, January 23, 2015.

62.   Anne Gearan, "After Meeting Morsi, Kerry Releases Immediate Aid to Egypt," *Washington Post*, March 3, 2013, https://www.washingtonpost.com/world /middle_east/after-meeting-morsi-kerry-releases-immediate-aid-to-egypt /2013/03/03/07295f38-841b-11e2-98a3-b3db6b9ac586_story.html.

63.   David D. Kirkpatrick, "Angry at Public and Officials, Security Forces Strike in Egypt," *New York Times*, March 7, 2013, http://www.nytimes.com/2013/03 /08/world/middleeast/angry-at-public-and-officials-police-strike-in-egypt .html?_r=0; Patrick Kingsley, "Egyptian Police Go on Strike," *Guardian*, March 10, 2013, http://www.theguardian.com/world/2013/mar/10/egypt -police-strike.

64.   "Egypt's Al-Gamaa Al-Islamiya Deploys Members in Assiut to 'Maintain Security,'" *Ahram Online*, March 13, 2013, http://english.ahram.org.eg /NewsContent/1/64/66755/Egypt/Politics-/Egypts-AlGamaa-AlIslamiya -deploys-members-in-Assiu.aspx; Mara Revkin and Yussef Auf, "Egypt's Fallen Police State Gives Way to Vigilante Justice," *Atlantic*, April 3, 2013, http://www.theatlantic.com/international/archive/2013/04/egypts-fallen -police-state-gives-way-to-vigilante-justice/274616/.

65.   Osman El-Sharnouby et al., "Intense Clashes at Egypt's Brotherhood HQ," *Ahram Online*, March 22, 2013, http://english.ahram.org.eg/NewsContent /1/64/67459/Egypt/Politics-/Clashes-erupt-at-Egypts-Brotherhood-HQ -amid-high-p.aspx; "Egypt Activist Says Brotherhood Leaders 'Incited Violence' against Her," *Ahram Online*, April 10, 2013, http://english.ahram .org.eg/NewsContent/1/64/68949/Egypt/Politics-/Egypt-activist-says -Brotherhood-leaders-incited-vi.aspx.

66.   "Egypt's Prosecutors Summon Opposition Figures Accused in Attacks on Brotherhood HQ," *Ahram Online*, March 25, 2013, http://english.ahram.org .eg/NewsContent/1/64/67698/Egypt/Politics-/Egypts-prosecutors-summon -opposition-figures-accus.aspx.

67.   Evan Hill, "Special Report: The Bad and the Ugly; Political Violence in Moqattam," *Tahrir Squared*, March 25, 2013, http://tahrirsquared.com/node /3669. While the prosecutor did not question or accuse any Brotherhood leaders following the Moqattam clashes of March 22, 2013, three of Brother- hood leader Khairat al-Shater's guards were summoned regarding assault accusations.

68.   Sahar Azzam, "Brotherhood Pages on 'Facebook' Call for Siege of Media Production City Tomorrow" (AR), *Masrawy*, March 23, 2013, http:// www.masrawy.com/News/News_Egypt/details/2013/3/23/79981 /صفحات-إخوانية-على-فيس-بوك-تدعو-لمحاصرة-مدينة-الإنتاج-الإعلامي-غدا.

69.   "Islamists Besiege TV Channel HQ for Disseminating False Information," *Middle East Monitor*, March 25, 2013, https://www.middleeastmonitor.com /news/middle-east/5583-islamists-besiege-tv-channel-hq-for-disseminating -false-information.

70.   Kareem Fahim and Mayy El Sheikh, "Egyptian Satirist Posts Bail as Author-

ities Press Case," *New York Times*, March 31, 2013, http://www.nytimes.com
/2013/04/01/world/middleeast/bassem-youssef-posts-bail-as-egyptian
-authorities-press-case.html.

71. "Egypt Foreign Currency Reserves Up for First Time in 5 Months," *Ahram
Online*, May 8, 2013, http://english.ahram.org.eg/NewsContent/3/12/70958
/Business/Economy/Egypt-foreign-currency-reserves-up-for-first-time
-.aspx.

72. Ulf Laessing, "Egypt Lifts Cooking Gas Price before IMF Visit," Reuters,
April 1, 2013, http://mobile.reuters.com/article/idUKBRE9300E220130401
?irpc=932.

73. Nehal Mounir, "Electricity and Energy Ministry to Cut Down on Summer Time Electricity Flow," *Daily News Egypt*, April 8, 2013 http://www
.dailynewsegypt.com/2013/04/08/electricity-and-energy-ministry-to-cut
-down-on-summer-time-electricity-flow/.

12. The Rebellion

1.   Eric Trager, "Tired of the Brotherhood, Egyptians Want the Military Back—
but Only Temporarily," *Atlantic*, April 10, 2013, http://www.theatlantic.com
/international/archive/2013/04/tired-of-the-brotherhood-egyptians-want
-the-military-back-but-only-temporarily/274856/.

2.   Egypt elections: ElBaradei Warns of Chaos," BBC, February 24, 2013, http://
www.bbc.com/news/world-middle-east-21566270.

3.   "Egypt: Poll Shows 82 Percent in Egypt Want Army to Return to Power,"
Aswat Masriya, March 17, 2013, http://allafrica.com/stories/201303170221
.html.

4.   Essam al-Sheikh, "Baseera: Low Percentage Approves of the President's
Performance" (AR), *Al-Gomhuria*, April 7, 2013, http://www.gomhuriaonline
.com/main.asp?v_article_id=78914&v_section_id=1#.VjeVmXiJndk.

5.   Mohamed Abdu Hassanein, "Fears of 'Ikhwanization' of Military," *Asharq al-
Awsat*, March 20, 2013, http://english.aawsat.com/2013/03/article55296303.

6.   I am paraphrasing the military leadership's mood. This is not an actual
quotation.

7.   Interview with US official, January 23, 2015.

8.   Evan Hill and Muhammad Mansour, "Egypt's Army Took Part in Torture and
Killings during Revolution, Report Shows," *Guardian*, April 10, 2013, http://
www.theguardian.com/world/2013/apr/10/egypt-army-torture-killings
-revolution.

9.   Sarah El Deeb, "Egypt Leader and Military Chief Put Tensions Aside," Associated Press, April 12, 2013, http://bigstory.ap.org/article/egypts-military
-warns-against-slandering-it.

10. "Baladna Bil-Masry: Tamarod; Signatures to Withdraw Confidence from
President Morsi" (AR), YouTube, April 28, 2013, https://www.youtube.com
/watch?v=OST4yYdiKk4.

11. Hend Kortam, "More Governorates Call on Army to Manage State," *Daily*

News Egypt, March 4, 2013, http://www.dailynewsegypt.com/2013/03/04
/more-governorates-call-on-army-to-manage-state/.

12. Interview with Mouhib Doss, October 9, 2014.

13. Shadi Hamid, "Morsy and the Muslims," *Foreign Policy*, May 8, 2013, http://
foreignpolicy.com/2013/05/08/morsy-and-the-muslims/.

14. "Who's Who: Egypt's New Ministers," *Ahram Online*, May 7, 2013, http://
english.ahram.org.eg/News/70884.aspx; "Planning Minister: Negotiations
with the International Monetary Fund on the Loan Matter Ongoing" (AR),
Masress, May 8, 2013, http://www.masress.com/almasryalyoum/1725276;
"Egypt's Finance Minister Appoints Adviser to Lead IMF Talks," Reuters, April 30, 2013, http://www.reuters.com/article/egypt-imf-shehata
-idUSL6N0DH3PT20130430.

15. Nada Badawi, "Egyptian Pound Slumps to Seven against US Dollar," *Daily
News Egypt*, May 19, 2013, http://www.dailynewsegypt.com/2013/05/19
/egyptian-pound-slumps-to-seven-against-us-dollar/.

16. Nada Badawi, "Experts Predict Higher Inflation Rates amid Unchanged Interest Rates," *Daily News Egypt*, June 23, 2013, http://www.dailynewsegypt.com
/2013/06/23/experts-predict-higher-inflation-rates-amid-unchanged-interest
-rates/.

17. Hesham Amr Abdel Halim et al., "Darkness of the Renaissance' Prevails in
Egypt and 'Electricity': 'It's Grabbing Us'" (AR), *Al-Masry al-Youm*, May 22,
2013, http://today.almasryalyoum.com/article2.aspx?ArticleID=383350;
Patrick Kingsley, "Egypt 'Suffering Worst Economic Crisis since 1930s,'"
Guardian, May 16, 2013, http://www.theguardian.com/world/2013/may/16
/egypt-worst-economic-crisis-1930s.

18. Rana Muhammad Taha, "Tamarod Collects over Two Million Signatures,"
Daily News Egypt, May 12, 2013, http://www.dailynewsegypt.com/2013/05
/12/tamarod-collects-over-two-million-signatures/.

19. Mohamed Abdel Qader, "Shura Ignores Morsi's Promises to the Judges" (AR),
Al-Masry al-Youm, May 15, 2013, http://today.almasryalyoum.com/article2
.aspx?ArticleID=382467.

20. Ahmed Shalabi, "Ahmed Maher Detained at the Airport on Charges of Inciting Protests in Front of the House of the Interior Minister" (AR), *Al-Masry al-
Youm*, May 10, 2013, http://www.almasryalyoum.com/news/details/314606.

21. Shaimaa Fayed and Maggie Fick, "Two Egyptian Journalists, Critical of Mursi,
Face Trial," *Aswat Masriya*, May 19, 2013, http://en.aswatmasriya.com/news
/view.aspx?id=9d62337f-386e-46d4-91dc-ad713b6d3350.

22. Basil El-Dabh, "TV Presenters Investigated for Tamarod Support," *Daily
News Egypt* (May 21, 2013): http://www.dailynewsegypt.com/2013/05/21/tv
-presenters-investigated-for-tamarod-support/.

23. "Tamarod Campaign Gathers Seven Million Signatures," *Egypt Independent*,
May 29, 2013, http://www.egyptindependent.com/news/tamarod-campaign
-gathers-seven-million-signatures.

24. Basil El-Dabh, "Al-Sisi: The Army Does Not Interfere in Political Affairs,"

Daily News Egypt, May 12, 2013, http://www.dailynewsegypt.com/2013/05 /12/al-sisi-the-army-does-not-interfere-in-political-affairs/.

25. Fathia al-Dakhakhny, "Morsi Turns to Protect the Safety of the Kidnapped and the Kidnappers in 'Liberating the Soldiers of Sinai'" (AR), *Al-Masry al-Youm*, May 16, 2013, http://www.almasryalyoum.com/news/details/317252.

26. Wael Ali and Mohamed Maher, "Delegation from 'National [Council] for Human Rights' to Determine the Safety of Conditions in 'Scorpion' Prison" (AR), *Al-Masry al-Youm*, May 17, 2013, http://www.almasryalyoum.com/news /details/317695; Zeinobia, "And Our Soldiers Are Not Released Yet in #Sinai 'Updated,'" *Egyptian Chronicles*, May 17, 2013, http://egyptianchronicles .blogspot.com/2013/05/and-our-soldiers-are-not-released-yet.html.

27. "Sinai Abduction: Egypt President Morsi Rules Out Talks," BBC, May 19, 2013, http://www.bbc.com/news/world-middle-east-22592623; Zeinobia, "Kidnapped Soldiers Appear in Video 'Updated,'" *Egyptian Chronicles*, May 19, 2013, http://egyptianchronicles.blogspot.com/2013/05/kidnapped -soldiers-appear-in-video.html.

28. Zeinobia, "And the Soldiers Are Back and Free," *Egyptian Chronicles*, May 22, 2013, http://egyptianchronicles.blogspot.com/2013/05/sinais-hostage-crisis -day7-statements.html.

29. Fady Salah, "Morsi Discusses Renaissance Dam in Ethiopia," *Daily News Egypt*, May 25, 2013, http://www.dailynewsegypt.com/2013/05/25/morsi -discusses-renaissance-dam-in-ethiopia/; "Ethiopia Diverts Flow of Blue Nile," Al Jazeera, May 29, 2013, http://www.aljazeera.com/news/africa/2013 /05/2013528212950410935.html.

30. Joel Gulhane, "Dam Report Presented to Morsi," *Daily News Egypt*, June 2, 2013, http://www.dailynewsegypt.com/2013/06/02/dam-report-presented -to-morsi/.

31. Liam Stack, "With Cameras Rolling, Egyptian Politicians Threaten Ethiopia over Dam," *New York Times*, June 6, 2013, http://thelede.blogs.nytimes.com /2013/06/06/with-cameras-rolling-egyptian-politicians-threaten-ethiopia -over-dam/.

32. Aya Batrawy and Maggie Michael, "Egypt Warns All Options Open for Ethiopia Dam," Associated Press, June 10, 2013, http://bigstory.ap.org/article /egypts-pm-ethiopian-dam-act-defiance.

33. Interview with US official, January 25, 2015.

34. Manar Mohsen, "Tamarod Closes In on Signature Goal," *Daily News Egypt*, June 12, 2013, http://www.dailynewsegypt.com/2013/06/12/tamarod-closes -in-on-signature-goal/.

35. Menna Mourad, "Tagarod Campaign to Counter Tamarod," *Daily News Egypt*, May 13, 2013, http://www.dailynewsegypt.com/2013/05/13/tagarod -campaign-to-counter-tamarod/.

36. Mara Revkin, "The Egyptian State Unravels," *Foreign Affairs*, June 27, 2013, https://www.foreignaffairs.com/articles/egypt/2013-06-27/egyptian-state -unravels.

37. Louisa Loveluck, "Egypt's Gathering Economic Gloom Leaves Millions Facing Food Shortages," *Guardian*, June 6, 2013, http://www.theguardian.com /global-development/2013/jun/06/egypt-economic-gloom-food-shortages; Amina Ismail, "With Electricity and Water in Short Supply, Egyptians Grow Tense," McClatchy, June 24, 2013, http://www.mcclatchydc.com/news /nation-world/world/article24750286.html; Ben Hubbard, "Anger at Egypt's Leaders Intensifies in Gas Lines," *New York Times*, June 26, 2013, http:// www.nytimes.com/2013/06/27/world/middleeast/anger-at-egypts-leaders -intensifies-in-gas-lines.html.

38. Eric Trager, "Egypt Will Erupt Again on June 30," *New Republic*, June 24, 2013, https://newrepublic.com/article/113590/egypt-june-30-demonstrations -unlikely-end-well.

39. Interview with Mahmoud Rashad, June 10, 2013.

40. Trager, "Egypt Will Erupt Again"; interview with Ahmed Sobea, June 6, 2013.

41. Interview with Ashraf Thabet, February 25, 2013; interview with Magdy Selim, February 27, 2013.

42. Interview with Ashraf Thabet, February 25, 2013; interview with Ahmed al-Kattan, June 10, 2013.

43. AFP, "Top Muslim Cleric Al-Qaradawi Urges Sunnis to Join Syria War," *Ahram Online* (June 1, 2013): http://english.ahram.org.eg/NewsContent/1/64 /72857/Egypt/Politics-/Top-Muslim-cleric-AlQaradawi-urges-Sunnis-to-join -.aspx.

44. Aya Batrawy, "Correction: Egypt-Syria Story," Yahoo News, June 14, 2013, http://news.yahoo.com/correction-egypt-syria-story-174634201.html.

45. Tom Perry, "Mursi Cuts Egypt's Syria Ties, Backs No-Fly Zone," Reuters, June 15, 2013, http://www.reuters.com/article/us-syria-crisis-egypt-mursi -idUSBRE95E0HA20130615.

46. "Sheikh Mohamed Hassan Demands Morsi Close Egypt's Door to Shiites" (AR), *Al-Youm al-Sabaa*, June 15, 2013, http://www.youm7.com/story/2013 /6/15/#1115851/الشيعة-أمام-مصر-باب-يغلق-مرسي-يطالب-حسان-محمد-الشيخ.VtMpJDZOJFJ.

47. Hamza Hendawi, "Egypt Seen to Give Nod toward Jihadis on Syria," Yahoo News, June 16, 2013, http://news.yahoo.com/egypt-seen-nod-toward-jihadis -syria-202608813.html.

48. "Egypt's Newly Appointed Governors: A 'Who's Who,'" *Ahram Online*, June 17, 2013, http://english.ahram.org.eg/News/74199.aspx.

49. "Popular Uprising against 'Brotherhood Governors': 'Alarm' from Al-Gharbiya" (AR), *Al-Masry al-Youm*, June 19, 2013, http://today.almasry alyoum.com/article2.aspx?ArticleID=386685.

50. Ben Hubbard and Mayy El Sheikh, "New Governor Is a Shock to Some Inside Egypt," *New York Times*, June 16, 2013, http://www.nytimes.com/2013/06 /17/world/middleeast/new-governor-shock-to-some-inside-egypt.html; Maggie Fick, "Ex-Militant to Run Bloodied Luxor Tourist Region," Reuters, June 17, 2013, http://www.reuters.com/article/us-egypt-mursi-islamist -idUSBRE95G0IP20130617.

51. Mariam Iskander, "Tourism Employees Protest New Luxor Governor," *Daily News Egypt*, June 20, 2013, http://www.dailynewsegypt.com/2013/06/20/tourism-employees-protest-new-luxor-governor/.

52. "Controversial New Luxor Governor Quits," Al Jazeera, June 23, 2013, http://www.aljazeera.com/news/middleeast/2013/06/20136231395844915.html.

53. "'Guidance Office' Delegation Fails to Convince Salafist Call to Back Morsi on Friday of 'Renouncing Violent'" (AR), *Al-Mogaz*, June 17, 2013, http://almogaz.com/news/politics/2013/06/17/960779.

54. "Updated: Egypt's Islamists Rally to Support President Morsi," *Ahram Online*, June 21, 2013, http://english.ahram.org.eg/NewsContent/1/64/74585/Egypt/Politics-/Updated-Egypts-Islamists-rally-to-support-Presiden.aspx; Reem Abdellatif and Matt Bradley, "Egyptian Moves to Detain Brotherhood Leaders," *Wall Street Journal*, July 10, 2013, http://www.wsj.com/articles/SB10001424127887323740804578597321211486136.

55. "Ambassador Anne W. Patterson's Speech at the Ibn Khaldun Center for Development Studies," Embassy of the United States, Cairo, June 18, 2013, http://egypt.usembassy.gov/mobile/pr061813a.html.

56. Mohamed Haggag, "'Brotherhood' Studies Results of Shater's Meeting with the American Ambassador" (AR), *Al-Youm al-Saba'*, June 20, 2013, http://www.youm7.com/story/2013/6/20/-الإخوان-تدرس-نتائج-لقاء-الشاطر-بالسفيرة #1124556/الأمريكية.VtMpeTZOJFK .

57. Interview with US official, January 23, 2015. Al-Shater's quotation is based on the US official's recollection and is meant as a paraphrase, not a word-for-word quotation.

58. Nathan J. Brown, "Will June 30 Be Midnight for Morsi's Cinderella Story," *Foreign Policy*, June 27, 2013, http://foreignpolicy.com/2013/06/27/will-june-30-be-midnight-for-morsis-cinderella-story/.

59. Ahmed al-Masry, "Number of Injured Muslim Brothers in Desouk Rises to 357" (AR), *IkhwanOnline*, June 20, 2013 (no longer available online); "Unidentified Burn Nour Party Headquarters in Al-Mahalla and Steal Some of Its Contents" (AR), *Al-Masry al-Youm*, June 23, 2013, http://www.almasryalyoum.com/news/details/224641.

60. Shaimaa Fayed and Alastair MacDonald, "Egyptian Army Steps In to Demand Political Truce," Reuters, June 23, 2013, http://www.reuters.com/article/us-egypt-protests-idUSBRE95M08E20130623.

61. "Statement from Islamist Parties and Forces" (AR), Facebook, June 24, 2013, https://www.facebook.com/photo.php?fbid=553844294677031&set=a.553830854678375.1073741910.185332328194898&type=1&theater.

62. Hany al-Waziri, "Urgent: 'Brotherhood' Declares a State of Maximum Alert within Its Ranks in Preparation for Morsi's Important Decisions in Facing the Opposition" (AR), *El-Watan*, June 26, 2013, http://www.elwatannews.com/news/details/210086.

63. "Text of President Mohamed Morsi's Speech" (AR), *Aswat Masriya*, June 27, 2013, http://www.aswatmasriya.com/news/view.aspx?id=6bc27c5a-6109

-46d1-92e3-408ecd92d0b3; "Translation: President Mohamed Morsi's Address to the Nation," Atlantic Council, June 28, 2013, http://www.atlantic council.org/blogs/egyptsource/translation-president-mohamed-morsi-s -address-to-the-nation.

64.   "Further Unrest across Egypt's Delta, Morsi Speech Fails to Placate Critics," *Ahram Online*, June 27, 2013, http://english.ahram.org.eg/NewsContent/1/64 /75065/Egypt/Politics-/Further-unrest-across-Egypts-Delta,-Morsi-speech-f .aspx.

65.   "Egypt's NSF Rejects Morsi Speech, Presses Demand for Snap Elections," *Ahram Online*, June 27, 2013, http://english.ahram.org.eg/NewsContent/1/64 /75126/Egypt/Politics-/Egypts-NSF-rejects-Morsi-speech,-presses-demand -fo.aspx.

66.   Interview with Gamal Heshmat, March 23, 2014; interview with Amr Farag, October 8, 2014; interview with Ashraf Abdel Ghaffar, October 8, 2014.

67.   Mohannad Sabry, "Deadly Violence Breaks Out in Egypt ahead of June 30 Protests," *Al-Monitor*, June 29, 2013, http://www.al-monitor.com/pulse /originals/2013/06/egypt-violence-ahead-of-june-30-protests.html.

68.   David Hearst and Patrick Kingsley, "Egypt's Mohamed Morsi Remains Defiant as Fears of Civil War Grow," *Guardian*, June 30, 2013, http://www.theguardian .com/world/2013/jun/30/egypt-mohamed-morsi-defiant-civil-war.

69.   Interview with Mouhib Doss, October 9, 2014.

70.   "Police Club: The Security Is Neutral and Our Mission Is to Secure Peaceful Demonstrators and Not Any Partisan Facilities" (AR), *Aswat Masriya*, June 20, 2013, http://www.aswatmasriya.com/news/view.aspx?id=deda01ca -95ea-4da3-aaf0-07582e6791be.

71.   Ibrahim Ahmed, "In Pictures: Interior Ministry Puts 'Police of the People' Posters on Central Security Vehicles" (AR), *Al-Youm al-Saba'*, June 28, 2013, http://www.youm7.com/story/2013/6/28/-الشعب-شرطة-ملصقات-تضع-الداخلية-بالصور #1137460/المرك-الأمن-مدرعات-على.VtMqEjZOJFJ.

72.   David D. Kirkpatrick and Mayy El Sheikh, "Morsi Spurned Deals, Seeing Military as Tamed," *New York Times*, July 6, 2013, http://www.nytimes.com /2013/07/07/world/middleeast/morsi-spurned-deals-to-the-end-seeing-the -military-as-tamed.html?_r=0.

73.   David D. Kirkpatrick and others, "By the Millions, Egyptians Seek Morsi's Ouster," *New York Times*, June 30, 2013, http://www.nytimes.com/2013 /07/01/world/middleeast/egypt.html?_r=0; Shaimaa Fayed and Yasmine Saleh, "Millions Flood Egypt's Streets to Demand Mursi Quit," Reuters, June 30, 2013, http://www.reuters.com/article/us-egypt-protests -idUSBRE95Q0NO20130630.

74.   Interview with Mohamed Ali Bishr, October 14, 2014.

75.   "Celebratory Carnival with Cake and Fireworks for the New Year of the President's Rule" (AR), Facebook, June 30, 2013, https://www.facebook.com /photo.php?fbid=505968886142126&l=fb5fe25f1d.

76.   Interview with Amr Farrag, October 8, 2014.

77.   Krishnadev Calamur, "Egypt's Military Lays Down Ultimatum as Unrest
      Spreads," NPR, July 1, 2013, http://www.npr.org/sections/thetwo-way/2013
      /07/01/197606521/egypt-unrest-grows-protesters-storm-ruling-party-office;
      "Statement from the General Staff of the Armed Forces" (AR), Facebook,
      July 1, 2013, https://www.facebook.com/Egy.Army.Spox/posts/33471140665
      9848.
78.   Interview with US official, January 23, 2015.
79.   Interview with Emad Abdel Ghafour, October 11, 2014.
80.   Kirkpatrick and Sheikh, "Morsi Spurned Deals."
81.   David D. Kirkpatrick and Ben Hubbard, "Morsi Defies Egypt Army's Ul-
      timatum to Bend to Protest," *New York Times*, July 2, 2013, http://www
      .nytimes.com/2013/07/03/world/middleeast/egypt-protests.html?_r=0;
      "Egypt: Deadly Clashes at Cairo University," Human Rights Watch, July 5,
      2013, https://www.hrw.org/news/2013/07/05/egypt-deadly-clashes-cairo
      -university.
82.   "Word of the President Mohamed Morsi to the Egyptian People 2 July: The
      Legitimacy Speech" (AR), YouTube, July 2, 2013, https://www.youtube.com
      /watch?v=O0Uqap-cX8Y.
83.   Nouran El-Behairy, "Al-Sisi Calls for Green Light to Fight 'Terrorism,'" *Daily
      News Egypt*, July 24, 2013, http://www.dailynewsegypt.com/2013/07/24/al
      -sisi-calls-for-green-light-to-fight-terrorism/; "Testimony by Ahmed Fahmi,
      Egyptian Upper House Speaker, Regarding General Sisi's Claims," *Ikhwan-
      Web*, July 25, 2013, http://www.ikhwanweb.com/article.php?id=31180;
      Zeinab El Gundy, "Former Egypt PM Qandil Defends Morsi," *Ahram Online*,
      July 25, 2013, http://english.ahram.org.eg/NewsContent/1/64/77370/Egypt
      /Politics-/Former-Egypt-PM-Qandil-defends-Morsi.aspx.
84.   Kirkpatrick and Sheikh, "Morsi Spurned Deals."
85.   Jeffrey Fleishman and Manar Mohsen, "Egypt Military Cracks Down on
      Muslim Brotherhood," *Los Angeles Times*, July 4, 2013, http://articles.latimes
      .com/2013/jul/04/world/la-fg-egypt-crackdown-20130705.

Conclusion: Broken Brothers

1.   David D. Kirkpatrick and Kareem Fahim, "Army Kills 51, Deepening Crisis in
      Egypt," *New York Times*, July 8, 2013, http://www.nytimes.com/2013/07/09
      /world/middleeast/egypt.html.
2.   Samuel Tadros, "The Brotherhood Divided," *Current Trends*, August 20, 2015,
      http://www.hudson.org/research/11530-the-brotherhood-divided.
3.   Eric Trager, "Why the Brotherhood Won't Back Down," *Foreign Affairs*,
      July 11, 2013, http://www.foreignaffairs.com/articles/139572/eric-trager/why
      -the-brotherhood-wont-back-down.
4.   Maged Atef, "'Assafir Meets the Leaders of the 'Rabaa' Sit-In: We Are Pre-
      pared to Offer One Hundred Thousand Martyrs" (AR), *Assafir*, July 31, 2013
      (no longer available online).
5.   Mohamad Salama Adam, "From Inside the Brotherhood Nahda Sit-In," *Mada*

Masr, July 24, 2013, http://www.madamasr.com/sections/politics/inside
-brotherhood-nahda-sit; Ali Abdel Mohsen, "An Account of Abuse in Rabea,"
Mada Masr, July 28, 2013, http://www.madamasr.com/sections/politics
/account-abuse-rabea.

6.   Kareem Fahim and Mayy El Sheikh, "Egyptian General Calls for Mass Protests," *New York Times*, July 24, 2013, http://www.nytimes.com/2013/07/25
/world/middleeast/egypt.html?_r=0.

7.   Kareem Fahim and Mayy El Sheikh, "Crackdown in Egypt Kills Islamists as
They Protest," *New York Times*, July 27, 2013, http://www.nytimes.com/2013
/07/28/world/middleeast/egypt.html.

8.   Mostafa Salem, "Rabaa and Nahda a Threat to National Security: Cabinet,"
Daily News Egypt, July 31, 2013, http://www.dailynewsegypt.com/2013/07/31
/rabaa-and-nahda-a-threat-to-national-security-cabinet/.

9.   Interview with Hazem Beblawi, October 12, 2014.

10.   The Egyptian government reported that over six hundred Morsi supporters
were killed. Human Rights Watch puts the number at over eight hundred.

11.   Gomaa Amin, "Islam Is the Religion of the Nation and the Reason for Its Renaissance" (AR), *Yanabeea*, July 29, 2014, http://www.yanabeea.com/details
.aspx?pageid=8625&lasttype=6.

12.   Eric Trager, "Egypt's Invisible Insurgency," *New Republic*, March 19, 2014,
https://newrepublic.com/article/117072/egypts-young-islamists-use
-facebook-organize-violence; Eric Trager and Marina Shalabi, "Egypt's Muslim Brotherhood Gets a Facelift," *Foreign Affairs*, May 20, 2015, https://www
.foreignaffairs.com/articles/egypt/2015-05-20/egypts-muslim-brotherhood
-gets-facelift.

13.   Trager and Shalabi, "Egypt's Muslim Brotherhood Gets a Facelift."

14.   Tadros, "Brotherhood Divided."

15.   Amr Bargisi and et al., "Khairat al-Shater on 'The Nahda Project' (Complete
Translation)," *Current Trends in Islamist Ideology*, April 10, 2012, http://www
.hudson.org/research/9820-khairat-al-shater-on-the-nahda-project-complete
-translation-.

16.   Mariam Iskander, "Essam El-Erian Attacks the UAE during the Shura Council
Meeting," *Daily News Egypt*, June 17, 2013, http://www.dailynewsegypt
.com/2013/06/17/eassam-el-erian-attacks-the-uae-during-the-shura-council
-meeting/; David D. Kirkpatrick, "Leaks Gain Credibility and Potential to
Embarrass Egypt's Leaders," *New York Times*, May 12, 2015, http://www
.nytimes.com/2015/05/13/world/middleeast/leaks-gain-credibility-and
-potential-to-embarrass-egypts-leaders.html?_r=0.

SELECTED BIBLIOGRAPHY

'Abduh, Muhammad. *The Theology of Unity*. Ishaq Musa'ad and Kenneth Cragg, trans. London: George Allen & Unwin, 1966.

Abouel Fotouh, Abdel Moneim. *Witness to the History of the Islamist Movement in Egypt, 1970–1984* (AR). Cairo: Dar al-Shorouk, 2010.

Aburish, Said K. *Nasser: The Last Arab; A Biography*. New York: Thomas Dunne Books, 2004.

Al-Awadi, Hesham. *In Pursuit of Legitimacy: The Muslim Brothers and Mubarak, 1982–2000*. London: Tauris Academic Studies, 2004.

al-Banna, Hasan. *Five Tracts of Hasan al-Banna (1906–1949): A Selection from the Majmu'at Rasa'il al-Imam al-Shahid Hasan al-Banna*. Charles Wendell, trans. Berkeley: University of California Press, 1978.

Arafat, Alaa al-Din. *The Mubarak Leadership and the Future of Democracy in Egypt*. New York: Palgrave Macmillan, 2009.

Awis, Fawzi. *Defectors from the Brotherhood: A Look into the Organization's Rule* (AR). Cairo: Sama House for Publication and Distribution, 2013.

Blaydes, Lisa. *Elections and Distributive Politics in Mubarak's Egypt*. Cambridge: Cambridge University Press, 2011.

Cambanis, Thanassis. *Once upon a Revolution: An Egyptian Story*. New York: Simon & Schuster, 2015.

Clinton, Hillary Rodham. *Hard Choices*. New York: Simon & Schuster, 2014.

Cook, Steven A. *Ruling but Not Governing: The Military and Political Development in Egypt, Algeria, and Turkey*. Baltimore: Johns Hopkins University Press, 2007.

Ghonim, Wael. *Revolution 2.0: The Power of the People Is Greater than the People in Power; A Memoir*. Boston: Houghton Mifflin Harcourt, 2012.

Habib, Mohamed. *The Muslim Brotherhood: Between the Rise to Power and Eating the Legitimacy* (AR). Cairo: Sama for Publishing and Distribution, 2013.

International Monetary Fund. *World Economic Outlook, April 2012: Growth Resuming, Dangers Remain*. Washington: International Monetary Fund, 2012.

Kandil, Hazem. *Inside the Brotherhood*. Cambridge: Polity Press, 2015.

Kassem, Maye. *In the Guise of Democracy: Governance in Contemporary Egypt*. Reading, UK: Ithaca Press, 1999.

Kean, Thomas H., and Lee H. Hamilton. *The 9/11 Commission Report*. New York: W. W. Norton, 2004.

Khalil, Ashraf. *Liberation Square: Inside the Egyptian Revolution and Rebirth of a Nation*. New York: St. Martin's, 2011.

Kurzman, Charles, ed. *Modernist Islam, 1840–1940: A Sourcebook*. Oxford: Oxford University Press, 2002.

Mitchell, Richard P. *The Society of Muslim Brothers*. Oxford: Oxford University Press, 1993.

Osman, Tarek. *Egypt on the Brink: From Nasser to Mubarak*. New Haven: Yale University Press, 2010.

Pargeter, Alison. *The Muslim Brotherhood: From Opposition to Power*. London: Saqi Books, 2013.

Qutb, Seyyid. *Milestones*. Damascus: Dar al-Ilm, n.d.

Raslan, Hany, and Rada Mohamed Helal. *The New Wafd Party (AR)*. Cairo: Al-Ahram Center for Political and Strategic Studies, 2010.

Salem, Ahmed. *The Islamists' Difference: The Islamist–Islamist Disagreement* (AR). Beirut: Namaa Center for Research and Studies, 2013.

Sallam, Hesham, ed. *Egypt's Parliamentary Elections: A Critical Guide to a Changing Political Arena*. Washington: Tadween Publishing, 2013.

Steavenson, Wendell. *Circling the Square: Stories from the Egyptian Revolution*. New York: Ecco, 2015.

Tadros, Samuel. *Motherland Lost: The Egyptian and Coptic Quest for Modernity*. Stanford, CA: Hoover Institution Press, 2013.

———. *Reflections on the Revolution in Egypt*. Stanford, CA: Hoover Institution Press, 2014.

Vatikiotis, P. J. *The History of Modern Egypt: From Muhammad Ali to Mubarak*. 4th ed. Baltimore: Johns Hopkins University Press, 1991.

Wickham, Carrie Rosefsky. *The Muslim Brotherhood: Evolution of an Islamist Movement*. Princeton, NJ: Princeton University Press, 2013.

Zollner, Barbara H. E. *The Muslim Brotherhood: Hasan al-Hudaybi and Ideology*. London: Routledge, 2009.

INDEX

Figures and tables are indicated by f and t following page numbers. All names of people, places, organizations, and so on, starting with "al-" or "el-" are alphabetized by the subsequent part of the name.

Abdel Aziz, Mohamed, 208
Abdel Ghafour, Emad, 97, 125, 164, 202
Abdel-Latif, Hatem, 194
Abdel-Maged, Assem, 216
Abdel-Rahim, Gamal, 169
Abdel Rahman, Ahmed, 231
Abdel Rahman, Omar, 147–48, 200
'Abduh, Muhammad, 45
Abedin, Huma, 150
Abouel Fotouh, Abdel Moneim: background of, 127–28; election results, 137, 137t; expulsion from Muslim Brotherhood, 128; presidential candidacy of, 5, 128–30, 134–35, 136–37t
Abouel Fotouh, Saber, 113, 203
Abu Bakr, Hossam, 194
Abu Hamed, Mohamed, 112
Abu Ismail, Hazem, 129
Abuzeid, Mahmoud, 21, 69
Adib, Amr, 210
al-Afghani, Sayyid Jamal al-Din, 44–45
Afghanistan war, 42
Ageez, Fathi, 143
Ahmadinejad, Mahmoud, 200
Al-Ahram (newspaper): military taking control of (July 2, 2013), 224; poll on Morsi and other presidential candidates (2012), 135, 136t; Salama appointed as editor in chief, 169
al-Ahrar, 81
Akef, Mehdi, 63
akh 'amal (active brother) status of Muslim Brotherhood membership, 50–51, 102
Algeria, 61

Aly, Yasser, 145, 164, 201
Amin, Gomaa, 230
al-Amin, Mohamed, 219
Anan, Sami, 125, 159–61, 163, 165, 175
anti-Christian violence. *See* Copts
anti-Morsi protests. *See* demonstrations and protests; Tahrir Square protests
anti-Mubarak protests. *See* Tahrir Square protests
anti-Semitism of Morsi, 200–201
anti-Western sentiment: al-Banna fostering, 46–47; Morsi holding, 88, 147, 171–72; Muslim Brotherhood continuing with, 85–89, 116, 121, 200; US and Iraq war as catalyst for, 15; US and Israel as focus of, 14
April 6 Youth Movement, 16, 18, 23–24, 82, 83, 104, 209
Arab–Israeli War (1948), 39
Arab–Israeli War (1973), 58, 167–68
Arab Spring: democracy and, 8, 37, 86–87, 140; instability following, 62; major players in, 6; momentum of revolutionaries after, 60; Muslim Brotherhood's taking opportunities afforded by, 1, 68; Obama administration's enthusiasm for, 87; Obama administration's reaction to, 38, 86; revolutionaries falling into disarray after, 75; rural clans and tribes' weaknesses revealed by, 139; the West's optimism about, 34, 37. *See also* Tahrir Square protests
Asala party, 97
Askar, Al-Sayyid, 113
al-Assad, Bashar, 214

al-Assar, Mohamed, 185
assassinations and attempted assassinations, 39.
    See also Sadat, Anwar
autocracy: Morsi's failure in, 2, 193, 194; Morsi's
    power grab, 175–87, 200, 202, 210; revolution-
    aries fearing restitution of, 67; Shura Council
    and, 121–22; al-Sisi government as, 232
al-Awa, Selim, 129, 164, 225
al-Azhar University: Constituent Assembly and,
    123; demonstrations (2006), 19, 64; institu-
    tional independence for, 117
Azmi, Zakaria, 72

Badeen, Hamdy, 159
Badie, Mohamed, 22, 116, 117, 119, 130, 134, 200
al-Badry, Yousry, 193
Bahgat, Ahmed, 219
al-Banna, Hassan, 45–48, 74; on "all-embracing
    concept" of Islam, 46–48, 95, 155; lack of spe-
    cifics on how Islamized nation would function,
    131, 155; Muslim Brotherhood's focus on teach-
    ings of, 49, 68; on non-Islamist adversaries,
    213; Renaissance Project and, 152; al-Shater
    adhering to al-Banna's program of Islamizing
    the state, 131; on West as barrier to Islamizing
    agenda, 117
al-Barr, Abdel Rahman, 154
Battle of the Camel (February 2, 2011), 31–33,
    58, 60; acquittal of former officials of orches-
    trating, 168
al-Bayoumi, Rashad, 62
BDP (Building and Development Party), 97,
    111, 113
al-Beltagy, Mohamed, 24, 65, 119
Ben Ali, Zine el-Abidine, 18
bin Laden, Osama, 39, 86
Bishr, Mohamed Ali, 77, 129, 165, 194
el-Bishry, Tarek, 62
British colonies in Middle East/North Africa, 44
Brooke, Steven, 40
Brown, Nathan, 42
Burns, William, 116, 117

caliphate, reestablishment of, 47–48
Cambanis, Thanassis, 248n10
Carney, Jay, 201
Central Security Forces. See police
chain of command of Muslim Brotherhood,
    51–55, 53f
children's rights, 110

China, 166
Christians: as appointees to Shura Council, 190;
    new constitution and rights of, 179; al-Shater
    criticizing as Morsi opponents, 218. See also
    Copts
Clapper, James, 37–38
Clinton, Bill, 172
Clinton, Hillary, 87–88, 115, 148, 150, 158, 172
Clinton Global Initiative, 172
Coalition of Revolutionary Youth, 67
Committee on Collaboration among Political
    Forces, 15
conspiracy theories: Christian conspiracy, 196;
    former Mubarak regime officials in conspir-
    acy within state institutions, 133, 139; Israel
    engaged in conspiracy in Sinai situation, 150;
    judiciary conspiring with SCAF, 140; Morsi
    blaming conspiracies for country's troubles,
    219, 228; Muslim Brotherhood blaming con-
    spiracy for Morsi ouster, 234; train collision
    (2013) caused by "hidden hands," 196; US and
    Israeli conspiring with Ethiopia to build Nile
    dam, 211; US-financed conspiracy, 88, 120
Constituent Assembly: boycott of, 123; drafting
    a new constitution, 66, 67; formation and
    composition of, 122–23; Morsi empowering
    himself to appoint, 159, 163; Morsi forbidding
    dissolution of, 176; protests over (October 12,
    2012), 168; at standstill in drafting a new
    constitution, 178–79; Supreme Administrative
    Court suspending, 123; withdrawal of non-
    Islamists, 179
constitution: Constituent Assembly to draft a
    new constitution, 66; Morsi's power grab and,
    175–87; Morsi's proposed new constitution's
    provisions, 178–80; referendum on new
    constitution, 178, 180, 186–87, 189; revolution-
    aries' demands for representative committee
    to draft, 89; el-Salmi Document (2011) enun-
    ciating principles for drafting of new consti-
    tution, 102–4; supraconstitutional principles,
    Muslim Brotherhood protest against, 91,
    97–98; theocratic nature of new constitution,
    179; timing of writing new constitution, 70,
    89, 178. See also supraconstitutional principles
constitutional amendments: 2007 amendment
    prohibiting religious political parties, 60; Ar-
    ticle 189, 66, 67; committee appointed to draft
    (February 2011), 62; Muslim Brotherhood's
    support for, 66–67; referendum (March

2011), 61, 65, 67–68; SCAF proposing, post-Mubarak, 57, 61, 65–66; *shari'ah* as "source of all law," 66
"continuous revolution," 205
Cook, Steven, 58
Copts: as candidates for Shura Council, 190; Constituent Assembly and, 123; fearful of Muslim Brotherhood's government, 148; financial control of church, 180; forced evacuations of, 180; Morsi courting in election campaign, 138; al-Shater criticizing as Morsi opponents, 218; violence against (2011), 17, 88–89, 115, 138, 183
corruption: election rigging, 17, 19, 42, 78; al-Ganzoury government criticized for, 124; in Mubarak regime, 14, 20, 22, 30, 219; in Muslim Brotherhood, 247n8; Muslim Brotherhood as remedy to, 154; politics and, 46; Tahrir Square protests against (2011), 26
counterterrorism. *See* terrorism
coup to remove Morsi. *See* Morsi ouster

Darrag, Amr, 209
el-Deeb, Khaled, 284n4
democracy: Arab Spring and, 8, 37, 86–87, 140; FJP election (2011–12) and, 33, 116; Morsi viewing possible ouster as sabotaging, 219; Muslim Brotherhood's views on, 10, 19, 39, 41–44, 55, 85–87; resolution of political disputes and, 217; US advocating as position for Muslim Brotherhood and Morsi, 86, 104, 116, 200, 201, 217; US advocating as position for post-Morsi Egypt, 233
Democratic Alliance for Egypt, 84–85, 97–101, 107, 112
Democratic Front Party, 23
demonstrations and protests: anti-Israel protests (2012), 173; anti-Morsi protests (2012), 168; arrest of Maher for (2013), 209; al-Azhar University demonstrations (2006), 19, 64; Coptic protests (2011), 88–89, 115; million-man march to end Morsi presidency (June 2013), 208; million-man march to support Morsi and *shari'ah* (2012), 178; million-man march to support Morsi presidency (June 2013), 214; Mohamed Mahmoud protests (November 18, 2011), 104–5, 115, 183; Muslim Brotherhood pro-Morsi protests (June 28, 2013), 220–21; police refusal to suppress anti-Morsi protests (2013), 7, 202; post-coup protests by Muslim

Brotherhood (July & August 2013), 227–29; pro-constitutional revision protests (December 2012), 180; promilitary protests (July 24, 2013), 229; Rabaa al-Adawiya mosque pro-Morsi protests (June 21, 2013), 216; Suez anti-Morsi protests (January 25, 2013), 196–97; Tamarod anti-Morsi protests (June 30, 2013), 2, 213, 222–24. *See also* Tahrir Square protests
Determination Friday (July 8, 2011), 90–91
el-Din, Ahmed Gamal, 195
Donilon, Tom, 186
Doss, Mouhib, 221
Al-Dustor (newspaper), 192, 205

economy and finance: al-Banna's views on, 46; currency crisis, 195, 209; Islamic banks and *shari'ah*-compliant finance tools, 194; military control over, 58–59, 102, 163, 207; Morsi's administration facing calamity, 166–67, 195, 203–4, 207, 209, 212–13; Muslim Brotherhood's commitment to improving, 64, 74; ongoing difficulties (2015), 234; post-Mubarak instability and, 124, 167; Renaissance Project and, 152; al-Sisi's rescue of, 232–34; sovereign Islamic bonds, 195–96; Tahrir Square demonstrations (2011), effect on, 27; Tamarod threatening economic devastation unless military remove Morsi, 213; US aid to and investment in Egypt, 170, 202. *See also* International Monetary Fund (IMF)
EGIS (Egyptian General Intelligence Service), 159, 173–74
Egyptian Bloc (party alliance), 100, 106, 107
Egyptian–Israeli peace treaty (1979), 8, 84, 88, 115, 147, 157, 169, 172, 174, 200
Egyptian Media Production Cities, Islamist sit-in at, 203
Egyptian Social Democratic Party (ESDP), 100, 111–12, 205
Egypt Party, 81
ElBaradei, Mohamed, 16–17, 23–24, 105, 177, 205
El Dahshan, Mohamed, 32
election laws: amendment of parliamentary elections law (2013), 198–200, 204; amendment of presidential election laws (January 2012), 117–18
elections. *See* parliamentary elections *by year*; presidential election *by year*
electricity outages, 166, 203–4, 209, 212, 232

El-Watan (newspaper), 194
emergency laws, 59, 62, 65, 110
el-Erian, Essam, 21, 33–34, 67, 79, 164, 250n40;
   dissolved parliamentary body and, 284n4;
   FJP monitoring and, 111; on martyrs killed in
   demonstrations, 114; parliamentary elections
   (2011) and, 101; as parliament committee
   chair, 113; on Port Said Massacre (February
   2012 soccer riot), 118; as Shura Council
   majority leader, 191
ESDP (Egyptian Social Democratic Party), 100,
   111–12, 205
Ethiopian dam construction on Nile, 211
Ezzat, Mahmoud, 25, 94, 111

Facebook. *See* social media activism
Fadila party, 97
Fahmy, Ahmed, 191, 225
Al-Faraeen network, 192, 205
Farouk, King, 58
el-Fattah, Alaa Abd, 60
feloul ("remnants" of Mubarak's former ruling
   party), 7, 66, 99
finance. *See* economy and finance
FJP. *See* Freedom and Justice Party
foreign policy: military and, 147; Morsi's presidency and, 169, 201–2; post-Mubarak, 84, 86
Fouda, Yosri, 79, 138
France: colonies in Middle East/North Africa,
   44; Muslim Brotherhood, relations with,
   88–89; occupation of Egypt, 44
Freedom and Justice Party (FJP): attitude
   toward Nour Party, 97; Constituent Assembly
   and, 122–23; creation of, 68, 110; criticizing
   and ordering protests over Battle of the
   Camel verdict, 168; expansion of, 80; Morsi as
   chairman of, 79, 81; other parties seeking to
   form coalition with, 84; parliamentary elections (2011) and, 99–101, 269n21; parliament
   committee chairs (2012) and, 112; relationship
   to Muslim Brotherhood, 79–81, 111; selection
   of candidates for 2011 elections, 101–2; Shura
   Council, appointments to, 191; Shura Council,
   majority in, 121–22; youth activists' demands
   on, 69
Freedom House, 120
Free Egyptians, 100
Free Officers Revolution (1952), 58, 61, 84
"Friday of Rage" (January 28, 2011), 25–28,
   34, 58

fuel shortages and prices, 166, 195, 203, 212,
   220, 232

Gallup survey (2010) on economic conditions, 14
al-Gamaa al-Islamiya: Abouel Fotouh's presidency campaign supported by, 135; Building
   and Development Party as political wing
   of, 97, 111; Morsi catering to, 147; Muslim
   Brotherhood making appointments from,
   113, 191, 216; police duties assumed by, 203;
   responsive to Muslim Brotherhood's call for
   protestors, 104, 218; as US-designated terrorist group, 96
Gami'atunah ("Our University"), 16
al-Ganzoury, Kamal, 105, 119, 120, 124–25, 135
Gaza and Hamas-Israel conflict (2012), 172–74
Gaza war (2008–9), 172
al-Gazzar, Helmy, 124
General Shura Committee (Muslim Brotherhood), 53, 110, 113, 127, 128, 129–30, 165; post-
   coup arrest and imprisonment (2013), 230
get-out-the-vote efforts of Muslim Brotherhood,
   106, 136, 141, 189
Ghad party, 9, 24, 191
el-Gheriany, Hossam, 129, 164
el-Ghobashy, Mona, 43
Ghozlan, Mahmoud, 88, 111, 119, 121, 182
Al-Gomhuria (newspaper), 169, 206
Graham, Lindsey, 120–21
gubernatorial appointments, 155, 164–65, 215–16
Guidance Office: anti-Morsi protests (2012), reaction to, 182; change in stance on running for
   political office, 79; in dialogue to end Tahrir
   Square standoff (2011), 32; FJP monitoring
   and, 111; "Friday of Rage" (January 28, 2011)
   and, 25–28; gubernatorial appointments by
   Morsi and, 165; al-Katatny and, 110; leadership
   role of, 53; leaders' responsibilities, 54; mobilization for protests in Arab Spring, 18; Morsi
   and, 77–78, 194; parliamentary elections
   (2011) and, 106; post-coup arrest and imprisonment (2013), 230; SCAF authority and,
   120; al-Shater and, 63; on Tahrir demonstrations (2011), 22–23; Tahrir Square anti-SCAF
   protests (June 20, 2012), 142; youth activists
   organizing in opposition to, 69. *See also* General Shura Committee

Habib, Mohamed, 152
Habib, Rafik, 164, 183

el-Haddad, Essam, 120, 164, 186, 223–24
el-Haddad, Gehad, 178
Hamas, 110, 157, 159, 172–74
Hamed, Mohi, 164
Hamed, Yehia, 209
Hamid, Shadi, 41, 43
Haqqī ("My Right"), 16
Hassan, Mohamed, 215
Hegazy, El-Morsi, 194, 195–96
Hegazy, Safwat, 216
Heshmat, Gamal, 196
Hezbollah, 215
Hoyer, Steny, 110
al-Hudaybi, Hassan, 40; *Preachers Not Judges*, 40
human rights, 65, 102, 233. *See also* inclusion
Human Rights Watch, 310n10
Hussein, Mahmoud, 111, 154
al-Husseini, Saad, 23, 89, 113, 165, 197

Ibn Khaldun Center: Patterson talk at (June 18, 2013), 217; poll on military resumption of control (2013), 205–6
Ibrahim, Hussein, 113
Ibrahim, Mohamed, 195
ideology. *See* Islam and Muslim Brotherhood; Muslim Brotherhood; Salafists
IMF (International Monetary Fund), 125, 166–67, 170, 194, 196, 209
inclusion: Kefaya's ideological diversity, 16; Morsi's campaign promises of, 138, 143, 155; Morsi's failure to govern by principles of, 164–65, 168–69; Muslim Brotherhood reformists in favor of, 5; Obama administration urging, 149, 168, 186, 233; open to negotiations with opposition, as Morsi claim of inclusion, 220
incompetence of Muslim Brotherhood, 6, 151–55, 207, 212–13, 220–23, 226, 234
insulting the presidency, 192–93, 203, 210
Interior Ministry: anti-Morsi support from (June 2013), 221; crackdown on Muslim Brotherhood (1995), 42; failure to protect Morsi from demonstrators (December 4, 2012), 182, 195; Morsi restrained from making Muslim Brotherhood appointment to, 156, 195; Muslim Brotherhood leveling charges of usurping legislative power at, 118, 119; in post-Mubarak period, 7; resources exhausted in run up to April Spring demonstrations, 26; siding with protestors against Morsi (June 28,

2013), 221; Tahrir Square protestors removed by order of (November 2011), 104; as target in removal of Mubarak, 29, 57, 58
international media: on Morsi and other presidential candidates (2012), 136; Morsi asserting Jewish control over US media, 201; Muslim Brotherhood courting, 33, 198; revolutionary activists and, 59
International Monetary Fund (IMF), 125, 166–67, 170, 194, 196, 209
International Republican Institute (IRI), 120
Iran, 166, 169, 200, 214–15, 233
Iraq: civil war in, 232–33; US invasion of (2003), 15, 42
IRI (International Republican Institute), 120
ISIS (Islamic State of Iraq and Syria), 233–34
Islamic Development Bank, 196
Islamic Resistance Movement. *See* Hamas
Islamism and Muslim Brotherhood: 2011–12 elections considered mandate for Islamism, 112–13, 271n43; "all-embracing concept" of Islam, 46–48, 55, 73, 155; constitutional revision under control of Islamists, 122–23; ideology of Islamism, 47–48, 64, 73–75, 87, 106, 148, 247n8; interpretation of Islam, 3, 55; lack of specifics on how Islamized nation would function, 131, 151–55, 234; Morsi presidency and, 151–57; new constitution and, 179–80; opponents considered to be enemies of Islam, 4; political mission to Islamize society, 73, 83, 93–94, 151; Salafists' view of Islam vs., 6; al-Shater as presidential candidate focusing on Islamizing the state, 131; theocracy and, 55, 123, 179
Islamist Bloc (party alliance), 100–101, 106, 107
"Islam Is the Solution" posters, 106
Ismail, Farid, 113
Israel: Arab–Israeli War (1948), 39; Arab–Israeli War (1973), 58, 167–68; Hamas and, 172–74; jihad against, 20, 41, 86; Morsi's presidency and, 173–74, 290n22; Operation Pillar of Defense (2012), 173; Sadat's peace efforts with, 81; Six-Day War (1967), 58; stability of 1979 peace accord with, 8, 86, 88, 116, 147, 157–58, 172, 174, 200, 290n22. *See also* Palestinians, Egyptian support of
Israeli embassy in Giza, protests at (2011), 89, 157–58
Istanbul, Muslim Brotherhood in exile establishing division in, 231, 233–34

al-Jabari, Ahmed, 173

jihad and jihadi: al-Assad attacks by, 215; al-Hudaybi not advocating, 40; Muslim Brotherhood youth cadres calling for, 231; Qutb advocating, 39; rift between Muslim Brotherhood and jihadists, 40; Sinai attacks by, 157–59

Jordan, 233

Judges Club, 177

judicial branch: monitoring of parliamentary elections, 42, 106, 176; Morsi impinging on, 175–76; Morsi naming judges to be investigated, 219; Shura Council seeking to amend laws on (2013), 209

Justice and Freedom Movement, 18, 23, 24

Kamel, Omaima, 164

Kamel, Osama, 165

Kandahar Friday (July 29, 2011), 91, 97–98

Kandil, Hazem, 3, 6, 247n8

Karama Party (Nasserists), 24, 111

al-Katatny, Saad, 22, 30, 32, 79, 250n40; background of, 109–10; as chair of Constituent Assembly, 123; dissolved parliamentary body and, 150, 284n4; on al-Ganzoury's government's failures, 124; Hoyer meeting with (2007), 110; Kerry and Patterson meeting with (2011), 115; Kumar meeting with (2011), 88; NGO raids in Cairo (December 2011) and, 121; parliamentary elections (2011) and, 99, 101; as secretary-general of Freedom and Justice Party, 110; as speaker of parliament, 113–14, 135; as spokesman for Muslim Brotherhood's leadership, 109–10

al-Kazzaz, Husain, 164

Kefaya (Popular Campaign for Change), 15–16, 82–83, 208

Kerry, John, 115, 117, 202, 233

Khalil, Ashraf, 30, 32

al-Khayat, Adel, 216

kidnapping of security officers in Sinai (May 2013), 210–11

Kumar, Prem, 88

Kuwait, 232

labor strikes: Judges Club calling for, 177; Al-Mahalla al-Kobra textile factory strike (2008), 16; under Mubarak, 14; Muslim Brotherhood and, 20–21; pervasive, post Mubarak fall, 98; police strike (March 7, 2013), 202, 212

Law of Political Exclusion to bar Mubarak regime officials from running for national office, 132, 133, 139

Leiken, Robert S., 40

Libya, 157, 203, 232; ISIS in, 233; US embassy attack in Benghazi, Libya (2012), 170–71, 172

Lotfy, Islam, 77

Luxor terrorist attack (1997), 216

Lynch, Marc, 41, 43–44, 283n61

Al-Mahalla al-Kobra workers strikes (2008), 20

Maher, Ahmed, 16, 209

Malek, Hassan, 30, 63, 64

al-Masry, Walid, 221

McCain, John, 121

media: criticism of and calls for removal of Morsi, 192–93, 205, 207; Islamist attacks and threats on, 203, 216; on June 30, 2013 protests, 222; Morsi naming in threats on, 219; post-Morsi ouster, effect on Muslim Brotherhood outlets, 225; prosecutor-general accusing of criminal incitement or insult to government, 192–93, 203, 210; revolutionary activists and, 59; SCAF taking control of, 58; Tamarod campaign (2013), coverage of, 208; torture of anti-Morsi protesters prompting criticism from, 183. See also international media

Mekki, Mahmoud, 129, 163–64

Meshal, Khaled, 174

Middle East Media Research Institute, 200

Middle East Studies Association, 9

military: as alternative to Morsi government, 205–7, 210, 212; control of country after Morsi ouster (July 3, 2013), 228–29; control of country by constitutional declaration (February 13, 2011), 57; economic power of, 58–59, 163; gubernatorial appointments by Morsi from, 165; independent judiciary, 180; instability requiring military intervention, 184–85; Mukhaymer's appointment to lead Defense and National Security Committee, 113; Muslim Brotherhood's concern over relationship with, 33; new constitution and, 180, 184; reaction to Tahrir Square demonstrations (2011), 27–28; el-Salmi Document (2011) protections for, 102–3; Syrian civil war and, 215; ultimatum to Morsi government, 223–24. See also al-Sisi, Abdel Fattah; Supreme Council of the Armed Forces; Tantawi, Mohamed Hussein

ministries, control of, 156
minorities' rights: Christians and Jews under new constitution, 179. *See also* Copts
"moderate" Islamism: Muslim Brotherhood as moderate relative to Salafists, 107; Muslim Brotherhood not qualifying as, 55; Muslim Brotherhood's behavior construed as, 38–43
modernists, 44–46
Mohamed Mahmoud protests (November 18, 2011), 104–5, 115, 183
Morsi, Abdullah, 137–38
Morsi, Mohamed: anti-Semitism of, 200–201; anti-US sentiment of, 88, 147, 171–72; background of, 77–78; Burns meeting with (2012), 116, 117, 274n41; Clinton meeting with (2012), 150, 158; in dialogue to end Tahrir Square standoff (2011), 32; elected as president (2012), 1–2, 141, 145; FJP monitoring and, 111; instructing Web editor not to call for 2011 revolution, 21; interview of (while Mubarak in power), 9; al-Katatny compared to, 109; Kerry and Patterson meeting with (2011), 115–17; meeting with Abdel Ghafour, 97; on Muslim Brotherhood forming political party, 62; in negotiations with other political forces to gain presidency, 143; Obama call to (2012 election), 140; opponents, treatment of, 4; parliamentary elections (2011) and, 101, 105; as presidential candidate for first round, 130, 133–34, 136–37t; as presidential candidate for second round, 137–41; refusing to compromise to allow al-Ganzoury to stay in power, 125; Tahrir Square protests (2011), reaction of, 25, 30; on US acceptance of Muslim Brotherhood in power, 117. *See also* Morsi ouster; Morsi presidency
Morsi ouster, 2, 4, 205–26; announcement of ouster (July 3, 2013), 225; concessions rejected by opposition, 224; effect on Muslim Brotherhood immediately after, 225; internal purges promised to forestall, 219–20; loss of support, ix, 205; military as alternative to Morsi government, 205–7, 210, 212; military ultimatum to Morsi government, 223–24; Muslim Brotherhood's misreading of situation, 220–21, 226; negotiations with opposition, Morsi claiming he is open to, 220; referendum on presidency, proposal for, 225; refusal of Morsi to resign, 224–25; resigna-

tions from Morsi's political circle, 223–24; al-Sisi meeting with Qandil and Morsi to obtain Morsi's concessions, 224; threats to opponents to forestall, 219. *See also* post-Morsi (2014–15) al-Sisi regime
Morsi presidency, 145–204; cabinet appointments, 156–57, 194–97, 208–9; Clinton meeting with (2012), 172; dissolved parliamentary body and, 146, 149–50; firing and replacing Tantawi and SCAF leaders in exchange for full political power, 159–60, 207; foreign aid sought by, 166–67; full executive and legislative authority residing in, 159, 163–74; gubernatorial appointments, 164–65, 215–16; Hamas and, 172–74; Hu Jintao meeting with, 166; hundred-day plan formulated by Muslim Brotherhood for, 165–67; inclusion, failure to govern by principles of, 149, 164–65, 168–69; internal shake-ups (2013), 194–97, 208–9; Iran visit (August 2012), 169; Israel and, 173–74, 290n22; judiciary power, impinging on, 175–76; Kerry meeting with (2013), 202; lack of coherent policy, 151–55, 207, 212–13, 234; media criticism of, 192–93; military intervention to restore social stability, 184–85; ministries, control of, 156; NSF meeting, al-Sisi trying to facilitate with, 185; oath of office and, 145–46; opportunity to implement *shari'ah* and Islamize government, 151–57; parliamentary elections (2013) and, 199–200; political capital of, 159; power grab of unchecked authority, 175–87, 205; in power struggle with SCAF, 145–46, 157, 284n4; presidential team of, 164; prosecutor-general, appointment of, 175; Tahrir Square speech (June 2012), 146–47; undefined powers of, 145, 149; US relations and, 147–51; vice-president, appointment of, 163–64, 169. *See also* constitution; demonstrations and protests
Moussa, Amr, 67, 129, 135, 136–37t, 177
mua'skarat (Muslim Brotherhood's educational camping trips) to prepare for political campaign (2011), 93, 96
mu'ayyad (supporter) status of Muslim Brotherhood membership, 49
Mubarak, Gamal, 14, 28, 72
Mubarak, Hosni: arrest of, 72; blockade on Hamas-controlled Gaza, 172; concessions offered by, 30; Morsi and, 77–78, 138; Muslim Brotherhood, repression of, 13, 18–19, 61,

Mubarak, Hosni (*continued*)
63–64, 82; Muslim Brotherhood's policy of non-confrontation under, 83; Muslim Brotherhood's willingness to retain as president, 254n96; negotiating exit terms (2011), 32, 34; opposition parties to, 9; ouster of, 1–2, 27–28, 30–32; political opposition, control over, 81–82; public frustration with, 14; Salafists, repression of, 97

Mubarakists, 31, 58, 181, 208, 217. *See also feloul*

Muhammad, Prophet, 45, 73; controversial video portrayals of, 170–71

muḥibb (lover) status of new recruits, 48–49

Mukhaymer, Abbas, 113, 118

municipal elections, 194

muntasib (affiliate) status of Muslim Brotherhood membership, 49

Muslim Brotherhood: *akh 'amal* (active brother) status, 50–51, 102; approach to taking power, 5–6, 32–35; blacklisting of author by, 10; characteristics and goals of, 3–4; children's introduction to, 48; considered as terrorist by al-Sisi government, 233; creation of political party by, 62, 68; dissent not tolerated in, 73–74; dues, payment of, 51; election (2012) and, 1, 4; exclusivism of, 4, 6; in exile and division established in Istanbul, 231, 233–34; Fifth Conference (1939), 46; flat organization structure used during election campaigns, 136; founding of, 45–46; future of, 234; history of, 1–2, 39, 45–46; ideology of, 3, 10, 44–48, 73, 231; internal disagreements post-coup (2013), 230; interviewing members of, 9–11, 235–45; legacy of regime in Egypt, 234; long-term view of Islamist goals, 230; loyalty of youth members, 70; motto of, 46; *mu'ayyad* (supporter) status, 49; *muḥibb* (lover) status of new recruits, 48–49; *muntasib* (affiliate) status, 49; *muntaẓim* (organizer) status, 49–50; Nasser's repression of, 126; nationwide chain of command, 51–55, 53f; no longer a viable threat to al-Sis regime, 234; number of members, 247n5; oath of members, 50–51, 258n56; oath of *shu'abah* officials, 52; opponents considered to be enemies of Islam, 4; organizational structure affording advantage to, 4, 55, 74, 75, 80, 106, 136, 137, 202; in post-Mubarak transition, 60–62; professional operations infrastructure, 54; recruitment and internal promotion policies, 3, 5, 10, 48–51,

231–32; removal of Morsi from presidency, reaction to, 2; rise and collapse in post-Mubarak Egypt, 2–3, 7–8; *shu'abah* (branch) structure, 52, 142; in Tahrir Square and ouster of Mubarak (2011), 25–35; *tarbiah* process to indoctrinate members, 48–51, 50f, 54–55, 155; unified structure and uniformity of, 3–4, 6, 55, 106, 134, 231; *usar* (families) structure, 4, 51–52, 101, 106; viewed as "moderate" Islamist organization, 38–43; viewed internally as divisive vs. cohesive, 4–5; violence and, 11; website of, 63; youth cadres replacing old guard by early 2015, 231. *See also* Freedom and Justice Party; Guidance Office; Islamism and Muslim Brotherhood; Morsi ouster; Morsi presidency; Renaissance Project

Muslim Sisters (female division of Muslim Brotherhood), 54

Muwafi, Murad, 159

Myrick, Sue, 37

Naaman, Salah, 279n8

al-Nahda Square, military vs. Muslim Brotherhood at (July & August 2013), 220, 228–29

Napoleon Bonaparte, 44

Nasser, Gamal Abdel, 39, 96, 117, 126

Nasserists, 15, 24, 71, 81, 84

National Defense Council, 180

National Democratic Institute (NDI), 120

National Democratic Party (NDP). *See feloul*

National Police Day, 18

National Salvation Front (NSF), 177, 184, 185, 189–91, 197

nationwide chain of command within Muslim Brotherhood, 51–55, 53f

NDI (National Democratic Institute), 120

NDP (National Democratic Party). *See feloul*

neighborhood watch groups, 28–29

"A New Vision from Within" conference (March 2011), 69

Nides, Thomas, 170

Nile dam construction by Ethiopia, 211

9/11 Commission, 39

nongovernmental organizations (NGOs), raids on (December 2011), 120–21

non-Islamists: anti-Morsi role of, 177, 178; Battle of the Camel, reliance on Muslim Brotherhood in, 32; Clinton visit, protests against, 150; Constituent Assembly boycott by, 123, 129, 179; Egyptian Bloc formed by, 100, 106, 107;

FJP forming parliamentary coalition with, 111; FJP/Morsi appointments and, 112, 156, 164, 191; international media coverage of, 35; joining Muslim Brotherhood in protesting against SCAF, 133; lack of coherent policies, 202; Morsi ignoring, 197–98, 208; Muslim Brotherhood not wishing to cooperate with, 20, 60, 78, 98; Nour Party allying with, 197; praise for Muslim Brotherhood youths for standing up to Guidance Office, 69; in presidential election (2012), 137, 137*t*, 148; al-Qassas coordinating with, 13, 16–17, 21; resigning from government roles, 178–79, 183; role of, 47; Shura Council elections and, 190; US opinion of, 8, 150, 202; weak voter turnouts, 122. *See also* National Salvation Front (NSF); Tamarod campaign; Wafd party; youth activists

Nour, Ayman, 132

Nour Party: Abouel Fotouh endorsed as presidential candidate by, 135; Constituent Assembly and, 122; Democratic Alliance for Egypt, leaving alliance of, 98; FJP working with, 111–12, 119; in Islamist Bloc, 100, 107; military praised by, 114; Morsi appointments from, 164, 214; Morsi courting in his presidential campaign, 134, 214; Port Said protests (January 25, 2013) and, 197; Salafist Call establishing, 97; in Shura Council, 121; split with Watan Party, 202

NSF (National Salvation Front), 177, 184, 185, 189–91, 197

Nuland, Victoria, 148, 186

al-Nuqrashi, Mahmoud, 39

Obama administration: Arab Spring, misjudgments in reaction to, 38; Arab Spring enthusiasm of, 86–88; engagement as policy toward Egypt, 8, 87–88, 110, 115–16, 148, 185–87, 200–201, 216; on Israel-Egypt relations, 200; Israel-Hamas conflict, urging Egypt to facilitate cease-fire in, 173–74; Morsi's failing leadership and, 216–18; Morsi's presidency and, 147–51, 168, 169–72, 285n15; Muslim Brotherhood, views on, 7–8, 38, 114–16; NGO raids in Cairo (December 2011) and, 121; SCAF, views on, 114–15; al-Sisi government as strategic partner, 233; Tamarod protests (June 30, 2013) and, 217; warning against military coup to topple Morsi, 206

Okasha, Tawfiq, 192

Omar, Manal, 193

Omran, Ahmed, 164

Ouda, Bassem, 194

Palestinian Authority, 172

Palestinian intifada (2000), 15, 173

Palestinians, Egyptian support of, 14–15, 88

Pargeter, Alison, 4–5

Paris Peace Conference (1918), 84

Parliament, 43, 111–12, 119, 135. *See also* Shura Council

parliamentary elections (pre-2011): 1984, 42, 84; 1987, 42, 84; 1990 boycott, 42; 1995, 42; 2000, 42, 77, 152; 2005, 18, 63, 84, 109; 2007, 19; 2010, 14, 17, 19; allocation of workers and farmers in parliament, 71, 98; judicial monitoring of, 42, 106, 176

parliamentary elections (2011–12), 93–107; Muslim Brotherhood's reversal of position not to field full slate of candidates, 100–101; results, 107; SCAF announcing plans for, 57, 98–99; victory of Muslim Brotherhood, factors contributing to, 106; violence preceding, 104–5; Wafd calling for postponement, 105

patriotism, 57

Patterson, Anne, 115, 116–17, 217

Peres, Shimon, 290n22

police: gubernatorial appointments by Morsi from, 165; National Police Day, 18; participating in anti-Morsi protests (June 30, 2013), 222; private police options proposed by Muslim Brotherhood, 203; pro-Palestinian demonstrations and (2000), 15; refusal to suppress anti-Morsi protests (2013), 202; relationship with Muslim Brotherhood, 7; strike (2013), 202, 212; Tahrir Square protests (2011) and, 24, 26–27, 104; Tahrir Square protests (2012) and, 177; US and Iraq war protests and (2003), 15. *See also* violence

Police Officers Club, 221

politics: al-Banna's views on, 46; Muslim Brotherhood banning its members from joining any other parties, 68; Muslim Brotherhood emerging as leading force in (2011), 107; Muslim Brotherhood's 2007 political platform, 78; Muslim Brotherhood's promise not to pursue presidency and parliamentary majority, 61, 78, 100–101, 126; political parties in opposition to Mubarak, 81–83. *See also specific political parties and elections*

Port Said Massacre (February 2012 soccer riot), 118–19, 196–97

Port Said protestors: January 25, 2013, 196–97; June 28, 2013, 221

Posner, Michael, 120

post-Morsi (2014–15): arrest and imprisonment, 230; economy, 232–34; military control, 228–29; Morsi and Muslim Brotherhood blaming conspiracies, 219, 228, 234; Muslim Brotherhood in exile and division established in Istanbul, 231, 233–34; Muslim Brotherhood's misunderstanding of situation, 228; al-Sisi regime, 227–34

postrevolutionary positions: Muslim Brotherhood and, 60–62, 68, 90–91; Renaissance Project and, 72–75; revolutionary activists and, 59–60, 90–91; SCAF and, 57–59, 89, 91. *See also* constitutional amendments

presidential election (2012), 1, 4, 127–44; Abouel Fotouh as candidate, 5, 128–30; Morsi as candidate, 130, 133–34; Muslim Brotherhood plans for holding, 61, 104, 119; Muslim Brotherhood reversing itself on putting forth its own candidate for, 128–30, 279n8; round 1 results, 136–37, 137*t*; SCAF plans for, 57, 105, 119; al-Shater as candidate, 130–31

presidential election (2014), election of al-Sisi, 232

presidential powers, constitutional amendments on, 65

al-Prince, Hassan, 165

prisoners, release or resistance during Tahrir demonstrations (2011), 27, 30

prosecutor-general: accusing media critics of criminal incitement or insult to government, 192–93, 203, 210; call of Morsi opposition to fire, 197; Morsi's appointment of, 175; Morsi's offer to fire, 225

protests. *See* demonstrations and protests; Tahrir Square protests

public opinion: on military resumption of control (2013), 205–6; on Morsi government, 204; Mubarak, frustration with, 14; on Muslim Brotherhood's governance, 207–10; Tahrir Square revolutionaries, resentment toward, 91. *See also* demonstrations and protests; Tahrir Square protests

al-Qaeda, 37–39; Muslim Brotherhood and, 41–42, 86

Qandil, Abdel Halim, 193

Qandil, Hesham, 156, 170, 174, 224, 225

al-Qaradawi, Yusuf, 214

al-Qassas, Anas, 21, 70

al-Qassas, Mohamed, 13–16, 18–19, 21–22, 30, 69

Qatar, 167, 195, 209

al-Qazzaz, Khaled, 164, 215, 223–24

Qur'an, 45–46, 48, 49–50. *See also shari'ah*

Qutb, Sayyid, 39–40, 78, 127

Qutbists, 127–28

Rabaa al-Adawiya Square, protests at (July & August 2013), 220–21, 223, 225, 227–29; massacre at, 229

Rashad, Mahmoud, 213

RDP (Reform and Development Party), 111–12

Red Sea resorts, terrorist attacks on, 157

referendum. *See* constitution; constitutional amendments

Reform and Development Party (RDP), 111–12

religious discrimination, 179; Morsi's statement of religious tolerance, 201. *See also* Copts

Renaissance Project, 72–75, 131, 134, 152–55, 153*f*, 158, 165, 194, 195

revolutionary activists. *See* youth activists

Revolutionary Socialists, 24

Revolution Continues Alliance, 107

Rida, Rashid, 45

rural clans and tribes, 7, 138, 139, 219

Saad, Mahmoud, 193

Sabahi, Hamdeen, 177

Sabry, Abdel Fattah, 213

Sadat, Anwar, 81, 96, 167–68

Sadat, Mohamed Anwar Esmat, 112

Said, Khaled, 17

salaf (companions of Prophet Muhammad), 96

Salafist Call, 66, 96, 97, 101

Salafists: awaiting presidential election results (June 24, 2012) and ready to fight, 144; constitutional amendments and, 66; in Democratic Alliance for Egypt, 84; government overhaul (2012) and, 119; history of movement, 96–97; ideology of, 96; July 29, 2011 protest, Muslim Brotherhood joined by, 91, 97–98; Morsi and, 1, 134–35, 214; Muslim Brotherhood compared to, 6, 96–97; parliamentary elections (2011) and, 101; post-Mubarak politics and, 97; Shura Council, appointments to, 191. *See also* Nour Party; Watan Party

Salama, Abdel-Nasser, 169

Saleh, Sobhi, 62, 71, 113

el-Salmi, Ali, 102

el-Salmi Document (2011), 102–4, 141

Salsabeel (computer company), 63

Satloff, Rob, ix

Saudi Arabia, 166, 214, 232

SCAF. *See* Supreme Council of the Armed Forces

SCC. *See* Supreme Constitutional Court

sectarian violence, 98

secularism and liberalism, Islamists opposed to, 91

shadow parliament (2010–2011), 17, 21–22, 24

Shafik, Ahmed: judge in Shafik election fraud case singled out by Morsi, 219; Obama call to (2012 election), 140; as presidential candidate first round, 129, 132, 135, 136–37*t*, 137; as presidential candidate second round, 1, 137–44, 189; as prime minister under Mubarak, 32, 57; resignation (March 3, 2011), 64; revolutionaries and Muslim Brotherhood seeking removal of post-Mubarak government, 59–60, 62

al-Sha'ir, Akram, 113

Shalit, Gilad, 159

Sharaf, Essam, 64–65, 105

shari'ah: Copts' rights and, 89; literalist interpretation by Salafists, 96; modernists and, 45–46; Morsi election campaign downplaying commitment to implement, 138, 155; Muslim Brotherhood advocating for legislation to comply with, 78; Muslim Brotherhood's desire to base new constitution on, 122–23; Muslim Brotherhood's intent to implement, 95–96, 151, 154; as "source of all law," 66, 116, 134, 179

al-Sharnouby, Abdel Galil, 21

al-Shater, Khairat: arrest and imprisonment of, 19; on al-Azhar independence law, 117; background, 62–64; barred from running for president by SPEC ruling, 132–33; FJP monitoring and, 111; on global Islamist order to counter the West, 94–95; al-Katatny compared to, 109; long-term approach of, 232; on low political aspirations of Muslim Brotherhood, 85; Morsi replacing, 78; *New York Times* letter, 171; Patterson meeting with (2013), 217; as presidential candidate of Muslim Brotherhood, 130–33; on presidential election (2012), 119, 143; prison stay and hero status of, 64; refusing to compromise to allow al-Ganzoury to stay in power, 125; release from prison, 30, 62,

64; Renaissance Project and, 72–75, 152, 232; on Suleiman as presidential candidate, 132

Shehata, Abdullah, 194, 209

Shehata, Rafaat, 159

Shehata, Samer, 43

Sherdy, Mohamed, 210

Sherif, Safwat, 72

Shiites, 96, 179, 214, 215

shu'abah (branch) structure of Muslim Brotherhood, 52, 142

Shura Council: appointments to, 190–91; elections (2012), 121–22; judicial reform (2013) and, 209; media and, 193; Morsi ceding legislative authority to, 190; Morsi restricting judiciary's right to dissolve, 175–76; parliamentary elections law (2013) and, 198–200, 204; resignations to protest Morsi's presidency (2013), 221. *See also* parliamentary elections *by year*

Sinai Peninsula: ISIS in, 233–34; jihadi attacks (August 2011), 157–58, 169; kidnapping of security officers (May 2013), 210–11; al-Shater on volatile situation in, 218

al-Sisi, Abbas, 160

al-Sisi, Abdel Fattah: calling for meeting for dialogue between NSF and Morsi, 185; calling for negotiations before June 30, 2013 protests, 218; Morsi, relationship with, 163, 207, 210; Morsi appointing as defense minister, 159–60; Morsi ouster and, 2, 225; Muslim Brotherhood, relationship with, 227; Obama meeting with (2014), 233; on Port Said protests (January 25, 2013), 197; as president (2014), 232; Tamarod protests and relationship with Morsi, 221–22; wife of, 160, 288n61. *See also* post-Morsi (2014–15) al-Sisi regime

Six-Day War (1967), 58

Sobea, Ahmed, 214

Sobhy, Sedky, 159

Socialist Labor Party, 81

social media activism: anti-Mubarak, 13, 16, 17, 18; FJP using for parliamentary elections campaigning, 198; Muslim Brotherhood's view of, 20; pro-Morsi advocates calling for cleansing of anti-Morsi factions, 178; al-Sisi using, 218; torture of anti-Morsi protesters and, 183

social services provided by Muslim Brotherhood, 4, 14, 38, 78; FJP offices handling, 80; neighborhood watch groups and, 28; parliamentary elections campaigning and, 198

Soliman, Ahmed, 152

SPEC (Supreme Presidential Elections Commission), 130, 132, 139, 143–44

Stacher, Joshua, 9, 43

Stack, Liam, 110

State Security: Morsi's relationship with, 78; Salafists during Mubarak era kept in check by, 97; al-Shater's relationship with, 63; threatening Muslim Brotherhood, 20, 26, 250n40

Steavenson, Wendell, 248nn10–11

Stevens, Chris, 171

Suez Canal, 15, 18, 58

Suez protests (January 25, 2013), 196–97

Suleiman, Omar, 30, 32, 34, 131–32, 137

Sultan, Farouk, 144

supraconstitutional principles: Muslim Brotherhood's opposition to, 91, 103; protest against (July 29, 2011), 97–98; revolutionaries' promoting, 91; el-Salmi Document mirroring, 102

Supreme Constitutional Court (SCC): Constituent Assembly and, 123; constitutional amendments on powers of, 65; dissolution of Mubarak-era Parliaments, 99, 140; dissolution of Muslim Brotherhood–dominated Parliament, 1, 140, 150; Morsi's power grab, effect on authority of, 175–76; parliamentary elections law (2013), disapproval of, 198–99; refusing to rule on Constituent Assembly's constitutionality, 180–81

Supreme Council of the Armed Forces (SCAF): al-Azhar independence law and, 117; concessions to Muslim Brotherhood, 62, 64; constitutional declaration (February 2011) and, 57; constitutional declaration (March 2011) and, 70, 103, 114, 122, 141; constitutional declaration (June 2012) and, 141–42; constitutional revision and, 70, 89; Morsi seeking unity with, 207; Muslim Brotherhood, relationship with, 6, 61, 75, 90, 97, 114, 117–20, 129; Muslim Brotherhood attacking on keeping al-Ganzoury in power, 125–26, 135; NGO raids (December 2011) and, 120–21; Nour Party, relationship with, 97; parliamentary elections (2011) and, 102–5; post-Mubarak control, 57, 89, 98; presidential election (2012) and, 105, 143; el-Salmi Document (2011) and, 102–4; transitional strategy, 57–59, 70; violence against protestors, 11, 23, 104–5, 115

Supreme Council of the Judiciary, 177, 209

Supreme Guide, 53–54

Supreme Presidential Elections Commission (SPEC), 130, 132, 139, 143–44

Syrian civil war, 214–15, 233

Tadros, Samuel, 180, 248n10

Tagammu party, 9, 67, 81, 100

Tahrir Square protests: 2011 anti-Mubarak (Arab Spring), 21–29; 2011 weekly Friday demonstrations, 62, 65; January 25, 2011 anti-Mubarak, 18, 25; January 28, 2011 (Friday of Rage), 25–28, 34, 58; February 2, 2011 (Battle of the Camel), 31–33, 58, 60, 168; May 27, 2011, 90; July 8, 2011 (Determination Friday) anti-SCAF, 90–91; July 29, 2011 (Kandahar Friday), 91, 97–98; November 18, 2011 anti-SCAF, 104; April 13, 2012 anti-Suleiman's candidacy, 132; April 18, 2012 anti-SCAF, 133; April 27, 2012 anti-SCAF, 133; June 5, 2012 anti-Shafik's candidacy, 139; June 20, 2012 anti-SCAF, 142; June 29, 2012 Morsi taking oath of office, 146; July 10, 2012 in support of Morsi, 149–50; November 22 & 27, 2012 anti-Morsi, 176–77; December 4–5, 2012 anti-Morsi, 181–83; January 25, 2013 anti-Morsi, 196; June 30, 2013 anti-Morsi, 2, 220–24; cameras to monitor, 118; clearing of demonstrators (March 2011), 65; clearing of demonstrators (summer 2011), 91; Mubarak's attempts to negotiate his exit and, 32, 34; Muslim Brotherhood maintaining order in (2011), 28–30; "snowball" strategy of protestors (2011), 24

Tamarod campaign (2013), 207–10; June 30, 2013 protests, 213, 220–24; military stance on, 221; Morsi attempting to counter, 211; Morsi not realizing extent of support for, 222–23

Tantawi, Mohamed Hussein: announcing SCAF plans to transfer power via elections, 105; ceding legislative authority following elections, 117; Clinton meeting with (2012), 150–51; in control following Mubarak, 57; al-Ganzoury's government supported by, 120; military ranks' dissatisfaction with, 160; Morsi firing, 159; Morsi retaining as defense minister, 157; revolutionaries protesting against government of, 71; visiting Sinai with Morsi, 158 *tarbiah* process to indoctrinate Muslim Brotherhood members, 48–51, 50*f*, 68, 155; *akh 'amal* (active brother) status, 50–51; as factor in parliamentary elections (2011) victory of Muslim Brotherhood, 106; *mua'skarat* (educational camping trips), 93, 96; *mu'ayyad* (supporter) status, 49; *muhibb* (lover) status, 48–49; *muntasib* (affiliate) status, 49; *muntazim* (organizer) status, 49–50; purpose of, 54–55

terrorism, 8; House of Representatives' Permanent Select Committee on Intelligence, testimony on, 37; Luxor terrorist attack (1997), 216; Muslim Brotherhood and, 37–38, 41, 234; War on Terror, 38. *See also* ISIS; al-Qaeda

Toner, Mark, 121

torture, 39, 110, 183

totalitarianism. *See* autocracy

tourism, 124, 216, 234

traffic congestion and improvement, 138, 165–67

train accidents, 196

Tripartite Nile Basin Committee, 211

Tunisia, 17–20, 26–27, 87

Turkey, 167, 195, 233

Twitter. *See* social media activism

ulema (Islamic scholars), 45

unemployment, 14

United Arab Emirates, 214, 232

usar/usrah (families/family) structure of Muslim Brotherhood, 4, 51–52, 101, 106

US policy toward Egypt: advising Morsi to change course, 223–24, 225; democracy, US in support of, 86, 104, 116, 200, 201, 217; military aid, 8, 37, 147, 206, 233; Muslim Brotherhood, views on, 7–8, 37–38, 40–41, 87–88, 114–16, 217–18; NGO raids in Cairo (December 2011) and, 120–21; popular support in US for Egypt's protestors, 37; US embassy attack in Cairo (2012) and, 170–72. *See also* Obama administration

vice-presidency, Morsi making appointment to, 163–64, 169

violence: anti-Christian violence (2011), 88–89, 115, 138; anti-Morsi protests (2012), 168, 176–77, 181–83, 214; anti-Morsi protests (2013), 196, 202, 205; final anti-Morsi protests (June 30, 2013), 222; military using against Muslim Brotherhood after Morsi ouster,

227–29; in Moqattam (June 30, 2013), 222; in Moqattam (March 22, 2013), 203; Muslim Brotherhood's commitment to nonviolence, 41; Muslim Brotherhood's willingness to use, 214; parliamentary elections (1995) and, 42; Port Said Massacre (February 2012), 118–19; presidential election (2012) and, 143, 144; pro-Mubarak demonstrators vs. anti-Mubarak demonstrators (2011), 30–32; at protests, 11, 23, 104–5, 115; torture of anti-Morsi protesters, 183; protestors clash (June 28, 2013), 220–21, 310n10; US embassy attack in Benghazi, Libya (2012), 170–71, 172; US embassy attack in Cairo (2012), 170–72. *See also* jihad and jihadi

Al-Wafd (newspaper), 84

Wafd party: alliance with Muslim Brotherhood, 68, 84–85; author's access to, 9; in Mubarak era, 81; opposed to constitutional amendments, 67; parliamentary elections (1984) and, 42, 68; parliamentary elections (2011) and, 99–100, 105, 106; parliament deputy committee chairs (2012) and, 112

war, power to declare, 103, 141, 180

War on Terror, 38

Wasat Party, 129, 191, 218

Washington Institute for Near East Policy, ix

Watan Party, 202

weapons, availability of, 212

Western powers, acceptance of Muslim Brotherhood, 85, 88–89. *See also* Obama administration; US policy toward Egypt

Wickham, Carrie Rosefsky, 5, 43

Yassin, Osama, 23, 250n40, 284n4

Yemen, 233

Youssef, Bassem, 193, 203

youth activists: Abouel Fotouh and, 128; Arab Spring role of, 6; arrests of Mubarak regime officials demanded by, 71–72; calling for renewed protests (May 2011), 89; on constitutional amendments, 67; criticizing Muslim Brotherhood's post-Mubarak politics, 69; July 8, 2011 protests (Determination Friday), 90–91; Kefaya and, 15–16; Muslim Brotherhood's distrust of, 20–21; Muslim Brotherhood's goals shared by, 60, 62, 72; Muslim Brotherhood youth cadres desiring aggressive responses, 178, 216, 230; Muslim

ABOUT THE AUTHOR

Eric Trager is the Esther K. Wagner Fellow at the Washington Institute for Near East Policy, where his research focuses on Egyptian politics and the Muslim Brotherhood. His writings have appeared in the *New York Times*, the *Wall Street Journal*, the *Washington Post*, and *Foreign Affairs*, among many other publications. He has served as an adjunct professor at the University of Pennsylvania, where he received his PhD in political science in 2013, as well as the University of Michigan and the University of California. A native of Queens, New York, and a diehard Mets fan, Trager currently lives in Washington, DC, with his wife, Alyssa, and his sons, Max and Theodore.